OTHER A TO Z (
THE SCARECRO\   D1510251

The A to Z of the Green Movement

Miranda Schreurs
Elim Papadakis

The A to Z Guide Series, No. 91

The Scarecrow Press, Inc.
Lanham • Toronto • Plymouth, UK
2009

Published by Scarecrow Press, Inc.
A wholly owned subsidary of
The Rowman & Littlefield Publishing Group, Inc.
4501 Forbes Boulevard, Suite 200, Lanham, Maryland 20706
http://www.scarecrowpress.com

Estover Road, Plymouth PL6 7PY, United Kingdom

British Library Cataloguing in Publication Information Available

Library of Congress Cataloging-in-Publication Data

The hardback version of this book was cataloged by the Library of Congress as
follows:

Schreurs, Miranda A. (Miranda Alice), 1963–
   Historical dictionary of the green movement. — 2nd ed. / Miranda Schreurs,
Elim Papadakis.
      p. cm. — (Historical dictionaries of religions, philosophies, and movements ;
   no. 80)
   Includes bibliographical references.
   1. Green movement—Dictionaries. 2. Green movement—History—
Dictionaries. I. Papadakis, Elim. II. Title.
GE195.P36 2007
333.7209—dc22   2007008534

ISBN 978-0-8108-6878-6 (pbk. : alk. paper)
ISBN 978-0-8108-7041-3 (ebook)

⊗™ The paper used in this publication meets the minimum requirements of
American National Standard for Information Sciences—Permanence of Paper
for Printed Library Materials, ANSI/NISO Z39.48-1992.

Printed in the United States of America

Contents

Editor's Foreword

Many movements have come and gone without leaving an enduring mark on the political landscape. One significant exception, probably the most important in recent decades, has been the environmental movement, which has generated numerous political parties. Collectively known as the greens, they have actually absorbed a large number of issues and are joining with, and sometimes even edging out, more conventional parties. Moreover, they have gradually moved from the fringes of the political spectrum toward the center, and most of the older mainstream parties have—sometimes grudgingly, sometimes more enthusiastically—taken on green issues and even accepted green parties in broader coalitions. Thus, the green movement is considerably more visible and successful now than just a decade ago.

This major sea change fully justifies a new edition of *The A to Z of the Green Movement*, which must add a large number of new parties and other groups to those mentioned in the previous edition. It also has to consider some new issues as well as older ones that have come into greater prominence, usually because not enough was done to solve them and they are more threatening than ever. Since the green parties are often part of broader social and economic movements, and especially the environmental movement as such, they must be seen in the broader context of today's thinking and action and also considered in very different situations in specific countries. Along with entries on parties and issues, those on concepts are particularly important. The dictionary, the book's core, is preceded by a chronology that traces the green movement's history, and an introduction that sums up its progress thus far. Those wishing to know more should consult the extensive bibliography.

The first edition of *Historical Dictionary of the Green Movement* was written by Elim Papadakis, who is a professor in European studies at the Australian National University. He has written extensively on the field including several books, among them *The Green Movement in West Germany* and *Politics and Environment: The Australian Experience*. This book has built on that and, as noted, expanded and updated the coverage thanks to the efforts of another eminent specialist, Miranda Schreurs. She is an associate professor in the Department of Government and Politics of the University of Maryland, with a focus on environmental policy and law in Japan, East Asia, and Europe. Among her many publications, including coedited works on environmental security and cooperation in Pacific Asia and across the Atlantic, she has written *Environmental Politics in Japan, Germany, and the United States*. Thanks to her knowledge and enthusiasm, we can command an uncommonly broad view of a movement that concerns us all.

Jon Woronoff
Series Editor

Acknowledgments

Miranda Schreurs would like to thank a group of outstanding research assistants for their help with researching and drafting several of the entries that appear in this book.

Jennifer Arthungal worked on entries for Bangladesh, India, Pakistan, and Vandana Shiva and aided with the bibliography.

Anna Sheveland helped research and draft those for Brazil, Common Pool Resources, Common Property Regimes, Costa Rica, Latin America and the Caribbean Region, Love Canal, and Mexico.

Margaret Olsen, who has a strong interest in Africa, aided with research on Central Africa, Greenbelt Movement, Kenya, Nigeria, South Africa, and various African environmental groups.

Jessica Olive aided with the entries for Agenda 21; Asia Pacific Partnership on Clean Development and Climate; Basel Convention on the Transboundary Movement of Hazardous Wastes; Comprehensive Environmental Response, Compensation, and Liability Act (CERCLA); Convention on Biological Diversity; Convention on Long-Range Transboundary Air Pollution (CLRTAP); Kyoto Protocol; Love Canal; World Commission on Sustainable Development; Montreal Protocol on Substances That Deplete the Ozone Layer; United Nations Framework Convention on Climate Change; Vienna Convention on the Protection of the Ozone Layer; and World Summit on Sustainable Development.

Casey L. Hall assisted with entries for Cambodia, Thailand, and Vietnam.

Christine M. Shehata worked on the entry for Egypt.

Saso Markovski aided with data collection on green parties in Estonia, Latvia, and Lithuania.

Dorothy Dai aided with the entry for Ken Sara Wiwa and researching environmental websites. Vanessa Kulick assisted with the compilation of the bibliography.

Evelyn Chia did initial work on the list of environmental websites and initiated a list of environmental nongovernmental organizations in different parts of the world, which was subsequently built on by the research assistants listed above.

Marcus Schaper aided with the technical production of the manuscript.

Our special thanks also go to Jon Woronoff, who has patiently helped guide this project through to completion.

Nicole McCullough, as associate editor, has done a superb job of seeing the manuscript through the stages of copyediting, proofreading, and printing. We also wish to thank Ann Beardsley for her thorough job of copyediting and Marianne Stone for her meticulous job of proofreading.

Acronyms and Abbreviations

ACF	Australian Conservation Foundation
ACT	Australian Capital Territory
ALÖ	Alternative Liste Österreichs
ALP	Australian Labor Party
ASEAN	Association of Southeast Asian Nations
BAPA	Bangladesh Poribash Andolon
BEN	Bangladesh Environment Network
CFCs	Chlorofluorocarbons
CLRTAP	Convention on Long-Range Transboundary Air Pollution
CND	Campaign for Nuclear Disarmament
CSD	Commission on Sustainable Development
DDT	Dichlorodiphenyltrichloroethane
EDF	Environmental Defense Fund/Environmental Defense
EGM	Estonian Green Movement
EPA	Environmental Protection Agency
ERI	EarthRights International
EU	European Union
GEF	Global environment facility
GMO	Genetically modified organism
GNP	Gross national product
GPS	Grüne Partei der Schweiz
IISD	International Institute for Sustainable Development
INFOTERRA	International Referral System
IPCC	Intergovernmental Panel on Climate Change
IUCN	International Union for the Conservation of Nature and Natural Resources/World Conservation Union
JATAN	Japan Tropical Forest Action Network
LAC	Latin America and Caribbean

MIT	Massachusetts Institute of Technology
MOSOP	Movement for the Survival of the Ogoni People
MP	Member of Parliament
MPE	Mouvement populaire pour l'environnement
NAFTA	North American Free Trade Agreement
NATO	North Atlantic Treaty Organization
NDP	Nuclear Disarmament Party
NEAC	National Environmental Awareness Campaign
NEPA	National Environmental Policy Act
NGO	Nongovernmental organization
NPL	National Priority List
NRDC	Natural Resources Defense Council
ODA	Official development assistance
OECD	Organisation for Economic Cooperation and Development
OPEC	Organization of Petroleum Exporting Countries
PCB	Polychlorinated biphenyl
PEPO	Pakistan Environmental Protection Ordinance
POROSH	Poribest Rakkha Shopoth
PRC	People's Republic of China
PVEM	Partido Verde Ecologista de México
RAC	Resource Assessment Commission
RAN	Rainforest Action Network
RFSTE	Research Foundation for Science, Technology, and Ecology
SAM	Sahabat Alam Malaysia
SAMFU	Save My Future Foundation
SEAC	Student Environmental Action Coalition
UDF	United Democratic Front
UNCED	United Nations Conference on Environment and Development
UNCHE	United Nations Conference on the Human Environment
UNCLOS	United Nations Conference on the Law of the Sea
UNDP	United Nations Development Programme
UNEP	United Nations Environment Programme
UNESCO	United Nations Educational, Scientific, and Cultural Organization

UNFCCC	United Nations Framework Convention on Climate Change
UTG	United Tasmania Group
VGÖ	Vereinte Grüne Österreichs
WCED	World Commission on Environment and Development
WRI	World Resources Institute
WWF	World Wide Fund for Nature (World Wildlife Fund)

Chronology

1642 Matsumoto-han in Japan establishes forest preserves.

1666 Japanese Shogunate adopts edict against tree felling.

1798 "Essay on the Principle of Population" by Robert Malthus published.

1849 U.S. Department of the Interior established.

1853 New York authorizes creation of Central Park.

1863 Enactment of Alkali Act in Britain represents a novel attempt to curb emissions on a large scale.

1864 *Man and Nature* by George Perkins Marsh published; Yosemite Valley and the Mariposa Grove of Big Trees are assigned by act of U.S. Congress to the state of California for public use, resort, and recreation.

1865 Commons, Open Spaces, and Footpaths Preservation Society in Britain formed.

1867 East Riding Association for the Protection of Sea Birds in Britain founded.

1870 Association for the Protection of British Birds founded.

1872 Yellowstone National Park created in the United States; Robert Angus Smith introduces the concept of acid rain.

1879 Royal National Park in Australia created.

1881 Royal Society for the Protection of Birds in Britain founded.

1883 Natal Game Preservation Society in South Africa formed; American Ornithologists Union founded.

1885 Banff National Park in Canada created.

1886 New York Audubon Society founded.

1889 Society for the Protection of Birds in Britain formed.

1890 Yosemite National Park created in the United States.

1892 John Muir and his associates form the Sierra Club.

1894 Tongariro National Park in New Zealand created.

1895 National Trust in Britain founded.

1900 Convention for the Preservation of Animals, Birds, and Fish in Africa endorsed.

1903 Society for the Preservation of Wild Fauna of the Empire in Britain formed; first U.S. wildlife refuge on Pelican Island, near Florida, established.

1905 National Audubon Society in the United States formed; Grand Canyon National Park established in the United States.

1906 U.S. Pure Food and Drug Act enacted.

1907 Inland Waterways Commission in the United States established.

1908 Conference of Governors on Conservation held at the White House, Washington, D.C.

1909 Wildlife Preservation Society in Australia founded; Swiss League for the Protection of Nature created; Swedish Society for the Protection of Nature formed; North American Conservation Congress held in Washington, D.C.; International Congress for the Protection of Nature convened in Paris.

1913 Consultative Committee for the International Protection of Nature in Switzerland formed; British Ecological Society founded.

1914 Swiss National Park established; Mountain Trails Club in Australia formed.

1916 U.S. National Park Service established.

1918 Save the Redwoods League founded.

1919 National Parks and Conservation Association founded.

1922 International Committee for Bird Protection (later named International Council for Bird Preservation) founded.

1924 First Wilderness Area designated in Gila National Forest in New Mexico, United States.

1926 Council for the Protection of Rural England founded.

1929 Migratory Bird Conservation Act passed; U.S. Forest Service promulgates first formal wilderness policy.

1930 U.S. Food and Drug Administration created.

1933 International Conference for the Protection of Fauna and Flora held in London.

1934 International Office for the Protection of Nature created; Wild Bird Society of Japan founded.

1935 Wilderness Society founded in the United States.

1936 National Wildlife Federation founded in the United States.

1942 First atomic reactor at the University of Chicago completed.

1944 Soil Conservation Society of America founded.

1945 The United States drops atomic bombs on Hiroshima and Nagasaki in Japan.

1946 International Whaling Commission formed.

1948 International Union for the Conservation of Nature and Natural Resources (now known as the World Conservation Union [IUCN]) formed.

1949 *A Sand County Almanac* by Aldo Leopold published; United Nations Scientific Conference on the Conservation and Utilization of Resources held at Lake Success, New York.

1951 The United States begins testing nuclear weapons.

1952 Britain begins testing nuclear weapons; "killer fog" kills thousands in London.

1953 The Soviet Union begins testing nuclear weapons.

1954 The United States conducts a hydrogen bomb test on Bikini Atoll and radioactive dust falls on the population of the Marshall Islands.

1956 Clean Air Act enacted in Britain.

1957 National Council for the Abolition of Nuclear Weapons Tests and of the Emergency Committee for Direct Action against Nuclear War in Britain created in response to the conduct of nuclear tests on Christmas Island; article by J. B. Priestley entitled "Britain and the Nuclear Bombs" published in the *New Statesman*; International Atomic Energy Agency founded.

1958 Committee to launch the Campaign for Nuclear Disarmament (CND) formed; the first of a series of marches organized by the CND between Aldermaston and London.

1959 Antarctic Treaty signed with a view to using the territory for peaceful purposes only.

1960 Organization of Petroleum Exporting Countries (OPEC) formed.

1961 Around 150,000 people assemble in Trafalgar Square at the end of a Campaign for Nuclear Disarmament (CND) march from Aldermaston to London; World Wildlife Fund founded; Arusha Conference on Nature Conservation held in Africa; first compensation payments to victims of mercury poisoning at Minamata, Japan, provided.

1962 *Silent Spring* by Rachel Carson published; first World Conference on National Parks held in Seattle, Washington.

1963 Partial Nuclear Test Ban Treaty signed.

1964 U.S. Wilderness Act passed.

1966 U.S. Endangered Species Protection Act passed.

1967 Collision of the oil tanker *Torrey Canyon* with rocks off the southwestern coast of England leads to oil pollution on the shores of Cornwall and of Brittany; Environmental Defense Fund founded in the United States.

1968   African Convention on the Conservation of Nature and Natural Resources signed by 33 African states that were members of the Organization of African Unity; convention of the Biosphere Conference in Paris to discuss the impact of human beings on the environment; creation of the Club of Rome to examine the interrelationships between factors such as economic growth, the environment, population, resources, and industrialization; *The Population Bomb* by Paul Ehrlich and "The Tragedy of the Commons" by Garrett Hardin published.

1969   David Brower leaves the Sierra Club to form Friends of the Earth; Don't Make a Wave Committee in Vancouver, Canada, a precursor to the foundation of Greenpeace, formed; Union of Concerned Scientists founded.

1970   Friends of the Earth established in London and Paris; first Earth Day attracts around 20 million people to protests held around the United States; Environmental Protection Agency (EPA) created in the United States.

1971   Save the Whales created; Gaucha Association for the Protection of the Natural Environment founded, and a green social movement emerges in Brazil; *The Closing Circle: Nature, Man, and Technology* by Barry Commoner published; Greenpeace Foundation created following protests against nuclear tests off the coast of Alaska by the U.S. government; Department of the Environment, Canada, established.

1972   *The Ecologist* magazine publishes *A Blueprint for Survival* by Edward Goldsmith and his collaborators, and *The Limits to Growth* by Donella H. Meadows, Dennis L. Meadows, Jorgen Randers, and William W. Behrens III; protests by Greenpeace held against nuclear weapons tests by the French government in the Mururoa Atoll; United Nations Conference on the Human Environment, convened in Stockholm; United Nations Environment Programme, the first United Nations (UN) agency with headquarters located in a developing country, formed; Convention concerning the Protection of the World Cultural and Natural Heritage signed in Paris; ratification in London of the Convention on the Prevention of Marine Pollution by Dumping of Waste and Other Matter (London Dumping Convention) occurs; Negative Population Growth founded; dichlorodiphenyltrichloroethane (DDT) banned in the United States; citizens of Neuchâtel in Switzerland oppose the building of a new highway, contest the communal elections, and win 8 of the 41 seats in the local parliament; United Tasmania Group formed in response to the destruction of Lake Pedder in Tasmania in order to promote a hydroelectric system; citizens' initiative umbrella organization, Bundesverband Bürgerinitiativen Umweltschutz, founded in the Federal Republic of Germany; Values Party in Wellington, New Zealand, the first party to be established at the national level that champions both environmental protection and participatory democracy, formed.

1973   The Organization of Petroleum Exporting Countries (OPEC) initiates a steep increase in the price of oil, which leads Western countries to consider rapid expansion in the construction of nuclear power plants; the declaration by the electricity industry that it would build a nuclear power station near the village of Brokdorf in Schleswig-Holstein, Federal Republic of Germany, signals the beginning of a dispute that was crucial in the development of antinuclear protests in Europe; the Chipko Andalan protest movement involving mainly women in Indian villages emerges; Convention on International Trade in Endangered Species of Wild Flora and Fauna held; Écologie et Survie, which went on to contest elections to the National Assembly in Alsace, France, formed; the party called People in Britain, which later became the Green Party, founded; *Small Is Beautiful: Economics as If People Mattered* by E. F Schumacher published; Endangered Species Act enacted in the United States; Cousteau Society founded.

1974   René Dumont, as the representative of environmental groups, contests the French presidential elections on an environmental platform; Karen Silkwood, a worker at the Kerr-McGee plutonium plant, Oklahoma, dies in mysterious circumstances; Environmental Policy Institute founded in the United States; F. Sherwood Rowland and Mario Molina present the argument that the release of chlorofluorocarbons (CFCs) into the atmosphere destroys the ozone layer.

1975   Mass protests against the proposal to construct a nuclear power station at Kaiseraugst, Switzerland, held; *The Monkey Wrench Gang* by Edward Abbey published; Worldwatch Institute founded.

1976 Mass protests against the proposals to construct nuclear power stations at Brokdorf and at Wyhl, Federal Republic of Germany, held; Swedish Miljöverbund formed.

1977 Mass protests held against proposals to develop nuclear power installations at Grohnde, Kalkar, and Brokdorf in the Federal Republic of Germany and at Creys-Malville in France; *Soft Energy Paths: Towards a Durable Peace* by Amory Lovins published; Groupement pour la Protection de l'Environnement in Switzerland formed; Sea Shepherd Conservation Society founded; Green Belt Movement in Kenya emerges; chemical contamination discovered at Love Canal in Niagara Falls, New York; *Amoco Cadiz* causes oil spill off the French coast.

1978 United States bans the use of chlorofluorocarbons (CFCs) in nearly all aerosols; Grüne Partei Zürich in Switzerland formed; mass protests held against the nuclear power reprocessing plant at Gorleben, Federal Republic of Germany; Sahabat Alam Malaysia (Friends of the Earth in Malaysia) founded; Love Canal Homeowners Association formed.

1979 In protests against government policies on nuclear energy, around 100,000 people assemble in Hanover and around 150,000 in Bonn, Federal Republic of Germany, and discussions are held in Offenbach over the possibility of establishing a new political organization; in Switzerland, first green parliamentarian to a national legislature elected; a green list (political party) in Bremen is successful in gaining the first seats ever won by a green party in a state parliament in Germany; green parties or lists participate in the first elections to the European Parliament; accident occurs at the Three Mile Island nuclear power plant in Harrisburg, Pennsylvania; Convention on Long-Range Transboundary Air Pollution (CLRTAP) is signed by 33 countries, including Britain, Germany, and the United States; in Luxembourg green groups form an umbrella organization, the Alternative Leescht: Wiert Ich, to compete at elections; Citizens' Committee formed in the United States; approximately 75,000 people gather in Washington, D.C., to take part in a demonstration against nuclear power; *Gaia: A New Look at Life on Earth* by James Lovelock published; campaign against the construction of the Franklin Dam in Tasmania begins; Convention on the Conservation of Migratory Species of Wild Animals signed in Bonn.

1980 Die Grünen in the Federal Republic of Germany, of Ecolo in Belgium, and of the Citizens Party in the United States formed; approximately 80,000 people participate in an antinuclear protest rally at Trafalgar Square in London; Canada and the United States sign a Memorandum of Intent Concerning Transboundary Air Pollution; *The Global 2000 Report* to the president by the U.S. Council on Environmental Quality published; publication and widespread dissemination of the *World Conservation Strategy: Living Resource for Sustainable Development* occurs; Earth First! radical environmental group created in the United States.

1981 Brice Lalonde contests the French presidential elections on a green platform; Swedish Green Party, Miljöpartiet de Gröna, and of the Ecology Party of Ireland, formed.

1982 In Belgium Agalev detaches itself from Anders gaan leven and formally becomes a political party; Vereinte Grüne Österreichs formed in Austria; United Nations Convention of the Law of the Sea signed.

1983 Die Grünen in Germany gains 28 seats in the federal parliament; Dei Greeg Alternativ in Luxembourg, De Grønne in Denmark, Comhaontas Glas in Ireland, and De Groenen in the Netherlands, formed; following a resolution by the United Nations General Assembly, the World Commission on Environment and Development (WCED) is formed.

1984 Inaugural meeting of the World Commission on Environment and Development held; poison gas accidentally released from the Union Carbide pesticide plant in Bhopal, India; congress of European green parties at Liége in Belgium advocates a "Europe of the regions"; Les Verts in France founded; green parties acquire 12 seats in the European Parliament and call themselves the Green-Alternative European Link; *Fighting for Hope* by Petra Kelly and *Seeing Green: The Politics of Ecology Explained* by Jonathan Porritt published; formation of the Thirty Percent Club to tackle long-range transboundary air pollution; Committees of Correspondence formed in the United States.

1985   Scientists at the Villach Conference draw attention to the increase in the average temperature across the world over the past century (the greenhouse effect); Convention on the Protection of the Ozone Layer endorsed in Vienna; release of pesticides into the Rhine River following a fire in a Basel chemical storage facility destroys living things on a vast scale; Greenpeace member dies following the bombing by the French intelligence service of the *Rainbow Warrior* while it was moored at Auckland harbor in New Zealand; Die Grünen becomes member of a coalition government with the Social Democratic Party in Hesse between 1985 and 1987; Rudolf Bahro quits Die Grünen over the issue of animal rights; the British Ecology Party becomes the Green Party.

1986   A federation of green groups forms a national Swiss Green Party (Grüne Partei der Schweiz [GPS]), and in Italy green groups form a Federation of Green Lists, Federazione delle Liste Verdi; explosion occurs at the Chernobyl nuclear power plant near Kiev in the Soviet Union.

1987   Die Grünen gains 42 seats in elections to the federal parliament; in elections to the national parliament, green groups in Italy receive around one million votes (2.5 percent) and gain 13 seats in the lower house and 2 in the Senate; Agalev gains 7.3 percent of the vote and 6 seats in the lower house in Flanders; Montreal Protocol on Substances that Deplete the Ozone Layer signed; *Our Common Future* by the World Commission on Environment and Development published.

1988   Miljöpartiet de Gröna becomes the first new party in 70 years to gain representation in the Swedish Parliament; Antoine Waechter contests the French presidential elections on behalf of environmental groups; several candidates of the Green Party in Brazil gain seats in municipal elections in large cities; intellectuals, scientists, and artists form the Ruse Committee in Bulgaria; scientists and policymakers at the Toronto Conference call for a 20 percent reduction in carbon dioxide emissions by the year 2000; Brazilian environmental activist Chico Mendes murdered.

1989   Victims of Bhopal awarded $470 million in compensation; Brontosaurus in Czechoslovakia and, later, Green Party formed; *Exxon Valdez* oil tanker runs aground in Prince William Sound, Alaska; green independent candidates gain 17 percent of the vote in Tasmania, gain 5 out of 36 seats in the state parliament, and form an accord with a government led by the Australian Labor Party; green parties achieve their best-ever results in elections to the European Parliament, gaining 32 seats; the Green-Alternative European Link dissolved and the Green Group in the European Parliament formed; the Green Association is formed in Finland, though this subsequently divided into two separate strands, Vihreat (the Greens) and Vihreä Liitoo (the Green Association); Independent Union Ekoglasnost in Bulgaria formed; Ecologists-Alternatives Party and the Federation of Ecological Organizations in Greece formed; *Blueprint for a Green Economy* by David Pearce and his collaborators published; Convention on International Trade in Endangered Species of Wild Fauna and Flora bans ivory trade.

1990   Die Grünen fails to gain seats in the federal parliament, though a new group from East Germany, Bündnis 90, does gain eight seats; Groen Links (Green Left) in the Netherlands and the Green Party in Prague, Czechoslovakia, formed; Génération Écologie under the leadership of Brice Lalonde formed as a competing party to Les Verts in France; signatories to the Montreal Protocol meet in London (London Conference of the Parties to the Montreal Protocol), and 80 countries now agree to phasing out, by the year 2000, of chlorofluorocarbons (CFCs) and other chemicals that contribute to the depletion of the ozone layer.

1991   Die Grünen becomes member of a coalition government with the Social Democratic Party (as senior partner) in Hesse; green groups in Italy win 16 seats in the lower house and 4 in the Senate; formation of the Green Party USA; Environmental Protocol to the Antarctic Treaty (the Madrid Protocol) signed by 39 nations agreeing to a moratorium on mining in Antarctica; severe pollution of the Gulf region in the wake of the Gulf War due largely to oil well fires and oil spillage.

1992   United Nations Conference on Environment and Development (the Earth Summit) held in Rio de Janeiro leads to signing of the Framework Convention on Climate Change by 153 nations and by the European Union; most nations attending the conference also support the Convention on Biological Diversity, the Declaration on Environment and Development, and the enactment of Forest Principles; United Nations Commission on Sustainable Development formed; Basel Convention signed by 20 countries in order to prevent the illegal dumping or transportation of waste; 93 nations that signed the 1987 Montreal Protocol on Substances That Deplete the Ozone Layer agree to meet their targets by 1996 rather than 2000, the date set in the original agreement; Petra Kelly and Gerd Bastian are found dead in their home.

1993 European Federation of Green Parties agrees on a set of guiding principles at a conference held in Masala, Finland; the Green Party in the United Kingdom fields 566 candidates in local elections, who gain, on average, 5.7 percent of the vote; membership of the Sierra Club numbers over 550,000; North American Agreement on Environmental Cooperation signed; agreement to safeguard the Black Sea by six European nations signed; World Bank permits public inspection of any authorizations linked to environmental assessment of intended projects; Latvian Green Party enters ruling coalition.

1994 Die Grünen, in coalition with Bündnis 90, gains 7.3 percent of the vote and 49 seats in the federal parliament and displaces the Liberal Free Democrats as the third-largest party; in elections to the European Parliament the number of seats won by green parties drops to 22; Die Grüne Alternative in Austria secures 7 percent of the vote in national elections and 13 seats; Miljöpartiet obtains 5 percent of the vote and 18 seats in the Swedish Parliament; green candidates poll over a million votes in local elections in the United States; the Constitution of the Federal Republic of Germany is amended to include a specific commitment to environmental protection; United Nations Conference on Population and Development held in Cairo, Egypt; declaration by the International Whaling Commission of Antarctica as a permanent sanctuary for whales occurs.

1995 In Sweden Miljöpartiet de Gröna gains four seats in elections to the European Parliament; Vihreä Liitoo secures 6.5 percent of the vote and nine seats in the Finnish Parliament; Agalev secures 4.4 percent of the vote in national elections; Die Grüne Alternative obtains 4.8 percent of the vote in Austrian national elections and 6.8 percent in elections to the European Parliament; Die Grünen becomes member of coalition governments with the Social Democratic Party in Hesse and in North Rhine Westphalia; first Conference of the Parties to the Framework

Convention on Climate Change held in Berlin, Federal Republic of Germany; membership of the World Wildlife Fund (WWF) numbers well over five million; plan developed by the World Bank and international conservation groups to protect marine biological diversity in 155 Marine Protection Areas; over 100 countries ratify a United Nations Global Fishing Pact to curb the decrease in fish reserves; environmental activist Ken Saro-Wiwa and eight others are executed in Nigeria; a sodium leak at the Monju fast-breeder nuclear reactor in Japan leads to its temporary shut-down.

1996   Australian Greens formed and Bob Brown elected to the Senate in federal elections; green independent candidates gain 11 percent of the vote and four seats in Tasmania; Vihreä Liitoo attracts 7.6 percent of the vote and gains a seat in the European Parliament; first presidential convention of the Association of State Green Parties in the United States held; second Conference of the Parties to the Framework Convention on Climate Change held in Geneva.

1997   Les Verts in France gains seven seats in elections to the National Assembly; membership of the European Federation of Green Parties consists of 28 political organizations from 24 countries, and seven other political associations comprise a group of applicants to join the federation; third Conference of the Parties to the United Nations Framework Convention on Climate Change held in Kyoto establishes the Kyoto Protocol, which sets a target of a 5.2 percent reduction in the greenhouse gas emissions of industrialized states by 2012 relative to 1990 levels; Dominique Voynet of Les Verts becomes environment minister in France; Greenpeace, suffering from severe budgetary problems, is forced to make massive cuts to its staff; Ecologist Green Party of Mexico wins a Senate seat.

1998   Bündnis 90/Die Grünen invited to join in a coalition with the Social Democratic Party in Germany; India conducts a series of underground nuclear tests, the first by any country in 20 years; Estonian Greens lose their party registration; Federation of Green Parties of Africa formed; Rainbow and Greens Japan launched.

1999   Oaxaca Declaration calls for formation of a Global Green Network of Green Parties; Green Party of Great Britain wins its first seat in the European Parliament; Green Party of South Africa formed; Verena

Diener becomes first green president of a cantonal in Switzerland; Audie Bock elected as first green representative to the California State Assembly; fatal accident occurs at Tokaimura nuclear fuel reprocessing plant in Ibaraki, Japan; European Federation of Green Parties-European Free Alliance doubles its representation to 48 of 626 seats; Ecolo enters into a coalition government in Belgium; antiglobalization protests in Seattle that coincide with an International Monetary Fund and World Bank meeting turn violent; Indian National Green Party is registered.

2000 Convention on the Protection of the Alps enters into force; antiglobalization protests held in Washington, D.C., and Prague, the Czech Republic; Asia Pacific Green Politics workshop held in Brisbane, Australia; David Brower, first full-time executive of the Sierra Club, dies; Cartagena Protocol of the Conventional on Biological Diversity adopted; George W. Bush elected as president; Ecologist Green Party of Mexico joins the conservative National Action Party in an alliance that brings Vicente Fox into the presidency.

2001 Ecologist Green Party of Mexico leaves the alliance with the National Action Party; George W. Bush pulls the United States out of the Kyoto Protocol, eliciting harsh criticisms in Europe and Japan; the European Union (EU) establishes a Renewable Energy Directive that calls for the share of renewable energies in electricity production to increase to 21 percent in order to reach an overall target of renewable energies accounting for 12 percent of energy consumption by 2010; Cyprus Green Party gains first national member of Parliament (MP); Global Greens founded; Green Party of the United States established; September 11 attacks on the World Trade Center and the Pentagon shock the world; U.S.-led war against the Taliban initiated in Afghanistan.

2002 Latvian Green Party enters ruling coalition; Brazil establishes Tumucumaque National Park, the world's largest tropical forest park; Green Party of Pakistan founded; John Eder elected to Maine State House of Representatives in the United States; World Summit on Sustainable Development held in Johannesburg, South Africa, where world leaders confirm their commitment to implementation of Agenda 21 and the realization of the Millennium Development Goals; first Association of Southeast Asian Nations (ASEAN) +3 (China, Japan, Republic of Korea) environment ministers meeting held; the Bush administration announces its Clear Sky Initiative to cut sulfur dioxide, nitrogen oxide, and mercury emissions, but the plan does not include carbon dioxide; in France, Noël Mamère wins 5.2 percent of the presidential vote.

2003 Mayors for Peace campaign launched; Benin Green Party enters national parliament; Wangari Maathai founds Mazingira Green Party of Kenya; Green Party of Nigeria formed; Global Greens founded; war on terrorism used to justify U.S. bombing of Bagdad; Saddam Hussein captured.

2004 Cyprus, the Czech Republic, Estonia, Hungary, Latvia, Lithuania, Malta, Poland, Slovakia, and Slovenia join the European Union (EU); Green Party of Bangladesh launched; Convention on Persistent Organic Pollutants enters into force; European Green Party formed out of the European Federation of Green Parties; Germany sends 13 delegates to the European Parliament; Korea Greens founded; Indulus Emsis, founder of the Latvian Green Party, becomes the first green prime minister in the world; Wangari Maathai wins the Nobel Peace Prize for her efforts to promote sustainable development; Poland's Green Party (Zieloni) set up; Spanish Greens join the Green group in the European Parliament for the first time; Orange Revolution in the Ukraine.

2005 Hurricane Katrina destroys much of New Orleans, raising many environmental justice concerns; Red-Green coalition in Germany comes to an end; Asia Pacific Green Network launched; Asia Pacific Partnership on Clean Development and Climate started by the United States and joined by Australia, China, India, Japan, and South Korea; the European Union (EU) initiates its carbon emissions trading program; Ginette Skandrani evicted from Les Verts in France as a Holocaust denier; Kyoto Protocol enters into force; Women's Global Green Action Network established.

2006 Czech Greens win six seats in the national parliament; European Green Party publishes plan for Green Future for Europe; Italian Greens enter Romano Prodi's ruling coalition; in midterm elections, the Democrats take back the majority in U.S. Congress, promising to initiate a more environmentally proactive legislative agenda; Die Grünen become Austria's third-largest party; Chinese State Environmental Protection Administration announces that China has 2,700 registered environmental groups.

2007 Bulgaria and Romania join the European Union (EU); the Intergovernmental Panel on Climate Change releases its fourth assessment reports on the state of knowledge regarding climate change and its damaging consequences; Al Gore's *An Inconvenient Truth* awarded best documentary film in the Oscars.

Introduction

Human beings have been concerned about nature and their place in it for millennia. The endurance of ancient societies has been based partly on their success in living in alignment with nature. Although the relationship between aboriginal inhabitants of different regions and the natural environment has sometimes erroneously been portrayed as entirely harmonious, this romantic view is not without foundation. For instance, in Australia there was a vast difference between Aboriginals and Europeans in the nineteenth century in terms of their impact on the environment and of the technologies they used to exploit it. This has led some political activists to argue that Aboriginals waged "the longest and most successful conservation campaign" in history because they chose "to become part of the environment" rather than to destroy it in the name of progress (Burnam Burnam 1987).

The primary focus of this historical dictionary is on green campaigns and movements. While some attention is given to the movements of the nineteenth century (in the wake of the so-called great transformation that involved political upheavals as well as the rapid development of industrial capitalism and a free market economy), the primary focus is on the twentieth century, and in particular the period since World War II that has seen both the further expansion of Western democratic free market economies and the questioning by some of the assumptions that underpin them. Here the term "green movement" refers to organized attempts by modern associations to change attitudes, values, and perceptions about the relationship between human beings and nature. Although disquiet about the consequences of human action on the natural environment can be traced back to the ancient Greeks and Romans (McCormick 1995, xi), the emergence of interest groups, political parties, and mass social movements focusing primarily on environmental issues is a fairly recent phenomenon.

The origins of the green movement can be traced back to the nineteenth century. In this period, individuals, groups, and organizations began campaigning for the conservation and preservation of natural areas and the protection of wildlife species. Efforts to combat pollution also began. Among the most prominent groups concerned about environmental protection to emerge at this time were the Commons, Open Spaces, and Footpaths Preservation Society founded in 1865 in Britain and the Sierra Club established in 1892 in the United States of America. These groups achieved notable successes, especially in influencing legislation for environmental protection, including the dedication of major national parks. Over the next several decades many new conservation and preservation groups were formed.

It was not until the 1960s, however, that the green movement in its more modern incarnation emerged. The green movements that arose at this time maintained the concerns with conservation, preservation, and industrial pollution held by earlier generations, but added to their agenda new issues, including justice, equality, participatory democracy, and sustainability. They also were more aware of and concerned with the larger structural factors that are behind pollution and resource degradation.

There were close connections between the New Left of the 1960s (the student movements, the anti–Vietnam War protests, and civil rights movements) and the green movements that arose to address environmental degradation and react against nuclear energy. Many participants in the radical movements of the 1960s became involved in environmentalist groups in the 1970s. There has likewise been a degree of thematic continuity. One example is the connection between protests for peace in the lead-up to the War in Iraq and campaigns in the 1950s against nuclear weapons. Some questions, like the preoccupation with individual self-fulfillment and self-expression by many participants in the student protests of the 1960s, developed into broader concerns like those of the women's movement, civil rights, equality of opportunity, and access to power.

One of the major differences between the period since World War II and earlier experiences is the level of public support for environmental protection. It is only since World War II that action to protect the environment has been sustained by the readiness of significant sections of the population to take political action. This has entailed support for citizens' initiatives, regional, national, and international social movements, new political organizations, and the traditional political parties. The latter have, in recent years, been willing to assume a large portion of the agenda first promoted by the green movement. The eagerness of traditional political organizations to adopt many of the policies of the green movement is matched by a broadening of the social bases of support for environmental protection. Over the past several decades, support for the green movement has been notable among certain social groups, including the young, the relatively affluent, and the well educated. Lately, however, the social bases of the green movement have increasingly come to reflect those of the broader community.

In referring to the green movement, there is an implicit assumption of similarities not only in the social bases for support of certain forms of political action and political agenda but of equivalence in sources of inspiration for such action and of similar preoccupations. While this can be shown to be the case, it is also important to point out that there is great diversity in approaches to addressing environmental problems and in how people perceive the relationship between human beings and nature.

There is a further issue. The agenda of green political groups and organizations includes much that is not specifically green, even though these preoccupations or values can be accommodated by what Goodin (1992) refers to as a "green theory" or philosophy of value. Among these values are the focus on postmaterialism (see Inglehart 1990), the notion of nature as irreplaceable, the ideas of sustainability and sustainable development, the long-term consequences of our current actions, and the connection between environmental protection and ideas of the emancipation of oppressed groups (for instance, minorities, the poor, and women). Goodin describes these values as corollaries to a green theory of value. More problematic, in his view, is the association between various personal lifestyles, especially those that focus on a holistic approach (be it to medicine, diet, or religion), and the green agenda for changes in policies. At any rate, the following account will be framed by three sets of considerations: the philosophies underpinning the diversity of values that influence the actions of participants in the green movement; the political organizations, including social movements, political parties, and interest groups that attempt to articulate the concerns of the green movement; and the issues raised by the green movement.

CONCEPTUAL BASES FOR THE GREEN MOVEMENT

Commitment to environmentalism manifests itself with different levels of intensity and in a variety of ways. Persons who are regarded as being radical or fundamentalist in their outlook may espouse a nonanthropocentric philosophy. In other words, they may take the viewpoint that nonhuman forms of life are valuable irrespective of their importance to human beings. They may also engage in militant opposition to established political institutions. This is not necessarily the norm. Many members and supporters of green political associations may prefer to work through traditional channels of the political system (such as major political parties and interest groups), even though they share certain broad objectives (for example, the preservation of the environment) with the radical activists.

INFLUENTIAL WRITERS

One way of accounting for or understanding the ways of thinking that predominate in the green movement is to consider the views of influential writers. The success of social movements has always depended on the capacity of intellectuals, scientists, and writers to develop new concepts that might change perceptions and then influence behavior. Among the most dramatic and successful efforts to bring about a transformation of that kind was the publication in 1962 of *Silent Spring* by Rachel Carson. This work became a source of inspiration to millions of people. The term "silent spring" was used to characterize the devastating consequences of the continued use of chemical insecticides and pesticides like dichlorodiphenyltrichloroethane (DDT) on wildlife and its habitat. The book provoked strong opposition from the chemical industry, which tried unsuccessfully to have it banned. The extraordinary popularity of the work contributed to the establishment by President Kennedy of a special panel of the Science Advisory Committee that supported the arguments presented by Carson about the hazards of pesticides.

Another highly influential treatise was, a decade later, *A Blueprint for Survival*, published by the editorial board of *The Ecologist* magazine. Like *The Limits to Growth*, published by the Club of Rome in the same year, *A Blueprint for Survival* advocated radical changes. Whereas *The Limits to Growth* urged governments to initiate drastic policies to reduce industrial and agricultural investment, reduce the birthrate, and transfer wealth from more developed to less developed countries, *A Blueprint for Survival* focused on radical changes in lifestyles in order to ensure the perpetuation of the planet. In particular, it advocated the formation of decentralized social structures as a way to ensure greater participation in decision making and encourage innovation. Anticipating the aims of the green political movements over the coming decade, the book argued for small, self-regulating communities in which people might achieve more fulfilling personal relationships. Like the authors of *The Limits to Growth*, they advocated greater controls on population growth. An important distinction between the two books was the focus in *The Limits to Growth* on the role of elites in bringing about change and on scientific models for understanding the problems arising from economic growth, industrialization, and environmental degradation.

Arguments about *The Limits to Growth*, particularly the focus on population growth, were of course anticipated in the late eighteenth century by the Reverend Thomas Malthus in *An Essay on the Principle of Population* and were echoed in the late 1960s in a book that received immense publicity, *The Population Bomb* by Paul Ehrlich. The issue of population growth is unresolved within the green movement. Some writers have argued for strong measures, including financial disincentives to procreation, as well as educational campaigns. In an essay on "The Tragedy of the Commons," Garrett Hardin argued that the principle of freedom in the use of common land had become anachronistic. Among the measures he proposed for restricting access to the commons and for preventing the overuse of scarce resources were constraints on the right to beget children.

Another important concept utilized by the green movement has been the notion of "small is beautiful," derived from the title and arguments of a book written by E. F. Schumacher. Schumacher developed an influential argument that questioned the appropriateness of large-scale ventures. This coincided with the interest among many activists in the green movement in forming decentralized and small-scale organizations that might facilitate participation and democratic decision making. Schumacher was also concerned about the impact of large-scale developments on the environment, again a very popular theme among supporters of the green movement.

WAYS OF THINKING ABOUT THE ECONOMY

The challenge issued by Schumacher impinged on prevailing ways of thinking about the economy. The questioning by the green movement of the dominant approaches to conceptualizing the economy has led to a number of reforms. Some governments have introduced carbon taxes with a view to reducing emissions that add to the warming of the Earth's atmosphere, the so-called greenhouse effect. Others have, for decades, tried to enact the principle that requires the polluter to pay for the damage caused. The idea is that all the expenses, including the cost of trying to repair the damage to the environment, should be taken into consideration and that in the final instance the price for products will reflect entirely the environmental and social costs.

Another important tactic used by the green movement in applying pressure on governments not to proceed with a wide range of projects is to evoke the strict application of the so-called precautionary principle. In other words, the green movement has often ensured the stringent application of safety standards to new projects. In areas such as the development of nuclear power, this has meant that governments have decided not to proceed with a particular project.

The green movement has also challenged how we define economic benefits, and several efforts have been undertaken to revisit how we measure the economic performance of a country. Traditionally the focus has been on the gross national product. However, in the wake of arguments about *The Limits to Growth* and the destruction wrought by industrial society, economists sympathetic to the green movement have attempted to devise new standards for measuring the performance of a nation, particularly in terms of the health of the population and other aspects of the quality of life. These efforts have the potential to enable citizens to influence government action and behavior since they question the basic premises of many policy decisions.

An important concept used to justify the reshaping of some policies and the perpetuation of some prevailing practices has been the notion of sustainable development. This concept has been widely used since the

1980s following the report by the World Commission on Environment and Development entitled *Our Common Future*. The report coincided with growing concern among Western nations about the dangers posed by environmental destruction and the enduring problems faced by less developed nations in meeting the basic needs of their populations. The term "sustainable development" was defined by the commission as meeting "the needs of the present without compromising the ability of future generations to meet their own needs." The commission attempted to show how a focus on economic growth would not necessarily damage the environment if it were guided by the principles of ecology. The idea of sustainable development has been used to forge close links between economic and environmental concerns by governments, businesses, and environmental groups. Governments have used the notion of sustainable development to try and shape debates about the environment and thereby diminish the electoral influence of some green political organizations. Although there has been much criticism of the concept by the latter, many supporters of the green movement have become involved in efforts to implement sustainable development.

Discussions about sustainable development have stimulated efforts to place a value on the environment. Among others, economists have tried to achieve this through the introduction of pollution charges and carbon taxes and, as indicated earlier, through questioning conventional ways of measuring economic costs and benefits. One initiative to bring about change in perceptions and policies was the publication by David Pearce and his associates of *Blueprint for a Green Economy*, which mapped out measures for achieving sustainable development by placing values on the environment, including water and the atmosphere, that have had no price attached to them and have therefore been overexploited.

Another approach to reconceptualizing prevailing economic practices and beliefs has been the idea of green consumerism. In a book entitled *The Green Consumer Guide*, John Elkington and Julia Hailes argue for the possibility of combining a comfortable lifestyle with environmental protection by buying products that do not destroy the environment. In certain respects, this approach is in alignment with both the enactment of government policies and the aspirations of many supporters of the green movement. Still, some people are skeptical about the possibility of tackling serious environmental problems simply through the substitution of products. Rather than focus on the substitution of products, some green economists such as Herman Daly have promoted the notion of a "steady-state" economy.

This implies support for a sustainable economy or for sustainable development. Daly argues for this from the perspective of the laws of thermodynamics: in other words, from the basis that in a closed system, energy is neither produced nor consumed but only modified. Daly argues, among other things, that in our society the rate of modification of existing matter is greater than the rate of replacement by solar energy. In order to address this problem Daly has advocated the creation of a steady-state economy with defined limits to the size of population and the creation of wealth.

Like many supporters of the green movement, Daly has questioned the values that underpin the focus on economic growth and material prosperity. This call has been echoed by Thomas Princen, Michael Maniates, and Ken Conca in their book, *Confronting Consumption*, which argues that it is the consumerism of the industrialized north and the structures that support it that are a major factor behind the ecological destruction in many parts of the world. These authors share a concern with issues like social justice. In revisiting how we measure economic performance, the green movement has often raised the question of social justice. Many green political parties have advocated the introduction of a guaranteed minimum income in lieu of the existing system of social security and tax relief. While this scheme may have certain merits, the green movement has so far been unable to deal adequately with two major objections to the idea— namely, the cost of implementing it and the disincentives it might create to people seeking employment.

Another dimension of the economic strategies proposed by the green movement has been the introduction of the idea of alternative energy as a framework for new policies. Green political organizations have drawn attention to the possibilities of using renewable energy sources such as solar, wind, and biofuels. An influential example of this way of thinking is *Soft Energy Paths: Towards a Durable Peace* by Amory Lovins. Lovins's idea that the development of benign, or "soft," technologies could contribute to the formation of a less coercive and centralized social system than the prevailing one was well received by many in the green movement. These technologies would apparently allow for the evolution of a more participatory political culture. Without necessarily accepting these arguments, traditional political and industrial organizations have become willing to explore the possibilities for using solar, wind, water, or biofuels. Examples include Brazil, which obtains a large share of its energy from ethanol derived from sugar cane, and the European Union, which has passed directives promoting a shift toward alternative energies throughout its member states.

FUNDAMENTAL PRINCIPLES AND CONCEPTS

The focus by the green movement on economic considerations and social justice represents an important element in its agenda for change. Another significant aspect of the development of the green movement is a discussion about the fundamental principles that might shape a green society.

One of the distinctions frequently used to characterize different approaches within the green movement is that between "deep" and "shallow" ecologists. The term "deep ecology" was invented in 1972 by the Norwegian philosopher Arne Naess. Shallow ecologists are said to be interested primarily in preserving resources for the benefit of human beings in developed nations. By contrast, deep ecologists concentrate on the intrinsic value of the environment, hence on a nonanthropocentric focus, valuing nature for its own sake and resisting the notion that human beings can be understood as separate from their environment. Like the biocentrists, deep ecologists advocate unity with nature and the preservation of all forms of life. Among the most significant divisions within the green movement is the one between the proponents of an anthropocentric perspective and those who urge others to accept the intrinsic value of nature.

This conflict manifests itself, for instance, in the discussion of the rights of animals. Deep ecologists have argued that animals have moral rights. Hence, supporters of groups such as Earth First! concentrate as much on the defense of the Earth and of all species of plant and animal life as on protecting individual human lives. The defense of the moral rights of animals is made in a book entitled *The Case for Animal Rights* by Tom Regan. Still, some of these efforts to argue for the basic moral rights of animals are often too intricate for most supporters of the green movement.

Other arguments are easier to follow: for instance, the concern about a loss of community. The idea of a loss of community is linked by many in the green movement to the rise of industrial society and the alienation of one person from another. This is a popular theme in writings by prominent intellectuals in the green movement. In *Socialism and Survival*, the late Rudolf Bahro argued that the interest of the human species should become the core point of reference for understanding the problems we confront and that social change could only be achieved if one went beyond the concept of class enunciated by Karl Marx. There is a parallel here with the arguments of deep ecologists, who questioned an anthropocentric approach to nature.

In order to reverse the loss of community, leading figures in the green movement such as Bahro advocated a more spiritual approach and the development of communal lifestyles. Bahro was also willing to propose a fairly controversial means of embracing such a lifestyle: he championed a model based on the practices of the Benedictine Order of monks. Another vision for a green society, not too dissimilar to that espoused by Bahro, was articulated by Kirkpatrick Sale, who used the concept of a decentralized bioregional society. The idea is that people will live in accord with the rhythms of the land or the discrete territory defined by natural boundaries. The focus is not on reshaping nature but on adapting to it. The planned outcome would be a more balanced economic and social system that would enable people to enjoy more leisure, develop communal bonds, and live in proximity to nature.

Many of these ideas had been anticipated by earlier generations. For instance, in *A Sand County Almanac*, published in 1949, Aldo Leopold developed an ethic for the relationship between human beings and their environment that went beyond the predominant focus on economic relationships and posited the extension of the notion of community to include the soil, water, plants, and animals. Moreover, like Rachel Carson in *Silent Spring*, he presented a gloomy portrait of the damage being inflicted on the environment.

The notion of reversing trends toward industrialization and development has also been an important theme in the pronouncements by leading figures in the green movement. In a publication entitled *The Great U-Turn: De-Industrializing Society*, Edward Goldsmith argues against the construction of cities, factories, highways, and airports. In certain ways this represents a radical response to the claims about *The Limits to Growth.* A similar line of argument is pursued by writers who maintain that affluent lifestyles are unsustainable and that we need to redistribute resources from wealthy to poor countries and reverse trends in economic development.

The connection between ideas about biocentrism and the rise of social movements arises in various ways. Take the interest in ecology among some supporters of the feminist movement: this group has been often referred to as the ecofeminist wing of the green movement. Ecofeminists have suggested that women may be more inclined to support the aims of the green movement because they are inherently closer to nature than men. This has then been linked to arguments about patriarchy and the propensity of men, rather than women, to destroy the natural environment.

The focus by ecofeminists on the nonmaterial characteristics of the relationship between human beings and nature reflects an enduring interest among the progenitors of the green movement. Pioneers like John Muir in the United States and Myles Dunphy in Australia anticipated in their writings the contemporary interest in the spiritual qualities of nature. This theme is echoed in postmaterialism or postmaterial values as well as in deep ecology. Some writers have condemned industrial society on the grounds that it fragments life. They draw a sharp contrast between industrialization and a holistic approach that includes spirituality, particularly the aesthetic, caring, and loving aspects of existence. Still, the notion of spirituality does not feature in an explicit manner in the pronouncements of green political organizations and is often regarded with suspicion by them.

While the terms "deep ecology" and "shallow ecology" have been used to differentiate between the approaches of green thinkers, activists, and sympathizers, the terms "fundamentalist" and "realist" have been utilized largely to refer to different factions within green political organizations. The terms were first used to describe groups that emerged in Die Grünen in Germany. The fundamentalists in the party were generally opposed to cooperation with traditional political parties, particularly to any notion of forming coalitions with them. The fundamentalists believed that they had a better understanding of the social movements that had given rise to the formation of green political parties than the realists. Whereas the realists appeared to accept that parliamentary politics involved compromise, the loss of the spontaneous character of the green movement, and an emphasis on professionalism, the fundamentalists argued for grassroots participation in the party, including the possibility of recall of delegates, rotating them out of office and achieving agreement through consensus rather than through majoritarian voting. In most green parties, the outcome of protracted struggles for power between fundamentalists and realists has been a victory for the latter. At any rate, most supporters of green parties have been in favor of cooperation between green and traditional political parties in order to accomplish at least some of the goals of the green movement. This trend has manifested itself in the increasingly large number of cases where green parties have entered into coalition governments. Bündnis 90/Die Grünen joined the ruling coalition in Germany from 1998–2005. In recent years, Greens have been parts of governing coalitions in Belgium, the Czech Republic, Finland, France, Germany, Georgia, Italy, and Latvia.

Though bruised in the electoral arena, the fundamentalists, like the deep ecologists, reflect the vigor of the green movement. This vigor is maintained by the infusion of new ways of thinking. Some ideas, like the Gaia hypothesis that was posited by James Lovelock in the 1970s, continue to provide inspiration to the green movement in questioning enduring ways of perceiving the environment. Though Lovelock has recognized that his belief in the existence of a complex system that can act as a "single living entity" (Mother Earth) cannot be tested scientifically, his argument continues to attract both supporters and detractors of the green movement, particularly since it implies that nature, if not the human species, has the capacity to survive the attack on it by human beings.

The tension between realism and fundamentalism also reflects persistent themes in socialist, or left-wing, politics. There has often been a close connection between the development of the green movement and left-wing politics. An important parallel has been the notion of social ecology. Whereas deep ecology is concerned about the exploitation of the environment, social ecology, as understood by anarchist-writer Murray Bookchin, represents the view that efforts to dominate nature originate in people's attempt to dominate their fellow human beings. The hope by Bookchin is that the green movement will seek to develop new social structures based on direct democracy rather than on the power of centralized and hierarchical bureaucracies. There is some overlap between these ideas and those of fundamentalists in green parties.

Another important theme in the development of the green movement has been that of peace and nonviolence. Many groups in the antinuclear protest movement that emerged in the 1970s presented nonviolence as one of the axioms guiding their activities, and this notion was adopted by Die Grünen in Germany as one of its four core principles. As with the Chipko Andalan movement in India, many other supporters of the green movement have been influenced, in this regard, by the writings and practices of Mahatma Gandhi and his followers in the campaigns against British rule in India. Still, green activists have not always agreed on precise forms of civil disobedience. These actions can range from noncompliance with tax regulations, to blocking the entrance to nuclear power installations to prevent the transportation of nuclear waste materials, to acts of sabotage as propounded by members of Earth First!

Despite these important and fundamental differences in approaches, the green movement has contributed to and been part of a huge shift in perceptions about how we relate to the environment. Detailed explanations for the rise of the green movement are too numerous to list here. Among those that have been widely used is the notion that postmaterialism explains changes in values. Though the distinction between material and postmaterial values can be traced to ancient times, recent empirical studies suggest that materialist and postmaterialist values were strongly associated with conflicts over environmental protection and economic development.

The notion of a shift in values is closely linked to the green movement's focus on the quality of life and on redefining what this means. This can entail rejecting economic growth and industrial development as the principal measures of the quality of life. Apart from a strong focus on environmental protection and preservation, the green movement has stimulated discussions on the quality of life in the workplace, in family relationships, and in local communities. This debate has had a significant impact on traditional political organizations, which have developed agendas that cover issues pertaining to immigrants, homosexuals, minorities, single parents, and women. In addition, the green movement has been influential in persuading governments to extend the notion of quality of life to include in an explicit manner the notion of the stewardship of nature.

GREEN SOCIAL MOVEMENTS, POLITICAL PARTIES, AND INTEREST GROUPS

For many political groups and movements, environmental protection was at first only a small part of a broader agenda that included issues like the democratization of society, the defense of civil rights, and the pursuit of social justice. However, the issue of environmental protection has become a significant theme in many of these associations. The notion of protecting the environment has, of course, been used to broaden the appeal of these movements and served as a focal point for a heterogeneous constituency. More than any other issue, environmentalism has provided new social movements with opportunities for reshaping the political order, challenging assumptions about economic growth and industrial development, and drawing attention to different types of values.

Within new social movements, citizens' initiatives, and interest groups, the focus on the environment has become the key theme. In addition, established organizations, notably political parties, have been selective in how they have adapted to the challenge by new social movements. They have primarily focused on the growing concern about the environment. They have also been reluctant to adopt aspects of environmentalism that may undermine economic imperatives and electoral considerations.

In terms of political action and political change, the most striking manifestation of a shift in perspective and a counter to prevailing trends has been the formation of social movements, interest groups, and political parties and the challenges posed by them. The impact of environmentalism on Western democracies is reflected in the great efforts by churches, trade unions, business and commercial interest groups, state bureaucracies, governments, and political parties to incorporate and respond to the demands of the green movement. The process of adaptation has become so widespread that one can now refer to the culture of environmentalism as one of the most significant elements in contemporary politics and society. This does not mean that the demands of environmentalists have been met or imply that traditional institutions have successfully defused the potential for conflict between environment and development.

THE RISE OF THE GREEN MOVEMENT

The following account focuses primarily on the contribution to the green movement by social movements, political parties, and interest groups since World War II. An important stimulus to protest action was provided by campaigns conducted in the 1950s by associations like the Campaign for Nuclear Disarmament. This postwar movement against testing nuclear weapons anticipated social movements like the ones that protested the war in Vietnam and, from the 1970s, fought against the deployment of nuclear weapons. The latter contributed to a revival of the Campaign for Nuclear Disarmament in the 1970s, and it was no coincidence that the organization became affiliated with interest groups such as Friends of the Earth and Greenpeace and political associations like the Ecology Party.

The rise of the green movement, though most concentrated and visible in the formation of new political associations (as well as the revival of some old ones) in western Europe, was not confined to one continent. Reflecting the international character of the movement, political organizations and interest groups arose on most continents in the 1970s. In Latin America, the Gaucha Association for the Protection of the Natural Environment in Brazil emerged in 1971. From 1974 on, hundreds of green groups were formed throughout Brazil, and the first members of the green movement were elected to state assemblies in 1982. In Japan, in the 1970s, spurred by the plight of the victims of Minamata mercury poisoning, thousands of environmental citizens' movements arose to protest the severe pollution afflicting their country and pry open a decision-making system that tended to focus on the concerns of business to the exclusion of society. In India one of the most interesting initiatives to boost awareness about environmental problems was the creation in 1973 of the Chipko Andalan movement (involving mainly women in villages). The protestors were principally concerned with preventing logging firms from destroying forests, which were a vital source of fuel and food. To achieve their goals the protestors used the methods of nonviolent resistance advocated by Gandhi. The Chipko Andalan movement secured some important concessions from the government. Further significant initiatives were the movement to prevent logging in Malaysia led by Sahabat Alam Malaysia (the Friends of the Earth organization in Malaysia) and the Green Belt Movement for planting trees in Kenya.

Still, while environmentalists in Australia and New Zealand have laid claim to being the first to create green political parties in substance if not in name (e.g., the Values Party formed in New Zealand in 1972 and the United Tasmania Group formed in Australia in 1972) and in the United States the now-defunct Citizens' Party shared many of the goals of the green parties that began forming in Europe, until the 1990s, green political parties were primarily a western European phenomena.

In the 1960s citizens' initiatives began to emerge in western Europe. They arose at the local level and tended to deal with issues that had been neglected by traditional political parties and associations. A notable feature of these initiatives was the desire to involve people in decision making. The citizens' initiatives played a central role in the rise of protests against nuclear power projects from the 1970s. An important factor in the development of green political movements and parties out of these citizens' initiatives was the effort by Western governments to develop nuclear power. Protests were regularly initiated at a local level by small communities anxious about the impact of radiation on agricultural products. Though local in origin, these responses rapidly led to the defense of entire regions and their cultures against the plans of central governments. Protests in the Federal Republic of Germany became the most famous, as they spread from small rural communities to large cities with radical political groups. They also attracted supporters from other countries. These protests laid the basis for the formation of green lists and parties competing at local, regional, and then national elections.

Not only were these groups protesting nuclear power, they were demanding grassroots democracy. Although divided over some issues, green political parties and other groups took strong stances on issues such as the humane treatment of animals; protection of wildlife; opposition to intensive animal husbandry and animal experimentation; the use of animal products, especially when it places an entire species under the threat of extinction; and opposition to hunting animals for recreational purposes.

The impact of the green movement on traditional political associations was so great that some of the leading figures in these organizations adopted significant elements of the green agenda. Among the many political leaders who were prepared to promote some of the ideas of the green movement were Prime Minister Gro Harlem Brundtland of Norway, who chaired the World Commission on Environment and Development from 1984 on; British Prime Minister Margaret Thatcher, who, in 1988, used an address to the Royal Society to express concern about issues like the greenhouse effect, the depletion of the ozone layer, and acid rain; and Australian Prime Minister Bob Hawke, who, from 1983 to 1990, placed the environment high on the political agenda and introduced many reforms. More recently, British prime minister Tony Blair has made addressing climate change one of his leading priorities and the former U.S. vice president Albert Gore has sought to galvanize the world into action through his educational documentary on climate change, *An Inconvenient Truth.*

However, prior to the efforts of established politicians to adopt much of the green agenda, leading figures in the green movement had already made important contributions. Even though these leading figures often found it hard to win the trust of the grassroots activists, the media ensured that they became famous. Petra Kelly was for a long time the most celebrated person in the green movement. Following her involvement in protests against the Vietnam War in the 1960s and in the German Social Democratic Party in the 1970s, she became a founding member of Die Grünen. Kelly herself shared many of the misgivings among activists about involvement in parliamentary politics and dubbed Die Grünen an "antiparty" that should not form coalitions with traditional parties. Still, she became entangled in arguments about the professionalization of green politicians and found it hard to accept that the principle of rotation of delegates out of office would also be applied to her. Like Kelly, other green politicians had to grapple with the tension between the demands for the accountability or rotation of delegates and the requirements of professional politics. But unlike Kelly, other leading green politicians, such as Joschka Fischer in the state of Hesse in the Federal Republic of Germany and Brice Lalonde in France, were prepared to make compromises in order to cooperate with traditional political organizations.

The creation and further development of green political parties reflected these deep tensions between the realists and the fundamentalists. However, there were also strong unifying elements, and it is remarkable how much green parties shared in terms of a common philosophical agenda across nations and continents even though circumstances varied from country to country.

THE DISTINCTIVE DEVELOPMENT
OF NATIONAL GREEN PARTIES

There were several key factors that contributed to the distinctive development of particular green parties. First, there were some important differences in emphasis on particular issues. For instance, in Australia there was a much stronger focus than that in many European countries on the protection of wilderness areas; many of these tracts of land were eventually nominated for World Heritage listing. The issue of nuclear power played a much more crucial role in some countries, notably the Federal Republic of Germany, than in others in mobilizing opposition to established government policies. The newly forming green parties in Africa have an understandably strong concern with health issues, and in particular HIV/AIDS.

Second, traditional patterns of political behavior and institutional practices that had evolved in different countries or regions had a significant impact on the fate of green political associations. For example, in Britain the "winner-takes-all" electoral system has made it extremely difficult for new political parties or for small parties to gain representation in Parliament. Similarly, while the United States has given rise to a powerful green movement, it has not been able to form a strong green party. The U.S. electoral system presents a major hurdle to the participation of new political organizations in presidential campaigns, and green associations have performed poorly in presidential contests. While Ralph Nader did make it as a third Green Party candidate in the 2000 presidential election, he received only 2.7 percent of the vote and may have contributed to the electoral loss of Democratic presidential candidate Albert Gore. In other countries, green parties have been able to benefit from the existence of electoral systems based on proportional representation. Another factor has been the capacity of traditional political organizations to engage in dialogue with or to co-opt new political movements.

The emergence of competent leaders who were able to innovate or seize on opportunities for change has been another important consideration. In some countries, certain individuals, expert communities, or intellectuals have played a crucial part in articulating concerns about the environment or the quality of life and in bringing together those who are disaffected with established political practices. In Belgium, for instance, the emergence of a green movement can be traced back to, among other factors, a Christian movement initiated by Luc Versteylen, a Jesuit priest and teacher. Among the key concerns of Versteylen and his associates was the meaning of the education offered to young people and of the values connected with a competitive, consumer society. These deliberations led to the formation of the Anders gaan leven movement, first in Antwerp and later in the provinces. This movement experimented with alternative lifestyles, attempted to achieve grassroots democracy, and engaged in campaigns to protect the environment. It also provided the basis for a new political organization, Agalev. Like Anders gaan leven, Agalev had as one of its primary aims getting young people to think about their problems and position in society. After competing in local and regional elections, Agalev participated in elections to the European Parliament in 1979. In 1982 Agalev separated itself from Anders gaan leven and formally became a political party.

The development of green political organizations in Belgium also shows how prevailing institutional practices and traditions shape such groups. In this case, cultural, religious, and ethnic differences intersect with green politics. Whereas Agalev represents the Flemish community, the other Belgian Green Party, Ecolo, represents the Walloon population.

France offers another illustration of the institutional factors that shape the development of green political parties. As in many other European countries, the origins of the green movement in France include a strong tradition of nature conservation groups, radical student groups that emerged in the 1960s, and citizen protests against the development of nuclear power. The French political system also presented both unique opportunities for and constraints on the development of green parties. In addition, several political leaders who had a decisive impact on the shape of these parties emerged. Although the green party Les Verts was formed in 1984, there were difficulties in uniting the green movement. There were clashes within the leadership, particularly over the questions of cooperating with traditional political organizations and of balancing two sets of considerations: the retention of many of the ideals of grassroots movements and the need to engage in pragmatic politics. In 1990 a second green party, Génération Écologie, was formed under the leadership of Brice Lalonde. In 1993 the parties presented a united front at the presidential elections. Although they did well, winning 7.6 percent of the vote, they were not able to win any seats in the National Assembly. With the 1997 election however, they succeeded in sending eight delegates to the National Assembly and in placing Dominique Voynet in the position of environment minister.

It has not been unusual for more than one green party to emerge in a country. In Belgium this reflected religious and ethnic divisions. In other countries, divisions occurred along the lines of political ideology. As in France, two green parties have formed in the Netherlands. The first, De Groenen (The Greens), was founded in 1983 and has not been very successful in electoral terms. The second, GroenLinks (Green Left), represented an electoral alliance of left-wing parties in 1989, before turning itself into a new political party in November 1990. One of the main differences between the two parties has been the extent to which they focus mainly on environmental issues or have a broader agenda for social change.

In some countries, green political issues were first promoted as a primary issue on the political agenda by radical reformist parties prior to the formation of a national green party. In Italy the agenda of the green movement had first been advanced by minor parties such as the Radical party and Worker Democracy. In Australia the platform of the Australian Democrats had long included environmental concerns as a fundamental issue.

When considering the development of green parties, Australia and New Zealand are interesting for a number of reasons. Green political organizations originated here earlier than in many European countries. These parties draw attention to the diversity of issues that can be used to launch campaigns for environmental protection. They also highlight the importance of political associations that did not bear the name "green party" even though they focused primarily on environmental issues. In both countries green political organizations were formed as early as 1972. The United Tasmania Group was one of the first green political organizations ever to compete in state elections. Formed in the same year as the New Zealand Values Party, its purpose was to challenge government policies that led to flooding Lake Pedder in order to create a hydroelectric system. The manifesto of this political association was compatible with many of the broader aims of the green movement, including participatory democracy, more harmonious relationships between human beings and nature, and social justice. The New Zealand Values Party was one of the first endeavors by political activists to establish themselves at a national level on a platform that advocated both environmental protection and participatory democracy. Ideas from Europe and the United States about *The Limits to Growth* and *A Blueprint for Survival* permeated the manifesto of the new party. Its manifesto was called *Blueprint for New Zealand*.

Although green parties now exist in most developed countries and in several less developed ones, their fortunes have been mixed or subject to rapid change. Institutional factors and the response of traditional political organizations have played an important part in these processes. In many countries green parties have made little impact in elections, either because of the rules and regulations that govern the process or because traditional political organizations have successfully adapted to the challenges issued by the green movement. In Sweden the greens simply took longer to effect a political impact than similar parties in other countries did. The Swedish Miljöpartiet de Gröna was founded in 1981. After seven years, in 1988, it made a significant breakthrough and became the first new party in 70 years to gain representation in the national parliament. Like other green parties, it has had to struggle to retain its position. In 1991 it did not gain any seats. Yet, in 1994 this situation was reversed when it gained 18 seats. After the 1998 parliamentary elections, the Social Democrats invited the Miljöpartiet de Gröna and the Left Party into a coalition government. In the 2006 elections they won 5.24 percent of the vote and 19 seats. The reasons for the success of Miljöpartiet de Gröna include its capacity to develop a position on other issues (in this case, opposition to membership in the European Union and the widespread mistrust of professional politicians) as well as, paradoxically, portray itself as a more traditional party with realistic policies and goals. In the 1995 European Parliament elections Miljöpartiet polled an impressive 17.2 percent and gained four seats. This matched the notable performance of the British Green Party, which polled 15 percent of the vote in the 1989 European Parliament elections. However, because of the electoral system the Green Party received no seats. This situation again draws attention to the difficulties posed for minor parties by electoral systems. Despite strong support for the green movement in Britain, there is little prospect of a green party gaining electoral representation. Instead, green issues have increasingly been articulated by the traditional parties, and the primary sphere of influence of the Green Party has been in elections to local and district councils.

Bündnis 90/Die Grünen in the Federal Republic of Germany is one of the most successful green parties in Europe, and certainly the one that has received the most attention and publicity. This is partly due to the high visibility obtained by the party as part of the Red-Green coalition under Helmut Schröder from 1998 to 2005. Joschka Fischer of Die Grünen served as foreign minister and was considered Germany's most popular politician for much of this time. In its position as junior partner in the coalition, Bündnis 90/Die Grünen pushed hard on issues it held dear. It succeeded in passing legislation for the phased shutdown of Germany's nuclear power plants. It also won support for ecological tax reform, which raised taxes on polluters, making it possible to cut income taxes. Germany also maintained its position as a frontrunner on climate change legislation during this time.

The visibility of the party, however, extends back to earlier times before the unification of Germany. After its election into Parliament in 1983, Die Grünen pushed for regulatory change on a wide variety of issues, including the highly visible problems of acid rain and nuclear energy, which in the post-Chernobyl era took on a new significance. The party was also a prominent voice in the peace movement during the Cold War. The program of Die Grünen, with its emphasis on peace, ecology, equality, and antinuclear energy, became a model for other parties.

Yet the formation, development, and agenda of the party have also served to highlight many of the dilemmas confronting green parties in general. In its earlier days, prior to the unification of Germany, Die Grünen experienced conflicts over adherents' dual membership in Die Grünen and other political parties, the professionalization of the party and how it should treat its most prominent figures, the limits and possibilities of implementing direct or grassroots democracy and the imperative mandate, and the possibility of coalitions with other parties, notably the Social Democrats. The party also struggled over its failure to actively support German unification and how to deal with the different values and agenda of the greens in East Germany, which were often far more supportive of capitalism than were members of Die Grünen. Internal party debates were also intense regarding the decision by the Red-Green coalition to support the sending of troops as part of a peacekeeping mission to Bosnia.

Another arena for parliamentary activities and influence by Die Grünen was the European Parliament. When elections to the European Parliament were first held in 1979, the green movement throughout Europe had scarcely begun to organize itself to contest elections on either a regional or national level. In 1984 Die Grünen gained 7 of the 12 seats that went to green parties in the European Parliament and joined their fellow greens in forming Green-Alternative European Link. Much like Die Grünen transformed environmental politics in Germany, the green parties have had a noticeable impact on the direction of European politics. In Germany, Die Grünen's success in transforming German environmental programs was less a result of any bills it introduced into the Diet, than it was as a result of the influence the party exerted on the traditional parties. The traditional parties felt threatened by the Green's sudden rise, and did their best to co-opt their agenda by picking up many of their agenda items. Similarly, just by their presence, the Green-Alternative European Link attracted attention to environmental concerns at the European level.

The influence of green parties in the European Parliament has grown substantially with time. In 1984, green parties for the first time entered the European Parliament with 12 representatives. In 1989 they improved their position to 27 seats. In 1994 they dipped to 21 but with the expansion of the European Union (EU) to include Sweden, Austria, and Finland their numbers improved to 26 and subsequently three other parliamentarians chose to join the group, raising their number to 29. After the 1999 election, they surged to 48 seats, and after some reshuffling following the 2004 election, they were still at a strong 42. They are the fourth-largest political group in the European Parliament.

In an effort to achieve greater coherence, the green parties in the Parliament decided in 1993 to form the European Federation of Green Parties. In 1999, they aligned with the European Free Alliance, a group of parties espousing self-determinacy for Scotland, Wales, and Catalonia, while sharing the green's goals of democracy. In 2004, with the EU expanding its membership to include a group of eight central and eastern European states and two southern European ones, the European Federation of Green Parties/European Free Alliance decided it was important to strengthen their unity. They therefore formed the European Green Party. Since that time, the European Green Party has worked to strengthen their common vision. The European Green Party accepts the European Union as an international project for peace and human rights. It desires to transform the EU into a model of sustainability and a safeguard of the European social model. Beyond this, it calls for enhancing the democratic characteristics of European institutions and promoting the sense of community.

Nevertheless, there is still considerable diversity among the green parties. Greens tend to share a commitment to democracy and decentralization, gender equality, peace, and sustainability. Their positions on the formation of the EU and other similar regional economic and political blocks, however, vary significantly. As a matter of policy, green parties contested some of the trends toward European unity, arguing instead for a "Europe of the regions." This was consistent with their focus on decentralization and autonomy and their distrust of huge, centralized bureaucracies. While these issues served to unite green parties, there were disagreements among their delegates over the value of working in the institutions of the EU; these disputes reflected the tensions that emerged between realist and fundamentalist factions at the national level. While some, such as the Swedish Miljöpartiet are opposed to their government's participation in the EU, others like Les Verts in France and GroenLinks in the Netherlands supported the passage of the European Constitution despite strong domestic public opinion against it. Thus, while the European Greens may be the first major international political party in the world, in many ways it remains more a federation than a unified party. In 2006, the European Greens had member parties and organizations from 31 European countries. There were also several observer organizations.

Still, as the EU over time has become increasingly institutionalized and influential both vis-à-vis national and international policy, many of even the most skeptical of the green parties toward the EU experiment have focused their attention on ways in which they might influence the development of the EU's institutions and policy decisions. A key issue for them has been strengthening of the role of the European Parliament as the sole elected body in the EU. They have also demanded greater adherence to the subsidiarity principle, which calls for decisions to be made at the lowest governmental level practical for addressing a problem. This is consistent with their preference for decentralization. They also have pushed for a strengthening of the community's focus on alternative energies, safe foods, climate change, sustainability, and quality of life issues.

The influence of the green movements and parties in western Europe on the development of green movements in other parts of the world is unmistakable. Green parties were largely a European phenomenon into the late 1980s. Since the collapse of communist and authoritarian governments in central and eastern Europe, Africa, Latin America, and East Asia, however, the possibilities for green movements and parties has improved substantially. The political landscape has altered and this has provided activists with new possibilities. One of the striking phenomena in the period since 1990 has been the rapid spread of green parties to most parts of the world. The question for the coming decade will be whether these parties, the vast majority of which are basically politically impotent, will be able to strengthen their political standing.

The area where the spread of green parties has been most rapid has been in central Europe, especially among the new member-states of the EU. All of the 12 states that joined the EU between 2004 and 2007 (Bulgaria, Cyprus, Czech Republic, Estonia, Hungary, Latvia, Lithuania, Malta, Poland, Romania, Slovenia, Slovakia) have formed a green party or green political organization in the post-1989 period. The success of the parties, however, has varied enormously. At one extreme is Hungary where greens struggle to survive as a party. At the other is Latvia, which had the world's first prime minister from a green party. Only in a handful of these countries have green politicians succeeded in winning representation in national parliaments.

This is despite the fact that in many former eastern European communist countries, environmental movements played a critical role in the struggle against the regimes. The visibility of environmental movements in the late 1980s struggle against the communist governments led many to predict that green movements would continue to play a major role in politics. Initially, it looked like this might indeed be the case as green parties sprang up throughout the region. Yet, as the states began to go through the difficult transitions from socialism to capitalism and communism to democracy, public attention quickly shifted to economic problems. People were more concerned with the economic collapse, the closing of industries, and the wide-scale unemployment they saw around them than with the sizeable pollution problems that still affected them.

This was the case in Hungary, for example. In the mid-1980s, environmental groups emerged to protest some of the development decisions of the communist rulers. The Danube Circle, for example, fought against the building of the Gabcikovo Nagyamaros hydroelectric dam. These groups became increasingly critical of the state and provided a forum for political debate in an otherwise tightly controlled system. In 1990, as the communist regime was collapsing, the green movement coalesced and formed the Hungarian Green Party. In the first elections in the postcommunist Hungary, however, it failed to win a sufficient share of the votes to gain any representatives. This led to an internal struggle and in 1993 the party was transformed into a far right, anti-immigrant party. Environmentalists disassociated themselves from the party and quickly regrouped, forming the Green Alternative (Zöld Alternatíva). The party, however, has struggled to gain acceptance and win supporters. In 2000, it tried to improve its status by changing its name to Green Democrats (Zöld Demokraták), but seemingly to little avail.

A somewhat analogous situation prevailed in Czechoslovakia. As in Hungary, the environmental movement in Czechoslovakia played an important role in the eventual downfall of the communist regime. It was one of several movements that during the mid-1980s questioned the policies and structure of the communist regime. Environmental organizations included Brontosaurus, the Czech Union of Nature Protectionists, and the Slovak Union of Protectionists of Nature and the Countryside. A Green Party formed in 1989. Also, like in Hungary, the party failed to capitalize on its role in bringing down the communist system. The agenda of the greens became less relevant as the government struggled with the economic and social consequences of the fall of communism and the introduction of a free market system. The party failed to win sufficient votes to win representation in Parliament. The development of green (and other) political associations in Czechoslovakia was further complicated by the divisions between the Czechs and the Slovaks. Once the country dissolved into two separate states, the Czech and Slovak Republics, distinct green parties emerged in each.

Green parties have had difficulty in the political arena throughout most of the region, in Bulgaria, Estonia, Lithuania, Poland, Romania, and Slovakia. In the 1990s attention in eastern Europe was directed toward economic development and reconstruction, often along the lines of a free market system modeled on the United States. Green movements struggled in this environment. There are some signs, however, that the future of the parties may not be all dim. Greens have done well in recent years in the Czech Republic and Latvia. In January 2007, after more than half a year of political uncertainty following an indecisive election, the Czech Greens (Strana zelených) were reluctantly invited into a coalition government by President Vaclav Klaus (even though Klaus in a 2007 speech to the U.S. House of Representatives called environmentalism a threat to freedom and said that "Communism was replaced by the threat of ambitious environmentalism"!). The Czech Greens won 6 percent of the vote in the June 2006 election, winning them six seats in Parliament. In the case of Latvia, the leader of the Latvian Greens, Indulis Emsis, became prime minister in 2004 when the existing government collapsed.

While on the whole in the transition states of central and eastern Europe, green issues have been on the back burner, dedicated green activists continue to push environmental agendas. There have been various vigorous green political campaigns, as in Ruse, Bulgaria, where there were strong protests against pollution from chlorine emissions at a factory in Giurgiu, a town across the Danube in Romania. Green political organizations, like the Ruse Committee, the Independent Union Ekoglasnost, and the Bulgarian Green Party, have all contributed to the powerful articulation of environmental concerns.

Green parties are also gaining toeholds in other parts of the world. In recent years, green parties or protoparties have formed in Africa (e.g., in

Benin, Kenya, Nigeria, and South Africa); Asia (e.g., Bangladesh, India, Pakistan, Japan, South Korea, and Taiwan) and Latin America (e.g., Brazil and Mexico). In most of these places, the green parties are still too small or too new to have entered electoral campaigns. They are expressions of intent by environmental activists who believe that establishing a political wing of a green movement is important to achieve their vision. In a few countries, however, green parties are making electoral inroads. This has been the case in Benin, Brazil, and Mexico. In 2003, the Green Party of Benin was able to send three delegates to Parliament. That same year, the Ecologist Party of Mexico did sufficiently well in the election to the Chamber of Deputies to send 17 representatives. After the 2006 election, there were 13 green party representatives in the Chamber of Deputies in Brazil.

As green parties form in other parts of the world, they too are beginning to form federations in order to try to strengthen their voice and to cooperate on key objectives. Thus, there is now a Federation of Green Parties of Africa, an Asia Pacific Green Network, and a Federation of the Green Parties of the Americas. Perhaps most significantly, in 2001 the Global Greens were formed as a network of the green parties and organizations from around the world.

INTEREST GROUPS FORMED BY ELITES

Eminent people, political activists, and sympathizers of the green movement in various countries have organized themselves into effective interest groups. Apart from the more popular image of a grassroots movement, the green movement on different continents includes initiatives by small groups of prominent people. For instance, the Club of Rome, which commissioned the highly influential report *The Limits to Growth,* was begun by Aurelio Peccei, an entrepreneur who brought together industrialists, scientists, economists, politicians, and bureaucrats to debate the connection between environmental and economic issues and the political and social implications of changes in these areas. The Club of Rome, like the Business Council for Sustainable Development, formed in 1990, has exercised significant influence in the area of environmental and industrial policies.

Another example of the impact of a small but well-organized group of prominent people is the International Union for the Conservation of Nature and Natural Resources (IUCN) (formed by conservationists in 1948 and known, until 1956, as the International Union for the Protection of Nature). This organization has been instrumental in bringing about cooperation between government and nongovernmental organizations (NGOs). In the 1970s it formulated a World Conservation Strategy and was active in developing the notion of sustainable development as well as in helping to convene the United Nations Conference on the Human Environment (UNCHE) in 1972. The IUCN also played a central role in the creation of the World Wildlife Fund (WWF) as well as in conservation initiatives in Africa. These initiatives included the African Convention on the Conservation of Nature and Natural Resources signed by 33 African states in 1968, and the African Special Project, which sought, with the assistance of African governments, to promote conservation and the economic, cultural, and scientific value of wildlife.

One of the most significant agencies coordinating the efforts of nongovernmental, as well as governmental, organizations to address environmental issues is the United Nations. Among the initiatives of this agency is the United Nations Educational, Scientific, and Cultural Organization's (UNESCO) work toward bringing experts together in order to establish a sound basis for gathering information on the state of the environment. This agency had a pivotal part in convening the Intergovernmental Conference of Experts on the Scientific Basis for Rational Use and Conservation of the Biosphere in 1968. This initiative also served to pave the way for the 1972 UNCHE. Another UNESCO project was the 1971 Man and the Biosphere Program, which brought together experts from many countries to acquire more information on the condition of the environment and on the impact of human interventions.

The 1972 UNCHE represented an important milestone in uniting government and nongovernmental organizations, with official delegates from 113 countries. This gathering highlighted both important differences between and opportunities for cooperation among developed and less developed nations. Apart from passing resolutions on a wide range of issues including whaling and the testing of nuclear weapons, the conference created the United Nations Environment Programme (UNEP). The aim of this program is to develop further the cooperation that had been achieved between government and nongovernmental organizations. It has focused on increasing knowledge about ecological systems, assisting in natural resource management, and providing expertise to less developed nations. UNEP has contributed to the design of international treaties, including the Framework Convention on Climate Change and the Convention on Biological Diversity that were signed at the 1992 United Nations Conference on Environment and Development (UNCED).

This conference, held in Rio de Janeiro, represented a mammoth effort to bring together organizations from all arenas to address some of the most pressing environmental issues. Despite the reservations expressed by many commentators about the capacity of such a gathering to bring about effective changes in policies, the conference drew considerable attention to questions of environmental protection and economic development. It also led to the signing of several agreements, including those on the implementation of sustainable development (Agenda 21), a Framework Convention on Climate Change (which outlined principles that would underlie efforts to deal with problems like global warming), the Convention on Biological Diversity, the Declaration on Environment and Development, and the enactment of Forest Principles. Five years after the conference, in 1997, the Kyoto Protocol to the Framework Convention on Climate Change was signed. It finally entered into force in 2005.

In 2000, at the United Nations Millennium Summit, world leaders agreed to establish a program for combating hunger, disease, illiteracy, environmental degradation, and discrimination against women. These goals, which have come to be known as the Millennium Development Goals, were reconfirmed at the 2002 Johannesburg Earth Summit.

Among the factors that determined the issues taken up by UNCED in 1992 and a decade later in Johannesburg was the report *Our Common Future* produced by the World Commission on Environment and Development (1984–1987). This highly influential publication gave weight to the notion of sustainable development and to notions of equity and justice. In many ways it was an embrace of many of the goals and ideas that arose from the green movement.

NONGOVERNMENTAL INTEREST GROUPS

While in some countries, green parties have been at the forefront of green activism, in many places the green movement has at its core nongovernmental interest groups (also commonly known as nongovernmental organizations [NGOs]). A variety of groups have emerged and relied on different tactics to influence governmental, corporate, and societal behavior.

Some green groups, particularly the more radical ones, have focused on direct action. They remain highly skeptical of efforts to link a preoccupation with economic development to environmental protection. Among the most radical groups in the green movement are Greenpeace founded in 1971, the Sea Shepherd Society formed in 1977, and Earth First! formed in 1980. All three organizations promote some form of direct action, which can involve breaking the law, although they are not always approving of each other's approaches. Of the three organizations, Greenpeace has been the most successful in attracting public attention to environmental problems, although the organization's influence has been declining since the early 1990s as its direct action techniques fail to win the same level of attention that they once did.

The formation of Greenpeace reflects the close links between the protests of the 1960s and the green movement. It was formed by activists who, following their involvement in demonstrations against the Vietnam War, campaigned against the testing of nuclear weapons in the atmosphere around the Aleutian Islands. Greenpeace specialized in provocative actions designed to capture the attention of the media. Their protests were carried out by small groups of professional activists and involved risky actions such as their 1973 attempt to penetrate the sites of nuclear tests. However, after experiencing a precipitous decline in its support base in the 1990s, Greenpeace has become a more conventional environmental group. While it still engages in direct action, it is also heavily involved in conventional lobbying activities. It claims that in pursuing its mission, it uses "research, lobbying, and quiet diplomacy" as well as "high-profile, nonviolent conflict." Its campaigns now focus on climate change, marine and forest protection, disarmament, opposition to genetically modified organisms, an end to the nuclear age, and sustainable trade.

Greenpeace is rather unconventional in the context of the democratic participation espoused by many champions of the green movement. Although the organization had a vast number of supporters in many countries, it has been run on strictly hierarchical lines with strong central control. In fact, one of the problems that has faced the organization is the criticism that it has become too large and bureaucratic and functions too much like the multinational corporations it criticizes. In contrast to Greenpeace, Earth First! better fits the popular image of a green movement based on grassroots or direct democracy. However, Earth First! distanced itself from the mainstream of the green movement through its commitment to the principles of biocentrism and deep ecology and its radical actions. It sabotaged equipment used for development projects. This has at times provoked outrage, since actions such as the insertion of metal spikes into trees in order to damage chain saws can cause serious injury to workers operating this equipment. Earth First! epitomized the more militant groups that emerged and came to be known as ecoterrorists. In the mid-1990s Earth First! renounced the use of violence, but this led to a split in the organization and the formation of the even more militant Earth Liberation Front, which gained notoriety for burning a ski resort in Colorado.

On the more conventional side, the Sierra Club embodies the strong traditions of the green movement in the United States. It has focused on lobbying government to protect and preserve the environment, particularly to create national parks. In the early 1990s the club had well over half a million members and had considerably broadened its agenda to incorporate issues like the protection of endangered species, population growth, and the greenhouse effect. Friends of the Earth, created in 1969 by David Brower, who had been forced to resign from the position of executive director of the Sierra Club, maintained the notions of democratic participation and grassroots involvement advocated by the student and other radical movements of the 1960s. Branches that emerged throughout the Western world were given considerable independence in how they organized themselves and in setting their own agenda.

The WWF (known both as the World Wildlife Fund and the World Wide Fund for Nature) is another highly influential lobbying group. Assisted by dignitaries such as Prince Philip, the Duke of Edinburgh, it has become one of the most successful organizations in raising funds for conservation projects and promoting dialogue between nongovernmental organizations and agencies of the United Nations. It has also shaped the conservation policies of many governments. In 2006 it had almost five million supporters and primary offices and associates in 40 countries. The WWF supports numerous projects in these countries and has been extremely effective in disseminating information about conservation issues.

Another strand of the green movement are organizations like the Natural Resources Defense Council (NRDC), which have made regular use of the courts to challenge governmental decision-making procedures, to pressure the Environmental Protection Administration to enforce environmental laws, or to draw attention to environmental injustices. The NRDC has 1.2 million supporters, giving the organization substantial clout. It has been able to mobilize many of its supporters as online activists. Whereas the NRDC has scientists and lawyers as its core staff members, Environmental Defense (EDF), another highly effective and influential NGO, relies heavily on environmental economists. Like the NRDC, EDF makes common use of the courts. It has its origins in a lawsuit that was aimed to end the use of DDT in order to protect osprey, bald eagles, and peregrine falcons. While it continues to make regular use of litigation to achieve its environmental protection goals, it also uses its in-house expertise to formulate legislative proposals. The 1990 U.S. Clean Air Act sulfur dioxide emissions trading system originated in EDF.

Of course, not all groups are as big, rich, or well known as these. There are now thousands of NGOs around the world that espouse many of the goals and values of the green movement. The structure, size, and approaches of these groups are often dependent on the political system in which they operate. Their goals, moreover, are usually closely tied to the pressing concerns facing their own countries, rather than more distant populations. Thus, in densely populated and rapidly developing countries such as Korea, organizations like Green Korea United or the Korean Federation for Environmental Movement (KFEM) tend to focus their attention on preventing environmentally destructive development plans and promoting open and democratic decision making in Korea. These organizations, while relatively large in size (Green Korea United had a membership of 15,000 in 2002 and KFEM, 85,000), are nowhere near as rich as the large environmental NGOs in the United States and Europe. They have relied on demonstrations, lobbying, and educational activities to advance their goals. Yet, in the absence of a green political organization, these groups function as the green movement in Korea.

In neighboring Japan, there are also many green interest groups. They tend to be very small in terms of size, however. Typically they only have a few dozen to a few hundred members. The largest groups (WWF Japan and the Wild Bird Society) both have less than 50,000 members. While the situation of the green interest groups has been improving with the passage of new legislation easing the rules governing nonprofit organizations and greater governmental acceptance of the role that can be played by NGOs, the groups remain limited in their ability to influence policy developments.

THE IMPACT OF SHIFTS IN VALUES

Green political organizations and social movements are significant sources of political change because they reflect shifts in values and perceptions. Support for green groups rose steadily throughout the advanced, industrialized world in the 1980s, particularly among the young and those with higher education. The shift in values was accompanied by a loosening of the connection between political conflicts and divisions based on social class and the erosion of support for the major parties based on these divisions (Dalton 1996). Paradoxically, the emergence of new movements and political associations echoes the expectation that political institutions and organizations, notably those that evolved during the formation of the welfare state in the nineteenth century, remain heavily involved in regulating the actions of powerful groups in society and in shaping the social behavior of all individuals.

People still turn to traditional political organizations because the green movement does not appear to present a viable alternative form of government. In addition, there is the inertia of established institutional practices and traditions, particularly those associated with the electoral system, the media, and the connections between industry, bureaucracy, and government. Although the new green parties have been elected into parliaments all over the world, they remain minor players.

However, a transformation is occurring within the major parties, which have been receptive to some of the ideas of environmentalists.

Although the efforts of the traditional parties have often been superficial, there has been a deeper action, one that acknowledges shifts in values and reflects a willingness to enact new policies, appoint supporters and leaders of new political movements to positions of influence, and, perhaps most importantly, focus attention on the principles underlying political decisions. All these responses have contributed to maintaining expectations that governments either can, or at least ought to, meet new challenges.

GREEN POLITICAL ISSUES

The focus on different issues, by the green movement as well as by the media, political parties, and interest groups, changes over time. In the 1980s, a strong correspondence arose between some of the preoccupations of social movements and those of traditional political parties trying to address the green agenda. The prominence of some issues appears to follow a pattern of different "cycles of attention." To a degree, data seem to support this theory by Anthony Downs (1972) whereby interest in issues, including concern about the environment, moves through various stages, culminating in their displacement from the political agenda. In reality, the notion of an "issue-attention cycle" offers only a partially satisfactory account of interest in the green program since environmental issues have remained high on the political agenda over a long period of time. In Australia, for instance, reporting on topics like sustainable development reflects both cycles of attention and the widespread interest in this issue created by political and intellectual elites (Papadakis 1996).

Apart from the enduring character of green issues on national political agendas, one can also observe the emergence of a green program on a global scale. This phenomenon can be illustrated by the concern about the threat to African wildlife, particularly among groups like the WWF. Initiatives by such organizations represent a response to the consequences of the late nineteenth-century colonization of regions such as East Africa by Britain and Germany. As far back as 1900 national governments like those of Britain, France, Germany, Italy, Portugal, and Belgium had signed the first-ever international environmental accord, the Convention for the Preservation of Animals, Birds, and Fish in Africa.

Apart from governmental endeavors to deal with the global impact of environmental destruction, the media has, in recent times, contributed to raising awareness of issues that affect people across the boundaries defining nations or continents. Hence, media coverage of catastrophes that occur in distant locations has led to an understanding of the significance of the green movement and of the responsibilities of Western nations and multinational corporations. This is illustrated by reports on the death of thousands of people at Bhopal, India, in 1984 following the release of poison gas from the Union Carbide pesticide plant. Victims of the disaster had to wait five years before receiving any compensation from the multinational Union Carbide Corporation based in the United States.

Other issues may paradoxically divide or unite the green movement. In 1985 Rudolf Bahro, a leading figure in Die Grünen, left the party in protest of the qualified support this political association gave for the invasive experimentation of animals if it could lead to even one human life being rescued. On the other hand, animal rights has been a significant feature of campaigns to change perceptions about the relationship between human beings and nature.

The question of nuclear power has not only united the green movement but also provided a vital spur to the formation of green political organizations. Following the 1973 decision of the Organization of Petroleum Exporting Countries (OPEC) to increase the price of oil sharply, Western countries sought to substitute nuclear power for imported oil. This provoked strong opposition, and several powerful social movements followed the lead of the green antinuclear protest movement in the Federal Republic of Germany. The opposition was given an added impetus by a near disaster at the Three Mile Island nuclear power plant in 1979 and the 1986 catastrophe at the Chernobyl nuclear power plant near Kiev in the Soviet Union. The accident at Chernobyl highlighted the difficulty of dealing with the global consequences of human interventions into the environment at the national level as radioactive clouds spread across many European countries and induced governments to impose bans on the consumption of some foods.

Another issue that has come to symbolize the need and opportunity for international cooperation is the destruction of territory once occupied by a wide range of species and of these species themselves. Efforts to stem the threats of extinction and preserve biodiversity are intensifying. An important early contribution to addressing this issue was the

Convention on International Trade in Endangered Species of Wild Flora and Fauna signed in 1973 by a small number of countries, which in subsequent years has attracted many more government endorsements. Still, the question of how to deal with the threat of extinction of a vast number of plant and animal species remains an issue high on the agenda of the green movement as well as of government agencies and industrial interests. The formation of the Convention on Biological Diversity aims to take conservation efforts in this direction. There is growing concern that the extinction of plant and animal species will lead to a loss of genetic resources that might have been used to cure illnesses as well as to resolve other problems.

THE LIMITS TO GROWTH

Among the issues that were first used to raise green awareness was the question of the "limits to economic growth." The publication in 1972 of *The Limits to Growth*, a study commissioned by the Club of Rome, focused the attention of millions of people on the problems arising from economic growth, industrialization, environmental degradation, population change, and the depletion of natural resources. The study made use of computers and complex models to predict the pattern of economic change over the next century. The appeal of *The Limits to Growth* was also emotional and served as a point of reference for people who, since the 1960s, had either participated in or been sympathetic to the aims of environmental groups and social movements that arose on university campuses, especially against the war in Vietnam. Environmentalist opponents of the prevailing industrial system were interested in the study's prediction that, if the prevailing patterns of exponential economic growth were to continue, there would be a catastrophe by the end of the twentieth century arising from the rapid depletion of resources, pollution of the environment, shortages in food supply, and growth in world population. Although critics of the study pointed to its failure to take into account the possibilities of devising strategies to address these threats, the book became one of the most successful efforts to raise interest in and awareness of environmental problems.

Like *The Limits to Growth*, *The Global 2000 Report*, commissioned by the U.S. government and published in 1980, attempted to evaluate trends in environmental destruction, especially those that would occur if current practices were not replaced by more cooperation between nations. Though critical of the methods and assumptions of studies like *The Limits to Growth*, *The Global 2000 Report* also examined the connection between population growth, the state of the environment, and the depletion of natural resources and made predictions about disasters that would arise because of human interventions in the environment.

Above all, debates similar to the one over *The Limits to Growth* stimulated ideas on how to deal with threats such as the inefficient use of resources like oil and other fossil fuels, traffic congestion, and the greenhouse effect. In an effort to make polluters pay for the damage they inflict on the environment, some governments, particularly in the EU, have introduced carbon taxes and carbon trading systems with the aim of reducing emissions that pollute the atmosphere and contribute to global warming.

THE ENVIRONMENTAL AGENDA OF THE GREENS

There are many environmental issues that have been championed by green movements. One of the first environmental issues to capture the attention of green movements and parties in Europe was acid rain. Acid rain is a form of pollution caused by emissions of sulfur dioxide and nitrogen oxide from industrial plants, coal-burning power stations, and cars. It can damage ecological systems and agricultural crops as well as corrode buildings and infrastructure. The Swedes were at the forefront of campaigns against acid rain, and already in the 1960s were applying pressure for governmental action across national boundaries. Their calls for action were picked up by green movements in Europe, especially once awareness grew that the effects of acid rain were more widespread than originally realized. The 1979 Convention on Long-Range Transboundary Air Pollution (CLRTAP) and the 1984 "Thirty Percent Club" of nations that committed themselves to reducing sulfur dioxide emissions by 30 percent over the period 1983 to 1993 were early initiatives to deal with acid rain. Initiatives of this kind were spurred on by the electoral success of green parties, particularly in countries like the Federal Republic of Germany. In 1990, the passage of the 1990 U.S. Clean Air Act amendments aimed at reducing sulfur dioxide and nitrogen oxide emissions through the introduction of an emissions trading system was also pushed by the green movement. More recently, the acid rain problems stemming from coal burning in China is mobilizing green activists in East Asia.

Another major issue that captured the attention of the green movement and propelled green issues high onto the political agenda was the destruction of the ozone layer. Scientists warned that depletion of the ozone layer, which blocks harmful ultraviolet radiation from the sun from reaching the Earth, could lead to a steep rise in incidences of skin cancer as well as damage the immune system of all species. Pressure from scientists and the green movement helped convince traditional political parties of the necessity of phasing out the use of chlorofluorocarbons (CFCs) and other ozone depleting gases. In 1987 countries that were producers and consumers of CFCs signed the Montreal Protocol on Substances That Deplete the Ozone Layer. The initial aim of the agreement was to curtail the use of CFCs by 50 percent by the year 2000, but subsequent scientific evidence of the seriousness of the problem led to a more rapid and total phase-out schedule.

Since the 1990s, green movements and parties have also paid more attention to the interrelated issues of protection of biodiversity and the promotion of safe foods. Green organizations are sounding the alarm bells regarding the rapidly deteriorating state of the world's oceans and the depletion of many commercial fish species. They have launched campaigns aimed at the protection of biologically rich tropical forests and promoted sustainable fishing and forestry practices. They have also championed organic farming as a means of reducing reliance on pesticides and environmentally harmful modern agribusiness practices. Along with this, they have typically opposed the introduction of genetically modified organisms into the food system for fear of their possible long-term health and ecological impacts. Their efforts were behind the formation of the Convention on Biological Diversity and the related Cartagena Protocol on Biosafety.

There are also many other concerns that have activated the green movement. Nuclear testing and nuclear waste disposal and transport have been focal issues. Distrustful of nuclear energy and concerned about global climate change, green organizations have long backed the development of alternative energies, including wind and solar power and biofuels, and cogeneration. Green groups have also reacted to massive pollution disasters, such as the crude oil spills by the *Torrey Canyon* in 1967 and the *Exxon Valdez* in 1989, when more than 10 million gallons spilled into Prince William Sound, Alaska.

While the green movement is not united in its views of capitalism (green movements in the former East bloc countries are in general more supportive of capitalism than are their counterparts in western Europe), they share a belief in the need to deepen environmental considerations in international relations. In general, the green movement has argued that nations have focused too much attention on the promotion of neoliberal economic agendas and free trade to the detriment of environmental protection and local communities.

Finally, although the green movement was not very active on the matter of climate change prior to the late 1980s, since that time in Europe, East Asia, and the United States, green groups have become increasingly active in addressing climate change, what many are calling the most vexing and serious environmental problem to face the planet. Indeed, for many organizations, climate change is now their single most important campaign issue. Over the past several decades, a strong scientific consensus has emerged that human activities, ranging from the burning of fossil fuels to large-scale deforestation, are contributing to the rapid warming of the Earth's atmosphere. The release of greenhouse gases (and most notably carbon dioxide) into the atmosphere are warming the Earth's surface temperature. The consequences of this could be catastrophic. Damage wrought by extreme weather patterns could cause droughts and floods, and a possible rise in sea levels could displace millions of people living in coastal areas and obliterate some island nations. Species that are not able to adapt could face extinction. Evidence of global warming was widely disseminated by scientists and the media already in the 1980s. At the 1992 UNCED, 153 nations and the EU signed the Framework Convention on Climate Change with a view to reducing greenhouse gas emissions. Five years later, they formed the Kyoto Protocol, which set a timetable and targets for greenhouse gas emissions reductions in the industrialized states. The agreement finally entered into force in 2005. This agreement is widely recognized, however, as little more than a first step. It calls for a reduction of 8 percent of EU greenhouse gases relative to 1990 levels by 2012 and 6 percent for Japan. Scientists, however, are warning that cuts on the order of 50 percent are necessary in the next few decades.

Moreover, the United States, the world's largest emitter of greenhouse gases, which had initially indicated its intentions of reducing its emissions by 7 percent of 1990 levels by 2012 at the 1997 Kyoto Conference, pulled out of the agreement in 2001. The U.S. action was widely condemned internationally. Australia also chose not to ratify the agreement.

The U.S. and Australian actions represent the scale of the struggle still facing green movements around the world. Their ability to influence political change is often dependent upon their ability to get their agenda items taken up by the larger and more powerful traditional political parties. While there are some signs in early 2007 that as a result of strong performance of the Democratic Party in the 2006 midterm election that green issues, and especially climate change and alternative energy, will gain a stronger position on the political agenda, the question is whether policy responses will go far enough. Whether or not other countries, like Australia or the many ratifiers of the Kyoto Protocol who look like they will not meet their emission reduction targets, can be persuaded to take more meaningful steps toward sustainability is uncertain.

Traditional political, social, and economic organizations have been selective in their response to challenges by the green movement. They have been reluctant to adopt aspects of environmentalism that may undermine economic requirements and electoral considerations. The heavy costs of environmental degradation, however, may become too big for many of even the most ardent adherents to neoliberal economic agendas to ignore. In fact, already most governments in the industrialized world have found it necessary to embrace at least some aspects of the green movement's agenda. Regulations controlling harmful pollutants, protection of endangered species, policies requiring environmental impact assessments, and rules governing access to environmental information have become commonplace in most industrialized nations.

Problems such as acid rain, ocean pollution, climate change, and biodiversity loss continue to raise crucial questions about current economic practices. The emphasis on growth and consumption that drives political, social, and economic behavior in most parts of the world suggests that the importance of the concept of sustainability has yet to be widely understood or embraced. Yet, as the environmental problems facing the planet become increasingly hard to ignore, governments may have little choice but to turn to the ideas that have been proposed by the green movement: sustainability, participatory decision making, safe foods, alternative energies, and international cooperation. While some elements of the green agenda are likely to remain controversial and anathema to some actors—such as their strong opposition to nuclear energy and genetically modified organisms—many of the goals of the green movement have the potential to become mainstream (e.g., support for alternative energies).

One of the biggest challenges for the green movement in the coming years, beyond influencing policy change in the United States, will be its ability to influence developments in countries like China and India, which in the coming years as a result of their huge populations and rapid industrial growth will become the world's largest consumers of many natural resources and producers of waste and emissions.

There are some positive signs. Environmental awareness is growing in many parts of the world. There has been a virtual explosion of environmental movements since the 1990s in Asia, Latin America, and Africa. There are also many protogreen parties and some green parties that have formed in these parts of the world. The form that green activism takes, however, may be less important than the impact that green activists can have on policy outcomes. The formation in recent years of international networks of environmental movements and green organizations (e.g., Global Greens) suggests that the movement is trying to strengthen its own ability to influence change in different parts of the world and at the global and regional levels.

THE DICTIONARY

– A –

ABOLITION 2000. This is a network of over 2000 organizations in 90 countries that was established in 1995 on the 25th anniversary of the Nuclear Nonproliferation Treaty. Its goal is to rid the world of nuclear weapons through the establishment of an international treaty. In 2003, Abolition 2000 launched a new initiative, together with the Mayor of Hiroshima: Mayors for Peace.

ACID RAIN (ACID POLLUTION). The question of how to combat acid rain has been a long-standing source of tension among national governments. This issue has also become a significant focal point of campaigns by environmental groups, and was a key issue of early green movements and parties.

Acid rain is a form of pollution caused by emissions of sulfur dioxide gas and nitrogen oxide gases from industrial plants, coal-burning power stations, and cars. Coal and oil are the main sources of these gases.

Though primarily transported by rain, the acids also travel in snow, sleet, and fog. Pollution by acids has been noted for centuries in the British Isles. In 1880 smog in London brought about the deaths of 1,200 people. Similarly, in 1952 the deaths of over 4,000 people were attributed to smog over Greater London.

Since the 1880s Scandinavians have been concerned about acid pollution from **Great Britain** transported by the weather. Early in the 20th century, damage to lakes and rivers and the loss of fish in Scandinavian countries have been ascribed to acid pollution from other regions. In 1948 the Swedish government created a network of observers to record levels of acid pollution across Europe. Concern about this issue was given further stimulus when, in the 1960s, Svante Oden, a Swedish soil scientist, exposed the connection between acid pollution and damage to thousands of lakes. Oden also suggested that the situation was getting progressively worse as a result of pollution generated as far away as Great Britain and central Europe. He used the term *acid rain* in describing these changes.

Pressure for international action to deal with the problem arose first in Scandinavia, notably in **Sweden** and **Norway**. The problem of acid rain induced the Swedes to bring their misgivings to the United Nations, resulting in the **United Nations Conference on the Human Environment (UNCHE),** held in Stockholm in 1972.

The tensions between the Scandinavians and their neighbors were matched by the disquiet among Canadians about acid pollution from the **United States.** In Europe, Great Britain and West **Germany** resisted efforts by the Scandinavians to organize a convention with legally binding obligations to reduce air pollution that traveled across national borders. A weak version of these demands for curbing pollution was eventually signed by 33 countries in 1979 (**Convention on Long Range Transboundary Air Pollution [CLRTAP]**).

Scandinavian countries, concerned about the ineffectiveness of this initiative, lobbied for a 30 percent reduction of sulfur dioxide emissions over the period 1983 to 1993. This led to the formation of the so-called Thirty Percent Club in 1984. By 1985 the club had 21 members, including many east European nations, all of whom committed themselves to lessening emissions by at least 30 percent.

In the early 1980s Scandinavian efforts for international agreements received a significant political boost when public opinion in West Germany was sensitized to the widespread destruction of native forests by acid rain. The success of **Die Grünen** in German elections contributed to a shift in direction among the political elites. Even Great Britain, which first refused to join the Thirty Percent Club, committed itself to a policy of reducing emissions over a longer time frame. The issue of acid rain was high on the agenda of national governments and green groups such as **Friends of the Earth, Greenpeace,** and the **World Wide Fund for Nature (WWF)** in Europe and North America throughout the 1980s and 1990s.

In 1980 **Canada** and the United States signed a Memorandum of Intent Concerning Transboundary Air Pollution. This led to the creation of working groups to study the problem. Still, throughout the 1980s, neither country could agree on the implementation of an effective policy to deal with the acid rain falling on Canada, much of which came from the United States. Within the United States, there also were significant problems with acid rain produced in the Midwest but affecting the Northeast. After a decade of inaction, the George H. W. Bush administration proposed the 1990 Clean Air Act amendment. The legislation has led to a vast reduction in sulfur dioxide and nitrogen oxide emissions through the use of an **emissions trading** system.

Acid rain problems have been gaining increasing attention in East Asia since the late 1980s, largely as a result of the heavy reliance on coal use in the **People's Republic of China**. China is now the world's second-largest producer of sulfur dioxide, exceeded only by the United States. The emergence of transboundary acid rain problems in East Asia has led to the formation of the East Asian Acid Rain Monitoring Network, which, as its name suggests, is monitoring the sources and consequences of acidic deposition in East Asia. **Japan** established a Green Aid Plan to promote technology transfer to China to reduce the acid rain problem and improve energy efficiency. Environmental groups have also formed around this issue.

ACTION! NETWORK. This is an Internet gateway to environmental, health, and population advocacy centers for over 170 organizations. It is sponsored by **Environmental Defense** and is designed to promote Internet activism by aiding individuals in contacting their legislative representatives on critical environmental matters.

ACQUIS COMMUNAUTAIRE. The entire body of law and court decisions of the European Union (EU) is known as the *acquis communautaire*. As one condition for acceptance into the EU, candidate countries must demonstrate that they have transposed this entire body of law into their own regulations. Chapter 22 of the *acquis communautaire* was devoted to the environment. As a result of this requirement, the 10 countries that joined the EU in 2004 (Cyprus, the **Czech Republic**, **Estonia**, Hungary, **Latvia**, Lithuania, **Malta**, **Poland**, **Slovakia**, and Slovenia) plus those that joined in 2007 (**Bulgaria** and **Romania**) greatly strengthened their environmental regulatory framework in a remarkably short period of time. The challenge for the coming decade will be adequate enforcement of the new laws and programs.

AFRICAN AMERICAN ENVIRONMENTALIST ASSOCIATION. A nonprofit environmental organization dedicated to protecting the environment, enhancing human, animal and plant ecologies, promoting the efficient use of natural resources and increasing African American participation in the environmental movement.

AFRICAN CONVENTION ON THE CONSERVATION OF NATURE AND NATURAL RESOURCES. A convention signed in Algiers in September 1968 by 33 African states that were members of the Organization of African Unity. The convention came into force in 1969 and was largely the product of efforts by the International Union for the Conservation of Nature and Natural Resources, now known as the **World Conservation Union (IUCN)** to promote conservation and the well-being of the population. Like many other conventions, however, little or no provision was made for the administration or implementation of the recommendations.

AFRICAN SPECIAL PROJECT. An initiative by the **World Conservation Union (IUCN)** to promote **conservation** and the economic, cultural, and scientific value of wildlife. The IUCN solicited the involvement of political elites in African states that had either gained independence or were about to do so. It organized the Pan-African Symposium on the Conservation of Nature and Natural Resources in Modern African States (held in Arusha, Tanganyika, in September 1961). The meeting was supported by the United Nations. The African Special Project provided a unique opportunity for African nations to articulate their views on the connection between conservation and their economic development. The African Special Project formed the basis for a dialogue that led to the signing of the **African Convention on the Conservation of Nature and Natural Resources** in 1968.

AFRICAN WILDLIFE. The threat to wildlife in sub-Saharan **Africa** has long been a concern of conservationists and remains crucial in mobilizing support for groups such as the **World Wildlife Fund (WWF).** Ever since the late 19th century, when **Great Britain** and **Germany** colonized East Africa, governments have been anxious about the destruction of wildlife by white settlers, professional hunters, and the indigenous population. Concern about preservation of game animals led to the signing, in 1900, of the first-ever international environmental accord, the Convention for the Preservation of Animals, Birds, and Fish in Africa. The convention was signed by Great Britain, **France**, Germany, **Italy**, **Portugal**, and the Belgian Congo.

In 1903 the goal of preserving wildlife also formed the rationale for the foundation of the first international environmental organization, the Society for the Preservation of Wild Fauna of the Empire, which focused on territories and colonies ruled by Great Britain. The plight of African wildlife was highlighted in several popular works by the German naturalist C. G. Schillings. These initiatives, however, did not reverse the trend of mass destruction. In 1933 Great Britain organized an International Conference for the Protection of Fauna and Flora, seeking to protect the natural habitat for wildlife. Most colonial powers then signed a convention on the Preservation of Fauna and Flora, though it was not legally binding on the signatories and lacked any mechanism for implementation. The 1973 **Convention on International Trade in Endangered Species of Wild Flora and Fauna (CITES)** was in part developed due to rising awareness of the threats that trade in species and species' parts posed to wildlife survival. *See also* AFRICAN WILDLIFE FOUNDATION.

AFRICAN WILDLIFE FOUNDATION. Founded in 1961, the African Wildlife Foundation is the leading international organization focused on protecting **African wildlife** and promoting conservation through community conservation and conservation enterprise techniques.

AGALEV. *See* NETHERLANDS.

AGENDA 21. Agenda 21 is an agreement for the promotion of **sustainable development** in the 21st century that was adopted by governments at the **United Nations Conference on Environment and**

Development (UNCED) in 1992. This agreement has 40 chapters covering measures governments should pursue to promote sustainable development across such topics as international cooperation, natural resources, combating poverty, consumption patterns, population, the atmosphere, the oceans, indigenous peoples, women, nongovernmental organizations (NGOs), technology transfer, education, public awareness, and training, as well as integrated decision making and international institutional arrangements. Implementation is to happen at the international, national, regional, and local levels. Some governments have legislated Local Agenda 21, as was recommended in chapter 28 of Agenda 21.

The **Commission on Sustainable Development (CSD)** was established in December 1992 in order to ensure that all member-states devise national plans of action to implement Agenda 21. Each year, member-states are to report to the CSD on implementation measures.

Progress at meeting the goals of Agenda 21 was assessed in 1997 by the United Nations General Assembly meeting in a special session. A number of gaps were identified in regards to poverty, increasing globalization, and a continued deterioration of the global environment. The *Johannesburg Plan of Implementation*, agreed at the **World Summit on Sustainable Development** held in Johannesburg, **South Africa** in 2002, confirmed the United Nations commitment to "full implementation" of Agenda 21, in addition to the Millennium Development Goals and other international agreements.

ALLIANCE OF SMALL ISLAND STATES. This group of small island and low-lying coastal countries formed an alliance in 1991 based on their shared environmental concerns, and in particular their vulnerability to the effects of a rise in sea level caused by **climate change**. The idea behind the alliance is to strengthen the voice of small—and for the most part poor and vulnerable—states in international negotiations. The alliance has 43 states and observers (as of 2006) spread across the oceans and coastlines of Africa, the Caribbean, Indian Ocean, Mediterranean, Pacific, and South China Seas. They do not have a permanent secretariat or charter; instead they work together through their missions to the United Nations in New York. Members include Antigua and Barbuda, Bahamas, Barbados, Belize, Cape Verde, Comoros, Cook Islands, Cuba, Cyprus, Dominican Republic, Fiji, Federated States of Micronesia, Grenada, Guinea-Bissau, Guyana, Haiti, Jamaica, Kiribati, Maldives, Marshall Islands, Mauritius, Nauru, Niue, Palau, Papua New Guinea, Samoa, Singapore, Seychelles, Sao Taome and Principe, Solomon Islands, St. Kitts and Nevis, St. Lucia, St. Vincent and the Grenadines, Suriname, Tonga, Trinidad and Tobago, Tuvalu, and Vanuata.

ALTERNATIVE ENERGY. Interest in alternative energies has been central to the platforms of green movements and parties, not only because of their concern about environmental damage caused by **nuclear energy** and pollution from fossil fuels but also because alternative energies are frequently more decentralized and can empower local peoples. Green political movements and parties have been quick to point to the possibilities of using renewable energy sources such as solar, wind, and water power.

Writers such as Amory Lovins, the author of *Soft Energy Paths*, have linked this preoccupation with alternative forms of energy to arguments about "soft" technologies (which are said to be sustainable, benign, flexible, and resilient) to the creation of a less coercive and centralized social system than the prevailing one. Alternative energy sources would be used to solve some of the economic and environmental problems arising within industrial societies, and the possibility of a more participatory culture, that might be associated with the use of technologies that require less centralized control, could be explored.

The notion of alternative energy remains a powerful one in the agenda of the green movement and has exercised some influence on traditional political organizations and on policymakers. Concerns about the climate change have invigorated efforts to promote alternative energies. There are several alternative energy success stories. **Denmark** produces close to one-fifth of its electricity from wind. **Germany** and **Spain** are the European leaders in installed wind capacity. They were getting respectively, 5 and 8 percent of their electricity from wind in 2005.

Brazil has become an internationally acclaimed success due to its promotion of ethanol, produced from sugar cane, as a viable fuel alternative to oil. The Brazilian Ethanol Program was launched in 1975 following the international oil crisis. While early on it faced a number of challenges, including dependency on government subsidies and falling demand due to market uncertainty born of insufficient production levels, the program has succeeded in creating a cost-effective and widely used gasoline alternative. Currently, ethanol's market share in Brazil is substantial (as of 2004, 20–25 percent of Brazilian cars operated solely on ethanol) and continues to rise. As a result of this booming industry, Brazil is expected to be entirely energy independent by 2007.

Environmental movements have been strong advocates of Europe's push toward alternative energies. When **Germany**'s Red-Green coalition was elected in 1998, they introduced a legislative agenda that included a green tax reform, a renewed emphasis on renewable energies, and the phase out of nuclear energy. The European Union (EU) established a Renewable Energy Directive in 2001 that calls for the share of renewable energies in electricity production to increase to 21 percent in order to reach an overall target of renewable energies accounting for 12 percent of energy consumption by 2010. In March 2007, the EU agreed to a target of having 20 percent of overall energy consumption from renewables (wind, solar, biomass, and hydro) by 2020.

Renewable energy is spreading to developing countries as well. **India** has become one of the world's leading users of wind and solar energy, and in 2006, the **People's Republic of China**'s renewable energy law, which aims to increase renewable energy capacity to 15 percent of total energy capacity by 2020, went into effect. With energy prices on the rise and global demand for energy rapidly increasing, environmental groups and green parties are calling for even higher renewable energy targets. *See also* BLUEPRINT FOR SURVIVAL, A.

ALTERNATIVE LISTE OSTERREICHS (ALO). *See* AUSTRIA.

AMAZON. The Amazon is the world's largest rainforest and richest biological area. The Amazon River Basin includes parts of **Brazil**, Bolivia, Colombia, Ecuador, Guyana, Peru, and Suriname. Rapid deforestation has occurred as a result of swidden agriculture (the cutting and burning of plots of forest for subsistence-scale cultivation), agribusinesses (cattle ranching, commercial agriculture), logging, infrastructure development, and deliberate burning. **Chico Mendes'** Forest People's Alliance focused on saving the Amazon, which was under tremendous pressure. In addition to suffering from exploitive development projects, more than two decades of destructive infrastructure development in the Amazon and harmful agricultural, land, and colonization policies of the Brazilian government had taken a heavy toll on the forests and their native inhabitants. Efforts aimed at protecting the forests, preventing further destruction and deforestation, and promoting **sustainable development** continue to galvanize and mobilize the movement today.

Due to its ecological importance, Amazon rainforest protection and justice for the indigenous peoples of the region are of major concern to many green groups, including the Amazon Alliance, Amazon Watch, and the **Rainforest Action Network (RAN)**.

ANIMAL RIGHTS. The question of the status of animals has both united and divided the green movement. In 1985 **Rudolf Bahro** quit Die Grünen in West **Germany** when the party qualified their support for animal rights by stating that invasive experimentation on animals was admissible if even one human life could be saved. Green political parties and groups have usually taken a far stronger line than traditional political organizations and interest groups on issues such as the humane treatment of animals; protection of wildlife; opposition to intensive animal husbandry and animal experimentation; the use of animal products, especially when it places an entire species under the threat of extinction; and opposition to hunting animals for recreational purposes.

The principal division among supporters of the green movement has been between those who have, from an anthropocentric point of view, sought to protect animals and those who have argued that animals have moral rights. The latter have either described themselves or been described as **deep ecologists**. There are also parallels between this approach and the one adopted by radical environmental groups such as **Earth First!** which place as much, if not more, emphasis on the defense of the Earth and all species of plant and animal life than on saving individual human lives.

Tom Regan's *The Case for Animal Rights* is a seminal work in the defense of animal rights. Regan focuses on mammals aged one year or more that have developed perception, memory, desire, belief, self-consciousness, and a sense of the future before elaborating on why some animals have basic moral rights, which he distinguishes from "acquired" moral rights (in other words, rights that are procured by law, by voluntary action on the part of individuals, and by virtue of one's position in institutional arrangements). Although these efforts to argue for the basic moral rights of animals have been only partially understood or rejected by large parts of the green movement, the issue of animal rights has been a significant feature of campaigns to change perceptions about the relationship between human beings and nature.

ANTARCTICA. This vast area in the Southern Hemisphere has been a source of contention as different nations compete for the opportunity to exploit its natural resources. The freezing climate of this continent has rendered it inaccessible to humans and ensured the preservation of a pure environment. In 1959 a small number of countries signed the Antarctic Treaty with a view to using Antarctica only for peaceful purposes, mainly scientific research, and excluding attempts to undertake nuclear tests or the disposal of radioactive materials. The countries that first laid claim to the territory and signed the treaty (Argentina, **Australia**, Chile, **France**, **New Zealand**, **Norway**, and **Great Britain**) were joined in this agreement by **Belgium**, **South Africa**, **Japan**, the **United States**, and the former Soviet Union. Other countries have since signed the agreement. Subsequent demands by other nations to exploit the territory led, in 1991, to the signing of an Environmental Protocol to the Antarctic Treaty (the Madrid Protocol), which placed a 50-year moratorium on mining in the region. The protocol was signed by 39 nations. Nongovernmental organizations (NGOs) and various green parties have been fairly successful in campaigning for the preservation of Antarctica against efforts to exploit its natural resources (including oil) that could have a devastating effect on wildlife in the region. The Madrid Protocol reversed a 1988 decision by the signatories of the Antarctic Treaty (the Convention on the Regulation of Antarctic Mineral Resource Activities) to permit exploration for mineral resources.

ANTIGLOBALIZATION MOVEMENT. The rise of the multinational corporation, the globalization of culture, loss of local identity, and the inequalities that have persisted (and in some cases worsened) among and within countries as international trade and investment have expanded have spawned an antiglobalization movement. The antiglobalization movement is opposed to the neoliberal economic agenda of the West (the **United States**, Europe, and East Asia). The antiglobalization movement has partaken in protests against the World Trade Organization, the World Bank, the International Monetary Fund, the G8, the World Economic Forum, and the regional free trade blocks (e.g., the European Union [EU], the Free Trade Area of the Americas) and on issues such as genetically modified organisms (GMOs), child labor exploitation, and pollution transfer from rich to poor countries. Huge antiglobalization demonstrations have been held on such occasions as the World Trade Organization meeting in Seattle in 1999, the International Monetary FUnd (IMF)–World Bank meetings in Washington, D.C., and Prague in 2000, and the G8 summit in Genoa, **Italy**, in 2001. After a protestor was killed by police in Genoa, tens of thousands of people took to the streets in protest in Rome, Florence, Bologna, Palermo, and other cities across Italy.

The movement sees the spread of global capitalism as a threat to global democracy because of its empowerment of corporations at the expense of people and their ability to make choices about their own lives and communities. It also opposes the loss of local cultures that have accompanied the spread of industrial and corporate structures and argues that while globalization has helped to make some corporations, individuals, and countries wealthy, it has left many communities and countries impoverished.

Large segments of the antiglobalization movement, for example, have a distrust of GMOs and global agribusiness. Activists such as **Vandana Shiva** argue that GMOs threaten the future of traditional crops and seed variety, and that while global corporations may benefit from the sale of GMO crops, local communities often suffer. Some within the movement, such as the Frenchman José Bové, have used direct action techniques to protest GMOs (such as the dismantling of a McDonald's in southern **France** and the destruction of GMO crops). The movement has pressured European and other governments, including **Japan**, to refuse products that contain GMOs.

ANTINUCLEAR PROTESTS. In 1973 the Organization of Petroleum Exporting Countries (OPEC) sharply increased the price of oil. Western countries responded by creating an International Energy Agency. Among other options, this agency devoted serious attention to increasing the supply of energy from nuclear power generators. In **France**, **Belgium**, and **Germany**, governments outlined plans for a vast increase in nuclear power plants. Although the highest percentage of nuclear-generated electricity produced in Europe was in France and Belgium, opposition was most fierce in West Germany.

The conflict over nuclear power in Western countries was a key factor in the advance of the green movement in the 1970s and the formation of green parties in the 1980s. Antinuclear protests normally involved small communities concerned about the effects of radiation on local produce. To some extent, this reflects the so-called NIMBY ("not in my backyard") syndrome. In other words, people opposed a project only because it was going to be located in their vicinity. They were not committed to preventing the project if it was located elsewhere. However, this account of motivations tends to underestimate the capacity of people to link particular concerns about industrial development that affect their **quality of life** with a broader preoccupation about the impact of economic values on the environment. Moreover, protests against nuclear power in France and West Germany often became linked to regional issues and the defense of a particular culture against dominance by urban centers. In **Great Britain** there was a strong association between protests by the **Campaign for Nuclear Disarmament (CND)** against nuclear weapons in the 1950s and 1960s and the perceived danger of nuclear power generation for civilian purposes. Hence, there was rapid growth in the membership of the CND in the late 1970s and early 1980s.

In the Federal Republic of Germany the mobilization of the population in several small communities rapidly expanded into national and international protest movements. For instance, the 1975 protests in Wyhl by a community concerned about damage to the vineyards that were their livelihood escalated into widespread antagonism toward three things: the collusion between the state government of Baden-Württemberg and industrial interests, the deployment of the police to solve political problems, and the dominant political parties.

Similar protests, on a much larger scale, occurred in **Brokdorf**, Schleswig-Holstein (1976); Grohnde, Lower Saxony (1977); and Gorleben, Lower Saxony (1978). Huge demonstrations also occurred at Kaiseraugst in **Switzerland** and at Creys-Malville in France (in July 1977). At some rallies many of the participants were from other countries, notably the Federal Republic of Germany. The largest gatherings were in that country. For instance, in March 1979 around 100,000 people participated in a protest rally against nuclear power in Hanover, the capital city of Lower Saxony, and in October 1979, around 150,000 people in Bonn staged the largest ever protest rally in the Federal Republic of Germany. During the same month, over 1,000 environmentalists met in Offenbach to discuss the possibility of establishing a new political organization that later became known as Die Grünen.

The connection between protests against nuclear power and new political movements and parties was evident throughout western Europe. In West Germany **citizens' initiatives** focused increasingly on this issue and were brought together under an umbrella organization called the Bundesverband Bürgerinitiativen Umweltschutz (Federal Association of Citizens' Initiatives for Environmental Protection), which was founded in 1972. The Organization for Information on Nuclear Power was formed in **Denmark** in 1974, the Initiative against Nuclear Power Plants arose in the **Netherlands** in 1973, and Action against Nuclear Power was founded in **Austria** in 1974. The Swedish Milj6verbund, formed in 1976, paved the way for the Milj6partiet de Gr6na, a green party founded in 1981.

Apart from mass protests across western Europe, public opinion about nuclear power was influenced by events and movements across the world. In **Australia**, a decision by the Australian Labor Party Conference in 1984 to allow the opening of a uranium mine led to the formation of the **Nuclear Disarmament Party (NDP)**. Within six months, the NDP had 8,000 members and attracted 643,000 (7 percent) first-preference votes in elections to the Senate, thereby accumulating an even higher proportion of votes than did parties such as Die Grünen in West Germany around the same time. In the **United States**, in May 1979 approximately 75,000 people gathered in Washington, D.C., to take part in the largest demonstration against nuclear power in that country.

Throughout the 1970s groups in the United States such as the Clamshell Alliance had engaged in civil disobedience to prevent the construction of the Seabrook nuclear power plant in New Hampshire. Over 1,400 people were arrested at the site in October 1976. Another event that brought the issue of the safety of nuclear power to public attention was the death of Karen Silkwood in 1974. Silkwood died in a mysterious car accident while on her way to meet a newspaper reporter and a union official, to whom she was going to present evidence of serious safety infringements at the Kerr-McGee plutonium plant in Oklahoma. Her concerns appeared to be warranted following the closure of the plant. Another stimulus to worldwide protests against nuclear power was an accident, in March 1978, at the **Three Mile Island** plant in Harrisburg, Pennsylvania, which resulted in the emission of radioactive gases and the mass evacuation of the local population.

The accident coincided with the release of a Hollywood film called *The China Syndrome*, which presented a dramatic and plausible account of the serious difficulties that could arise in a nuclear power plant. The worst fears of opponents to nuclear power were realized less than a decade later. On 26 April 1986 there was an explosion at the **Chernobyl** nuclear power plant near Kiev in the **Ukraine**, then part of the Soviet Union. It is estimated that 30 people died very soon after the explosion, several hundred others had to be treated for the severe effects of radiation, and over 130,000 inhabitants had to be evacuated from the region.

Antinuclear activism has spread to other parts of the world as well. A criticality accident at the Tokaimura nuclear fuel processing plant in 1999 is recognized as the third-worst nuclear accident in history. It was caused by a mistake of the workers at the plant in Ibaraki, **Japan**. Three workers were exposed to high levels of radiation and two died within a few months of the accident. This accident on top of a number of other safety issues at nuclear facilities in Japan have intensified antinuclear activism and made difficult the government's plans to build more nuclear power plants.

Despite the protests and the accidents, two contrasting trends are apparent. First, the main stumbling block to the development of nuclear power appears to be high costs and public opposition. Second, the nuclear industry has derived some encouragement from concern about **climate change** and the **greenhouse effect** and the assertion that nuclear power may, in some respects, be a "cleaner" source of energy.

ASIA PACIFIC GREENS NETWORK. The Japanese green activist group, the **Rainbow and Greens**, hosted an international meeting in Kyoto, **Japan**, in 2005 to formally launch the Asia Pacific Greens Network. The idea is to facilitate international exchange among greens in the Asia Pacific region. The meeting was attended by representatives of established green parties and green groups that are involved in electoral politics at some level. The meeting followed the Asia Pacific Green Politics Workshop held in Brisbane, **Australia**, in 2000. Twenty-seven green parties and organizations from 23 countries were accepted as provisional members. An Asia Pacific Young Greens Network was also launched at the Kyoto meeting.

ASIA PACIFIC PARTNERSHIP ON CLEAN DEVELOPMENT AND CLIMATE. This is an informal climate change agreement among **Australia**, the **People's Republic of China**, **India**, **Japan**, the **Republic of Korea**, and the **United States** and was introduced on 28 July 2005 at the **Association of Southeast Asian Nations'** **(ASEAN)** regional forum. The agreement focuses on technology development and voluntary measures for greenhouse gas emissions reductions. Critics argue that its voluntary approach makes it toothless.

ASSOCIATION OF SOUTHEAST ASIAN NATIONS (ASEAN). Initiated in 1967 on the model of the European Economic Community, there are now 10 countries that are members of ASEAN: Brunei Darussalam, Cambodia, Indonesia, Laos, **Malaysia**, Myanmar, the Philippines, Singapore, **Thailand**, and Vietnam. Importantly, as a result of ASEAN, cooperation in Southeast Asia is moving beyond the bilateral to the multilateral level. The initial goal of ASEAN was to promote peace and stability among historic rivals. Slowly, environmental concerns have also crept onto the agenda. The United Nations played an important stimulating role in this process. The **United Nations Environment Programme (UNEP)** pushed the establishment of a Sub-Regional Environmental Programme in Southeast Asia in 1977.

In the 1980s ASEAN issued several environmental declarations, calling for cooperation on raising environmental awareness in the region; the creation of a list of sites in the region that should be recognized as special heritage parks and reserves; and regional cooperation in protection of the seas and tropical forests and addressing land-based pollution, air pollution, and urban pollution.

ASEAN's environmental activities picked up noticeably in the 1990s, especially in response to the haze problems caused by wide-scale slash-and-burn agriculture in Indonesia, a problem that gained international attention in 1997 and 1998 and again in the early 2000s when the fires burned out of control and caused problems not only for Indonesia but throughout much of Southeast Asia. The formation of the Agreement on Transboundary Haze Pollution marks the first such agreement in the world and may be an important step in moving ASEAN toward the acceptance of legally binding international environmental agreements.

The first ASEAN +3 (**Japan**, the **People's Republic of China**, and the **Republic of Korea**) environment ministers meeting was held in November 2002. This was an important, if still early, step in promoting greater regional environmental cooperation in East Asia.

ASEAN's work has received mixed reactions from the few green parties of the region. The Green Party of Aotearoa, **New Zealand**, has opposed its efforts to establish a free trade agreement because of ASEAN's failure to make adequate progress on labor, human rights, and environmental protection. The Taiwan Green Party, on the other hand, has supported ASEAN's efforts to promote a neutral and peaceful zone in Southeast Asia and to establish a nuclear-free zone.

AUDUBON SOCIETY. Founded as a national organization in the **United States** in 1905, the Audubon Society was named after the naturalist John James Audubon. Audubon was the renowned author of *Birds of America*, completed in 1837. The Audubon Society was first formed in New York in 1886 with the aim of preventing poaching and hunting of birds and wildlife, and it gained public attention during a campaign to prevent the use of birds' feathers in hats. It has since grown into an organization with more than 500,000 members and has broadened its focus on questions of pollution of land, waterways, and oceans.

AUSTRALIA. The origins of green political organizations in Australia can be traced to the appearance in the 1970s of community group opposition to specific developments. A striking example of a popular protest movement was the radical Green Ban movement, which involved cooperation between industrial workers and middle-class environmentalists in New South Wales. Workers from the militant Builders Labourers Federation joined in protests against plans for development and the destruction of parklands, established communities, and historical buildings. The unions imposed work bans on projects they considered to be environmentally hazardous. Forty-two bans were applied over a four-year period (from 1971 to 1975) and blocked development projects valued at hundreds of millions of dollars.

These protests in Sydney were predated by a momentous campaign that arose on the island state of Tasmania, in response to the impending destruction of Lake Pedder to promote a hydroelectric scheme. The **United Tasmania Group (UTG)**, which was created in response to the failure by traditional political parties to consider the full implications of this action, was among the first green political organizations in the world to compete in state elections. The conflict over the flooding of Lake Pedder is widely believed to have contributed to the upsurge of green political organizations and is regarded as a source of inspiration for many leading activists in more recent campaigns. In addition, it gave rise to associations such as the Save Lake Pedder Committee (1967), a group with a far more radical orientation than environmentalist associations of the past. Although the protest groups were ultimately unsuccessful in preserving Lake Pedder, they precipitated the growth of a movement that eventually influenced the national agenda on environmental policies.

The program of the UTG contained some of the classic tenets of green political organizations, including a critique of the "misuse of power" as well as a focus on social justice and on participatory democracy. The emphasis on values such as grassroots participation had a far-reaching impact on organizations that followed the UTG, for example, the Tasmanian **Wilderness Society** (later renamed the Wilderness Society). This organization, formed in 1976, became one of the most influential groups in the development of the green movement and provided a loose, yet highly effective, organizational structure for mobilizing protestors. Groups such as the Wilderness Society helped get the environment onto the national political agenda, as, for example, in the campaign between 1979 and 1983 to prevent the creation of the **Franklin Dam**.

Another association that has played a crucial part in mobilizing support for green political organizations is the **Australian Conservation Foundation (ACF)**. Both the Wilderness Society (through its mobilization of activists) and the ACF (through its adoption of a more radical stance) were to influence environmental policies, first in the Australian Labour Party (ALP) and later in other established parties, notably the Australian Democrats.

Apart from providing a focus for green campaigns, Tasmania also had an electoral system that made it easier than in most other states for minor parties to secure representation in the state parliament. The breakthrough came in 1989, when five green independent candidates, who polled 17 percent of the vote across the state, were elected to the House of Assembly, which is made up of 36 members. The independents also held the balance of power and signed a momentous "accord" with the ALP. The greens agreed to support an ALP government in exchange for some major policy concessions, notably the extension of wilderness and forest areas covered by **World Heritage** protection and **national park** status, guarantees of staffing and other resources for the green parliamentary delegates, access to parliamentary committees and reforms in parliamentary procedures, and standing orders to ensure greater transparency of the financial interests of parliamentary delegates.

Many of these measures were implemented, particularly those pertaining to the protection of forests and wilderness. The accord accelerated a shift in values; environmental considerations were taken into account much more consistently than in the past in political and other institutional processes and decision making. The accord did not entail the formation of a coalition government, however, and the ALP was able, in effect, to govern on its own. The party remained constantly under pressure by green delegates who questioned the slow pace of reforms. After 18 months the accord fell apart after a dispute over the closure of schools and differing perceptions on how to deal with economic and environmental issues, notably the question of whether to apply quotas on the export of wood chips from Tasmania.

The formal disintegration of the accord in September 1991 was directly linked to arguments over the wood chip quota.

The ALP remained in government until February 1992, and by then many voters had become disillusioned with the Labor-Green experiment. Although the vote for the ALP in the 1992 election was its lowest ever, the green independents retained their five seats. However, the latter's share of the vote was reduced to 13.4 percent, and a new Liberal government was elected on a platform that opposed many green reforms. In 1996 the greens lost another seat in Tasmania, and their share of the vote declined to 11 percent.

Tasmania and Western Australia are the two states in which green political organizations have managed to secure sufficient support to send representatives to the federal upper house, the Senate. The origins of the Western Australia Green Party reflect both failures and successes of other green political associations, including the short-lived upsurge of the **Nuclear Disarmament Party (NDP)** in the early 1980s. The demise of organizations such as the NDP contributed to the long delay in the formation of a national green party. For a long time the gap was filled by the Australian Democrats.

The Australian Democrats were founded in May 1977 by Don Chipp, a former minister in the federal Liberal government. The primary justification for the formation of the Democrats was to keep the traditional parties "honest." The party soon developed a strong profile on green issues, focusing at first on the questions of uranium mining and the nuclear industry, always concentrating on protecting the environment as a fundamental objective. Its national constitution formulated, in 1978, as core objectives: "To accept the challenge of the predicament of mankind on the planet with its exponentially increasing population, disappearing finite resources, and accelerating deterioration of the environment" and "To seek the transition to a sustainable economy, in equilibrium with world resources and eco-systems, with a minimum of dislocation by planning the necessary changes in good time, and by increasing public awareness of the problem ahead." Like many green political organizations, the Democrats emphasized participatory democracy, including the involvement of party members in determining policy guidelines.

Apart from the UTG and the Western Australia Green Party, the Democrats were the only other minor party that succeeded in exploiting the environment as an election issue. In 1990 the Democrats appealed to environmentalists by adopting, in their advertising, the widely recognized triangular symbol used in the campaign against the Franklin Dam almost a decade earlier. They also claimed to be "the original environmental party" and to have fought consistently for environmental protection. In the first assertion they ignored the formation of the UTG in 1972. On the issue of consistency, their leader, Senator Janine Haines, suggested that the Democrats had always been far ahead of other parties on environmental matters. Haines drew attention to initiatives by the Democrats such as the introduction of the first bill to save the Franklin, the first bill to ban all ozone-depleting substances by 1995, a bill to rescind the sales tax on recycled paper, and campaigns in the 1970s to combat soil salinity and degradation.

In 1990 the Australian Democrats achieved their best results in a federal election (12.6 percent of first-preference votes in the elections to the Senate). They continued to do reasonably well over the course of the next decade, but as a result of party infighting, the party lost voter appeal, and in the 2004 federal election, their support plummeted to 1.2 percent of the vote. Many of the party's supporters on the left gravitated to the Australian Greens.

In 1992 a new political organization called the Australian Greens formed as a confederation of the eight separate state and territory Greens (Greens South Australia, Greens Western Australia, Tasmanian Greens, Queensland Greens, Greens Victoria, Northern Territory Greens, Canberra Australian Capital Territory (ACT) Greens). The state Greens have retained considerable autonomy, but the formation of a national party has provided the greens with more visibility. The rise of the Australian Greens coincided with the decline of the Australian Democrats.

In 1992 as a member of the Western Australia Green Party, Christabel Chamarette became a senator in the Australian Parliament. Following the March 1996 federal election, she lost her seat, but the Greens maintained a Senate presence with the election of Bob Brown, a leading figure in the Australian Greens. The Greens did well in the 2004 parliamentary election; they were able to acquire four Green senators: Bob Brown (Tasmania), Christine Milne (Tasmania), Kerry Nettle (New South Wales), and Rachel Siewert (Western Australia). *See also* DIRECT DEMOCRACY.

AUSTRALIAN CONSERVATION FOUNDATION (ACF). Formed in 1965, the ACF was the first truly national environmental organization in **Australia**. Prominent politicians, administrators, and dignitaries (including the Duke of Edinburgh and the Chief Justice of the High Court, Sir Garfield Barwick) played a pivotal role in its formation. Efforts by these prominent figures to encourage changes in perceptions reflected the growing awareness, at least among conservation groups and sections of the political and administrative elites, of the dangers of environmental degradation. It initially lobbied for conservationists. However, it did not mobilize its support for militant direct action campaigns.

Like other voluntary organizations, the association received some support from the federal government. In 1964 it received A$1,000 from the Department of the Prime Minister. By 1990, under a Labour government, this figure had risen to A$175,631. During the campaigns to save Lake Pedder in Tasmania and to prevent the construction of the **Franklin Dam**, the ACF became more militant. In 1983 it joined a coalition of 800 conservation groups to oppose the latter project.

From a modest 1,017 in 1967, membership in the association rose to 5,154 in 1971. In the 1980s there was a further rapid rise in membership from 11,046 in 1982 to 21,400 in 1991. In 2000, the association had approximately 60,000 supporters.

The ACF has long operated as a powerful lobby group, and it continued to exert influence on policymakers when, in 1991, it was invited to participate in consultations over ecologically **sustainable development** and received large amounts of financial support from the federal government in order to carry out the necessary research. Like other green groups, the association argued that the government was placing too much emphasis on economic values. Throughout the 1980s and early 1990s, the association effectively lobbied the government for a wide range of issues, including specific concerns over the protection of forests and wilderness areas as well as broader policy issues such as **climate change** and sustainable development.

The ACF counts as among its success stories the establishment of numerous **national parks**, the prevention of drilling and mining in natural areas (including the Great Barrier Reef and **Antarctica**), the stopping of plans to dam rivers, winning new support for the National

Heritage Trust, and the passage of legislation preventing nuclear waste dumping.

Like the **Wilderness Society**, the ACF has played an important part in endorsing candidates of green parties, as well as of the Australian Democrats and of the traditional political parties at federal and state elections.

AUSTRIA. The emergence of the green movement in Austria is similar to developments in other countries as regards the connection with campaigns by social movements and by **citizens' initiatives**. In one such campaign, opponents succeeded in blocking the construction of a nuclear power plant in Zwentendorf near Vienna. In a referendum conducted in 1978, most people voted to ban **nuclear energy**. In 1984 the green movement succeeded in preventing the building of a hydroelectric power plant at Hainburg on the Danube.

An exceptional aspect of green politics in Austria is the formation of political organizations in an environment dominated, more than in most countries, by a corporatist style of policymaking, a long and relatively successful partnership between labor and business groups and the government.

The Vereinte Grüne Österreichs (VGÖ) (United Greens), a moderate and reformist green party, was formed in 1982. It gained its main basis of support from campaigns against nuclear power. The Alternative Liste Österreichs (ALÖ) (Alternative List), a more radical green party, was also formed in 1982. Support for this party arose principally from social movements, including those that campaigned for peace and nuclear disarmament and on issues directly affecting less developed countries.

As early as 1977, citizens' lists (Bürgerliste) contested local elections in Salzburg and attracted 5 percent of the vote. Following the referendum on nuclear power in 1978, green groups did not form a political party in time for the 1979 national elections. When they competed in the 1983 national elections, the VGÖ and ALÖ only attracted 1.9 and 1.4 percent of the vote, respectively. By contrast, in 1986, by presenting a united front under the title Die Grüne Alternative (Green Alternative), the two parties gained 4.8 percent of the vote and eight seats in the national parliament. Moreover, in that year, one of the leading figures in the green movement, Freda Meissner-

Blau, competed in the presidential elections. Although she received only 5.5 percent of the vote, this was sufficient to force a second-round contest between candidates for the conservative People's Party and the Socialist Party.

The ALÖ was, in many respects, not dissimilar to Die Grünen in **Germany**, and borrowed heavily from its platform. It had close links to new social movements and emphasized participation by activists. The VGÖ was a much more conservative organization, and much of its program, apart from environmental questions, resembled that of traditional political organizations. However, most of its supporters, like those of the ALÖ, voted for the coalition rather than their individual party.

There was initially a clear contrast between the respective programs and policies of the VGÖ and ALÖ. The former concentrated on the individual citizen, support for the family, and civil liberties. It had, in many respects, an antistatist program, emphasizing deregulation and privatization in economic affairs and a less interventionist role in social policy. By contrast, the ALÖ favored statutory intervention in all these areas, including such measures as nationalization and regulation of incomes. Moreover, the ALÖ seized on issues articulated by social movements, notably their preoccupation with peace and nuclear disarmament. Die Grüne Alternative took up some of the concerns expressed by the VGÖ, though it also developed more fully ALÖ policies on the economy, reforming the political system, health and social security, peace, and many other questions.

In 1993, the united party adopted the official name, Die Grünen-Die Grüne Alternative. They are commonly called Die Grünen. Since this time, they have grown to become one of the strongest green parties in Europe. In 1994 Die Grünen increased its share of the vote to 7 percent and its representation to 13 out of 183 seats in the national parliament. Although the party suffered a setback in 1995 when it attracted only 4.8 percent of the vote and lost four seats, in 1999 they returned their share to 7.4 percent of the vote (14 MPs). In 2002, after the collapse of the ruling right-wing coalition government, they upped their share of the vote to an impressive 9.47 percent (17 seats). They briefly entered into negotiations with the Christian Democratic Österreiches Volkspartei about forming a coalition government, but the negotiations collapsed due to sharp political disagreements. Voters rewarded the party's decision and its opposition to the conservative governments that have dominated Austrian politics in recent years. Running on a platform that included a new energy policy, green job investments, education for women, organic food, social justice, and a global foreign policy, Die Grünen became Austria's third-largest political party after winning 11.05 percent of the vote (21 MPs, of whom 12 are women) in the October 2006 parliamentary election.

In the 1990s the question of reform of the political system included issues such as greater citizen involvement in policymaking, as well as in determining the direction of schools; work conditions; and strengthening the role of Parliament. Special attention was paid to the rights of social minorities and disadvantaged groups. Die Grünen opposed Austria's application for membership in the European Union (EU). Once this effort failed, it did not undertake to work for the withdrawal of Austria but to influence the union from within. Die Grünen has since become a member of the **European Green Party**. Die Grünen's 2001 party platform laid out six basic principles: **ecology**, solidarity, self-determination, **grassroots democracy**, feminism, and **nonviolence**.

Die Grünen has performed strongly in local and regional elections as well. In the 2003 regional election in Tyrol, the party garnered 15.59 percent of the vote (five seats). In Upper Austria, Die Grünen was brought into government, gaining the post of environment minister after winning 9.06 percent of the vote in the 2003 election. The regional government has since introduced antidiscrimination legislation and supported renewable energies. In Vienna, Die Grünen won 14.63 percent of the vote in 2005. As of 2006, Die Grünen was represented in nine regional governments and had about 1,000 municipal councilors. They also did well in the 2004 **European Parliamentary** elections, winning 12.89 percent of the vote (two seats).

A major campaign issue for Die Grünen and the broader environmental community in Austria during the 1990s and into the 2000s was opposition to the start up of the Temelin Nuclear Power plant in the **Czech Republic**. Temelin was already under construction at the time of the collapse of the Soviet empire in 1989. The Czech government, after updating safety designs and incorporating American nuclear reactor design elements into the plant, determined the plant was safe and decided to move forward with its operation. As the Bohemian plant is near the Austrian border, there was great concern in Austria. Austrian protesters, often led by Die Grünen, mobilized against the plant, blocking border crossings between the two countries and collecting over 900,000 protest signatures. In the end, their protests failed as the European Commission refused to hold up Czech membership in the EU based on this issue as the protesters had demanded. The Temelin plant went into operation beginning in 2000.

– B –

BAHRO, RUDOLF (1935–1997). Following his exile from East **Germany**, Rudolf Bahro, an intellectual and critic of the communist regime, became a leading figure in the formation of Die Grünen in West Germany. At first he espoused the possibility of combining socialism with environmental concerns. However, he rapidly became disillusioned first with socialism and then with the pragmatic reformers, or realists, in Die Grünen. Bahro increasingly articulated the position of fundamentalists within the party, before promoting **spirituality** and leaving Die Grünen in 1985 in protest at the compromises they were making over issues such as animal experimentation.

Bahro was at first welcomed by the political establishment in the Federal Republic of Germany as an exile from the autocratic regime in East Germany. However, his criticism of the latter did not mean that he was an enthusiast for capitalism. Drawing on his Marxist intellectual heritage, he expressed fears about the problem of alienation (rather than exploitation) arising from a capitalist economic system. In *Socialism and Survival* he referred to the loss of community associated with industrial society and to the alienation of one person from another. He also argued that the interest of the human species should become the core point of reference for understanding the problems we confront and that social change could only be achieved if one went beyond the concept of class enunciated by Karl Marx.

Bahro had shifted from being a fairly conventional Marxist to aligning himself with utopian socialists and communists. Influenced by arguments about *The Limits to Growth*, he also began to abandon socialism and to question attempts by environmentalists to reform the capitalist system. In *Building the Green Movement* he promoted the notion of drastically reducing consumption in Western societies. He also presented more fully his rejection of parliamentary politics and espousal of **spirituality**. Bahro agreed with the fundamentalists that the involvement by Die Grünen in parliamentary politics meant it was becoming just like any other traditional political party, losing touch with the grassroots, and abandoning many of the core principles of the green movement. Bahro was especially annoyed at the decision of Die Grünen not to oppose all experimentation on animals, and he left the party after it had agreed that "if even one human life can be saved, the torture of animals is permissible."

Bahro was aligning himself with **deep ecologists** and their rejection of anthropocentrism. He also elaborated on his own spiritual approach and how society might be transformed through the creation of communal lifestyles that resembled, in certain respects, the social organization of the Benedictine Order of monks. Bahro argued that this communal form of social organization presented a cultural alternative to the prevailing focus on industrialism and capitalism. He also suggested that the new movement would differ from the original Benedictine Order by rejecting a monotheistic idea of God (which had originated in despotic and hierarchical systems) and abandoning the separation of the sexes and sexual oppression. The retreat by the green movement into spirituality would, according to Bahro, eventually provide a much deeper and sounder basis for transforming social institutions and realizing the potential of the greens.

Although Bahro had identified some of the tensions and difficulties that arise when a new movement attempts to bring about social change, his withdrawal from contemporary politics and criticism of prevailing lifestyles were met with skepticism by many people within the green movement. Still, his involvement in the movement demonstrated the possibilities for dramatic shifts in perceptions of the relationship between different ideologies (including socialism, capitalism, and environmentalism) and the importance of notions of culture and spirituality in this process. There are parallels between Bahro's focus on these notions and the idea of a shift in values from materialism to **postmaterialism**. Bahro's strong stance on opposing technology and reducing consumption may simply reflect a more consistent and fundamentalist viewpoint than is acceptable to many in the green movement. *See also* ANIMAL RIGHTS.

BANGLADESH. Bangladesh is the world's eighth most populous state, but one of its poorest on a per capita basis, ranking 175 out of 229 in the U.S. Central Intelligence Agency's world ranking list in 2006. The country faces wide-scale poverty, income inequality, a burgeoning population, disease, lack of resources, environmental destruction, and recurring floods. As the population of Bangladesh soars, so does the amount of poverty: over half of the population is impoverished and illiterate.

Despite Bangladesh's poverty, environmental movements have started to form. In 1997 a citizens' forum, known as the Poribesh Rakkha Shopoth (POROSH), formed to address the pollution problems of Dhaka, one of the most polluted cities in the world. The following year, nonresident Bangladeshis set up the Bangladesh Environment Network (BEN). In 2000 BEN joined with POROSH to host the International Conference on Bangladesh Environment in Dhaka. The conference discussed Bangladesh's major environmental issues and drew widespread media attention. A merger of BEN and POROSH created Bangladesh Poribesh Andolon (BAPA) (Bangladesh Environment Movement), the beginning of the civic environmental movement. Efforts to form a Green Party are underway as well. In June 2004, a Green Party of Bangladesh was launched in Dhaka. Whether or not the party can make it in a country overflowing with political parties, however, remains to be seen.

BASEL CONVENTION ON THE CONTROL OF TRANS-BOUNDARY MOVEMENTS OF HAZARDOUS WASTES AND THEIR DISPOSAL. The Basel Convention is an international treaty drafted in 1989 in response to public outcries against the indiscriminate dumping of hazardous waste. The convention went into force in 1992. It intends to reduce the movement of hazardous waste between nations and to prevent the "trade" in waste that resulted in the dumping of developed countries' hazardous waste into lesser developed countries.

Hazardous waste is potentially dangerous because, if spilled accidentally or managed improperly, it can cause severe health problems and destroy water and land for many years. The convention covers toxic, poisonous, explosive, corrosive, flammable, and infectious hazardous waste. Under the convention, the movement of hazardous wastes can take place only with written notification by the exporting state to the importing state, the approval of the importing state, and a requirement that every shipment must have a movement document from the point at which the transboundary movement began to the point of disposal.

There are, moreover, absolute bans on the export of hazardous wastes to certain countries. For example, **Greenpeace** International demanded that a naval aircraft carrier, the *Clemenceau*, which was being towed to **India** for scrapping, return to **France**, which is a signatory to the Basel Convention, due to the hazardous materials on board, including 500 tons of asbestos.

Transboundary movement is allowed to take place if the exporting state does not have the ability to dispose of the hazardous waste in an environmentally sound manner. Each party to the convention must fill out an annual questionnaire about the specific country's generation and the export and import of hazardous waste.

The convention focuses on the "environmentally sound management" of hazardous waste through an "integrated life-cycle approach." This means controlling the generation, storage, transport, treatment, reuse, recycling, recovery, and disposal of hazardous waste. The convention also tries to lower demand for products that result in hazardous waste.

In order to help countries implement the Basel Convention, Regional Centres for Training and Technology Transfer have been established in countries such as Argentina, the **People's Republic of China**, **Egypt**, and El Salvador. The centers provide guidance on technical, technological, and enforcement issues. The centers also encourage cleaner production technologies and environmentally sound waste management practices.

BELGIUM. Belgium is culturally and linguistically divided, and this has influenced the development of green movements in the country. The two largest linguistic groups in Belgium are the French speakers living in the southern region of Wallonia and the Dutch (Flemish) speakers of Flanders in the North. Because of the ethnic and cultural divisions, there are no longer any truly national parties in **Belgium**. Political parties tend to be organized around regional issues. Mirroring these divisions, two green parties were formed: Agalev ("for an alternative way of life") representing the Flemish community and **Ecolo** representing the Walloons. Agalev has since changed its name to **Groen!**

BENIN. Environmental nongovernmental organizations (NGOs), women's movements, and youth groups spawned the formation of Benin's Green Party in 1995. In 2003, the Green Party as part of the Star Alliance, an oppositional political party comprised of the Builders and Managers of Freedom and Democracy, the Union for Democracy and National Solidarity, and the Greens, sent three delegates to Parliament.

BHOPAL. This city in **India** will be remembered as the setting for a catastrophe that began on 3 December 1984 following the release of poisonous gas from the Union Carbide pesticide plant. The gas, comprised mainly of methyl isocyanate, killed at least 2,500 people immediately, though some estimates put the death toll at four times that number. About 250,000 inhabitants of the slums around the factory suffered extreme discomfort (including temporary blindness and burning lungs). Many more died from the effects of the poisonous gas in the following years. After a lengthy court battle, victims were awarded US$470 million in compensation in February 1989, a figure well below original demands. On the twentieth anniversary of the disaster, the International Campaign for Justice in Bhopal, of which **Greenpeace** is a member, was demanding that Dow Chemical, the new owner of Union Carbide, assume liability for the long-term health impacts and loss of livelihood suffered by the community.

BIOCENTRISM. Biocentrism developed as a reaction to the concept of human conquest of nature associated with the industrial revolution and scientific progress. It entails a focus on oneness with nature and on the dangers of human distance from and interference with the natural environment. The biocentric view of the world was given a significant boost in the 19th century both by romantic poets and writers and by scientific studies such as Charles Darwin's work on the evolution of animal species. *See also* BIOREGIONALISM.

BIODIVERSITY. Biological diversity or **biodiversity** refers to the variety of different species living on Earth and the natural patterns that their interaction causes. Over 1.75 million different species have been identified, although many scientists estimate that there are about 13 million species.

Concern with the preservation of biological diversity originated in the 19th century. Formal attempts to address the problem can be detected in the recommendations by the **United Nations Conference on the Human Environment (UNCHE)** (1972), in the World Conservation Strategy launched by the **World Conservation Union (IUCN)**, in the United Nations Educational, Scientific and Cultural Organization (UNESCO) Man and the Biosphere Program, and in the **Convention on International Trade in Endangered Species of Wild Flora and Fauna (CITES)**.

In the 1980s, various groups of experts began raising the alarm about the threat to biological diversity from population pressures, expansion of modern agriculture, deforestation, development, and introduction of alien species. More recently, concerns about the impacts of climate change on biological diversity have started to gain attention.

The Global 2000 Report, which was released in 1980, estimated that by the end of the 20th century, largely as a result of the destruction of tropical rainforests, hundreds of thousands of plant and animal species would become extinct. Concern by environmental groups and governments about this loss is based in aesthetic, moral, and utilitarian considerations. The cure for many illnesses may ultimately be found in plants that face the threat of extinction. There are also concerns about how the loss of genetic resources narrows the range of possibilities for dealing with problems, especially in agriculture, and about the destruction of rainforests without regard to the likely consequences on plant, animal, and human life. The seriousness of biodiversity loss spawned the **Convention on Biological Diversity**. *See also* BIOPROSPECTING; GLOBAL BIODIVERSITY HOTSPOTS.

BIOREGIONALISM. The vision of a decentralized society has been articulated in many different ways. The term *bioregionalism* is one such expression. It refers, in the words of Kirkpatrick Sale, to a society in which people live according to the rhythms of the land or the discrete territory defined by natural boundaries (flora, fauna, water, landforms, and climate soils). Rather than shape the land, humans would adapt to it. This, it is argued, would accelerate the formation of different cultures, different systems of government, and a more balanced or steady-state economic and social system. The perceived advantages of a bioregionalist society include an increase in leisure time, proximity to nature, the development of communal bonds, and the acceptance of the world "as it is" and of people "as they are" rather than a situation characterized by fragmentation, change, and violence. Contrary to the expectations of its proponents, the concept of bioregionalism has not been widely championed within the green movement. Still, some of the values that are said to be an integral part of bioregionalism have been significant in shaping aspects of its platforms, programs, and practices. *See also* BIOCENTRISM; *BLUEPRINT FOR SURVIVAL, A.*

BIOPROSPECTING. The search for medicinal and useful material substances in plants and animals is known as bioprospecting. Bioprospecting has become a controversial issue as most of the companies involved in bioprospecting are located in developed countries and much of the bioprospecting occurs in developing countries. Intellectual property rights issues have become entangled with bioprospecting as pharmaceutical and other companies often benefit from the indigenous knowledge of local people and medicine men and women when collecting plants and living organisms for research purposes.

Efforts to address these issues have been made with the establishment of **Convention on Biological Diversity** and the Cartagena Protocol on Biosafety. There have also been some efforts between companies and developing states to work out arrangements that provide the company with plant specimens in exchange for a percentage of any profits derived from medicines or other products developed from research conducted with that specimen. While the hopes for bioprospecting agreements, such as that between Merck and the National Biodiversity Institute (INBIO) in **Costa Rica** have been big, the long lead time to developing new drugs has meant that to date, Costa Rica has seen no royalties as a result of the agreement.

BIOSPHERE CONFERENCE. Assembled in Paris between 1 and 13 September 1968, the Intergovernmental Conference of Experts on the Scientific Basis for Rational Use and Conservation of the Biosphere was an initiative by the United Nations Educational, Scientific, and Cultural Organization (UNESCO) to foster international debate among experts about the impact of human beings on the environment. The themes broached at this conference anticipated and provided a firmer basis for the 1972 **United Nations Conference on the Human Environment (UNCHE)**. The Biosphere Conference focused mainly on the potential contribution of natural scientists toward addressing issues such as air and water pollution and the destruction of forests. UNCHE was to debate these issues in a broader socioeconomic and political context. The Biosphere Conference played an important part in voicing growing concerns about the scale of environmental destruction, focusing on the complex linkages between human activity and the environment, and raising awareness about the importance of collecting data on regional and international aspects of changes in the environment.

BLUEPRINT FOR SURVIVAL, A. In the early 1970s a number of parallel concepts drew attention to the threats posed by environmental destruction. *A Blueprint for Survival* was the title of an article published in 1972 by the editorial board of *The Ecologist* magazine led by Edward Goldsmith. Like *The Limits to Growth* published by the **Club of Rome**, *A Blueprint for Survival* was written to startle people into action. Sales of the book reached 750,000 copies. It called for radical changes in lifestyles in order to ensure the survival of the planet. The main proposal was the creation of a new, decentralized social system. This would supposedly facilitate more participation in decision making and cooperative attitudes than in a heterogeneous, centralized society and would lead to greater innovation both in agriculture and industry. Small, self-regulating communities might also be characterized by more fulfilling personal relationships, and there would consequently be less emphasis on consumption. Other possible benefits of decentralization would include self-sufficiency and a reduction in the use of expensive facilities such as large-scale sewage treatment plants. The authors also prescribed policies of stable **population growth**, more efficient use of energy, and less reliance on pesticides and fertilizers.

BOOKCHIN, MURRAY. *See* SOCIAL ECOLOGY.

BRAZIL. Brazil is the world's sixth most populated country, with close to 190 million inhabitants in 2006. The opening of political space that accompanied Brazil's democratic transformation in 1985 was crucial to the emergence of the country's environmental movement. The freer flow of information and civil dissent allowed in the new political system enabled the explosion of environmentally oriented nongovernmental organizations (NGOs) onto the scene. These early NGOs were largely local groups that sought to protect their environment from destructive and exploitive logging, damming, mining and other development projects undertaken by the Brazilian government, private corporations, foreign countries, and international institutions such as the World Bank.

Brazil's green movement has strengthened substantially as the country's democracy has deepened. Aid from international NGOs has also bolstered the efficacy of Brazil's environmental community. However, its base remains small and compared to their northern counterparts, Brazilian NGOs still lack adequate resources and support. Moreover, the country's pervasive poverty problem and pressure from the global capitalist market continue to exert tremendous pressure on Brazil's natural resources.

The foundation of the Gaucha Association for the Protection of the Natural Environment in 1971 marked the appearance of a social movement directly concerned about green issues in Brazil. The rise of a green movement was connected to diffuse protest actions over questions such as the rights of women and indigenous groups and, above all, the restrictions on freedom imposed by the military regime between 1968 and 1974. With the easing of these restrictions in 1974, hundreds of environmentalist groups emerged over the following decade. Many of the leaders of the Brazilian ecological movement were in exile in Europe during the 1970s and were influenced by European social movements. Apart from addressing the problems connected with extremely rapid expansion in the size of cities and with industrial development, the green movement concentrated on the defense of the rainforests and drawing attention to the immense problem of soil erosion. The extent of some of these problems has meant that many traditional organizations, notably trade unions or professional associations, have often articulated popular concerns about damage to the environment. Support for the green movement itself came largely from the middle classes, especially from the growing number of people living in cities and those who were obtaining a university education and entering white-collar occupations.

The military regime's relaxation of some of its control over political activity allowed environmentalists to contest elections, and beginning in 1982 members of the green movement were elected to state assemblies. With the ending of the military regime in 1985, several prominent ecologists, writers, actresses, and ex-exiles (including Fernando Gabeira) took the initiative to try to form a green party. They facilitated dialogue among environmental groups and in 1986 agreed to form a national green party (Partido Verde), though it was not formally registered until 1988. In the interim, it campaigned on a joint platform with the Workers' Party and received much coverage in the media, especially in relation to its "Speak Up Woman" feminist demonstration and its "Hug the Lake" human chain of 100,000 people around the polluted Rodrigo de Freitas Lake. In the November 1988 municipal elections, 20 candidates were successful in gaining seats in Rio de Janeiro, São Paulo, Santa Catarina, and Paraiba.

The party expanded into other areas, including the **Amazon**, where they had an ally (albeit not a party member) in **Chico Mendes**. Mendes took part in the Green's "Save the Amazon" demonstration in 1988, but was killed one month later. Soon afterward, Partido Verde fielded Herbert Daniel, a homosexual civil rights activist suffering from AIDS, as a presidential candidate. Daniel quit the race after his campaign had the desired affect of raising media attention to the AIDS issue. Thereafter, Fernando Gabeira ran as Partido Verde's presidential candidate. While the party received less that 1 percent of the votes in the first-term election, the campaign led to the organization of the Greens in other regions of the country. The Green's first federal deputy, Sidney de Miguel, was elected from Rio de Janeiro in 1990.

The 1992 **United Nations Conference on Environment and Development (UNCED)**, which was held in Rio de Janeiro, was an important turning point for the country's green movement as well as for Partido Verde. They hosted the First Planetary Meeting of Green Parties at the UNCED. The delegates to the meeting issued a joint statement calling upon the world's governments to aggressively tackle the looming crises of **global warming**, pollution, habitat loss, deepening poverty, and food production (e.g., the global fish catch). After the UNCED, Partido Verde elected 54 city councilors and three mayors in Rio de Janeiro, Salvador, and Natal. The party was also finally granted definitive registration status. In 1996, they upped their representation to 13 mayors and 200 city councilors.

At the national level, the party remains small; it emerged the eleventh-largest party in the National Congress after the 2006 election, when it won 3.6 percent of the vote (13 seats) in the Chamber of Deputies.

BROKDORF. The declaration in November 1973 by the electricity industry that it would build a nuclear power plant near the village of Brokdorf in Schleswig-Holstein, Federal Republic of **Germany**, signaled the beginning of a dispute that was crucial in the development of **antinuclear protests**. In August 1974 a local **citizens' initiative** collected over 30,000 signatures for a petition against the project. In October 1976, the electricity industry encircled the proposed site with barbed wire, triggering a series of demonstrations that led to bitter confrontations between the police and protestors. The conflict rapidly drew in militant groups from the city of Hamburg. The forceful reaction by the police also contributed to the escalation of violence.

The dispute attracted national and international attention to the possibilities of protest against the development of nuclear energy. The successful campaign against further work on the site at Brokdorf contributed to a shift in public opinion against the construction of nuclear power plants, and the membership of radical environmental groups grew rapidly afterward. In addition, traditional political parties, such as the Social Democratic Party in Hamburg and Schleswig-Holstein, began to reconsider their positions on the development of nuclear power at Brokdorf.

However, there were tensions within the labor movement, as many trade unionists perceived the campaign by green groups as a threat to the employment of workers. Campaigns such as the one against the proposed nuclear power plants at Brokdorf and Wyhl were crucial to the advance of Die Grünen in **Germany** and the emergence of protest movements and green political organizations in other countries.

BROWER, DAVID (1912–2000). One of the most tireless organizers of environmental groups, David Brower served as the first full-time executive director of the **Sierra Club** from 1952 until 1969. He was extremely popular among club members. David Brower was a pioneer in efforts to turn U.S. environmental groups into mass membership organizations. He helped to expand greatly the membership of the organization, which grew from 15,000 in 1960 to 113,000 in 1970, as he steered one of the most well-established conservation organizations in the world toward more radical engagement with the authorities. However, he was forced to resign in 1969 by opponents who pointed to the poor administration of financial resources. In the years prior to his resignation, the club had suffered significant financial losses and forfeited its entitlement to tax exemptions following political campaigns against government plans to build two dams in the Grand Canyon.

Brower moved on to establish **Friends of the Earth** and devote himself to mobilizing support and influencing public opinion. He was one of the most highly regarded environmentalists at the national and, through the growth of Friends of the Earth, international levels. In 1982 Brower founded the Earth Island Institute, an organization that linked a preoccupation with environmental protection to the question of human rights and economic development in emerging nations. *See also* UNITED STATES.

BRUNDTLAND COMMISSION. *See* BRUNDTLAND, GRO HARLEM; WORLD COMMISSION ON ENVIRONMENT AND DEVELOPMENT (WCED).

BRUNDTLAND, GRO HARLEM (1939–). Chair of the **World Commission on Environment and Development (WCED)**, at the time of her appointment, Brundtland was leader of the opposition Labor Party in **Norway**. She had been prime minister in 1981 and was elected to the same office for the period 1986 to 1989 and from 1990 to 1996. As chair of the WCED, Brundtland was immensely successful in promoting the concept of **sustainable development**, which was used in dialogue between less developed and more developed countries.

In the early 1990s as prime minister, Brundtland came under pressure from both environmentalists and Norwegian fishermen on the issue of whaling. Norwegian fishermen argued that their livelihood was being threatened by bans on whaling because the whales were consuming large quantities of fish. Environmentalists and governments of many developed countries argued for the continued protection of all whale species as mandated by the International Whaling Commission's moratorium on whaling that went into effect in 1986. Brundtland agreed to the resumption of commercial whaling of Minke whales in 1993.

BULGARIA. As in other former communist countries, the ascent of the green movement in Bulgaria was connected to concern about the exclusive focus on economic development, exploitation of natural resources, and the struggle against an oppressive regime. Once the old communist regime weakened, there was less emphasis on environmental protest and a new focus on economic development and social welfare. Nonetheless, the political and social movements for environmental protection were genuine and had a lasting impact. The most important manifestations of action for the environment are the formation of the Independent Union of Ekoglasnost and the Bulgarian Green Party and the advent of a protest movement that originated in the city of Ruse on the Danube and along the border with **Romania**. Like the protests in Ruse, which subsequently led to the formation of the Ruse Committee, Ekoglasnost emerged under the communist regime.

The main problem at Ruse was pollution from chlorine emissions at a factory in Giurgiu, a town across the Danube in Romania. The contamination, especially from 1986 onward, was so severe that thousands of people were hospitalized, and a significant proportion of the population either left Ruse or wanted to (but was prevented from doing so by the authorities). Eventually, in February 1988, approximately 2,000 local citizens staged a protest rally and thereby contributed to the formation of similar protest groups throughout the nation. The national focus on this issue prompted the March 1988 creation of the Ruse Committee by intellectuals, scientists, and artists (many of whom were members of the Communist Party). Most of these activists were based in the capital city, Sofia. The objectives of the association were to lobby the government to address the problems identified at Ruse, to draw on the assistance of national and international scientific experts, and to demand openness in government, especially in divulging the truth about environmental problems.

Members of the committee had to endure harassment and intimidation to such a degree that they were unable to organize any activities. Most went on to form the Independent Union Ekoglasnost on 22 March 1989. The authorities found it harder to suppress this organization, though it was severely restricted in some of its activities and often had to operate in a clandestine manner in order to disseminate information about environmental problems, particularly to the international media. Ekoglasnost even managed to carry out small-scale protests and lobby against larger projects, notably supported by the pharmaceutical industry, that were causing pollution and endangering the health of citizens.

Still, the demise of the old communist regime at the end of 1989 meant that the focus on environmental issues was overshadowed by an interest in political reforms. Ekoglasnost played a pivotal role in the formation of the Union of Democratic Forces in December 1989. However, the process of political liberalization presented Ekoglasnost not only with new opportunities to bring about social change but with dilemmas about how to organize itself. Over a period of two years it experienced three kinds of schism. In April 1990, after some argument, the association formed a parliamentary wing. In June 1991 the parliamentary delegates who had formed the Political Club Ekoglasnost found themselves under pressure by Ekoglasnost to withdraw from Parliament because of the dangers associated with signing a constitution that was being shaped, to a large degree, by the Communist Party. The parliamentary delegates then split from the social movement. Following the October 1991 elections, fortunes were reversed when the delegates associated with the Political Club Ekoglasnost failed to overcome the 4 percent electoral hurdle, while four delegates from the Ekoglasnost social movement were elected as part of the United Democratic Front.

The other main division among environmentalists seeking political reforms was the December 1989 foundation of the Green Party by a leading member of Ekoglasnost. This move, which appeared to have taken place with no prior discussion among members of Ekoglasnost, came as a surprise and was regarded as divisive. Despite opposition by Ekoglasnost, the party joined the United Democratic Front (UDF) and in the June 1990 elections secured 12 seats in Parliament. Other highlights for the Green Party included the election as mayor of Sofia (October 1990 to October 1991) of the leader of the party, Aleksandar Karakacanov; the 1991 election of another leading member of the party, Filip Dimitrov, to the post of president of the Coordinating Council of the United Democratic Front; and the appointment of two members to ministerial positions in the coalition government. In 1990 the Green Party had formed a network with 90 branches across the nation and 20 groups in Sofia.

Despite these early successes and the country's serious environmental problems (notably the pollution arising from industrial plants), focus on economic development and social welfare supplanted interest in environmental protection throughout much of the 1990s and 2000s. Moreover, the Green Party has suffered from its inability to establish an independent image as a party.

The Green Party split from the UDF for the 1991 election. Unfortunately for the party, it failed to win the 4 percent of the vote it would need to remain in Parliament. In 1994, the Greens joined a new coalition, the Democratic Alternative for the Republic, but they again fell shy of the 4 percent threshold necessary to win seats in Parliament. In the 1997 election, they joined yet another coalition, the Alliance for National Salvation; this time they won two parliamentary seats. In the 2001 and 2005 elections, the Green Party joined the Coalition for Bulgaria. While this coalition did quite well in both elections, winning respectively 17.1 percent (48 seats) and 34.2 percent of the popular vote

(82 seats), the Green Party was not one of the parties sending MPs to Parliament. After the 2005 election, the Green Party did get the position of Deputy Minister of Justice.

BÜNDNIS 90/DIE GRÜNEN. *See* GERMANY.

– C –

CAMBODIA. In the early 1990s, nongovernmental organizations (NGOs) began to form in Cambodia although the government treats them with suspicion. They receive their funding from United Nations' programs, other nations, and international NGOs. There is also a growing Buddhist **Ecology** movement. Cambodia has a tradition of Theravda Buddhism, in which the forests are considered sacred. Rooted in a Buddhist environmental ethic, Buddhist monks in Cambodia as well as other Asian Buddhist nations have begun to mobilize in an effort to stop deforestation and promote environmental awareness.

Mlup Baitong, which means "green shade" in Khmer, is one of the more prominent and well-organized Cambodian environmental NGOs. Established in 1998, it works to promote environmental awareness, conservation, and **sustainable development**. Mlup Baitong focuses on community-based initiatives and emphasizes the need for both sustainable and equitable use of natural resources. Its projects include a Buddhism and environment program, as well as community forestry, ecotourism, gender and the environment, school environment education, and a radio and environmental advocacy program.

CAMPAIGN FOR NUCLEAR DISARMAMENT (CND). Formed in January 1958, the Campaign for Nuclear Disarmament paved the way for social movements that protested against the war in Vietnam in the 1960s and campaigned against the deployment of nuclear weapons in the 1970s. All these movements signaled the upsurge of extraparliamentary activities that contributed to the emergence of the green movement. Many of the issues brought up by the CND later became an integral part of the agenda of green political parties. The

CND developed in **Great Britain** from the disquiet, initially among pacifist groups and prominent intellectuals, writers, and thinkers, about the development of atomic weapons, bombing of Hiroshima and Nagasaki in 1945, and development of the hydrogen bomb. Among the forerunners of the CND were a wide range of local initiatives against the development of nuclear weapons as well as the umbrella organizations the National Council for the Abolition of Nuclear Weapons Tests, created in February 1957, and the Emergency Committee for Direct Action against Nuclear War, formed in April 1957. The latter represented a response to the conducting of nuclear tests on Christmas Island by the British government.

The trigger to the formation of the CND was an article by J. B. Priestley entitled "Britain and the Nuclear Bombs" published in the *New Statesman* on 2 November 1957. Priestley was responding to divisions in the Labour Party over adopting a unilateralist policy as well as to the concern in the international community about the competition between the **United States** and Soviet Union in the nuclear arms race. Events such as the invasion of Suez by the British and the uprising in Hungary in 1956 also provided a focus for those who were anxious to reverse the apparent trends toward confrontation between East and West. Priestley's article served to bring together prominent people. The first executive committee of the CND included Canon John Collins as chair, Bertrand Russell as president, and Peggy Duff as organizing secretary. Groups such as the National Council for the Abolition of Nuclear Weapons Tests merged fully with the CND.

Five thousand people attended the inaugural meeting of the organization, held on 17 February 1958 in London. The aims of the campaign were to persuade people that Great Britain should take unilateral action to cease using and producing nuclear weapons and bring other countries to the negotiating table to do the same. Between 1958 and 1965 the CND organized marches between Aldermaston, the site of an installation for nuclear weapons, and London. These marches attracted tens of thousands of participants and a vast amount of publicity. At the conclusion of the march held in 1961, around 150,000 assembled in Trafalgar Square. Although commitment to the CND waned in the 1960s (due partly to changes in policy, such as the signing of the Partial Nuclear Test Ban Treaty in

1963 and divisions between militants who favored direct action and those who wanted the organization to remain primarily a pressure group), links were made with protests against the Vietnam War.

Further marches to Aldermaston in the 1970s strengthened the connection between the CND and the **antinuclear protest** movements. The CND was affiliated with the Ecology Party, **Friends of the Earth**, and **Greenpeace**, especially in campaigns against the deployment of nuclear weapons in Europe. CND membership rose sharply, from 4,000 in 1979 to 50,000 in 1982. The number of CND branches or groups around the country increased from 150 in 1979 to about 1,000 in 1982. There were also about 1,000 affiliated organizations. Significant campaigns were conducted against the expansion of the nuclear submarine fleet and placement of cruise missiles. A rally held in Trafalgar Square on 26 October 1980 attracted around 80,000 people. The CND increasingly became part of antinuclear protests throughout western Europe in the 1980s. The focus was not simply nuclear weapons but the entire nuclear industry.

In the 2000s, the CND has campaigned against the war in Iraq, nuclear reprocessing, the transport of plutonium, American plans for a missile defense system, and NATO's nuclear weapons.

Antinuclear weapons protests have erupted elsewhere in the world as the number of states with nuclear capabilities increases. **India**, the first state to conduct nuclear tests in 20 years when it performed three separate underground tests in May 1998, elicited statements of concern, a cutoff of aid, and withdrawal of official representatives from numerous countries around the world. Activists in Hiroshima, site of the world's first atomic bombing, have been particularly active in their protests. *See also* NUCLEAR DISARMAMENT PARTY (NDP).

CANADA. Canada is the second-largest country in the world after **Russia**, but has a population of only around 33 million, most of whom live within 100 miles of the **United States**' border. As a result, Canada still has large amounts of open and pristine land. The Canadian economy, however, depends heavily on resource extraction, including forestry, mining, gas, and oil. In recent years, the rising price of oil has made Canada's tar sands of great interest to developers, who have stepped up oil extraction in Alberta. The pollution and en-

CARBON TAXES • 43

vironmental degradation associated with the tar sands, however, has raised concerns in the country.

Canada has a strong environmental movement that was colored by developments in the United States. The National and Provincial Parks Association of Canada was set up in 1963, the **Sierra Club** in 1970, and the Canadian **Audubon Society** in 1971. Canada has also given birth to some major groups. **Greenpeace** has its roots in British Columbia, Canada's westernmost province. In 1971, a crew of 11 men set out in a hired fishing boat to Amchitka in the Aleutian Islands to protest U.S. nuclear weapons testing there, and later the French atmospheric testing at Mururoa in French Polynesia. They used the slogan "green peace" to represent their environmental concerns, and their hopes for a world free of the threat of nuclear war. In 1973, Greenpeace Foundation was set up in Canada. Greenpeace Foundation was involved in the famous 1975 at-sea protest of whaling and the campaign against the clubbing of seals in Newfoundland, an eastern province of Canada, beginning in 1976. The Greenpeace message took off, and Greenpeace organizations began to form around the world. The Sea Shepherd Conservation Society, founded in 1977 also has its roots in British Columbia. An activist group with early links to Greenpeace, it has as its mission the enforcement of international laws governing the world's oceans, where no enforcement exists. In 1979, the Sea Shepherd rammed a whaling ship, the *Sierra*, effectively disabling the ship. While originally allied in their efforts to oppose illegal whaling, poaching, shark finning, and the like, in the mid-2000s there was considerable tension between the Sea Shepherd Conservation Society and Greenpeace.

The Green Party of Canada was set up in 1983 and ran 60 candidates in the 1984 federal election. In 1997, they fielded 78 and in 2000, 111. In the 2004 election, they fielded 308 candidates and won 4.3 percent of the vote. They do not, however, have representation in either the federal Parliament or at the provincial level. There are Green Party branches in British Columbia, Alberta, Saskatchewan, Manitoba, Ontario, and Quebec. They all share a common vision of supporting green economics, progressive social planning, and responsible governance.

CARBON TAXES. Proposals for the introduction of taxes to modify behavior, in particular to reduce consumption of resources, have arisen in many developed countries. Concern about the **greenhouse effect**, inefficient use of resources such as oil and other fossil fuels, unrealistic pricing of resources, traffic congestion, and an interest in applying the **polluter pays principle** have led to the introduction of carbon taxes in several countries (e.g., **Denmark, Finland, Great Britain**, the **Netherlands, Norway, Sweden**). Efforts to introduce a carbon tax at the European Union (EU) level, however, have failed. The coal, oil, metal, and car industries tend to oppose these measures even though the taxes are often offset by reductions in other forms of taxation.

CARSON, RACHEL (1907–1964). The author of *Silent Spring* (1962), a work that is widely credited with providing a major impetus to the birth and growth of a more radical and vigorous form of environmentalism in the 1960s. Carson, following her studies in genetics at Johns Hopkins University and after teaching at that university and the University of Maryland, worked for the U.S. government as a marine biologist. In 1951 she published a best-selling study in natural history entitled *The Sea around Us*. Subsequently, she dedicated herself to writing and in 1955 published *The Edge of the Sea*. In the 1950s she became interested in and deeply disturbed by the impact of chemical pesticides and insecticides on wildlife and its habitat and on the dangers to human life. Using her skills as a writer and scientist, she produced, in *Silent Spring*, one of the most provocative and rousing accounts of the damage done to the natural environment by human beings.

CENTER FOR INTERNATIONAL ENVIRONMENTAL LAW (CIEL). CIEL is a nonprofit organization working in over 60 countries to use international law and institutions to protect the environment, promote human health, and ensure a just and sustainable society.

CENTRAL AFRICA. Covering the states of Burundi, Rwanda, Chad, and the Democratic Republic of Congo, Central Africa is rich in natural resources, including some of the most important tropical rainforests in the world. However, a long history of war, oppression, and corrupt governments have left the area in poverty, with little social infrastructure, and terrible environmental degradation.

The environmental issue in the region that has captured the most international attention is the plight of the endangered mountain gorilla. The population of the gentle and shy herbivores that Dian Fossey studied has dropped to dangerously low levels. After Fossey's murder in 1985, Rwandan biologist Eugene Rutagarama took up the cause of the gorillas. In 2001, he won the **Goldman Environmental Prize**. See also FEDERATION OF GREEN PARTIES OF AFRICA.

CHERNOBYL. A town near Kiev in the Ukraine, formerly part of the Soviet Union, and scene of the worst civilian nuclear power disaster. Following a failed experiment, the nuclear reactor at Chernobyl exploded and for 10 days released radioactivity into the atmosphere. Around 30 people died shortly after the explosion and over 130,000 had to be evacuated from the region. The explosion realized the worst fears of opponents to nuclear power and hardened public opinion against the development of nuclear power plants in many parts of Europe. Programs for the development of **nuclear energy** for civilian use were either cancelled or postponed in **Austria**, **Belgium**, the **People's Republic of China**, **Finland**, **Greece**, **Italy**, the Philippines, and **Spain**. Radioactive clouds containing zodine131, caesium134, and caesium137 traveled thousands of kilometers and affected 21 countries in Europe.

Twenty years after the accident, the international community is spending over a US$1 billion to repair the massive concrete sarcophagus that was built over the site to contain its radiation. The sarcophagus is corroding due to the radiation.

CHINA, PEOPLE'S REPUBLIC OF (PRC). Rapid economic development and a population of over 1.3 billion people have combined to make China one of the most polluted countries in the world. The severity of the pollution and natural resource degradation in China has started to awaken governmental awareness of the need to address pollution and promote **sustainable development** and has spawned the emergence of environmental movements and nongovernmental organizations (NGOs).

In 2006, the Chinese State Environmental Protection Administration announced that there were 2,700 registered environmental groups in the country. While environmental protesters are still suppressed, and even imprisoned at times, the state has become more accepting of environmental NGOs, possibly recognizing that they can help achieve its policy goals. Environmental protest is most likely to lead to suppression when it directly opposes important state goals. The Chinese government, however, risks international criticism for imprisoning activists. The imprisonment of Dai Qing in 1989 for writing a book in opposition to the building of the Three Gorges Dam, for example, sparked widespread international condemnation.

The first environmental NGO to register in China was the Academy for Green Culture (now called Friends of Nature) in 1994. Global Village Beijing and Green Home were then set up in 1996. These remain among the most important environmental NGOs in China.

When environmental groups first emerged in China, they were primarily focused on environmental education and nature conservation. Increasingly, they are becoming bolder and are protesting development plans that threaten the environment and human settlements. They are also protesting corruption among local government officials, which has contributed to environmental destruction. Importantly, protests in 2004 against the building of a series of dams along the Three Parallel Rivers in southern China did not end in arrests but rather in a decision by Chinese Premier Wen Jaibao to hold up their construction pending further assessments of their potential environmental and human impacts.

China's environmental NGO community still faces many hurdles, including difficulties in winning governmental approval of registration requests, fund raising, and a very watchful governmental eye. The Chinese government is well aware that environmental movements were active elements in the demise of some former East bloc states. *See also* GOLDMAN ENVIRONMENTAL PRIZE.

CHIPKO ANDALAN. The term *chipko* means "embrace" and refers to protestors who cling to trees in order to prevent loggers from felling them. The aim of the protestors, who are mainly women in Indian villages, is to protect their livelihoods, since the forests provide food and fuel and prevent soil erosion and flooding. The movement arose in April 1973 in the village of Gopeshwar, Uttar Pradesh. The successful protest against a logging company inspired many others, and the movement spread to different parts of the Himalayas and **India**. A notable feature has been the adoption of resistance and protest through **nonviolence**, inspired by the Gandhian concept of *satyagraha*. In 1980 the movement achieved a significant concession from the government, a 15-year ban on green felling in the Himalayan forests of Uttar Pradesh. Though still a long way from effecting fundamental changes in government policies, Chipko Andalan has been celebrated for using nonviolent protest and highlighting the predicament of communities in less developed countries as they address environmental issues and defend a traditional way of life.

CHLOROFLUOROCARBONS (CFCs). *See* OZONE LAYER.

CITIZENS' INITIATIVE. The term *citizens' initiative* has been used to describe the organization of **antinuclear protests** in the early phase of their development. In countries such as the Federal Republic of **Germany**, the origin of citizens' initiatives (Bürgerinitiativen) can be tracked to the citizens' associations (Bürgervereine) of the 1950s and 1960s. The latter were formed by leading figures in local communities to apply pressure for community projects. To a degree, they were an attempt to fill the vacuum left by traditional political parties that tended to neglect local interests. This void became even larger in the 1960s and resulted in the advent of student protest movements. The notion of citizens' initiatives was continued in the 1960s in the wake of these protests for greater participation by the citizens in decision making. Many citizens' initiatives turned to the reformist Free Democratic Party in the hope that it might be more effective than other major parties in articulating the people's aspirations for greater involvement in politics.

Campaigns such as those at Wyhl and **Brokdorf** against the development of nuclear energy were initially carried out mostly by local citizens' initiatives. The citizens' initiatives also had strong connections with the reform-oriented youth wing of the Social Democratic Party. Above all, the campaigns against the development of nuclear power led to the spread of citizens' initiatives that were supported by a powerful umbrella organization, the Bundesverband Bürgerinitiativen Umweltschutz (Federal Association of Citizens' Initiatives for Environmental Protection).

Citizens' initiatives have not only been influential in persuading traditional political organizations to reconsider their policies on the environment, but they have also played a pivotal part in the formation of green lists or parties. The candidates for green parties have often gained their political experience and expertise through involvement in citizens' initiatives. Participation in these associations contributed to the desire of activists in green parties to practice **direct democracy** at the local, regional, and even national levels. *See also* GERMANY.

CITIZENS' MOVEMENTS. Like **citizens' initiatives**, the term *citizens' movements* has been used to refer to the groups of individuals, usually at the local level, that joined together to protest environmental grievances. In **Japan** citizens' movements arose to protest Minamata mercury poisoning, *itai-itai* ("it hurts-it hurts") disease from cadmium poisoning, asthma problems in industrialized areas, loss of sunshine from the building of skyscrapers, food contamination, and construction projects.

CITIZENS PARTY. The now defunct Citizens Party resulted from the first major effort in the **United States** to form a green political organization to contest local and national elections. After informal discussions among prominent environmentalists and expressions of interest from members of environmental and other social movements, the Citizens Committee was formed in August 1979. The aim of the committee was to form a national Citizens Party, and over the next few months thousands of people from around 30 states became members of the fledgling organization and formed local chapters.

The official foundation of the Citizens Party occurred in April 1980 at a gathering of nearly 300 delegates. Despite reservations expressed by some members, the Citizens Party quickly prepared itself for the 1980 presidential elections. This had always been the intention of its founding members. However, this issue soon led to divisions within the organization. Several leading figures who questioned this focus on the presidential campaign subsequently resigned from the party. The first priority for those who remained was to engage in the onerous and expensive task of securing enough signatures to obtain a position on the ballot. Even though the Citizens Party only gained access to the ballot in 29 states and in the District of Columbia, it did cover three-quarters of the total population. At any rate, this was a considerable achievement in the context of the enormous institutional barriers that face any new party that tries to challenge the Republican and Democratic dominance over the political system. Achieving this goal depleted the resources available to the party for the electoral campaign, and in attracting 234,279 votes (0.27 percent), it fell far short of its stated goal of winning 5 percent of the vote. In the 1984 presidential elections the results were even less encouraging. The Citizens Party, which was in a state of rapid decline, attracted only 72,200 votes (0.1 percent). Yet, these results reflected neither the underlying strength of interest in environmental issues nor the much better prospects for the influence of green politicians at the local level.

At its inception, the Citizens Party sought to combine concerns about the democratization of the economic system and environmental protection. It also profited from the widespread **antinuclear protests** arising from the accident at **Three Mile Island**. The focus on other social issues, notably the rights of women and minorities, had the potential to broaden the base of the party but was not fully realized, particularly as a result of disputes between leading figures. At times, the struggles at the national level were reflected in conflicts among local chapters of the party. Yet it is at this level that the Citizens Party demonstrated the possibilities for political action by green parties in the political system of the United States.

CLEAN DEVELOPMENT MECHANISM. This is a flexibility mechanism of the **Kyoto Protocol** that permits the Annex I countries (Organisation for Economic Cooperation and Development [OECD] countries as of 1992) that are required by the Kyoto Protocol to reduce their greenhouse gas emissions to obtain credit toward their own reductions (certified emissions reductions) for taking action to reduce greenhouse gas emissions in developing countries. The idea behind this is that it may be more cost effective to reduce greenhouse gas emissions in developing countries than in developed ones.

CLEAN WATER ACTION. Formed in 1972 in the **United States**, this is a watchdog and advocacy organization with a membership of over

700,000 focused on clean, safe, and affordable drinking water and the empowerment of people to make democracy work.

CLEAN WATER NETWORK. An alliance of over 1,000 public interest organizations working to implement and strengthen U.S. clean water and wetlands policy.

CLIMATE CHANGE. This term is commonly used to refer to the changes in climatic systems that a majority of scientists believe are being caused by rising levels of greenhouse gases in the atmosphere. Whereas the term *global warming* points attention to rising average global temperatures, the term *climate change* focuses attention on the broader climatic implications of the **greenhouse effect**.

One early effort to evaluate changes in temperature was the World Climate Research Program, initiated in 1979 by the World Meteorological Organization and the International Council of Scientific Unions. By the mid-1980s scientists had become increasingly aware of the possibility of the warming of the Earth's atmosphere as a result of carbon dioxide and other greenhouse gas emissions. At the Villach Conference in 1985, scientists publicized the fact that there had been a slight increase in the average temperature across the world over the past century and that there did appear to be a correspondence between this finding and the rate of emissions of carbon dioxide and other gases. The most alarming finding was that if this trend continued, there could be significant increases in average temperature across the Earth and severe consequences. Drastic changes in weather patterns, including droughts, floods, and storms, would occur. Above all, scientists have speculated on the impact of climate change on regions covered with ice, notably the Arctic, and the consequent impact on sea levels. A vast proportion of the world's population living in coastal regions could be forced to relocate, and some countries, notably small islands in the Pacific Ocean, would vanish under seawater.

In 1988, at a conference held in Toronto, more than 300 scientists and policymakers from nearly 50 countries and international organizations noted that a 50 percent reduction in carbon dioxide emissions would have to be achieved in order to stabilize the atmospheric concentration of greenhouse gases. They suggested, as an initial target, a

20 percent reduction in carbon dioxide emissions by the year 2000. Fears about the greenhouse effect also coincided with speculation about the impact of chlorofluorocarbons (CFCs) on the depletion of ozone at high altitudes and the potential catastrophe that could be unleashed by the hole in the **ozone layer**.

Also in 1988, the World Meteorological Organization and the United Nations Environment Programme set up the Intergovernmental Panel on Climate Change (IPCC) to study and assess the risks associated with human-induced climate change based on the findings of thousands of peer-reviewed scientific and technical articles. The IPCC is divided into working groups that assess the physical basis of climate change (Working Group I); climate change impacts, adaptation, and vulnerability (Working Group II); and mitigation (Working Group III). Each working group has released several reports. The most recent assessment released by the IPCC's Working Group I in spring 2007 states that "warming of the climate system is unequivocal" and can be seen in rising global average air and ocean temperatures, the melting of snow and ice, and rising average sea level. In addition, the report concludes that it is very likely that rising average global temperatures are caused by anthropogenic greenhouse gas concentrations.

Concerns about the greenhouse effect were a major factor behind the organization of the **United Nations Conference on Environment and Development (UNCED)**, held in Rio de Janeiro in 1992, to bring together nation-states as well as businesses, industries, and nongovernmental organizations (NGOs). The **United Nations Framework Convention on Climate Change (UNFCCC)**, which had been initiated by the United Nations General Assembly in 1991, was signed by 153 nations and by the European Union (EU) at the 1992 UNCED. The 1997 **Kyoto Protocol** to the UNFCCC is the first international agreement with the aim of reducing greenhouse gas emissions.

In 2007 U.S. vice president Albert Gore's movie, *An Inconvenient Truth*, which introduces the subject of climate change, won the Academy Award for best documentary film.

CLUB OF ROME. At the instigation of Italian entrepreneur Aurelio Peccei, a group of 30 industrialists, scientists, economists, politicians, and bureaucrats met in 1968 to discuss issues of global concern, including environmental and economic issues. As a result of their first meeting, held in Rome, the group named itself the Club of Rome and set out to examine the dynamic interrelationships between economic development, the environment, population, resources, and industrialization. The group was also concerned about the political and social implications of changes in all these spheres. Though dealing with global issues, the Club of Rome was widely regarded as being primarily concerned with the interests of industrial and political regimes in developed countries. In 1970 the 75 members of the Club of Rome were drawn from 26 countries. Most were from more developed countries.

The impact of the Club of Rome on the environmental movement was ensured when a report it had commissioned in 1970 was published two years later under the title *The Limits to Growth*. The alarming findings of this report ensured sales of 20 million copies worldwide and secured the Club of Rome a place in the history of the green movement. The Club of Rome exercised significant influence on the agenda for debate over environmental policy, including the **United Nations Conference on the Human Environment (UNCHE)** held in 1972. The Club of Rome, while recognizing the exploratory nature of much of *The Limits to Growth* study, was intent upon provoking debate, especially among political and economic elites. It has since commissioned further reports and continued to exercise significant influence in the area of environmental and industrial policies.

COMMISSION ON SUSTAINABLE DEVELOPMENT (CSD). The CSD was established in December 1992 in order to monitor follow-up on agreements made at the **United Nations Conference on Environment and Development (UNCED)** held in Rio de Janeiro in 1992. The CSD specifically oversees implementation of **Agenda 21** and the Rio Declaration on Environment and Development. It also provides policy guidance for the Johannesburg Plan of Implementation. The CSD meets annually in New York in two-year cycles. Each cycle focuses on various themes and cross-sections of issues. *See also* WORLD SUMMIT ON SUSTAINABLE DEVELOPMENT.

COMMON-POOL RESOURCES. Public resources such as fisheries, air, and international waters are often referred to as common-pool resources. Common-pool resources are not privately owned; they are characterized by the access that many individuals have to their use. Individuals, groups, and countries may have little incentive to contribute or invest in the resource's protection or conservation in return for using it. Since denying noncontributing users access to the common-pool resource is either impossible or highly impractical, a problem that may arise is irresponsible or excessive use. This can lead to rapid depletion, pollution, or destruction of the resource. *See also* COMMON-PROPERTY REGIMES; "TRAGEDY OF THE COMMONS."

COMMON-PROPERTY REGIMES. Common-property regimes are a way of managing natural resources in such a way as to ensure their long-term sustainability. Common-property regimes are institutional arrangements in which a select group of individual parties share both the rights and responsibility to a natural resource. Common-property regimes are designed to prevent the depletion of **common-pool resources** that often arises from the tendency of local populations to overuse such resources, threatening their long-term sustainability. This is often referred to as the "Tragedy of the Commons." The conference of communal property rights on a group of users by way of common-property regimes is thought to provide incentives for responsible, efficient, and controlled use of resources.

While common-property regimes were once prevalent and established in communities around the world, economic and technological changes, as well as initiatives aimed at dissolving them undertaken by numerous governments, have led to widespread abandonment of the institution in favor of other arrangements.

COMMONER, BARRY (1917–). The author of *The Closing Circle: Nature, Man, and Technology*, Commoner is a biologist who has been associated with the University of St. Louis since 1947. Apart from his interest in plant pathology, Commoner has been prominent in campaigns against nuclear testing and for environmental protection. In the 1970s Commoner engaged in a highly publicized debate with **Paul Ehrlich** over the danger of **population growth**.

COMPREHENSIVE ENVIRONMENTAL RESPONSE, COMPENSATION, AND LIABILITY ACT (CERCLA). The U.S. Congress passed what is often referred to as Superfund legislation in 1980 in response to the **Love Canal** disaster and growing public pressure. Superfund included an appropriation of US$1.6 billion to clean up the nation's worst abandoned toxic and hazardous waste sites. CERCLA was later amended to include an additional appropriation of US$8.5 billion. Superfund was originally set up by hazardous waste taxes and general tax reserves. There were also two specific funds set up. The Hazardous Substances Response Fund, which is available for clean up of emergency spills, is financed by a tax on petroleum and chemical feed stock. The Post-Closer Liability Fund is available for already shut-down companies and is financed by a tax on hazardous waste.

Superfund legislation requires the Environmental Protection Agency (EPA) to compile a list of the **United States'** most dangerous hazardous waste sites, called the National Priority List (NPL). The NPL ranks sites according to their human health and environmental risks and begins cleanup on sites according to their ranking. As of May 2005, the EPA listed 1,604 sites on the NPL.

Superfund puts liability on the people responsible for the release of hazardous waste at these sites and establishes a trust fund for cleanup when no responsible party can be found. Organizations such as **Greenpeace**, **Friends of the Earth**, the **Sierra Club**, and the **United States Public Interest Research Group (U.S. PIRG)** have criticized the government for its slow pace in cleaning up Superfund sites.

CONSERVATION INTERNATIONAL. Founded in 1987 in the **United States**, this organization is primarily concerned with achieving **sustainable development** in less developed countries. Conservation International has organized agreements between less developed and wealthy nations that have made it possible for developing states to spend an agreed-upon sum on conservation measures instead of repaying part of their national debt to the developed nations. This arrangement is referred to as a **debt-for-nature swap**. The first such success by Conservation International was the exchange of a portion of Bolivia's national debt for preservation of part of the **Amazon** in 1987. It has been able to replicate this kind of achievement in negotiations with several other countries. *See also* WORLD WIDE FUND FOR NATURE (WWF).

CONSERVATIONISM. The key schools of thought in early U.S. environmentalism were conservationism and preservationism. Conservationism, heavily influenced by George Perkins Marsh, was a movement initiated in the 1890s by forester Gifford Pinchot, and later led by **Aldo Leopold.** The movement embodied Enlightenment ideals of rationality, science, and utilitarianism. Stressing the efficient utilization of resources, particularly sustained-yield forest management, it led to the early creation of government bureaucracies to manage resources, such as the U.S. Forest Service (established in 1905) to manage vast federally owned forest areas, and the Reclamation Service (established 1902, later the Bureau of Reclamation), to undertake irrigation of arid western regions for settlement and farming. This was an era that saw a flowering of scientific societies and organizations aimed at the rational study and management of natural resources. These included private scientific societies, such as the American Fisheries Society (1870), the American Forestry Association (1875), the American Ornithologists Union (1883), and the Audubon Society (1886). Elite outdoor clubs such as the Boone and Crockett Club (founded 1885) advocated for game conservation legislation, and their sportsmanship codes acted as a type of conservation policy. The 1890 U.S. Census Report ignited public opinion in favor of conservationism, calling attention to the quickly disappearing supplies of timber and arable land in the United States.

In response, the competing philosophy of preservationism, embodied in the views of naturalist and mystic **John Muir** (who cofounded the **Sierra Club** in 1892), was based on the Romantic ideologies of William Wordsworth and Jean-Jacques Rousseau, which held that wild, primitive, and ideal forms of nature deserve preservation in pristine form. Preservationism thus held that nature reserves and parks should be off limits to resource use, in contrast to the efficient utilization of resources for human benefit championed by the conservationists. These movements contributed to the establishment of a national parks system in the United States.

Many writers and painters helped to spread ideas about conservation and preservation. George Catlin, a Romantic landscape painter, traveled the **United States** frontier in 1832 and popularized wilderness areas that would later become **national parks**. Ralph Waldo Emerson's writings, such as the 1836 essay "Nature," greatly influenced Henry David Thoreau and other Transcendentalists. Naturalist John James Audubon contributed to early conservationism by writing on forest depletion and popularized appreciation of wildlife through his impressive paintings of birds.

Henry David Thoreau wrote extensively about appreciating and living in harmony with nature (such as in the 1854 *Walden*). In his essay "Civil Disobedience," he laid the foundation for **nonviolent** social movements resisting unjust policies, a strain of thought that led, through Mahatma Gandhi and Martin Luther King, to the later direct action tactics of environmental groups such as **Greenpeace**. "Direct action," bearing witness, and conscientious objection (such as to military service by religious groups such as the Quakers) became important threads in American thinking and hence, later, environmental campaigns.

George Perkins Marsh's 1864 *Man and Nature* noted the historical effects of unsustainable resource management and advocated the conservation of natural resources in keeping with ecological views. Marsh defined basic principles of conservation, describing scientifically the relationships among soil, water, and vegetation. His work contributed to the establishment of the National Forestry Commission in 1873. *See also* AUDUBON SOCIETY.

CONVENTION ON BIOLOGICAL DIVERSITY. At the **United Nations Conference on Environment and Development (UNCED),** world leaders agreed on the Convention on Biological Diversity. The convention was the first global agreement dedicated to the conservation and sustainable use of the world's biological diversity or **biodiversity**. Over 187 countries have since ratified the convention, whose goals include "the conservation of biodiversity, the sustainable use of the components of biodiversity, and the sharing of benefits arising from the commercial utilization of genetic resources in a fair and equitable way."

The convention is in charge of a variety of issues related to biological diversity, regulating access to genetic resources and biotechnology, impact assessments, conservation incentives, public education, financial resources, and the national reporting of implementation efforts.

The Cartagena Protocol to the Biodiversity Convention was adopted in January 2000. This protocol attempts to protect biological diversity from risks posed by genetically modified organisms (GMOs). It created an advanced informed agreement procedure for countries to be properly informed before importing GMOs into their borders. This protocol also established a Biosafety Clearing-House, which oversees the exchange of information on GMOs and helps countries with implementation. *See also* ANTIGLOBALIZATION MOVEMENT.

CONVENTION ON INTERNATIONAL TRADE IN ENDANGERED SPECIES OF WILD FLORA AND FAUNA (CITES). CITES restricts trade in endangered species. The convention was signed in 1973. In 2006 it accorded various levels of protection to approximately 30,000 plant and animal species. There are 169 parties to the convention.

CONVENTION ON LONG-RANGE TRANSBOUNDARY AIR POLLUTION (CLRTAP). In the mid-1970s the Soviet Union joined **Sweden** and **Norway** in calling for action on transboundary air pollution. This unusual coalition brought together downwind victims of air pollution. The Soviet Union was a net recipient of air pollutants emanating from its neighbors to the west, and especially **Poland**, **Czechoslovakia**, **Germany**, Hungary, and **Finland**. Although the Soviet leadership was not very concerned with **acid rain** as an environmental matter, they saw it as a useful issue upon which to promote their East-West détente initiative. Thus, at the initiatives of Scandinavia and the Soviet Union, efforts began under the auspices of the United Nations Economic Commission for Europe to establish a Convention on Long-Range Transboundary Air Pollution. Although Scandinavia was pushing for an agreement that would have required sulfur dioxide emissions reductions of 30 percent, **Great Britain** and Germany rejected this proposal. By this time, however, scientific evidence was accumulating that air pollutants could indeed travel thousands of kilometers before deposition occurred. After long negotiations, a least common denominator compromise was reached.

CLRTAP was the first international agreement of its kind to deal with air pollution in a regional area. It called upon states to reduce their transboundary air pollution as much as was economically feasible, report on their efforts to control emissions, and cooperate on research and monitoring of acid rain. All major western European states, the former Soviet Union and many of its satellite states, the European Community, **Canada**, and the **United States** signed the convention in 1979, which entered into force in 1983. Presently, it has 50 parties and it has since been extended by eight protocols that outline specific actions to be taken in order to cut a range of air pollutants.

CONVENTION ON PERSISTENT ORGANIC POLLUTANTS. This convention entered into force in May 2004 with 151 signatures and 124 parties. The purpose of the convention is to prevent the production, use, and export and import of designated persistent organic pollutants. Persistent organic pollutants are chemicals that remain in the environment for long periods of time; distribute over wide geographical areas through the air, water, or migratory species; fail to degenerate; accumulate in the fatty tissues of living organisms; and are toxic to humans and wildlife. The **United States** has signed but not ratified this convention.

CONVENTION ON THE PROTECTION OF THE ALPS. The Convention on the Protection of the Alps was signed in 1991 by the Alpine countries, ratified in Italy in 1999, came into force March 2000. It was signed by **Austria**, **Switzerland**, **France**, **Germany**, Monaco, Slovenia, Liechtenstein, and **Italy**.

COORDINATION OF EUROPEAN GREEN PARTIES. *See* EUROPEAN GREEN PARTY.

COSTA RICA. While concentrated soil and forest conservation efforts originated in Costa Rica in the early 1900s, for most of the 20th century concern over environmental destruction was limited to a vocal but very small group of agronomists. During the mid-1970s, a campaign for the establishment and expansion of a **national parks** system as a way of combating deforestation and growing threats to the country's diverse wildlife population began to spur broader public discussion and discontent concerning the country's environmental problems. At the same time, Costa Rica's first environmental nongovernmental organizations (NGOs) began to form, providing important organizational and networking avenues for environmental advocates. The movement took on deforestation, air and water pollution problems, and destructive development projects.

In the late 1980s and early 1990s, environmentalism became institutionalized in the political realm under the administration of Oscar Arias, which implemented a number of important environmental policy initiatives and established a new environment ministry. In few countries has the green movement been as successful in pressuring the government to adopt conservation policies as in Costa Rica. More than 25 percent of its national territory is now protected and sustained largely by ecotourism. Costa Rica has become a model of successful environmental conservation for the entire developing world.

CYPRUS GREEN PARTY. The Cyprus Green Party was created in February 1996. While it only received 1 percent of the vote in the May 1996 national parliamentary elections, in the December 1996 municipal elections, the party succeeded in electing its first Member of Council in Nicosia, the capital. The Cyprus Green Party campaigns on ending the Turkish occupation of Cyprus, protecting the Akamas peninsula, and dealing with the country's water shortages and traffic congestion. The party gained its first national member of Parliament (MP) in the 2001 parliamentary election after winning 2 percent of the vote. It repeated its performance in the May 2006 parliamentary elections.

CZECHOSLOVAKIA. Until 1989, prior to the "Velvet Revolution" that destroyed the communist regime, Czechoslovakia was under the influence and control of the Soviet Union. The possibility of an autonomous green movement and green political organizations was severely constrained. The pattern of damage to the environment was similar to other countries in eastern Europe, as environmental protection was accorded a much lower priority than economic development, and there were few or no opportunities for interest groups and other political organizations to influence this ordering of priorities.

Several organizations were formed, however, notably Brontosaurus, though they were only tolerated if they were connected to the Communist Party. Later, these organizations were used by activists opposed to the regime. The communist regime had enacted some laws to protect the environment, notably the 1967 Practical Measures against the Pollution of the Atmosphere. Although the law included penalties for polluters, they were ineffectual. Following the collapse of communism, more stringent measures modeled after those proposed by international organizations such as the World Health Organization and the European Union (EU) were introduced.

The **polluter pays principle** was reaffirmed and new policies developed on **sustainable development**, such as the General Environmental Law and General Act on the Environment enacted in 1992. Other landmark legislation included the 1991 Clean Air Act and the 1992 Act on Environmental Impact Assessment.

The rise and decline of Czechoslovakia's Green Party was linked as much to the rapid political changes that occurred from 1989 onward as to concern about damage to the environment. Formed in November 1989, the party was closely associated with the displacement of the communist regime. Its program for reforms focused primarily on the political system and democratic change rather than on the environment.

The connections between the new party and environmental organizations were slender. A very large proportion of the members of the new party had never belonged to environmental associations. These organizations had often been anything but subservient to the communist regime and included groups such as Brontosaurus, the Czech Union of Nature Protectionists, and the Slovak Union of Protectionists of Nature and the Countryside. In addition, they were used by many activists as a platform for opposing the communist government.

The formation of the Green Party in Prague was followed by the creation of green political organizations throughout the country. In February 1990 over 300 delegates attended the inaugural national congress of the new party. The fragmentation of the new political organization reflected divisions between ethnic groups and the difficulty that has confronted many other green parties in reconciling a focus on national politics with the emphasis on the grassroots. Divisions within the nation were mirrored in the structure of parliamentary representation. Elections to the two chambers of the federal assembly were structured along the following lines: in the Chamber of People, seats were allocated according to a ratio of the Czech and Slovak population; of the 150 seats in the Chamber of Nations, half went to the Czechs and half to the Slovaks. Elections were also held to a Czech National Council and to a Slovak National Council. The electoral system was structured to include both an element of proportional representation and one of multimember constituencies. There was one important rider: in the federal assembly and the Czech National Council, seats would only be allocated to parties that secured 5 percent of the vote; for the Slovak National Council, the hurdle was only 3 percent. In June 1990 elections to all these bodies, the Green Party did not fulfill its promise. It polled only 3.3 and 2.9 percent of the vote for the two assemblies, 4.1 percent in the election to the Czech National Council, and 3.5 percent (and six seats) in the Slovak National Council.

The environment had rapidly been eclipsed as an electoral issue by the focus on how to reinforce the rapid changes in the political system by developing the economy. The inherent weakness of the Green Party and its slight connection with environmental groups made it ineffectual in mobilizing a large number of potential voters. In local elections in November 1990 the Green Party, on average, did not perform much better than it had in June of that year. It did quite well, however, in areas that had suffered high levels of damage to the environment. In order to compete in the 1992 elections and overcome electoral hurdles, the Green Party, representing primarily Czechs and Moravians, joined a Liberal Social Union, which included the Socialist and Agrarian Parties. From then on, the party split into various groupings and suffered further decline. To make matters worse, a large proportion of the Green Party had been opposed to the coalition with the Agrarian Party. The latter was in favor of cooperative agriculture, which, in the eyes of many, had been largely responsible for immense damage to the landscape. For many environmentalists, the Agrarian Party was too left-wing in orientation.

A further difficulty that afflicted the Green as well as other parties was the tension between the Czechs and Slovaks. The Slovak wing of the party contested the 1992 elections on its own and secured 2.5 and 2.1 percent of the vote for the federal assembly and Slovak National Council, respectively. The Liberal Social Union polled 6 and 6.5 percent in the federal assembly and Czech National Council, respectively. Although several green deputies were thereby elected to these assemblies, the Green Party lost most of its members because of the coalition it had formed with other parties. Moreover, it was harmed by internal conflicts, its loose and deficient organizational structure, and the dominance of nonenvironmental questions on the political agenda.

The most significant of these issues was the nationalist tension between Czechs and Slovaks, which culminated in the division of the country into the **Czech Republic** and **Slovakia** on 1 January 1993. Other issues included the revival of the economy and, beginning in 1992, social problems such as unemployment, crime, and poverty. While the prospects for the Green Party were bleak, the possibilities for reforms in environmental policy were greatly enhanced following the transition from communism.

CZECH REPUBLIC. Formed on 1 January 1993, the Czech Republic joined the European Union in May 2004. The Czech Republic is among the first eastern European parliaments to have a green party enter Parliament. The Czech Republic suffered from severe air pollution, particularly in the Black Triangle region where the borders of Poland, eastern Germany, and the Czech Republic come together. Coal mining and heavy industry were concentrated in this region, and the environmental destruction these activities caused made this one of the most polluted places on the planet.

With such severe environmental problems in parts of the country, many environmental groups formed in the immediate years after the collapse of communism. Environmental concerns, however, gave way to economic ones as the Czech Republic struggled through the transition process. Many of these groups subsequently disbanded. Much of the environmental activism in the Czech Republic is now found at the local level. The environmental groups working in the Czech Republic are faced with a shortage of funds and personnel and a public whose primary attention is focused on matters other than the environment. Importantly, the environmental nongovernmental organizations (NGOs) now working in the Czech Republic do seem to be accepted by the state and are increasingly being incorporated into local decision-making committees.

The Czech Green Party (Strana zelených) was formed in 1990. They won three seats in Parliament when they ran in coalition with other parties in the 1992 election. Like much of the environmental movement, the party had a difficult time through much of the remainder of the decade. It did not contest the 1996 general elections, joined the European Federation of Green Parties in 1997, reorganized itself on a regional basis in 1999, and won one seat in the 2000 regional elections. After the party made a conscious effort to appeal to environmental organizations to work with the party to improve its chances of election to office, the Czech Green Party won seats in local councils in Prague, Brno, and Northern Bohemia. Jaromír Štetina was the first Green Party representative to be elected to the Senate in November 2004. The party gained two more local council seats in South Moravia in 2004.

The June 2006 elections were a turning point in the party's fortunes. In the elections, the Greens won six seats to the lower house of the Czech Parliament, 447 seats in local councilor elections, and six regional seats in the Prague city council. As the election produced no majority winner, and the minority government of the rightist Civic Democrats failed to win a confidence vote in October, on 9 January 2007 Czech president Vaclav Havel named a new government led by rightist prime minister Mirek Topolanek and including the centrist Christian Democrats, the Green Party, and the rightist Civic Democrats. Martin Bursik, the Green Party chairman, became environment minister and one of four deputy prime ministers. Several other ministerial posts went to the Green Party as well. *See also* AUSTRIA; CZECHOSLOVAKIA.

– D –

DALY, HERMAN. *See* STEADY-STATE ECONOMY; STEWARDSHIP.

DE GROENEN. *See* NETHERLANDS.

DE GRØNNE. *See* DENMARK.

DEBT-FOR-NATURE SWAPS. The concept of a "debt-for-nature" swap was invented in 1984 by Thomas Lovejoy, a U.S. biologist, who suggested that less developed and wealthy nations might come to the following arrangement: rather than repay part of their national debt to the developed nations, the developing nations would spend an agreed-upon sum on conservation measures or social programs. Under this arrangement, a nongovernmental organization (NGO) purchases the debt of an emerging nation at a large discount. The elimination of the debt is followed by an arrangement between the NGO and the emerging nation to ensure that the latter preserves a certain portion of land. *See also* CONSERVATION INTERNATIONAL; WORLD WIDE FUND FOR NATURE (WWF).

DECENTRALIZATION. *See BLUEPRINT FOR SURVIVAL, A.*

DEEP ECOLOGY. A differentiation between "deep" and "shallow" **ecology** was made by Norwegian philosopher Arne Naess in 1972. The term *shallow ecology* is used to refer to campaigns against pollution and the depletion of resources that have as their principal objective "the health and affluence of people in developed countries." The term *deep ecology* suggests a fundamentalist approach or a concern with **spirituality** in relating to the environment. In addition, as formulated by Naess, it focuses on the intrinsic value of nature. It attempts to posit a nonanthropocentric approach, an ideal in which nature is valued for its own sake, and the idea that human beings are located in but separate from the environment is renounced. As in **biocentrism**, the focus is on the possibility of unity with nature and the dangers associated with attempts by human beings to conquer the environment.

Naess develops the notion of "biospherical egalitarianism" to open a debate on how we should coexist with other forms of life and avoid killing, exploiting, and suppressing them. He links these ideas to the question of **quality of life** and of how, in overcrowded environments, humans and mammals suffer from neuroses, aggression, and the loss of traditions. He evokes the principles of diversity and symbiosis to support the retention of all species and argues for the principle of "live and let live" to replace the conventional principle of "either you or me" derived from arguments about the survival of the fittest. Deep ecology promotes diversity in all spheres of activity, including the economic, cultural, and occupational. This appears to be consistent with Naess's advocacy of autonomy and decentralization.

Although there have been many variations on the model of deep ecology conceived by Naess, his core ideas introduced issues that have remained central to discussions about the core principles and practices that should be adopted by the green movement in its efforts to transform social practices. Among the many objections to the deep ecology approach is the argument that any attempt to posit nonanthropocentric values is still based on attempts by human beings to devise or formulate values. Nonetheless, deep ecology has been influential in changing perceptions about the values attached to the nonhuman natural environment and how it might be preserved and protected through the efforts of the green movement and its sympathizers. *See also BLUEPRINT FOR SURVIVAL, A.*

DEFENDERS OF WILDLIFE. Founded in 1947 as Defenders of Fur Bearers, the organization's name was changed as its mission expanded to not only focus on the preservation of wildlife but also the preservation of habitat and **biodiversity**. It has a membership of close to 500,000. It is one of the most progressive organizations in the **United States** working on wildlife **conservation**.

DEINDUSTRIALIZATION. A common theme in writings by leading promoters of the green movement has been that of the problems associated with industrial society. This has led some to propose a radical shift in direction, away from industrialization, which is seen to destroy nature inevitably, toward deindustrialization, preventing the pillage of the environment.

This theme was most explicitly developed by Edward Goldsmith. His book *The Great U-Turn: De-Industrializing Society* opposes all efforts to build cities, factories, highways, and airports. Goldsmith also draws a distinction between the "real" world, which comprises the world of living things or the biosphere, and the "surrogate" world, which involves the destruction of forests, soil erosion, and the creation of pollution and toxic wastes. Goldsmith's proposals represent a radical response to the findings of studies such as *The Limits to Growth*, which points to the limits of the resources available for maintaining lifestyles in affluent societies. The argument for deindustrialization is also advanced by writers such as Ted Trainer who, in *Abandon Affluence!* argues that the Western way of life is unsustainable and contributes directly to poverty in less developed countries. In sum, he argues for the "dedevelopment" of wealthy nations in order to ensure that resources are redistributed to the poor and that the economic system can be reshaped in order to meet their needs. However, arguments about deindustrialization have not been widely accepted or promoted by the green movement.

DENMARK. Denmark is widely considered to be among the most environmentally progressive states in Europe. Nevertheless, the Danish greens, De Grønne, remain a small party. De Grønne were founded in October 1983 and first competed in local elections in 1985, attracting 2.8 percent of the vote and gaining 12 seats on municipal councils and six on provincial councils. In the 1987 and 1988 national elections, they attracted only 1.3 percent of the vote, and in the 1990 elections only 0.9 percent, insufficient to enter Parliament where there was a 2 percent of the vote electoral requirement for gaining seats. The relatively weak performance by De Grønne is partly attributable to the competition from other minor parties that had championed the goals of various new social movements in the 1970s. Another explanation is that other parties, notably the Socialist People's Party, had already shown a keen interest in environmental issues. Furthermore, unlike some of its neighbors, Denmark did not have a nuclear power program.

Because of the challenges for a new party to enter the Danish political scene, De Grønne decided in 1996 to join a coalition of other parties (Demokratisk Fornyelse or Democratic Renewal) opposed to the European Union (EU). This coalition received sufficient signatures to run for election to the national parliament, but the coalition did not do well in the election. De Grønne failed to get sufficient signatures to enter the 2001 and the 2005 elections.

The party has not faired well at the local level, either. Of the two seats the party had in 1998, one was lost after the party's vote dropped 0.1 percentage points to 4.7 percent and the other was lost after the Green representative resigned (although the seat is still in the hands of a local environmental list that includes De Groenen). In the 2005 European Parliamentary election, the party ran candidates for the June Movement and the People's Movement against EU, which together received approximately 23 percent of the vote (4 of 16 seats). The greatest support for De Grønne comes from younger people, those with higher levels of education, and urban dwellers. In its organizational structure, De Grønne has attempted to promote internal democracy and accountability to the membership. With this objective in mind, it holds several national congresses each year to which local branches of the party can send delegates. Like Die Grünen in **Germany**, De Grønne has based its platform on four principles: **ecology**, **nonviolence**, **direct democracy**, and social security. They are major supporters of nonnuclear renewable energies. There is also an emphasis on peace and disarmament. Like many other green parties, De Grønne has developed policies on the economy, social issues, and international relations, with a focus on unilateral disarmament, the abrogation of NATO, and the repudiation of Denmark's membership in the EU and in the euro.

DIE GRÜNEN. *See* GERMANY.

DIE GRÜNEN-DIE GRÜNE ALTERNATIVE. *See* AUSTRIA.

DIRECT DEMOCRACY. The term *direct democracy*, or *grassroots democracy*, is widely used by green political groups to distinguish their practices from those of traditional political organizations. The latter are seen as autocratic or promoting representative rather than participatory democracy. The focus on direct democracy in green parties reflects the interest among fundamentalists to retain the spontaneous character of the social movements from which they emerged and remain accountable to the grassroots of the organization. Direct democracy is seen as a means of preventing the emergence of a strong bureaucratic and professional culture in green political organizations. It also exhibits the enduring skepticism of many activists about involvement in conventional political action and parliamentary politics.

Among the most notable efforts to put direct or grassroots democracy into practice have been the endeavors of the fundamentalists in **Germany's** Die Grünen to limit the tenure of parliamentary delegates by rotating them out of office and to ensure that representatives remained directly accountable to the membership, in effect allowing members to dismiss them from their offices. The latter principle is often referred to as the imperative mandate. Green political organizations have constantly had to decide between their efforts to ensure greater accountability to the membership and the need to develop a higher degree of competence and professionalism to deal with the complex processes and decisions that arise in parliamentary politics.

Apart from the principle of rotation and the imperative mandate, green political organizations have attempted to promote direct democracy by trying to maintain close links with social movements, convening meetings that are open to all members of a political organization, and advocating consensus rather than majority voting on important issues. Another manifestation of the emphasis on direct democracy has been the granting to local and regional groups within green political organizations of a large measure of autonomy to draw up party programs, follow their own procedures for internal organization, and manage their financial affairs. There is a convergence here with notions of decentralization. The notion of direct democracy has also been used to bolster campaigns by green political organizations against the accumulation of offices, patronage, and corruption in parliamentary politics. *See also BLUEPRINT FOR SURVIVAL, A.*

DUBOS, RENÉ (1901–1983). Born in France, René Dubos worked as a biologist and philosopher in the **United States**. Renowned as the person who invented the expression "think globally, act locally," Dubos is coauthor, with Barbara Ward, of *Only One Earth*. This highly influential book, which took issue with the path of development pursued by advanced industrialized market economies, contributed to the shaping of the policy agenda of the United Nations, which had commissioned the work. For most of his career, Dubos taught at Rockefeller University in New York. He had also held posts at Rutgers University and Harvard Medical School. A recipient of the Pulitzer Prize, Dubos wrote extensively on the relationships between human beings and their surroundings, and his works include *The*

Wooing of Earth: New Perspectives on Man's Use of Nature and Celebrations of Life.

– E –

EARTH DAY. United States Democratic senator Gaylord Nelson from Wisconsin, an environmental advocate, called for a national teach-in about the environment, an idea that took off and led to an estimated 20 million people participating in the nation's first Earth Day celebration on 22 April 1970. Since then, Earth Day has become an annual celebration. The founders of Earth Day created the Earth Day Network, which works with over 12,000 organizations in 174 countries.

EARTH FIRST! The radical environmental group Earth First! was formed in 1980 in the southwestern **United States**. The group has often been compared with and described as more radical than **Greenpeace**. Both organizations focus on direct action, though Earth First! has had nothing like the success enjoyed by Greenpeace in gaining popular support and eliciting a sympathetic response from the news media. This is hardly surprising since Earth First! was formed as a strong reaction against conventional green groups and their ameliorative approach to environmental issues. Earth First! has also espoused **biocentrism** and **deep ecology** as well as an extremely loose organizational structure. In fact, it claims to be an international movement and a "priority" but not an organization.

The founders of Earth First! including David Foreman, its unofficial leader, were also strongly influenced by the ideas expressed by Edward Abbey in his well-known novel *The Monkey Wrench Gang.* Its fictional characters want to protect nature by engaging in acts of sabotage that involve wrecking equipment and machinery. Earth First! came to the attention of the media and the public in 1981 by scaring the authorities responsible for the Glen Canyon Dam through an imaginative act. They created the illusion of a crack in the wall of the dam by rolling a huge strip of plastic over it. Other actions by some members of the group were less benign and mirrored the ideas of activists Foreman and Bill Haywood, who together edited *Ecodefense: A Field*

Guide to Monkeywrenching. The guide promoted "monkeywrench-ing" (the destruction of machinery and equipment) as part of a cam-paign to sabotage the infrastructure being used to destroy wilderness areas. The proponents of monkeywrenching argued that it was nonvi-olent, not subject to any central control or direction, and carefully aimed at vulnerable elements of a project.

The monkeywrenchers regarded themselves as warriors defending the wilderness from industrial civilization. By striking at companies involved in activities such as logging, they aimed to force them out of business by increasing the costs of equipment repair and insurance premiums. Actions by supporters of Earth First! included the de-struction of equipment belonging to loggers and logging companies and, most controversially, the "spiking" of trees (the insertion of metal spikes into trees, damaging the chain saws used to cut them down). The authorities have argued that this poses a serious hazard to the loggers, though this has been denied by the activists. There have been deep divisions among supporters of Earth First! over the tactics used in support of their original motto: "No compromise in defense of Mother Earth!" For some, sabotage of power lines and equipment is entirely valid in defending the wilderness. Others advocate much stricter adherence to the principles of **nonviolence**.

The absence of organizational structures has left activists uncon-strained in pursuing a wide range of approaches to achieving their primary objective, namely, the protection of wilderness areas. Earth First! has repudiated organizational structures to a far greater extent than most environmental groups. There is no formal leader, no lead-ership structure, and no formal membership. Communication be-tween members is maintained through a magazine that appears about eight times a year, an annual meeting lasting one week, and an an-nual conference. One indicator of the size of the membership has been the subscription list of the magazine, which by 1990 had 6,000 subscribers plus sales of another 3,000 copies. Following a serious conflict among members in 1990, subscriptions fell to around 3,000. It is difficult to estimate how many people participate in Earth First! though groups are spread throughout the **United States**. A following has also developed in Europe as well as in **Canada** and **Australia**. Although much attention has been directed to some of the violent tactics employed by Earth First! supporters, their actions usually entail accepted forms of campaigning. These include using music and theater to entertain children and raise their awareness of environmental issues as well as standard approaches to lobbying for changes in policy.

Like other green political organizations, Earth First! has had to grapple with struggles between its founders, who have been fundamentally committed to deep ecology, and those members who have been concerned about the implications of their actions in terms of social justice and economic welfare. Developments within Earth First! parallel the conflict between fundamentalists and realists in many green political parties. In 1990 David Foreman withdrew from Earth First! on the grounds that the organization had taken on too many economic and social issues. Foreman was also concerned that many members were becoming less enthusiastic about the militant approach, for instance, the spiking of trees. Foreman felt that the focus on social issues damaged the initial and fundamental objective of the organization, namely, to focus above all else on the defense of the Earth.

In 1995, there was a split in the organization when Earth First! renounced the use of violence. A new group, **Earth Liberation Front**, then formed.

EARTH ISLAND INSTITUTE. Founded in 1982 by **David Brower**, Earth Island Institute provides organizational support to groups working for conservation, preservation, and restoration of the global environment. Earth Island Institute has launched over 50 environmental projects, including **Rainforest Action Network (RAN)**, International Rivers Network, and Urban Habitat. It led one of the largest consumer boycotts ever that led to the requirement that all tuna be dolphin safe.

EARTH JUSTICE. In 1965 the **Sierra Club** launched a campaign to save the Mineral King Valley in the Sierra Nevada from becoming a ski resort as planned by Walt Disney Productions. When the organization was unsuccessful at blocking the project through political channels, it filed its first lawsuit in 1969. A San Francisco attorney took the case through to the Supreme Court (1972). Although the Sierra Club technically lost the case, it was allowed to return to the lower courts to try again. In the meantime, Disney chose to pull out of the project and environmental groups won confirmation of their right to seek review of environmental disputes in the courts. Two of the volunteer attorneys who worked on this case (Don Harris and Fred Fisher) established the Sierra Club Legal Defense Fund in 1971. Fully independent of the Sierra Club, this nonprofit public interest law firm has provided free legal representation to citizen groups to protect and enforce U.S. environmental laws. They have represented the **Wilderness Society**, the **Audubon Society**, and **Natural Resources Defense Council (NRDC)**, among many others. They changed their name to Earth Justice in 1997.

EARTH LIBERATION FRONT. A group of disaffected members of **Earth First!** split off to form Earth Liberation Front. Like Animal Liberation Front, the group is willing to use sabotage to stop activities that harm nature. In its 1997 communiqué, the organization announced its adherence to social and **deep ecology** and seeks to achieve the collapse of industry and the undermining of the state. Earth Liberation Front became the subject of congressional hearings related to ecoterrorism.

EARTHRIGHTS INTERNATIONAL (ERI). ERI is involved in the defense of human rights and the environment in countries where few other organizations can safely operate. ERI works in issues pertaining to human rights natural resource management in Southeast Asia and the **Amazon**. It organizes human rights and environmental activists around these issues, documents human rights and environmental abuses, and litigates in U.S. courts (under the Alien Tort Claims Act) on behalf of victims in developing countries.

EARTH SUMMIT. *See* UNITED NATIONS CONFERENCE ON ENVIRONMENT AND DEVELOPMENT (UNCED).

ECOFEMINISM. As with many other social movements, sections of the feminist movement have developed a strong interest in **ecology**. The range of arguments about the connection between the concerns of feminists and the protection and preservation of nature is fairly diverse. Some themes, however, arise quite frequently. They include the assumption by many ecofeminists that women are inherently closer to nature than men. This ties in with arguments, contested within the feminist movement itself, about fundamental traits that can (or cannot) be ascribed to females rather than to males. Some feminist thinkers, such as Carolyn Merchant in her book *The Death of Nature*, have suggested that the distinction in Western societies between culture and nature caused women, who are seen as closer to nature, to be regarded as socially and culturally inferior to men.

Some ecofeminists have employed this argument about the proximity of women to nature to suggest that patriarchy, the control of a disproportionately large share of society by men, lies at the core of the devastation of nature. This argument is similar to that posited in social ecology about hierarchy as the source of environmental destruction. Some ecofeminists consider women to be more likely than any other group to become aligned with efforts to protect the environment. Not surprisingly, many of these assumptions are challenged by other feminists who question suppositions about the role of women and their potential contributions to all areas of social life.

ECOLO. The Belgian green party that represents the Walloon population was part of a coalition government at the federal level from 1999 to 2003. In the 2003 general election, however, Ecolo suffered a major set back, losing about half of its seats. The party, which had been visibly divided about entering into a coalition government, was viewed by voters as being torn and indecisive.

Ecolo (Écologistes Confédérés pour l'organisation de lutes originales) was founded in March 1980. Since the early 1970s, a variety of groups had been formed to contest elections either on a platform promoting **direct democracy**, including a group called Démocratie Nouvelle (New Democracy), or combining democratic and ecological principles, such as Combat pour l'Écologie et l'Autogestion. By the late 1970s, these groups and others such as Ecopol and Ecolog (which partly represented segments of the **Friends of the Earth**) had laid the foundations for Ecolo. Paul Lannoye, who left the Rassemblement Wallon (Walloon Union) in 1971 to form Démocratie Nouvelle, was a central figure in the development of Ecolo. The immediate spur to its creation was the success of a loose association called

EuropeÉcologie in the 1979 elections to the **European Parliament**. EuropeÉcologie did better than any other green party, attracting 5.1 percent of votes cast by the Walloons.

In 1981 Ecolo, with 5.9 percent of the Walloon vote, gained two seats in the Belgian lower house. It improved slightly on this performance in the 1985 and 1987 elections when it gained over 6 percent of the Walloon vote both times. In the 1984 elections to the European Parliament Ecolo secured 9.4 percent of the vote and a single seat. In the 1989 European elections, Ecolo did even better, winning 16.6 percent of the vote and two seats. Similarly, at the national elections it secured 13.5 percent of the ballot in Wallonia and 10 seats. However, like **Agalev**, Ecolo lost many supporters in 1995: its share of the national poll declined from 5.1 to 4 percent. The number of Ecolo delegates in the lower house was reduced as a consequence both of the election result and the reduction in the total number of seats available in the lower house from 212 to 150. Ecolo therefore lost four seats compared to 1991.

This important reversal in the fortunes of Belgium's green parties has been attributed partially to the fear of many green voters that lack of support for the Socialist Party, which was under siege because of various corruption scandals, would result in the dismantling of many important aspects of the social security system by the conservative opposition. *See also* BELGIUM; GROEN!

ECOLOGICAL FOOTPRINT. *See* ENVIRONMENTAL JUSTICE.

ECOLOGY. Originally a scientific term, *ecology* has been used to describe new political parties and social movements concerned about environmental issues as well as new ways of conceptualizing politics. In *What Is Ecology?* Denis Owen moves from its straightforward definition as the relationships between plants and animals and the environment in which they live to an argument about how human activities should not be considered separate from the living world, which is composed of both simple and complex systems of interrelationships. The notion of the connection between human beings and the rest of the living world has been a source of inspiration for supporters and sympathizers of the green movement. Owen states, "The first important lesson to learn is that man is part of nature and that the rest of nature was not put there for man to exploit, the claims of business, political and religious leaders notwithstanding." *See also* DEEP ECOLOGY.

EGYPT. As most of Egypt is a desert, its population of 79 million is very densely concentrated along the Nile River, the lifeblood of the country. Population pressures and economic development have combined to create a host of environmental concerns. A small number of environmental groups have formed in Egypt, although as a whole the environmental movement remains weak, as is the case throughout much of the Arab world. Examples of groups that have formed include the Association for the Protection of the Environment, which was set up in 1984 and focuses on recycling, waste separation, and composting, and the Centre for Environment and Development for Arab Region and Europe, formed in the mid-1990s and with its headquarters in Cairo.

EHRLICH, PAUL (1932–). Best known for his controversial views on **population growth** and its impact on the environment, Ehrlich is the author of *The Population Bomb*. A biologist who has worked at Stanford University since 1959, his views have always provoked strong reactions, including a fierce debate in the 1970s with another biologist, **Barry Commoner**. *See also* MALTHUS, THOMAS ROBERT.

EMISSIONS TRADING. The U.S. Clean Air Act Amendments of 1990 brought to prominence an idea that environmental economists had long advocated: an emissions trading scheme for sulfur dioxide emissions from power plants. The idea behind this concept is that firms can more efficiently determine where and how to make emissions reduction cuts than can governments through regulating specific technology standards or processes. In an emissions trading system, a government establishes a cap for total emissions allowed, but then leaves it to industry and the market to determine how emissions cuts are to be made. This is done through a system of pollution permits that can be bought and sold. At the start of such a system, firms are either allocated pollution permits or buy them in an auction. Firms that can do so inexpensively have an incentive to reduce their pollution in order to be able to sell off their permits. Firms that wish to expand, and thus pollute more, must either buy more pollution permits or make emissions cuts elsewhere in their system. Depending on the design of the system, when a trade occurs, a certain percentage of permits may be retired from the system. Environmental groups and others have bought up some pollution permits in order to retire them from the system, thereby driving up the cost of remaining permits and adding pressures on firms to further reduce their emissions.

This system proved highly successful at reducing sulfur dioxide emissions in the **United States**, although critics question the notion of a right to pollute that is implied by the system and point out the injustice of the system for those who are misfortunate enough to live next to a plant that does not reduce its emissions. In 2002, the George W. Bush administration announced the Clear Skies Initiative, a plan to use a cap and trade system to cut emissions of sulfur dioxides by 73 percent, nitrogen oxides by 67 percent, and mercury by 69 percent relative to 2002 levels by 2018. A group of New England states that are critical of the United States' federal government's failure to mandate emissions reduction cuts has initiated its own cap and trade system for carbon dioxide emissions.

The European Union (EU) was initially opposed to the idea of emissions trading within the **Kyoto Protocol** framework, arguing that emissions cuts should be made domestically. Opposition to the idea, however, turned into strong support as the costs and obstacles to fulfilling Kyoto Protocol targets became increasingly clear and the emissions trading system became better understood. In 2005, the EU initiated the world's first international carbon dioxide emissions trading system that encompasses 12,000 firms and power plants. Firms were allocated emissions permits based on anticipated carbon dioxide emissions for each country. In its first year, the system ran into problems as the cost of CO_2 permits dropped once it was announced that the **Czech Republic**, **Estonia**, **France**, the **Netherlands**, and the Walloon region had emitted less carbon dioxide than had been anticipated. If prices drop, the incentive for firms to reduce their emissions decline. This suggests a need to improve decisions on how to allocate carbon dioxide permits.

ENVIRONMENTAL DEFENSE. One of the big 10 environmental organizations in the **United States**, Environmental Defense was founded in 1967 and in the mid-2000s had a membership of 500,000. The group has its origins in efforts that began in New York State to stop the use of DDT to kill mosquitoes because of its adverse impacts on the eggs of osprey and other birds. The group eventually went national and after successfully ending the use of DDT in the United States, took up other campaigns, such as the protection of whales and the phase out of ozone-depleting **chlorofluorocarbons (CFCs)**. Environmental Defense sees its mission as protecting the rights of this and future generations to clean air, clean water, healthy food, and healthy ecosystems. Environmental Defense has a strong focus on issues of **environmental justice**, especially in the United States. Its campaigns currently focus on **global warming**, ocean protection, and healthy farms.

ENVIRONMENTAL JUSTICE. There are inherent conflicts of interest that arise in relation to economic development and environmental protection. These include conflicts among different groups within a society, between different generations, and between nations. Which groups are forced to live with the most serious pollution problems associated with development and industrialization? Which groups benefit the most from expenditures for environmental protection, and who is asked to pay the cost of protective or remedial measures? Is it fair for rich countries that polluted during their own development to expect developing countries to cut harmful emissions to protect the global environment at early stages in their economic development?

The foundations of the environmental justice movement go back to the civil rights movements of the 1950s, 1960s, and 1970s in the **United States** that called for the empowerment and fair and equitable treatment of peoples of color. The civil rights movement brought several important elements to the environmental justice movement in the United States, the most important of which were experience with direct action and a perception that the distribution of environmental hazards was not the result of chance or "neutral" decisions, but rather a product of the dominant social and economic structures of society. Also important to the rise of the environmental justice movement were the protest movements that arose in the 1970s and 1980s in relation to toxic pollution. The best-known example is **Love Canal**, a residential housing area built on top of a toxic waste dump that was evacuated when President Jimmy Carter declared it a disaster area.

The "antitoxics movement" also shared with the civil rights movement a belief that inequity could only be addressed if larger social and economic structures were confronted, and especially the power of corporate America. A milestone event in the environmental justice movement was the protests in 1982 against the State of North Carolina's decision to site a polychlorinated biphenyl (PCB) disposal landfill facility in Warren County, a poor and predominantly black community. The protests stimulated studies into the associations between environmental risks and population distribution by socioeconomic status and race, issues that had been neglected by the mainstream environmental groups in the United States.

Remarkably, the idea of environmental justice (and environmental racism) was really only brought to the highest political levels in the 1990s when a group of scholars brought to the attention of William Reilly, head of the Environmental Protection Agency (EPA), their studies that showed a disproportionate impact of pollution on minority populations. This led to the establishment of a Working Group on Environmental Equity that in 1993 was turned into the Office of Environmental Justice. The next year in June, President William J. Clinton signed an Executive Order on Environmental Justice, bringing an unprecedented level of political attention to the issue and acknowledging the need to "focus Federal attention on the environmental and human health conditions in minority communities and low-income communities with the goal of achieving environmental justice."

Many of the types of environmental justice concerns that the United States faced can be found in other societies where there are multiple racial and ethnic communities and class divides. Environmental and social justice movements are emerging in nations around the world. Examples include the protests of the Ogoni people in **Nigeria** against pollution caused by the multinational oil company Shell, which was drilling in their community; the protests of citizens in Koko, Nigeria, against the dumping of hazardous waste coming from Italy, and the protests of the Penang in Sarawak, Malaysia, against the logging of their tribal forests.

The concepts of the environmental justice movement are increasingly being applied to the international community as well. International environmental problems first began to attract serious attention in the early 1970s. At the time of the first **United Nations Confer-**

ence on the **Human Environment (UNCHE)** in Stockholm in 1972, there was much attention to the global population explosion. Rich countries tended to have lower **population growth** rates than developing countries. Calls by the rich nations to slow population growth for the protection of the planet, however, were lambasted by some developing countries as being inherently unjust, as it was the high consumption lifestyles of the rich countries that were causing the real strains on the planet. Certainly, the energy and resource consumption of individuals in rich countries is many-fold that of individuals in the **People's Republic of China, India**, or elsewhere in the developing world. Rich countries, however, tended to challenge these interpretations as they failed to account for the inefficiency of resource use in many developing countries (particularly true for energy).

The **climate change** negotiations have drawn great attention to issues of international environmental equity. Many developing countries have called upon the rich countries, which to date have been the largest producers of greenhouse gases, to take responsibility for addressing the problem and to provide technology and financial transfers to developing countries to help abate their growing emissions. There are also sovereignty concerns that come into play, such as with issues of biological preservation. Developing countries that have some of the richest biological diversity in the world have questioned the equity of demands placed upon them by richer countries to preserve their forests as much of the original deforestation in developing countries occurred during colonial times and rich nations exploited their own forests during their own early industrialization. These concerns were behind the development of the **Convention on Biological Diversity** and its associated Cartagena Protocol on Biosafety.

The political theorist John Rawls was among the earliest to focus attention on intergenerational equity, justice, and the rights of future generations. While there has been considerable debate on the question of whether or not rights can be assigned to individuals who do not yet exist, there is general agreement that we have an "obligation" to protect the world's natural resources. The famous **Brundtland Commission**'s 1987 report, *Our Common Future*, called upon nations to promote **sustainable development** in order to ensure the long-term survival of the human species and so that future generations would be afforded the same opportunities as current generations enjoy.

Finally, there is a gender perspective related to environmental justice. The United Nations Development Programme (UNDP) has argued that environmental pollution and natural resource degradation tends to affect the lives of women more harshly than men since, in many societies, it is women who are responsible for collecting firewood and water, which in many places are in scarce supply and thus, requires that women must travel long distances to find these basic necessities. It is also women who tend to be primary caretakers of the young and the old, and thus, they are often most aware of the effects of pollution on human health. Thus, promoting sustainable development can also improve the lot of women.

Yet, in many societies, women have traditionally had limited voice in policy formulation. Recognizing this and identifying it as a major challenge to effective environmental policy formulation and implementation, at the 1992 **United Nations Conference on Environment and Development (UNCED)**, a plan of action for sustainable development, known as **Agenda 21**, was formulated. One chapter of Agenda 21 speaks specifically to the importance of enhancing the role of women in environmental decision making. *See also* BIODIVERSITY; ECOFEMINISM; GREENHOUSE EFFECT.

ESTONIA. The Estonian Green Movement (EGM) that formed in 1988 to protest the Soviet Union's plans to mine phosphorite deposits along the country's northeast coast was one of the first independent popular political movements under Soviet rule in Estonia. In 1989, EGM joined **Friends of the Earth**, registered as a political party, and joined the **Coordination of European Green Parties**. The EGM also split in 1989, with the more politically minded members forming the Estonian Green Party. Although weakened by the split, the EGM won eight seats (out of 105) in the first multiparty election to the Estonian Supreme Council in 1990. One of their deputies, Arnold Rüütel, was nominated to be chairman of the High Supreme Council, and the chairman of the party, Tomaas Frey, became environment minister.

As has been the case in so many other transition states, the EGM did not do well as the country entered the hard years of political and economic transition, losing ground to major political parties. In the 1992 election they received only 2.6 percent of the vote (one seat in the Riigikogu [Parliament]). In 1992, the EGM and the Estonian Green Party merged to form the Estonian Greens (Erakond Eestima Rohelised). Since that time, the party has not done well, failing to meet the requirements (such as having 1,000 members) necessary to run as a party in parliamentary elections. They lost their party registration after the 1998 elections and have since functioned as a nongovernmental organization (NGO). They have had slightly better performance at the local level where they have had a few representatives elected to local councils. Since joining the European Union (EU) in May 2004, the Estonian Greens have been trying to gain a sufficient number of new members to reregister as a party.

EUROPEAN COORDINATION OF GREEN PARTIES. *See* EUROPEAN FEDERATION OF GREEN PARTIES-EUROPEAN FREE ALLIANCE.

EUROPEAN FEDERATION OF GREEN PARTIES-EUROPEAN FREE ALLIANCE. In 1984 the Green parties of **Belgium, France, Germany, Luxembourg,** the **Netherlands, Sweden, Switzerland,** and **Great Britain** formed the European Coordination of Green Parties. The coordination was established to lend coherence to the efforts of green parties to influence the direction of European politics.

With the European continent undergoing sweeping political changes as a result of the collapse of the communist East bloc, the coordination felt it was necessary to be able to speak in a single voice. Thus, in June 1993 at a conference held in Masala, **Finland,** the coordination was turned into the European Federation of Green Parties. The new federation agreed on a set of "guiding principles." These focused on the economy (patterns of consumption and production), citizenship (including a focus on equal rights for all individuals regardless of gender, age, race, religion, ethnic or national origin, sexual orientation, wealth, and health), democratization, and security. Some of these themes were articulated in a section entitled "the new citizenship," which called for the expansion of civil rights, democratic participation, human rights ("without discrimination on the basis of race, disability, gender, sexual orientation, religion, age or national or ethnic origin"), and protection for the rights of minorities. The federation opposed the strong reactions against newcomers to western Europe and called for a "humane immigration policy." It also supported proportional electoral systems.

The federation's principles included a pan-European strategy of ecological and social reform. Economic development was to focus on "cooperation not competition." Both free market economy and state-controlled economies were rejected, as they assumed no limits to economic growth. The European Greens emphasized "ecological sustainability, equity and social justice" and argued for "the protection of the diversity of ecological resources and the global commons." They also focused on the burden of debt affecting poor countries and the question of **population growth** and how it should be reduced. Europe was to foster more "self-reliant" national, regional, and local economies within a "Europe of Regions." Any attempt to measure the performance of the economy was to include all social and environmental costs, for instance, by imposing "ecological taxes" on resources such as nonrenewable energy and activities that threatened the environment. Recycling and repairing products were similarly emphasized.

The federation also proposed the conversion of the economy, for example, from the production of military equipment and the chemical industries toward new sectors such as those focusing on reducing the consumption of energy, recycling, public transport, agriculture, forestry, nature protection, and environmentally sound technology.

Other themes included a total ban on the construction of nuclear power plants, the phasing out of existing facilities, and the end to the EURATOM treaty. Forestry and agricultural practices would also be changed to prevent overproduction by the European Union (EU) and pollution and to protect endangered species and expand the size of forests.

The federation sought a more equitable distribution of wealth and resources between western, eastern, and central Europe and the introduction of environmental safeguards across the continent. The federation also envisioned a new European security system that would not be dominated by Western organizations such as the North Atlantic Treaty Organization (NATO). Rather, a peace-oriented Common Foreign Security Policy should be pursued and a European Civil Peace Corps created. The federation rejected nuclear weapons and called for a comprehensive test ban treaty. In 1999, a new grouping emerged when the European Free Alliance joined with the Greens to form the Greens/European Free Alliance. The European Free Alliance is a grouping of political parties that espouse democracy and independence or self-government (e.g., Plaid Cymru, Wales; Scottish National Party, Scotland; Republican Left of Catalonia; and For Human Rights in Latvia). The group has as its goals the promotion of fundamental human rights and environmental justice; deepening democracy through decentralization and enhancing people's participation in decision making; enhancing the openness of government; and reorienting Europe towards social, cultural, and ecological values, among other issues. The group has co-presidents to ensure gender balance. After the 2004 European Parliamentary elections, the European Greens-European Free Alliance had 42 members of Parliament and was the fourth-largest block in the **European Parliament**. *See also* CARBON TAXES; EUROPEAN GREEN PARTY; POLLUTER PAYS PRINCIPLE.

EUROPEAN GREEN PARTY. At its fourth party congress held in Rome, **Italy**, in 2004, the European Federation of Green Parties decided to form the European Green Party. Reflecting the democratization of much of central and parts of eastern Europe in the post-1990 period, the European Green Party had member parties from 31 countries in 2006: Die Grünen (**Austria**), Ecolo and **Groen!** (**Belgium**), Green Party (**Bulgaria**), **Cyprus Green Party**, Strana Zelenych (**Czech Republic**), De Grønne (**Denmark**), Erakond Eestimaa Rohelised (**Estonia**), Vihreät (**Finland**), Les Verts (**France**), Sakartvelo's mtsvaneta partia (**Georgia**), Bündnis 90/Die Grünen (**Germany**), Ecologoi-Prasinoi (**Greece**), Zöld Demokraták Szövetsége (**Hungary**), Comhoantas Glas (**Ireland**), Federazione dei Verdi (Italy), Latvijas Zala Partija (**Latvia**), Déi Gréng (**Luxembourg**), Alternattiva Demokratika (**Malta**), De Groenen and Groenlinks (**Netherlands**), Miljøpartiet De Grønne (**Norway**), Zieloni (**Poland**), Partido Ecologista "Os Verdes" (**Portugal**), The Green Party (**Romania**), Zelenaya Alternativa (**Russia**), Strana Zelenych (**Slovakia**), Stranka Mladih Slovenije (Slovenia), Los Verdes and Iniciativa per Catalunya Verdes (**Spain**), Miljöpartiet de Gröna (**Sweden**), Grüne/Les Verts (**Switzerland**), Partija Zelenykh Ukrainy (**Ukraine**), and The Green Party and Scottish Green Party (**Great Britain**).

In addition, there are a number of observer parties. These include the **Federation of Young European Greens**, Te Gjelberit (Albania),

Partit Verdes d'Andorra (Principat d'Andorra), Socialistisk Folkepartei (Denmark), Partidul Ecologist din Moldova "Aliante Verde" (Moldova), Green Russia (Russia), Zeleni (Serbia), and Yesiller (Turkey).

In an effort to establish a common vision, at the second Congress of the European Green Party, which was held in Geneva, Switzerland, in October 2006, an agreement was reached on a substantive set of policies that all member parties will base their plans on. Called a Green Future for Europe, the agreement opens with a preamble lamenting the problems facing the European Union (EU). These include the failure of the EU Constitution, declining budgetary support for the EU project, and a democratic deficit in EU decision making that leave many citizens feeling as if they have little voice in the shaping of policies that come to govern them. The agreement suggests that many of these problems are tied to the drive for economic globalization that does not pay adequate attention to the needs of the people and promotes unsustainable lifestyles.

The agreement supports the EU as an international project for peace and human rights. It also calls upon the EU to become a model for a sustainable future, a safeguard of the European social model, and a supporter of consumer rights, health, and a green economy. The agreement does not reject globalization, but rather calls for a just globalization that stands for democracy, diversity, equality, and the rule of law. It also calls for a strengthening of the role of the **European Parliament** by, among other things, the granting of the right to legislative initiative, and the allocation of a percentage of seats (e.g., 10 percent) in the Parliament to pan-European parties.

The 2006 Action Plan for the European Green Party (adopted in October 2005) focused on the need to work on strengthening the political position of green parties throughout Europe after a number of important defeats. These defeats included the NO referendums in France and the Netherlands on the EU Constitution and the loss of green representation in national governments. Whereas a few years earlier, green parties were represented in the governments of Italy, Finland, France, Belgium, Germany, Poland, Slovakia, and Ukraine, in late 2005 Latvia was the only government where Greens were still part of ruling coalition although in 2007, it appears that the Czech Green Party will be part of a ruling coalition in the Czech Republic.

See also EUROPEAN FEDERATION OF GREEN PARTIES-EUROPEAN FREE ALLIANCE.

EUROPEAN GREENS-EUROPEAN FREE ALLIANCE. *See* EUROPEAN FEDERATION OF GREEN PARTIES-EUROPEAN FREE ALLIANCE; EUROPEAN GREEN PARTY.

EUROPEAN PARLIAMENT. In 1979, when the first elections to the European Parliament were held, the green movement had only recently begun to make an impact on the political agenda, and none of the new green parties were successful in gaining seats. In 1984 green parties succeeded in capturing 12 seats. The dominant group in what came to be known as the Green-Alternative European Link was from the Federal Republic of **Germany**, with seven delegates from Die Grünen. The **Netherlands** and **Belgium** each had two representatives, and **Italy** had one.

In 1989 green parties achieved their best-ever results in elections to the European Parliament, gaining 32 seats. Although Die Grünen acquired eight of these seats, they were no longer the dominant group. There were nine delegates from **France**, seven from Italy, three from Belgium, and two from the Netherlands. **Portugal**, **Spain**, and **Denmark** had one each. Although among the most successful green parties in terms of share of the national vote, **Great Britain**'s Green Party gained no seats because of the constraints imposed by the electoral system in that country. In 1994 environmental issues were less prominent on the political agenda than they had been in 1989 when Europe was focused on assisting central and eastern European accession states in transforming their economies and polities. As a result there was a decline in the green parties' share of the European Parliament vote, and only 22 candidates were successful. Unlike most other green political parties, Bündnis 90/Die Grünen improved on their previous performance and once again emerged as the most powerful group, with 12 seats. Italy had three representatives, Belgium had two, and the Netherlands, Denmark, and **Luxembourg** each had one. The Danish delegate was not the representative of a green party. However, her party, the Socialist People's Party, became part of the Green Group in the European Parliament in 1992.

In the 1999 election, the newly formed Greens-European Free Alliance won 48 of 626 seats. This time, France's Les Verts sent the largest number of delegates (nine), followed by seven each from Belgium and Germany, six from Great Britain, four each from Spain and the Netherlands, two each from **Austria, Finland, Ireland,** Italy, and **Sweden.** After the 2004 election, the **European Greens-European Free Alliance** had 42 seats (13 from Germany, six from France, five from Great Britain, four from the Netherlands, three from Spain, and one or two each from Austria, Belgium, Denmark, Finland, Italy, **Latvia,** Luxembourg, and Sweden).

The ambivalence that characterized the approach of many green parties to parliamentary politics, especially prior to the 1990s, influenced their attitude toward the European Community/European Union (EU) and the relationship between various green parties. After the 1984 congress of green parties held at Liege in Belgium, they advocated a "Europe of the regions." This corresponded to their emphasis on decentralization and autonomy and arguments against hierarchical forms of governance. Green parties have also regarded with suspicion the development of large, centralized bureaucracies. Questions that united the green parties in their early years included their opposition to any attempts to achieve greater central control and coherence of the military, focus on the arms race, the goal of protection of the environment, and advocation of the rights of women and minority groups.

Some of the divisions that prevailed at the national level manifested themselves at transnational meetings. During their first term in office, between 1984 and 1989, most members of Die Grünen refused to adhere to the principle of rotation out of office on the grounds that this would undermine their efforts to gain and make use of their newly acquired expertise in operating within the political system. Green delegates also disagreed about the value of working in the institutions of the European Community: whether to attempt, in a pragmatic manner, to transform the institutions (to make them more transparent and accountable) or refuse to change fundamentally flawed structures. There are strong parallels here with the division in green parties between realists and fundamentalists.

Further conflict arose between members of Die Grünen (who wanted to promote both environmental protection and traditional left-wing themes such as social justice and democratization) and other green parliamentarians (who wanted to focus first and foremost on environmental issues). Following the 1989 elections, these conflicts intensified with the election of delegates from countries such as France and Italy who were able to challenge the dominance of the German representatives. There were also serious divisions among the latter over how they should implement forms of **direct democracy** and the question of the professionalization of politics.

As a result of these conflicts, the Green-Alternative European Link was dissolved, and in July 1989 a new association called the Green Group, supported by 29 green parliamentarians, emerged in the European Parliament. This group focused much more on environmental policy than on attempts to promote both environmentalism and a left-wing agenda. In the period following the **United Nations Conference on Environment and Development (UNCED)** and the coming into force of the Maastricht Treaty establishing the EU in 1993, efforts to establish a common program for the green parties in Europe intensified. The **European Federation of Green Parties** was formed in 1993 and the **European Green Party** a decade later.

While some national green parties remain opposed to all or parts of the European experiment, including the euro and the European Constitution, for many their focus is on how to "green" the agenda and workings of the EU. The focus is on such values as grassroots democracy, sustainability, environmental protection, citizen rights, and gender equality. In February 2005, at an extraordinary Council Meeting of the European Green Party, a majority of 51 representatives supported the EU Constitution. The seven votes against it came from Miljöpartiet de Gröna (Sweden), De Grønne (Denmark), Miljøpartiet De Grønne (**Norway**), and the Ecologist Greens (**Greece**). The reason for their support of the European Constitution was that it would provide greater transparency and that the EU could play a positive role in reaching the party's goals of social justice, ecologically **sustainable development**, peace, and European democracy.

The European Green Party-European Free Alliance's campaigns within the Parliament address such issues as stopping **climate change** through policies to address airline emissions, energy strategy, biomass and biofuels, and car pollution; food culture (greening trade, anti–genetically modified organisms); chemicals (promoting a toxic-free world), and preservation of the European social model. *See also* EUROPEAN FEDERATION OF GREEN PARTIES-EUROPEAN FREE ALLIANCE.

EXXON VALDEZ. The running aground of the oil tanker *Exxon Valdez* in March 1989 was one of the darkest moments in the succession of disasters of this kind. The responses of traditional political organizations to the related concerns brought up by the green movement have varied immensely. In some instances, there has been a huge effort by governments to shift public opinion in support of new, radical measures to prevent such potential catastrophes. In others, changes have been slow despite the obviousness of the problem. As early as 1922 the International Committee for Bird Protection (later named International Council for Bird Preservation) was worried about oil pollution of the oceans. Oil pollution increased in the 1960s, and incidents such as the *Torrey Canyon* spill in 1967 received worldwide publicity.

Despite efforts to regulate the oil industry, there has been a string of disasters. On 24 March 1989 more than 10 million gallons of crude oil spilled into Prince William Sound, Alaska, from the *Exxon Valdez*. For over two decades scientists, environmentalists, and local citizens had warned of the dangers of such an accident in Prince William Sound.

– F –

FAIR TRADE MOVEMENT. The fair trade movement is a reaction to the injustices that have accompanied the globalization of capital and trade. In an effort to promote both the economic well-being of small-scale farmers and artisans in developing countries and the use of organic and sustainable agricultural methods, a fair trade movement that includes many greens among it, has been gaining in strength since the 1980s. Fair trade works to cut out the middleman and return a greater share of profits from sales to the producer. It is a nonmarket mechanism for promoting social justice, democracy, and environmental protection. It has as its overarching goal the creation of a fairer international trading system, and thus, also works to eliminate agricultural tariffs that have a tendency to keep out products from developing countries. There is now a fair trade certification process to aid consumers in their purchasing decisions. The best known fair trade product is coffee.

FEDERATION OF GREEN PARTIES OF AFRICA. Green parties began to form in Africa as the continent began to democratize. They found it difficult to influence national politics on their own, however, and thus, in 1994 green parties from nine countries in West Africa and **Central Africa** met in **Nigeria** where they formed the African Greens Committee. In May 1998, they decided to strengthen the organization by forming the Federation of Green Parties of Africa at a meeting held in Nairobi, **Kenya**. The member parties include Les Verts du Benin (**Benin**), Rassemblement Des Ecologistes du Burkina Faso (Burkina Faso), Defense de l'Environmen Camerounais (Cameroon), Parti des Ecologistes Guinees (Guinea), Liga Guineese de Protocçao Ecologica, (Guinea-Bissau), Parti Pour la Protection de l'Environnement (Côte d'Ivoire), Mazingira Green Party (Kenya), Parti Ecologist du Mali, Movement République-The Green Way (Mauritius), Les Verts (Morocco), Rassemblement pour un Sahel Vert (Niger), Green Party of Nigeria, Les Verts (Senegal), Somalia Green Party, and Green Party of **South Africa**.

FEDERATION OF GREEN PARTIES OF THE AMERICAS. Established in 1997 with its headquarters in Mexico City, the Federation of Green Parties of the Americas has as its goal strengthening the cooperation among the green parties and movements of the region in addressing environmental, human rights, social justice, and peace. Member parties come from **Brazil**, **Canada**, Chile, Colombia, Dominican Republic, **Mexico**, Nicaragua, Peru, Uruguay, **United States**, and Venezuela.

FEDERATION OF YOUNG EUROPEAN GREENS. Formed in 1988 in Belgium, the Federation of Young European Greens brings together youth wings of Green parties and nongovernmental youth organizations from across Europe. With 33 member organizations as of 2006, the federation has been provided an office in the **European Parliament** by the **European Green Party**.

FINLAND. Throughout the 1980s, green groups contested elections without attaching themselves to a formally constituted green party. In February 1987 the Green League was formed, though this subsequently divided into two separate strands, Vihreät (the Greens) and

Vihreä Liitoo (the Green League). The main reasons for this division were the difficulties leading figures had in getting along with each other. There appeared to be little difference on policy issues between the two organizations. Vihreä Liitoo registered as a political party in 1988 and adopted a Green Manifesto in 1990.

In the mid-1970s green groups began to contest municipal elections in Helsinki and in the 1980 elections gained a seat on the council. At the 1983 national election, a green list of candidates was put forward and received 1.5 percent of the vote and two seats in Parliament. They improved on this in the 1987 national elections, with 4 percent of the vote and four seats. In 1991 Vihreä Liitoo secured 6.8 percent of the vote and 10 out of 200 seats. They achieved a similar result in 1995 (6.5 percent and nine seats). Following this, Vihreä Liitoo joined a coalition of five political parties and held the portfolio for the environment. The minister, Pekka Haavisto, was thus the first green parliamentarian ever to hold such a post in a national government. In the 1999 election, Vihreä Liitoo attracted 7.3 percent of the vote (11 seats) and in 2003, 8 percent (14 seats). The next elections are scheduled for 2007.

Since joining the European Union (EU) in 1995, Finland has consistently sent green delegates to the **European Parliament**. In 1995 the party obtained one of 16 seats allocated to Finland in the European Parliament (based on the results from the 1991 parliamentary elections) and in October 1996 was again allocated one seat, after attracting 7.6 percent of the vote. After both the 1999 and 2004 elections, Vihreä Liitoo was able to send two delegates to Strasbourg, the seat of the European Parliament.

Green political organizations originated from a variety of social movements in the late 1970s preoccupied with environmental issues, including the dangers of nuclear power. Among the major concerns was the preservation of Lake Koijärvi, a haven for many species of birds, which came under threat. Other issues that were important in the mobilization of support for green groups included the problem of sulfur emissions and **acid rain** and opposition to the development of more nuclear power plants and the wood pulp industry.

Vihreä Liitoo joined the European Green Coordination in 1989. The **European Federation of Green Parties** was formed in Finland in June 1993. Vihreä Liitoo supported the expansion of the EU to the east. They support European Tax Reform so that taxation of energy and raw materials are increased in order to be able to reduce the taxation of income and labor-related costs.

FOREMAN, DAVID. *See* EARTH FIRST!

FRANCE. The origins of the green movement in France are as diverse as those in many other countries. There is a strong tradition of nature conservation associations, and in the 1960s these groups became more politicized as they focused on issues such as the *Torrey Canyon* disaster (which affected the coast of Brittany) and government plans to develop Vanoise National Park for commercial gain. Further impetus was provided by the student uprisings of May 1968, which questioned traditional political parties and modes of political behavior. In the 1970s a strong **antinuclear protest** movement emerged as France became more dependent than almost any other country in the world on this form of energy. In 1977, at the height of these protests, a demonstrator was killed during a rally against the proposed site of a nuclear reactor at Creys-Malville.

One of the earliest attempts by green groups to compete in elections to the National Assembly occurred in 1973, when Écologie et Survie attracted 3.7 percent of the vote. However, in general, green groups fared worse in National Assembly elections than in presidential contests, attracting only 2.2 percent of the assembly vote in 1978 and 1.1 percent in 1982. Since the formation of Les Verts in 1984, the green's fortunes have improved somewhat. In 1993, Les Verts and Génération Écologie campaigned together and won 11 percent of the national vote. Les Verts received 3.6 percent of national votes cast in the 1997 National Assembly elections (seven seats) and 4.51 percent in 2002 (three seats). The party's image was tainted by the actions of some of its members. In 2005 after considerable criticism, the party expelled Ginette Skandrani who had participated in a holocaust-denial website.

At the local level, around 270,000 votes were cast for green groups in the 1977 elections, winning 30 seats on town councils. Due to changes in the electoral system, green groups gained 757 seats in town councils following the 1983 local elections, even though they attracted fewer votes (around 148,000) than in 1977. In 1989 green groups gained nearly twice as many votes as in 1983 and 1,369 seats on town councils. These elections were a significant breakthrough in the advance of green politics.

At the 1992 regional elections, following the 1990 formation of Génération Écologie, under the leadership of Brice Lalonde, as a competing party to Les Verts, both parties secured a similar proportion of the vote, 7.1 and 6.8 percent, respectively. Despite important differences in their organizational structure, compounded by the different styles of their leaders, Les Verts and Generation Écologie resolved to join forces in the 1993 elections to the legislative assembly and present a single candidate in each constituency. Though the greens secured a respectable 7.6 percent of the vote, they failed to obtain any seats in the national assembly. Thus, in addition to internal problems, they continued to have difficulty in overcoming the hurdles set by the electoral system. However, in the 1997 elections, they finally succeeded, gaining seven seats in the National Assembly.

Until 1984 green political groups were organized under two umbrella organizations, the Confederation Écologiste and Les Verts-Parti Écologiste. Other significant groups were the French section of **Friends of the Earth**, Réseau des Amis de la Terre, which was founded in 1970; a group called Écologie et Survie (Ecology and Survival), formed in March 1973 in Alsace; and the Mouvement Écologique, which like all the other groups was principally concerned about the expansion of the nuclear industry. The foundation of Les Verts in 1984 was an attempt to unify the diverse green groups. Les Verts is now the largest green party in France, but other green parties and groups persist (Génération Écologie, Mouvement Écologiste Indépendant, Citoyenneté Action Participation pour le XXIe siécle, CAP21).

In 1981 Brice Lalonde contested the presidential elections on a green platform and obtained 1,222,445 votes (3.9 percent). This was a significant improvement on the 337,800 votes (1.3 percent) for Réné Dumont who, as the representative of environmental groups, had contested the 1974 elections. In the 1988 elections Antoine Waechter gained 1,145,502 votes (3.8 percent). In 1994, the Greens broke with Waechter's policy of political nonalignment ("*ni droite, ni gauche*," "neither right, nor left"), shifting their policies notably to the left. Waechter left Les Verts and formed Mouvement Écologiste Indépendant (Movement of Independent Ecologists).

In 1995, Les Verts supported Dominique Voynet as a presidential candidate. She received 3.8 percent of the vote. In 1997, Voynet was invited to join the government of Lionel Jospin's Socialist Party and the Communist Party as Minister for the Environment and Regional Planning, a post which she held until 2001 when she resigned. She has since been designated Les Verts' presidential candidate for the 2007 election. In the 2002 presidential election, Noël Mamère won 5.2 percent of the vote.

In elections to the **European Parliament**, French green groups have had something of a roller coaster performance. They attracted 888,134 votes (4.7 percent) in 1979. Partly due to internal disputes, their share of the vote in the 1984 elections dropped to 3.4 percent (680,080 votes). By contrast, they performed well at the 1989 elections, with 10.6 percent of the vote. Les Verts became the largest group, with nine delegates, of all the green parties represented in the European Parliament. In the 1995 elections, however, the Union des Ecologistes and the Génération Écologie combined won only 2.95 percent of the vote and as a result had no members of Parliament. In the 1999 elections, in contrast, Les Verts attracted 9.7 percent of the vote (nine seats). The Mouvement Écologiste Indépendant attracted another 1.5 percent, bringing the total green vote to over 11 percent. In 2004, Les Verts dropped their number of seats to six after winning a smaller 8.43 percent of the vote. On the highly divisive issue of the European Union (EU) Constitution, Les Verts campaigned in favor of ratification.

Illustrating slowly changing perspectives on European citizenship, in the 1999 election for the European Parliament, the leader of the list for the party, Daniel Cohn-Bendit, was a noncitizen. Admittedly, he had been an active deputy in the European Parliament since 1994 but as a member of Die Grünen. Taking advantage of the European Parliament election laws that make it possible for a citizen of any member state to run for election to the European Parliament from anywhere in the EU, Cohn-Bendit ran as a noncitizen (albeit a well-known face in France since his days as a student leader of the protests that rocked the country in the late 1960s) at the top of Les Verts' list.

Support for Les Verts has come largely from young people and those employed in the academic sector, as well as from managers and white-collar employees who have acquired high levels of formal education. The structure of Les Verts is decentralized, and regional groups enjoy a high level of autonomy. As in many other green parties, members have shown distrust of leading personalities in the party, and several of these figures have had to make way for others.

Autonomy, solidarity, and **ecology** are key principles in the platform of Les Verts. They embrace the central green themes of the protection and preservation of "life" in the face of advanced industrial society's fundamental threats to the existence of human beings, plants, and animals. Les Verts have also presented an alternative economic program that explores the possibilities for work-sharing schemes in order to address the problem of unemployment, a **guaranteed minimum income**, and greater control of the economy by workers. There has also been an emphasis on cooperation with less developed countries and on peace and disarmament. Like other green parties, Les Verts has adopted **nonviolence** and civil disobedience as alternatives to conventional approaches to security.

By contrast, Generation Écologie adopted policies that could be regarded as antagonistic to Les Verts. Brice Lalonde supported the efforts of the West in the Gulf War. In addition, his group has given far less emphasis, at least initially, to participatory democracy. Many of the supporters of Generation Écologie came from the Socialist Party, and the tendency was to create an organization that resembled the dominant parties rather than one that articulated the style and objectives of new social movements.

The green parties have recently also begun to adopt a more pragmatic approach. Apart from an appreciation of the gains made by Génération Écologie, there has been a realization that the state of the environment, although not displacing the economy as the major preoccupation of voters, does concern most people and could be linked to dissatisfaction with the political system as a whole. *See also* DIRECT DEMOCRACY.

FRANKLIN DAM. In **Australia**, challenges to the institutional order by green groups rose in the late 1960s and had gained in intensity by the late 1970s, notably in the form of social movements such as the one opposed to the construction of the proposed Franklin Dam in Tasmania. The campaign against the Franklin Dam, waged between 1979 and 1983, is one of the most striking examples of a rise in popular awareness of environmental problems and of the tensions between central and regional governments. If the changes that occurred during the 1970s in the government's approach to environmental issues were meant to defuse conflicts, they were a failure. In 1983 environmental issues featured prominently in an Australian federal election for the first time.

The question of states' rights (that is, the rights of regional governments), which had preoccupied reformers for decades, now assumed a new significance. In the conflict over the proposed construction of a hydroelectric power system and the subsequent flooding of the Franklin and lower Gordon rivers, the Tasmanian government confronted environmentalists who pleaded for federal intervention and more central regulation of environmental policy. Though the Australian Labor Party (ALP) supported environmentalists against the Franklin Dam, it refused to address the issue of states' rights. In the 1983 federal election, the conservative (Liberal and National) parties stood for the individual state's right to set its own environmental policy. The Liberal government sought to avoid confrontation by offering the Tasmanian government US$500 million for the construction of a coal-fired thermal power plant instead of the dam. When this offer was refused, the ALP announced that it would oppose the construction of the dam if it were elected. The party offered help to the Tasmanian government to diversify the methods of electricity production and to expand the tourist industry in order to create employment. These policies were crucial in attracting green votes in the 1983 election.

Once elected, the ALP government offered the Tasmanian Liberal government alternative schemes for creating employment. The rejection of this offer led the federal government to use existing legislation to override states' rights. This decision has been interpreted as a major extension of the powers of the federal government. Still, the ALP government was reluctant to clash with state governments and finally came to an arrangement with the Tasmanian government, offering it compensation for money spent on the Franklin Dam project before it was halted, alternative employment programs, and subsidizing the supply of energy.

Though the ALP had sided with the green movement over the Franklin Dam, it was initially unable to respond to growing expectations of a more decisive environmental policy. It remained uncertain about taking sides between established interests, which favored development and the exploitation of states' resources, and the new green movements. Over time, the question of states' rights appeared to become less important than the long-term social and economic implications of environmental protection.

The pressure on governments to incorporate environmentalism became apparent during and after the dispute over the Franklin Dam. The expectations of green groups and their supporters exerted a decisive influence on ALP policies in the 1980s. Each new conflict over environmental policy appeared to increase both public awareness of environmental issues and the economic and political stakes.

The battle to protect the Franklin and Gordon rivers was significant for a number of other reasons. The Tasmanian **Wilderness Society**, later renamed the Wilderness Society, emerged from this campaign and provided a basis for getting the environment onto the national political agenda. The radicalism of the Wilderness Society epitomized the new generation of environmentalists, engaged in political activities. The campaign against the Franklin Dam also created new opportunities for coalitions between environmental groups. In a historic effort to coordinate and render more effective actions against the Franklin Dam, environmental groups formed a coalition that included the **Australian Conservation Foundation (ACF)**, state conservation councils, **national parks** associations, and 70 branches of the Wilderness Society. It rallied the support of around 800 conservation groups with up to half a million members. Environmentalists were successful in attracting media attention by inviting international figures such as David Bellamy to participate in their campaign. The arrest of 1,340 activists between January and March 1983 attracted widespread attention and accelerated the ascent of the green movement in Australia.

FREE THE PLANET! Developed from a student-led campaign that emerged in 1995 in opposition to the 104th U.S. Congress's "Contract with America," Free the Planet! has as its goal the expansion and strengthening of the student environmental movement. It has signed up several hundred high schools and colleges in Canada and the United States for clean energy on campuses.

FRIENDS OF THE EARTH. In 1969 **David Brower**, the executive director of the **Sierra Club** since 1952, parted company with this powerful organization and became the founder of Friends of the Earth. Although Brower had effectively been forced to leave the Sierra Club by members who felt that he was primarily responsible for some of its financial problems, he had been very popular, particularly because of his espousal of a more proactive stance in trying to change public policy. Brower was able to shape Friends of the Earth to attract the growing sections of the population that favored more direct forms of political action than those deployed by well-established environmental groups. Moreover, like the student and other protest movements of that era, Friends of the Earth sought a basis for support that transcended the boundaries of nation-states.

In keeping with the spirit of political involvement and participation by the grassroots, Friends of the Earth gave its established branches in other countries a high degree of autonomy in determining their campaign strategies and internal organization. Following the establishment of its first office in San Francisco, Friends of the Earth installed themselves in London and Paris in 1970 and subsequently in most Western democracies. In its 2004 annual report, Friends of the Earth International claimed to be the world's largest grassroots environmental network, linking an estimated 1.5 million members in 5,000 local activist groups in 71 countries.

Among the questions initially raised by Friends of the Earth were the protection of wildlife, prevention of pollution, and the development of **alternative energy** forms such as solar power. However, like many other green groups, they assumed many additional issues, such as green consumerism, protection of the **ozone layer**, promotion of green trade, global warming, and chemicals. Some of the leading figures in the green movement, such as Jonathon Porritt in England, have served as directors of national branches of Friends of the Earth. Apart from the extension of the Friends of the Earth into many other countries, in 1990, the organization coalesced with the

Environmental Policy Institute and the Oceanic Society. In 2005, it finalized a merger with Bluewater Network.

In the mid-2000s, Friends of the Earth campaigns included a wide range of environmental and social issues: **climate change**, desertification, Antarctica, **biodiversity**, trade, environment, **sustainability**, mining, and human rights.

– G –

GAIA HYPOTHESIS. The term *Gaia* is derived from the Greek word for Earth. The Oxford dictionary definition of Gaia refers to the Earth "as a self-regulating system in which living matter collectively defines and maintains the conditions for the continuance of life." The Gaia hypothesis has been promoted since the 1970s by James Lovelock, a British scientist who worked for the National Aeronautics and Space Administration on a project to discover whether or not there was life on Mars. Lovelock, in trying to establish the composition of the gases surrounding Mars, began to speculate about the process of maintaining life on Earth. In *Gaia: A New Look at Life on Earth*, Lovelock suggests that "life itself" shapes the composition of the Earth, the atmosphere, and the oceans and thereby challenges the customary view that "life adapted to the planetary conditions as it and they evolved their separate ways."

Lovelock acknowledges that his belief in the existence of a complex system that can act as a "single living entity" (Mother Earth) cannot be tested scientifically. Still, his argument, which has attracted considerable interest among some supporters of the green movement, is based on three crucial observations. First, for about 3.5 billion years and despite significant variations in the heat emitted from the sun, there has been very little change in the climate of the Earth. Second, the atmosphere appears to be not so much a biological product but a biological construction: "not living, but like a cat's fur, a bird's feathers, or the paper of a wasp's nest, an extension of a living system designed to maintain a chosen environment." Third, the atmosphere has appeared to have always been ideal for supporting life on Earth. This, he suggests, must be more than a highly improbable coincidence.

Lovelock therefore defines Gaia "as a complex entity involving the earth's biosphere, atmosphere, oceans, and soil; the totality constituting a feedback or cybernetic system which seeks an optional physical and chemical environment for life on this planet." The conclusion by many writers using the Gaia hypothesis is that nature will survive the onslaught on it by human beings. The question is whether or not human beings will withstand nature's response to their assault on it.

GEORGIA. Georgia's Green Party has had a difficult time since its formation in the early 1990s as it has been actively blocked from participation in various local elections. Nevertheless, it has been quite successful. Georgia was less industrialized than many other Soviet republics, but several of its cities, including Tbilisi, Kutaisi, and Rustavi, had some of the worst air pollution of any former Soviet territory. Georgia was also impacted heavily by the **Chernobyl** nuclear accident. The green movement and the Green Party in Georgia played a critical role in adding environmental concerns into the country's evolving democratic institutions. In 1991, the party won a seat in the Supreme Council of Abkhazian Autonomous Republic elections. After the Supreme Council collapsed at the national level in 1991, a State Council was formed, which included members of the Green Party in its Ecological Committee. In the November 1992 parliamentary elections, the Green Party succeeded in sending 11 representatives to Parliament. When in 1993 the Georgian environment minister resigned in protest that the government was ignoring environmental problems, the Green Party used its position in Parliament to pressure for changes. The following year, the Cabinet of Ministers created a new interdepartmental environmental monitoring program under the Ministry of the Environment.

The Green Party was from 1995–1999 part of the Citizens' Union coalition that won the election in 1995 and remained the governing coalition until 2003. It won two seats in Parliament and a representative of the party was appointed as chairman of the parliament committee for environment and natural resource protection.

In 1995, the Georgian Constitution was amended. Article 37 now guarantees Georgians the right to a healthy environment, obliges the state to protect nature for this and future generations, and requires the state to provide timely information on their living and work environment. Beyond this, the Green Party influenced the development of environmental legislation, including the prohibition of nuclear waste transport or the building of nuclear power plants.

Free and fair elections are still an issue in Georgia, however. In the 1996 Adjarian Autonomous Republic, the local Supreme Council, blocked the Green Party from running in the election until the Green Party succeeded in challenging this decision. The party, however, did not win any seats in the election.

In the 1998 local elections, the Greens ran independently. They fielded 3,000 candidates in 205 districts, and had 60 victories in 29 of those districts. In the 1999 parliamentary elections, the party ran independently. The party claims that as a result of irregularities in the election, the party failed to win any seats. It sued the government in Strasbourg over the election. In the 2002 local elections, the Green Party won 0.35 percent, but argued that the results had been rigged. Along with several other parties, they successfully challenged the results in court, resulting in a cancellation of the results. On a recount of the votes, however, the party's fortune did not improve.

Finally, while the party did well in the 2003 elections as part of a nine-party coalition under Eduard Shevardnadze that received over 20 percent of the vote, the elections were annulled due to the Rose revolution. The elections were denounced as having been grossly rigged in favor of Eduard Shevardnadze. The main democratic opposition parties demanded Shevardnadze's ouster. There were massive street demonstrations against Shevardnadze as well as those organized by Shevardnadze in his support. When Parliament nevertheless opened, opposition party representatives with roses in their hands seized the Parliament. A crisis ensued, and eventually Shevardnadze was forced to step down. The Supreme Court of Georgia annulled the election results.

The Green Party has since spoken out against constitutional changes that have weakened the power of Parliament and strengthened the role of the presidency, arguing that this is a weakening of democracy.

GERMANY. As in other western European nations, the predominance of economic development after World War II led to little emphasis on environmental protection as a core component of the national policy agenda. In the Federal Republic of Germany, the only hint of a change in focus came from the leader of the opposition Social Democratic Party, Willy Brandt. In a 1961 speech Brandt proclaimed the necessity for turning the sky over the Ruhr River blue again. Pollution in the German Democratic Republic was even worse.

It was not until the late 1960s, and then in West but not East Germany, that this exclusive attentiveness to economic development began to weaken. The formation of a coalition government between the Social Democratic and the Free Democratic (Liberal) Parties in 1969 was followed by the transfer of control over measures to combat pollution from the Ministry of Health to the Ministry of the Interior, which was eventually, in 1986, named the Ministry of the Environment, Nature Conservation, and Nuclear Safety.

Historically, however, the powers to legislate, manage, and regulate the environment have been vested in the states. There is also an enduring tradition in Germany of a legal basis for the protection of the environment. A key change to the involvement of the states in regulating environmental protection occurred in 1972 in the form of an amendment to the Constitution. This conferred on the federal government the power to enact legislation that, in effect, overrode the states in areas such as air and noise pollution and waste management. In addition, the federal government was able to issue guidelines on the enactment of state legislation on matters such as water quality and planning as well as the preservation and conservation of nature. Another significant action was the formation of the 1974 Federal Environmental Agency.

Despite these important changes, spurred on by key figures in both parties of the coalition, the predominance of economic considerations in policy making and the decision to expand massively the system of nuclear power plants brought a powerful counterresponse. This came in the form of **citizens' initiatives** for environmental protection, **antinuclear protests**, and the formation of a green political organization, Die Grünen.

In many ways, Die Grünen can be considered the mother of all green parties. While not the first green party to form or to win representation, the impact of Die Grünen has extended far beyond the German political landscape. Many green parties from around the world looked to Die Grünen for inspiration. Founded in January 1980 following widespread support for social movements opposed to the development of nuclear power and green groups contesting local and state elections, Die Grünen (The Greens) became the most celebrated manifestation of the upsurge of the green movement in Germany. Its formation as a political party was anything but a smooth process. At the preliminary meeting in Offenbach in October 1979 divisions emerged over issues such as dual membership in Die Grünen and other political parties, the focus on grassroots citizens' initiatives, electoral politics, and whether to adopt a conservative or socialist agenda. Prior to the formation of Die Grünen as a federal party, a coalition of green groups, Sonstige Politische Vereinigung: Die Grünen (Alternative Political Association: The Greens), had polled 3.2 percent in elections to the European Parliament (June 1979), and a green group in Bremen, Bunte Liste (Multicolored List), had for the first time secured seats in a state parliament (four seats and 5.1 percent of the vote).

Among the most influential people in the early stages of the formation of Die Grünen were Herbert Gruhl, a former Christian Democrat and member of Parliament (MP); **Petra Kelly**, who had been active in protests against the Vietnam War in the **United States**; Rudi Dutschke, a leading radical intellectual in the West German student revolt in the 1960s; and **Rudolf Bahro**, a dissident intellectual who had been expelled from East Germany.

Die Grünen's performance in federal elections improved progressively in the 1980s, from a shaky start in the 1980 elections (1.5 percent) to 5.6 percent of the vote and 27 seats in 1983 and 8.3 percent of the vote and 42 seats in 1987. Their success was bolstered by the increasing concern over **acid rain**, the destruction of forests, and the quality of air and water. By the mid-1980s, following a sequence of successes in regional and national elections, traditional (conservative, liberal, and socialist) political organizations, trade unions, and business groups realized that a fundamental shift in values and priorities had occurred. Even if economic considerations were still predominant, the environment was now widely regarded as a crucial issue in political deliberations. Following the Chernobyl nuclear accident, Germany created a Ministry for Environment, and Nature Conservation Nuclear Safety.

Die Grünen suffered a reversal of fortune in 1990 when it polled only 4.8 percent of the vote, thereby failing to gain any seats in Parliament because of the 5 percent electoral hurdle that applies in the Federal Republic of Germany. The principal reasons for their setback in 1990 were the failure to appreciate the significance of German unification to the electorate and the willingness of the major parties to incorporate many green issues in their programs. For a while Die Grünen was represented in Parliament only by Bündnis 90 (Alliance 90), that had been formed in East Germany. Bündnis 90 represented a coalition of citizens' initiatives concerned about environmental issues as well as the restoration of democracy.

Special rules had been introduced for the 1990 electoral contest, whereby the 5 percent electoral hurdle was applied separately in the eastern and western parts of Germany. Bündnis 90 polled 5.9 percent of the vote in East Germany and thus gained eight seats in Parliament. Moreover, the West German greens soon began to reassert themselves in numerous state elections. Die Grünen, in coalition with Bündnis 90, also performed very well in the 1994 federal elections, attracting 7.3 percent of the vote and 49 seats. Its success was doubly significant. It displaced the Free Democrats (who gained 47 seats) as the third-largest party and made an unprecedented recovery. No other party in the Federal Republic of Germany had previously succeeded in overcoming its complete exclusion from Parliament (following an electoral defeat) and regaining representation.

In elections in 1984 to the **European Parliament**, Die Grünen secured 8.2 percent of the vote and seven seats. In 1989 a "Rainbow Coalition" of greens gained 8.4 percent of the vote and eight seats.

At the state level, Die Grünen has attracted enough votes to secure continuous representation in most parliaments. Its share of the vote rose consistently in large states such as Baden-Württemberg, North Rhine Westphalia, and Rhineland-Palatinate and in city-states such as Berlin and Bremen throughout much of the 1990s. In 1996 the party held seats in all the state parliaments of western Germany and in Saxony-Anhalt in eastern Germany. Apart from regularly dislodging the Free Democrats as the third-largest party, Die Grünen was a member of a coalition government with the Social Democratic Party (as the senior partner), in Hessen between 1985 and 1987 and again from 1991–1999, in Berlin from 1989–1990 and again from

1999–2001, in Lower Saxony from 1994–1998, in Saxony-Anhalt from 1994–1998, in Hamburg from 1997–2001, in Schleswig-Holstein from 1996–2005, and in North Rhine Westphalia from 1995–2005. In September 1991, following the state election in Bremen, a coalition was formed between the Social Democrats, the Free Democratic Party, and Die Grünen. In a sharp reversal of fortunes for Die Grünen at the state level in the 2000s, their share of the vote dropped in many states. At the time of the federal elections in 2005, there were no longer any states where Die Grünen were in a coalition. As a result, Die Grünen began to take more seriously the possibility of forming coalitions with parties other than the Social Democrats. A step in this direction was taken in 2006 when Die Grünen accepted an invitation to join the Christian Democrats in a coalition in Frankfurt.

This was not the first time Die Grünen and the Christian Democrats toyed with closer cooperation. Support from the Christian Democrats resulted, for instance, in the November 1994 election of Antje Vollmer, a leading figure in Die Grünen, to the position of deputy parliamentary speaker. The Christian Democrats also became eager to involve members of Die Grünen in parliamentary committees. Black-Green coalitions formed in several urban areas, including Muelheim/Ruhr, Saarbrücken, and Cologne. These changes flowed from the increasingly precarious position of the Free Democrats, who had served as coalition partners for over a decade, and the growing influence of the "realists" or "Realos" with their more practical and compromising orientation rather than the "fundamentalists" or "Fundis" within Die Grünen.

The Christian Democrats also became more serious about environmental issues, such as with their support for the 1997 **Kyoto Protocol**. The current German chancellor, Angela Merkel, was environment minister under Helmut Kohl. In her role as president of the European Council in the first half of 2007, she has taken an aggressive stance on climate change.

Die Grünen's attraction was tied in part to its progressively broadened focus to include a wide range of economic and social issues. It cannot therefore be labeled a "one-issue" party; there were a cluster of issues that served to differentiate it from the other parties and mobilize electoral support. Apart from environmental issues, which have to some degree been adopted by the other parties, Die Grünen took the lead in opposing the use of military force in foreign policy, criticizing patronage and corruption in politics, advancing women's rights, and advocating a looser confederal structure for the European Union (EU). The issues of political reform, rendering decision-making processes more transparent, and combating the problems arising from the concentration of power have both benefited and harmed Die Grünen. Many voters have appreciated the party's efforts to uncover shortcomings in the political system; to practice grassroots or **direct democracy**, for example, to rotate office holders; and to reduce the privileges enjoyed by parliamentarians.

Some of these issues also reflect deep divisions within the party over whether to adopt some of the organizational practices of traditional political parties. Initially, the main ideological division within Die Grünen tended to be between conservative "pure" environmentalists and those who sought to link **ecology** with left-wing politics. Although the latter won out, a new division emerged, namely, between the fundamentalists, who did not wish to make compromises with established organizations as regards specific policies (such as the development of nuclear power) or with respect to sharing power (for instance, in a coalition government), and the realists, who adopted a more pragmatic approach to parliamentary politics. The conflict between the fundamentalists and realists has often been blamed for preventing the development of Die Grünen as a major political force.

Although Bündnis 90/ Die Grünen polled less well in 1998 (6.7 percent) than it did in 1994 (7.3 percent), the Socialist Party invited the Greens to form a Red-Green coalition with them. Gerhard Schroeder of the Social Democratic Party became chancellor, and Joschka Fischer, a central figure in the party, became foreign minister. Two other ministerial posts went to Bündnis 90/ Die Grünen: Consumer Protection, Food, and Agriculture (Renate Künast) and Environment (Jürgin Tritten). The Greens used their position in the coalition to push through ecological tax reform (reducing the tax burden on workers), while increasing its energy consumption (which was also intended to reduce energy consumption), a nuclear phaseout plan, and active promotion of renewable energies through special feed-in tariffs. Unlike some other green parties, Bündnis 90/Die

Grünen was a stronger supporter of the EU. Their decision to support German involvement in NATO operations in Bosnia proved a major break with the party's past position, and angered many Fundis. The Red-Green coalition remained in tact after the 2002 elections when the Green Party won 8.6 percent of the vote. The coalition dissolved after the 2005 election that brought Angela Merkel into the position of chancellor. This was due to the Socialist Party's poor showing, rather than that of Bündnis 90/ Die Grünen, which polled 8.19 percent of the vote and 51 members of Parliament. After the 2004 European Parliament election, the Greens won the right to send 13 delegates to Strasbourg.

Following the setback in the 1990 federal elections, the realists, who in the 1980s had already entered coalitions with the Social Democrats in states such as Hesse, began to gain the upper hand and remove some of the restrictions placed by the fundamentalists upon tenure of office and styles of political negotiation adopted by parliamentary delegates. Above all, the realists have been more successful than the fundamentalists in attracting support at the ballot box. This trend was reinforced by the coalition with Bündnis 90, which also espoused a pragmatic approach to parliamentary politics and for a time, between 1990 and 1994, was the only green party in the federal parliament.

It is important to emphasize that the focus on coalitions with other parties and a more professional approach to parliamentary politics (including a greater emphasis on achieving coherence and unity at the level of the party elite) does not mean that Die Grünen has abandoned some of its basic long-term goals that continue to set it apart from the major parties.

Apart from the importance of the federal structure, environmental policy making in the Federal Republic of Germany has been shaped by a tradition of formal cooperation between government and influential interest groups, notably industrial organizations. There is also an enduring and successful practice of informal cooperation among the government, the opposition, and bureaucracy. In the 1970s and early 1980s both the informal approach to cooperation and the formal corporatist system appeared to be working against the inclusion of new political movements. In response to pressure by the green movement and widespread skepticism about the appropriateness of the prevailing approaches to environmental questions, the federal government, led by the Christian Democrats, began to play a more active role than any previous government in considering the possibility of including Die Grünen in the informal processes of deliberation over policy and promoting environmental protection at a national and international level. At the national level, the government made some advances in improving the quality of air and water, even though there is still a great deal to be accomplished in these and other spheres, such as reversing the deterioration of forests.

In 1994 the Constitution of the Federal Republic was amended to include a specific commitment to protect "the natural foundations of life for future generations." The government also played a leading role in international fora, notably at the 1992 **United Nations Conference on Environment and Development (UNCED)**, in applying pressure on other countries to follow its lead in requiring a total ban of **chlorofluorocarbons (CFCs)** and pushing other members of the EU to implement commonly agreed-upon directives on environmental policy.

The federal government has also had to deal with new challenges, notably those arising from the unification of Germany and the environmental problems associated with East Germany. Although the Constitution of the (former) German Democratic Republic did include a clause on the protection of nature and plans for preventing pollution, no regulations were implemented. The most acute problems were the contamination of land and water caused by uranium mining over several decades, the decline in air quality largely due to the use of brown coal in power plants, and the safety of nuclear reactors.

The federal government has taken on these assignments by introducing to the former East Germany its own structures for environmental protection and establishing a specific time frame for achieving its objectives. This has led to a huge loss in employment in the east. Apart from subsidies based on higher taxes on citizens in the west, the federal government has funded numerous projects (and thereby created new jobs) to solve environmental problems. In addition, there were rapid moves to close down nuclear power plants in the east.

The government of the Federal Republic has also attempted to raise a considerable amount of revenue specifically to address environmental problems and has been among the leaders in introducing a carbon tax on those who contribute to carbon dioxide emissions. Although, as in most other countries, its focus is still very much on economic growth and production, the Federal Republic has begun to develop long-term strategies and apply the precautionary principle in dealing with concerns about the environment. There has been a shift toward more dialogue, a better-informed public, and the introduction of improved procedures for handling environmental issues. The government has also begun to play a more innovative and strategic role in environmental policy and promote international cooperation. *See also* NUCLEAR ENERGY.

GLOBAL 2000 REPORT, THE. *The Global 2000 Report* summarizes the findings of an investigation by the U.S. Council on Environmental Quality. The report was commissioned by the government and first published in 1980. It contains a critique of previous accounts of the current and future condition of the environment and its own analysis of trends. Like many of the critiques of *The Limits to Growth* thesis, the study questions prevailing presuppositions about political and social values as well as the availability of mineral reserves and fossil fuels. In particular, *The Global 2000 Report* points out that *The Limits to Growth* failed to produce accurate analyses of problems in particular regions and did not recognize that the type of economic growth that occurs can hugely influence the rate of depletion of natural resources.

In the same vein as *The Limits to Growth* and other reports, *The Global 2000 Report* draws attention to the many possibilities for disaster if prevailing trends are not addressed through cooperation between nation-states. In particular, the report points to the links between **population growth**, the state of the environment, and the depletion of natural resources. The report also gave a number of specific predictions for the year 2000: namely, an increase in the frequency of natural disasters caused by human interventions; the destruction of tropical rainforests, which would lead to the extinction of hundreds of thousands of plant and animal species; a 50 percent increase in the population of the world, with most of the growth taking place in poorer countries; an increase in the gap between rich and poor; and the diminution of resources such as land, water, and oil.

The Council on Environmental Quality published a further report, *Global Future: Time to Act*. This report outlines measures such as investment in renewable sources of energy and sustainable land use that could be implemented to address these problems. There is also an emphasis on improved coordination between government agencies as well as the establishment of new structures.

GLOBAL BIODIVERSITY HOTSPOTS. In an effort to draw public and policymakers' attention to the need to conserve the most biologically rich places on the planet, Norman Myers developed the concept of **biodiversity** hotspots, areas that are among the most biologically rich in the world but have already lost 70 percent of their original biodiversity. Expanding on Myers' works, **Conservation International** has designated a list of 34 regions worldwide where three-quarters of the world's most threatened mammals, amphibians, and bird are found. The **World Wide Fund for Nature (WWF)** has also created a separate conservation plan called Global 200. Global 200 identifies regions with exceptional biological diversity or unusual ecological or evolutionary life. WWF seeks to ensure that all distinctive ecosystems are represented in the list.

GLOBAL ENVIRONMENT FACILITY (GEF). The GEF was set up in 1991 to help developing countries fund projects and programs that protect the global environment. GEF projects are primarily managed by the **United Nations Environment Programme (UNEP),** the United Nations Development Programme (UNDP), and the World Bank. GEF grants support projects related to **biodiversity, climate change**, international waters, land degradation, the **ozone layer**, and persistent organic pollutants.

GLOBAL GREENS. Founded in 2001 in Canberra, Australia, Global Greens is the international network of green parties and movements. It has its roots in the First Planetary Meeting of Greens held at the **United Nations Conference on Environment and Development (UNCED)** and hosted by the Brazilian Green Party (Partido Verde). At the UNCED, a Global Green Steering Committee was formed; their first meeting was in January 1993 in Mexico City where they formed a Global Green Network. In the following years, there were sporadic efforts to turn this network into more than a name, through the publication of a Global Green Calendar, Global Green Bulletin, and Global Green Directory. In 1999, there was a renewed push for global green networking that led to the Oaxaca Declaration, which called for the formation of a Global Green Network of Green Parties to take "coordinated action on matters of common global concern."

GLOBAL WARMING. *See* CLIMATE CHANGE; GREENHOUSE EFFECT.

GLOBE INTERNATIONAL, GLOBAL LEGISLATORS' ORGANISATION FOR A BALANCED ENVIRONMENT. GLOBE International was formed in 1989 as an interparliamentary consultative group between the U.S. Congress and the **European Parliament** to exchange information and coordinate policy action on pressing environmental matters. By 2000, the group had expanded to include 700 legislators from around the world and established affiliate offices in Tokyo, Brussels, Cape Town, Moscow, and Washington, D.C.

GOLDMAN ENVIRONMENTAL PRIZE. Established in 1990 by Richard and Rhoda Goldman, it is the largest prize awarded to grassroots environmental activists. There are typically between six and eight awardees per year from around the world. One of the six recipients in 2006 was Yu Xiaogang. Yu was recognized for his successful efforts to promote watershed management along Lashi Lake that involved not only local authorities but also nongovernmental organizations (NGOs), and residents in the **People's Republic of China** for the first time. He was also recognized for his work educating local residents and government officials of the potentially harmful environmental and socioeconomic implications of a series of 13 dams that were planned to be built along the Three Parallel Rivers—the Nu, the Jinsha (Yangtze), and the Lancang (Mekong). As a result of his efforts, Premier Wen Jiao Bao put a temporary halt on the construction of the dams, which would have forever altered a United Nations World Heritage Site.

GOLDSMITH, EDWARD. *See BLUEPRINT FOR SURVIVAL, A*; DEINDUSTRIALIZATION.

GRASSROOTS DEMOCRACY. *See* DIRECT DEMOCRACY.

GREAT BRITAIN. One of the most striking features about the green movement in Great Britain is the inverse relationship between the strength of green political organizations and the degree of access afforded by the bureaucracy to environmental groups. The failure of the Green Party to win representation has often been attributed to the restrictive electoral system. At the same time, the administration has been open to ideas of environmental groups ever since the 1960s, and especially following the debate about *The Limits to Growth*, about the threats posed to the environment by pollution, and the expansion of the nuclear power industry.

British politics were dominated from 1979 until 1997 by Conservative governments. The preoccupation of the Conservative government with reducing the role of the state meant that there was initially little concentration on addressing environmental problems. Rather, the focus was on removing impediments to the operation of a free market. This resulted in a partial reduction in influence and access by environmental groups to government agencies. Although environmental groups did not sever their links with established institutions, they were, to an extent, forced to adopt a more militant approach and began to appeal directly to the public for support. They were able to exert influence, especially in public inquiries, in the system of parliamentary select committees (established in 1979) and through local authorities.

In 1979 the Liberal Party appeared to be the only one of the major parties to take environmental issues seriously and was certainly the only one to express strong doubts about the desirability of economic growth. By the mid-1980s, Great Britain, under the Conservative government led by Margaret Thatcher, had been labeled by many commentators as the "dirty man of Europe," partly because of its reluctance to implement directives by the European Union (EU) on environmental protection and partly because of the resolution shown by the government to promote economic development regardless of the social and environmental costs. The Conservative government came under pressure from its own ranks on issues such as the protection of rural land (the Green Belt), implementation of the Wildlife and Countryside Act, and **acid rain** and from a Royal

Commission on Environmental Pollution for being unresponsive to urgent problems and not coordinating work by different government agencies.

Additionally, the government was becoming aware of the drift of public concern about the environment and in 1984 introduced reforms in a number of areas, including greater coordination of the activities of government agencies to combat pollution, and statutory intervention to discourage certain farming practices and encourage preservation of the rural landscape. In 1985 the government came under further pressure, on this occasion from the Labour and Social Democratic Parties, which produced detailed policy statements on environmental protection. However, it was only after their third successive electoral victory, in 1987, that the Conservatives began to consider the environment a key issue on the political agenda. On 27 September 1988, in a speech delivered to the Royal Society, Margaret Thatcher used the growing concern about problems such as greenhouse gas emissions, the depletion of the **ozone layer**, and acid rain to place the environment high on the national political agenda for the first time.

Within the Conservative Party, the tide was also turning against certain aspects of its prodevelopment policies, particularly facilitating the decline of the influence of local authorities over planning and the aggressive approach to the development of land for housing. The environment minister, Nicholas Ridley, came under intense pressure for promoting free market policies in this area. Rather than concede to the environmentalists, he espoused the importance of market mechanisms in addressing environmental problems, notably the **polluter pays principle** and the need for **sustainable development**. Nonetheless, he was replaced by Chris Patten, who was far more interested in the preservation of the landscape, enforcing government controls over planning of the landscape, and engaging in dialogue with environmental groups.

Although there was a strong reaction among some Conservatives against softening the government's approach to economic development, in 1990 Patten directed the production of a White Paper entitled "This Common Inheritance." Though it contained few specific policy commitments, the document attempted to reinforce the new prominence given to environmental protection and to outline principles for action, including the precautionary principle, the notion of stewardship, sustainable development, and the value of both statutory intervention and market mechanisms.

Although the environment still did not feature as a key issue in electoral politics, at the level of government administration the influence of environmental groups and of scientific experts was on the rise. Among the major reforms was the creation in 1987 of Her Majesty's Inspectorate of Pollution to coordinate the inspection of pollution. At first the inspectorate had few effective powers. However, the introduction of the Environmental Protection Act in 1990 provided the inspectorate with the necessary legal basis for fulfilling some of its potential as a pivotal agency in regulating industry.

The ousting of the Conservative Party by the Labour Party in 1997 heightened the place of environmental issues on the policy agenda. Prime Minister Tony Blair promised to prioritize sustainability policies and in 2000 created the U.K. Sustainable Development Commission. The green movement has successfully placed pressure on Blair's government to take **climate change** and sustainable development seriously. After the **United States** pulled out of the **Kyoto Protocol** in 2001, the British government joined other European governments in condemning the U.S. action. Blair has made climate change one of his government's top priorities. This is seen by some as an effort by his administration to distance itself from the image of being too closely tied to the George W. Bush administration and by others, as an effort to create a legacy. Great Britain and **Germany** are the two countries in Europe that have managed to substantially reduce their greenhouse gas levels relative to 1990 levels. In March 2007, Blair's government introduced a bill that would require Great Britain to reduce its greenhouse gas emissions by 60 percent of 1990 levels by 2050. With this initiative, Great Britain is vying with Germany for leadership on climate change matters internationally.

Much as is the case in the United States, the green movement in Great Britain has had only limited success in forming a Green Party. Influenced by the debates about *The Limits to Growth* and by publications such as *A Blueprint for Survival* as well as by predictions of impending doom by writers such as **Paul Ehrlich**, a small group founded a party called People in 1973. In 1975 it became known as the **Ecology** Party. At the two 1974 general elections, the party called

People presented five and four candidates, respectively. Until 1979, there was little emphasis on electoral activity. In a further attempt to improve on poor electoral results, it was renamed the Green Party in 1985.

A cornerstone of People was the use of decentralization as a means for addressing the concerns found in *The Limits to Growth*. Among the issues that emerged in the late 1970s was the development of nuclear power, which became the focus for the Windscale Enquiry into the development of facilities to process nuclear waste, and the deployment of nuclear weapons, such as in the "dual track" decision by the North Atlantic Treaty Organization (NATO) in 1979 and the decision by the British government to acquire the Trident nuclear submarine as part of its own strategy for deterrence.

People's founding platform included an emphasis on a sustainable society based on stable **population growth**, a minimum of interference in ecological processes, and more efficient use of energy with a focus on conservation of resources. Although population is no longer a major theme, the Green Party continues to call for a greening of the economy; clean green energy; safe foods; and peace, justice, and security.

A pivotal concept in both its energy policy and various other policies, including assistance to less developed countries, has been the notion of self-reliance. The 1987 manifesto of the Green Party advocated the creation of a "steady-state, sustainable economy." Employment policy would focus on job sharing, and there would be general measures such as a **guaranteed minimum income**. There would be a much greater emphasis on the informal sector and small communities and networks. Underlying much of this is the concept of decentralization of government and the economy. In the 2000s, the manifesto of the party is "Real Progress" and the creation of a world that is just, fair, safe, and healthy.

The simple plurality electoral system in Great Britain, often referred to as a first-past-the-post system, makes it difficult for minor parties to gain any representation since the candidate with the most votes in a particular constituency is automatically elected, and there is no means for minor parties to have any representation in the Parliament unless they can secure a majority of votes in that electorate. The system does not allow for any element of proportional representation. However, at the 1979 general election, the Ecology Party presented 53 candidates in order to boost its public profile and take advantage of the access to national television that was permitted to parties contesting at least 50 seats. The party attracted on average only 1.5 percent of the vote for the 53 seats; however, it did gain national recognition as a result of the campaign. In the 1983 general elections the party attracted on average only 1 percent of the vote for 108 seats.

The disappointing performance was attributed to the emergence of another new party, the Liberal/Social Democratic Party Alliance. The alliance attracted many people who were disillusioned with the major parties. Even with a change in its name, the Green Party was not able to garner more than a small percentage of the vote. In the 1987 elections the Green Party received on average only 1.4 percent of the vote. In 1990, there was an amicable split of the Green Party into the Green Party of England and Wales, the Scottish Green Party, and the Green Party in Northern Ireland.

In the 1992 election Cynog Dafis, a candidate for both the Welsh nationalist organization Plaid Cymru and the Green Party in the Welsh constituency of Caredigium Gogledd Penfro, became the first ever green member of the Westminster Parliament. The Green Party of England and Wales has made some inroads in local elections. In the 2004 local elections it won 70 local council seats.

In 1989, the party profited from the prominence of issues such as the **greenhouse effect** and the depletion of the **ozone layer**, as well as from disillusionment with the dominant parties, notably the Conservatives, to win about 15 percent of the vote in elections to the **European Parliament**. As in many of these elections, the turnout was low (36 percent). Moreover, because of the first-past-the-post electoral system in place at the time, the party did not win any seats. The party did not fare as well during much of the 1990s, as it was rocked by internal divisions and other parties began to green their own platforms. A look at the membership of the party over time represents this well. In 1979 the Ecology Party had only 650 members. By 1981 membership had grown to around 6,000, mainly as a result of a deliberate strategy to raise the party's electoral profile and partly because of widespread concern about the development of nuclear power and weapons that began around 1979. Membership of the Green Party pinnacled around 20,000 in 1990, but dropped to 6,500 in 1992 and 4,500 in 1993. The anti–Iraq War status of the party may have helped revive its membership somewhat. In 2004, membership had risen to approximately 6,300.

The introduction of proportional voting for Great Britain in European parliamentary elections in 1999 may make it easier for the party to increase its visibility in the future. The Green Party won its first seat in the European Parliament in 1999. As of May 2006, there are two European Parliament members from the Green Party: Jean Lambert, who is the vice president of the Green/EFA Group in the European Parliament and Caroline Lucas, the Green Party's principal speaker. The Green Party also has two representatives in the London Assembly and one Green Party peer, Lord Tim Baeumont.

Jonathon Porritt is one of the most well-known members of the Green Party. In the 1979 European elections, he gained 4.1 percent of the vote in London Central, and was one of the few figures in the Green Party to attract attention from the national media. He cochaired the Green Party from 1980 to 1983; still a member of the Green Party, he was appointed as chairman of the U.K. Sustainable Development Commission in 2000. *See also* ALTERNATIVE ENERGY.

GREECE. Though far less developed than northern European countries, in the 1960s and 1970s Greece experienced very high rates of economic growth. The focus on economic development has left many pressing environmental problems unaddressed both in political debate and policy implementation. Until 1989 the established parties felt no pressure from environmentalist political organizations, and the poor performance by the latter since then has allowed the major parties to retain their focus on economic rather than environmental issues.

In policy, there is a conspicuous difference between legislation, or intent, and implementation, or practice. To a degree, Greece's 1981 membership in the then European Communities placed some pressure on the government to enact new legislation. The obstacles to its implementation were substantial, however. The Greek Constitution, framed in 1975 after the resignation of the military junta in 1974, provided for "the protection of the natural and cultural environment" by the state (Article 24). There were also pledges to protect forests. In addition, the government established a National Council for Physical Planning and Protection of the Environment in 1976. In the 1980s various governments formed ministries that combined the administration of environmental issues with other areas of responsibility. The net outcome of these initiatives, including the attempts to implement directives issued by the European Union (EU), has been far from favorable.

There are at least two major obstacles: first, the focus on economic development and the pressure to maintain the pace of industrialization, and second, the divisions in the structure of public administration and lack of coordination among government agencies. Many different ministries have had responsibilities pertaining to environmental protection. Often, protection of the environment is regarded as of secondary importance if there is a potential for dispute with industrial or economic interests. Still, there are indications that some government agencies, particularly at the local level, are exploring possibilities for **sustainable development**, particularly in the area of tourism and the need to prevent pollution in order to maintain this sector. Among the most pressing problems affecting Greece are air pollution (particularly the smog over Athens), deforestation, and noise pollution. Other issues that the government needs to address are the disposal of wastes, water pollution, and soil erosion.

A difficulty in dealing with these issues is the lack of public awareness about their urgency. The growth of environmental groups may alert more people to these problems and is certainly a novelty in the political life of the country. However, their access to policymaking is limited. Government agencies, through membership in the EU and international meetings, have nonetheless become more aware of measures that can be adopted to influence both business and industrial organizations, as well as individual citizens, to give greater consideration to the environment.

Thus far, environmental issues have not formed a significant part of Greek political life though, as in most European countries, attempts have been made to create new political organizations to address these questions. In 1986 environmental groups participated in local elections without much success. In 1988 some groups tried, without any lasting effect, to form a citizens' union. In 1989 some of these groups managed to form the Ecologists-Alternatives Party and competed in the June elections to the **European Parliament**. They polled only 1.1 percent of the vote and failed to secure any seats. In October 1989 a large number of environmental groups formed the Federation of Ecological Organizations, with a view to competing in a national election the following month. They retained the name Ecologists-Alternatives, and although they polled only 0.6 percent, they secured one seat in Parliament. In the national elections held in April 1990, their share of the vote rose only to 0.8 percent, and they retained one seat. In local elections in 1990 the environmentalists managed to gain seats on some municipal councils.

The Federation of Ecological Organizations' loose structure failed to unify its highly diverse member groups. Apart from arguments about organizational structures (centralized versus decentralized), there were disputes over fundamental principles (shallow versus **deep ecology**). These quarrels delayed the founding congress of the party until February 1992 and then came to dominate it. To confound matters, the sole parliamentary representative of the party detached herself from the organization and sat as an independent delegate. For a time, it looked as if it were the death knell of efforts to form a green party in Greece.

A decade later, however, Oikologoi Prasinoi (Ecologist Greens) was formed. The members of Prasini Politiki (Green Politics), which had represented Greek environmental interests in the European Federation of Green Parties prior to this, joined Oikologoi Prasinoi. The founding declaration of the party defines it as internationalist and pacifist, community-oriented, movement-oriented, feminist, anticonsumerist, antiauthoritarian, and alternative.

GREEN-ALTERNATIVE EUROPEAN LINK. *See* EUROPEAN PARLIAMENT.

GREEN BELT MOVEMENT. The driving force behind this movement is **Wangari Maathai**, who grew up in **Kenya** and studied in the **United States**. On her return to Kenya, Maathai became interested in altering the trend toward desertification of the landscape. An active member of the Kenyan National Council for Women, Maathai also has connections with prominent individuals in the **United Nations Environment Programme (UNEP)**. The first step toward the Green

Belt movement was taken on 5 June 1977, the day set aside for World Environment Day. Seven trees were planted in Nairobi. Apart from securing corporate sponsorship for tree planting—for instance, from Mobil Oil—Maathai ensured that her initiative was backed by organizations such as UNEP and by local political elites. Organizations such as the Danish Voluntary Fund for Developing Countries, the Norwegian Forestry Society, and the Spirit of Stockholm Foundation also provided valuable financial support. Hundreds of tree nurseries were established, employing thousands of people, mainly women, and involving participation by hundreds of thousands of schoolchildren. Apart from the success in reversing some of the damage inflicted on the landscape through the planting of millions of trees, the movement has raised awareness about the connection between development and environmental protection. It has also promoted a number of other goals, including the creation of employment opportunities in agriculture, improving the status of women, and undertaking research in collaboration with universities.

GREEN CONSUMERISM. Green consumerism entails enjoying a prosperous lifestyle without destroying the environment. For instance, in a best-seller entitled *The Green Consumer Guide*, John Elkington and Julia Hailes suggest that the choices we make in purchasing goods contribute significantly to the quality of the environment. Apart from offering specific advice on products, these advocates of green consumerism describe how major corporations have implemented radical changes in the manufacture of products such as aerosols to ensure that they do not contain chlorofluorocarbons that destroy the **ozone layer**. They also make several key points about how green consumers should select goods. For instance, the products should not pose a danger to anyone's health; should not have a critical impact on the environment as a result of their manufacture, use, or disposal; should not require large amounts of energy to manufacture, use, or dispose of; should not expend materials from species or environments that are at risk; should not entail cruelty to animals; and should not be counter to the interest of developing nations.

Some of the critics of green consumerism, such as Sandy Irvine in her book *Beyond Green Consumerism*, have recognized that the approach advocated by Elkington and Hailes can enable the green movement to exert immense pressure on business and industrial groups to change dramatically the entire process of production or risk losing their customers. However, along with many other proponents of *The Limits to Growth* thesis, Irvine is skeptical about the possibilities for overcoming some of the fundamental problems of our economic and social system. These critics argue that it is impossible, even for highly educated green consumers, to be fully cognizant of the involvement by a particular manufacturer or corporation in a wide range of activities, some of which may have an adverse impact on the environment. More significantly, they develop the following argument: in order to address environmental questions, we will need to do much more than substitute goods that have been produced, will be used, and will be disposed in ways that damage the environment with those that have a less deleterious impact on it. Rather, we will need to consume less.

Green consumerism, they maintain, perpetuates the illusion that we can maintain affluent lifestyles without harming the environment. In addition, the critics suggest that only fairly affluent people can afford the selectivity and lifestyle implied by the proponents of green consumerism. The main issue, however, centers on *The Limits to Growth*, diminution of energy and raw materials as a consequence of **population growth**, and reduction in land available for waste disposal. At present, however, there is growing support for green consumerism, especially in the context of arguments for **sustainable development** and the possibility of combining economic development with environmental protection. *See also* STEADY-STATE ECONOMICS.

GREEN MOVEMENT OF SRI LANKA. A consortium of 147 nongovernmental organizations (NGOs) in Sri Lanka that are concerned with environmental conservation and awareness and empowerment of the poorest segments of society. The consortium is a member of the **Asia Pacific Greens Network**.

GREENHOUSE EFFECT. Concern about the warming of the Earth's atmosphere as a result of industrial development has become widespread since the 1980s. The term *greenhouse effect* has been used to characterize the warming of the atmosphere as a result of water vapor and the emission of gases (carbon dioxide, methane, nitrous oxides, hydrofluorocarbons, perfluorocarbons, and sulfur hexafluoride) that prevent the escape of heat from the Earth's surface. Carbon dioxide is currently the largest contributor to the greenhouse effect. In the Earth's atmosphere, carbon dioxide and other greenhouse gases functions like a greenhouse; in other words, they provide a passage for light waves from the sun but restrict the escape of radiation from the Earth into the atmosphere. The main sources of carbon dioxide emissions are the burning of fossil fuels such as oil and coal, though other processes such as the burning of wood, agricultural activities, and deforestation also contribute to the problem. Over the past century, there has been a steep increase in the rate of carbon dioxide emissions and other greenhouse gases.

GREENPEACE. Greenpeace describes itself as "an independent, campaigning organization which uses **nonviolent**, creative confrontation to expose global environmental problems, and to force the solutions which are essential to a green and peaceful future." On the whole, Greenpeace has focused on direct protest actions. It has been more successful than any other organization in breaking the law and attracting the implicit support of the media and explicit approval of millions of people.

The origins of this environmental protest organization can be traced to the 1969 formation of the Don't Make a Wave Committee in Vancouver, **Canada**. This group, which included people who had protested the Vietnam War, launched a campaign against the testing of nuclear weapons over the atmosphere in the Aleutian Islands. The Greenpeace Foundation was created in 1971, the year in which protesters sailed an old fishing boat into the vicinity of Amchitka Island off the coast of Alaska, an area being used by the U.S. government to test nuclear devices. Apart from effecting a postponement and ultimately the abandonment of these tests, the protestors attracted media attention and a considerable amount of popular support. These events set the pattern for future successful action by Greenpeace. The organization would focus on a particular issue with a view to receiving maximum attention from the media. It would then conduct its protest in a highly organized and professional manner.

In 1972 Greenpeace carried out one of its most memorable protests when, backed by major volunteer associations such as the **Sierra Club**, **Friends of the Earth**, and the World Council of Churches and by the Canadian government, it launched a campaign against the testing of nuclear weapons by the French government in the Mururoa Atoll in the Pacific. Led by David McTaggart, a Canadian who later became director of Greenpeace International, a group of activists embarked on a voyage, sailing right into the nuclear test zone.

The risks undertaken by McTaggart and his crew, who sailed to within 50 miles of the site where a bomb was detonated, drew an enormous amount of attention to their cause. This was followed, in August 1973, by another attempt to enter a zone for testing nuclear weapons. On this occasion, French troops set upon the crew with force. Photographs of the beatings brought further adverse publicity for the French government, which, in November 1973, declared a pause in the tests. Greenpeace profited immensely from these events.

The determination of the French to continue with the tests provided an ideal focal point for Greenpeace's professional campaigns over the next 20 years. The most critical moment in this battle was the death of a member of Greenpeace in 1985 when the French intelligence service bombed the *Rainbow Warrior*, a ship owned by Greenpeace, while it was moored at Auckland harbor in New Zealand. The incident led to the resignation of Charles Hernu, the French Minister of Defense. It also increased the popularity of Greenpeace, which by now had conducted international campaigns on issues such as the protection of seals and whales as well as the transportation and disposal of nuclear waste. At the national level, Greenpeace carried out highly visible campaigns against pollution, for example, against the contamination of rivers by chemical companies. For instance, following its inquiries into the Ciba-Geigy factory in New Jersey in the **United States**, the company had to face numerous criminal charges and pay fines of more than US$4 million.

Support for Greenpeace grew at a rapid rate, especially in the late 1980s. Between 1981 and 1989 Greenpeace increased its worldwide revenue, raised largely from private donations, from US$1.2 million to US$100 million. In the early 1990s it had around 40 branches in 30 countries and claimed around five million supporters in 158 countries (although membership figures may have been exaggerated due to poor accounting). Approximately half of its supporters lived in the United States. In Europe, the two largest concentrations of supporters were in the Netherlands and **Germany**. In 1990 there were about 750,000 supporters in Germany alone. The 1990s, however, proved a difficult time for the organization. The organization had become too large and bureaucratic for many of its supporters. Its flamboyant tactics had lost their newness and appeal for others. Membership in Greenpeace USA plummeted. In the late 1980s, Greenpeace USA had 22 regional offices and a membership of around one million. With dropping membership and financial support, in 1997 the organization was forced to lay off three-quarters of its staff. In 2006, it had but two regional offices. Membership was down to around a quarter of a million. Membership in European branches dropped as well although not as dramatically as in the United States. In the mid-2000s international membership figures stood at roughly 2.5 million.

The victory of George W. Bush in the 2000 and 2004 elections has done the organization some good. The Bush White House's image as one of the most corporate friendly and antienvironmental of any administration has rallied support for Greenpeace and other environmental groups.

Its campaigns are now focused on addressing **climate change**, protecting forests and oceans, opposing genetic engineering, eliminating toxic chemicals, demanding peace and disarmament, and preventing the expansion of **nuclear energy**.

GREENS/EUROPEAN FREE ALLIANCE. *See* EUROPEAN FEDERATION OF GREEN PARTIES-EUROPEAN FREE ALLIANCE.

GROEN! Originally called **Agalev**, Groen! is one of two Belgian green parties. Reflecting the cultural and ethnic differences in **Belgium**, Groen! represents the Flemish community. By contrast, **Ecolo** has emerged as the voice of the Walloon population. The term *Agalev* derives from a movement called Anders gaan leven ("for an alternative way of life"). Agalev was founded in March 1982, though it originates in a Christian movement that began in 1970. The movement was initiated by Luc Versteylen, a Jesuit priest and teacher. His aim was to involve young people in reflection about their problems. Along with his collaborators, Versteylen questioned the value of the educational system and the competitive, consumer society. This formed the basis for the Anders gaan leven movement, which developed first in Antwerp and then in the provinces. The movement launched into grassroots action, including the promotion of alternative lifestyles and environmental protection. Later, a group from the movement, Agalev, contested local and regional elections.

In 1979 Agalev presented lists of candidates at the first elections to the **European Parliament** and obtained 2.3 percent of votes in Flanders. In 1981, with 3.9 percent of the votes, it gained two seats in the lower house of the Belgian Parliament and a seat in the senate. Success in local elections created a new momentum. In March 1982 Agalev detached itself from Anders gaan leven and formally became a political party. Throughout the 1980s, it steadily increased its support base, reaching 12.2 percent in the 1989 European elections and 7.8 percent of the vote in Flanders in the national elections. In the early 1990s, Agalev agreed to give its support to a constitutional amendment creating a federal system in Belgium in exchange for agreement on a tax on bottles, Europe's first ecotax.

After a slight drop in support in the mid-1990s as voters gravitated toward the Socialist Party after a series of scandals, in the 1999 European elections, Agalev's support rebounded and the party received 12 percent of the vote (two of 14 seats) and in the federal parliamentary elections, 11.1 percent (increasing its number of seats from five to nine). Just prior to the election, Belgium had been hit by a food contamination crisis when high levels of dioxin were found in chickens raised in the country. The green parties, with their focus on sustainable living, appealed to voters.

Because of their strong showing, Agalev and Ecolo were invited to join in a rainbow coalition government (socialists, liberals, and greens) at the federal level. Agalev's Magda Aelvot was made vice-prime minister and Minister for Public Health and the Environment and Eddy Boutmans became Minister of Development Cooperation. Agalev also joined in the regional government of Flanders, obtaining the posts of Minister for Well Being and Development Cooperation and Minister for Agriculture and Environment. During their time in government, Agalev and Ecolo succeeded in a plan to phase out **nu-**

clear energy and passing antidiscrimination legislation and legislation recognizing gay marriages.

Both Agalev and Ecolo, however, found the compromise required of coalition governments problematic. Magda Aelvot resigned her post in opposition to a deal to export arms to Nepal, which was then engaged in a civil war. Ecolo's uncompromising positions on policy matters, such as on the question of night flights over Brussels (which led to the resignation of the Ecolo Ministers of Energy and Transport when no compromise could be reached) and their opposition to tobacco advertising, which led to the cancellation of the Belgian Grand Prix, strained the coalition. Agalev distanced itself from Ecolo, but in the 2003 parliamentary elections, the party took a heavy hit. It fell to 2.5 percent of the vote, insufficient to enter Parliament (a 5 percent hurdle, which had been supported by Agalev, was introduced just prior to the election). At the European Union (EU) level, it also did poorly, winning only one seat.

In an effort to revitalize the party after its poor showing, Agalev changed its name to Groen! Several prominent members of the party, however, left after the party congress rejected the idea of forming a federal coalition with other Belgian parties.

GROSS NATIONAL PRODUCT (GNP). Concern about *The Limits to Growth* and damage inflicted on the environment by industrial society has given rise to a variety of suggestions for reconceptualizing economic performance. Green economists have called into question the conventional measures of performance, notably the use of GNP. The principal limitation of the exclusive focus on GNP is the failure to consider factors such as health, social, and some **quality-of-life** indicators; the neglect of the informal economy, which varies immensely in size in different countries; and, above all, the disregard for the environmental costs of economic development.

Instead of GNP, the traditional measure of wealth, green economists have argued for the inclusion of the above indicators and a more differentiated approach to promoting economic growth. In some sectors of the economy, economic growth may be highly advantageous, and in others it may be undesirable, especially because of damage to the environment. The green movement has begun to influence some governments and international agencies to the extent that greater effort has been applied both to measuring and publicizing performance along the lines suggested by green economists. Furthermore, techniques such as **carbon taxes** and **pollution charges** have been proposed for placing a value on the impact of various processes on the environment. *See also* STEADY-STATE ECONOMY; VALUING THE ENVIRONMENT.

GUARANTEED MINIMUM INCOME. A guaranteed minimum income is central to the platform and policies of many green political organizations. The guiding principles of the **European Federation of Green Parties** (as resolved on 20 June 1993 at the conference at Masala, Finland) stated that "every person has the right to free education, social protection, and a guaranteed social minimum income."

The connection was then made between the maintenance of a comprehensive social security system (which covered "the basic needs of all people" and did not rest on the notion of paid work) and the notion of "sustainability": "Sustainability will not be possible as long as poverty persists, or people live in material insecurity. We will ensure a guaranteed minimum income for every citizen through either a social assistance scheme or minimum wage legislation, or improved welfare benefits or the introduction of the basic income, or a combination of the above mentioned" (Clause 4.4). Die Grünen in **Germany** has long argued for a guaranteed minimum income that excludes any attempt to measure the financial assets of individuals or their employment record.

A comprehensive defense of such schemes has been elaborated by Paul Ekins in *The Living Economy*. Ekins states that a "basic income scheme" would have the following aims: to prevent rather than just relieve poverty, replace the prevailing system of social security and tax relief, and abolish some of the traps that arise from the current operation of the welfare state. These include, according to Ekins, the poverty trap (an increase in pay can lead to the withdrawal of crucial social security benefits), unemployment trap (if you do not work for low wages you lose all entitlements), idleness trap (which has apparently prevented people from undertaking voluntary work because they would otherwise be seen as technically not seeking formal employment, and thereby lose entitlements), and spendthrift trap (if you save above a certain amount of money you lose entitlements to social security benefits).

There are two fundamental criticisms of this universal scheme that aims to provide benefits at a higher level than the existing system. The first is that it would be very costly and thereby lead to higher taxes for everyone. The second is that for many people at the lower end of the socioeconomic ladder, it may provide a disincentive to seeking employment. At any rate, these ideas about a guaranteed minimum income reflect the strong emphasis in green political organizations on social justice and egalitarianism. The hope cherished by many green political activists is the guaranteed minimum income scheme, with its strong emphasis on universal rather than individually means-tested forms of social benefits, will engender a spirit of cooperation and serve as a defense against the forces of competition, which are often regarded as responsible for the destruction of the environment.

– H –

HARDIN, GARRETT. *See* "TRAGEDY OF THE COMMONS."

– I –

INDIA. The 1900s were a time of revolution for underrepresented groups in India, and it was at this time that environmental movements began. Modernization and industrialization caused increased deforestation and abuse of natural resources; as these initially affected most immediately the rural population, it was they who first created ecological movements.

In 1972, Jharkhand Mukti Morcha, or Jharkhand Liberation Front, literally meaning "forest area," emerged. Jharkhand desired to protect the rural community from natural resource and human labor capital exploitation. However, the movement diminished after being placated by Indira Gandhi's government's development programs.

One of India's most significant social movements was the **Chipko** ("embrace") **Andalan** Movement, which emerged in 1973. Unique because its major constituency was women, including the well-known ecofeminist **Vandana Shiva**, the Chipko Andalan Movement's members opposed commercial deforestation and would hug the trees so that contractors could not remove them. In Uttar Pradesh, the Chipko Andalan Movement had a major victory in 1980 when Prime Minister Indira Gandhi passed a 15-year ban on green felling. These protests and subsequent victories spread to other regions in India, including Karnataka, Rajasthan, and Bihar.

The struggle of fishermen in the southern state of Kerala in the 1980s symbolized an even more active form of protest against an increasingly industrialized and ecologically destructive state. The main reason for fighting was over the use of mechanized trawlers that caused increased destruction of marine ecosystems and excessive capture of young fish. Composed of clergy, nuns, and fishermen, the protests spread from Kerala up to the coastal city of Goa and back down to the south in Tamilnadu where violent clashes took place.

The Indian National Green Party, led by Prof. Dr. Priya Ranjan Trivedi, who is also the convener of the World Federation of Green Parties, was officially registered with the Election Commission of India on 7 January 1999. As a relatively young party, it is dominated by the major parties, but due to the range of opinions that the Indian National Green Party holds, from land reform to health care to environmental sustainability, it should be able to pull in a range of voters.

The promotional scheme of the party is aimed at the youth, with catch phrases such as "Catch them young" and "Each one teach one." Members believe that the youth can change the world if they learn to be both ecologically respectful and socially aware. The official charter of the Indian National Green Party has a list of beliefs and goals including **ecology**, democracy, social justice, peace, **sustainable development**, meaningful work, culture, information, global responsibility, and long-range future focus.

The party emphasizes the need to reduce the emissions of **greenhouse** gases and carbon dioxide into the environment, limit the amount of various types of waste that are both produced and expelled into the environment, and protect biological diversity (**biodiversity**). Great concern is placed on the depletion of natural resources, specifically due to the overuse of land in agriculture and mining. Education is also emphasized, and the party states that it is important that there be a national educational system whose focus is on teaching students the importance of global interdependence. Another aim of the party is to not only provide nationalized health care but to also prevent the spread of disease among the population. *See also* NARMADA DAM.

INDUSTRIAL SOCIETY. The term *industrial society* has been used by leading figures in the green movement to criticize a wide range of established political regimes, whether communist, capitalist, or liberal-democratic. The argument is simply that whatever their differences, these political regimes are committed to economic growth tied to industrialization, technology, and the expansion of the means of production. This theme was articulated by prominent personalities such as Jonathon Porritt and **Rudolf Bahro**. *See also* GROSS NATIONAL PRODUCT (GNP); *LIMITS TO GROWTH, THE.*

INGLEHART, RONALD. *See* POSTMATERIALISM.

INTERNATIONAL COALITION FOR LOCAL ENVIRONMENTAL INITIATIVES. Founded in 1990, this is a coalition of city, town, and local governments that have made a commitment to **sustainable development**. As of 2005 there were more than 475 members. The coalition shares information on sustainable development initiatives, provides training courses, and works to build local capacity to deal with global environmental problems.

INTERNATIONAL INSTITUTE FOR ENVIRONMENT AND DEVELOPMENT. Formed in 1971 and based in London, this international policy research institute partners with local organizations to conduct research and promote sustainable and equitable global development.

INTERNATIONAL INSTITUTE FOR SUSTAINABLE DEVELOPMENT (IISD). Based in Canada and opened in 1990, IISD has 150 people working in more than 30 countries and affiliates with 200 organizations worldwide. As a policy research think tank, IISD reports on international negotiations and provides policy recommendations toward **sustainable development** in the fields of international trade and investment, economic policy, **climate change**, measurement and assessment, and natural resources management.

INTERNATIONAL UNION FOR THE CONSERVATION OF NATURE AND NATURAL RESOURCES (IUCN). *See* WORLD CONSERVATION UNION.

IRELAND. The Ecology Party of Ireland was formed in 1981 by a Dublin schoolteacher, Christopher Fettes. The party received only 0.2 percent of the vote in national elections held in November 1982. In 1983 it was replaced by Comhaontas Glas (Green Alliance). However, it continued to have little impact in electoral terms. Christopher Fettes secured 1.9 percent of the vote in the 1984 elections to the **European Parliament**. In the 1985 local elections, the Green Alliance only gained 0.6 percent of the vote. In 1987, the party changed its name to the Green Party/Comhaontas Gas to clarify its image as a political party. The party's fortunes improved somewhat after this time. Roger Garland was elected from South Dublin as the Green's first delegate to the lower chamber of the Irish Parliament, known as the Dáil. Although he lost his seat in a subsequent election, Trevor Sargent was elected in 1992 to the Dáil from Dublin North. In the 1994 European Parliament elections, the Greens secured two of the 15 available seats (Patricia McKenna and Nuala Ahern). John Gormley was also elected in 1995 as the first Green Lord Mayor of Dublin. He subsequently became a delegate to the Dáil. Still, in the 1991 and 1999 local elections, the party was only receiving 2.4 percent of the national vote.

As has been the case with many other green parties, the Green Party's poor electoral performance led to the decision to restructure and select a leader, deputy leader, and chairman. The strategy worked, and in the 2002 general election, the party won six seats to the Dáil.

The Green Party/Comhaontas adopted at its founding seven principles: society's impact on the environment should not be ecologically disruptive, resources should be conserved, the subsidiarity principle of decision making (taking decisions at the lowest level that is effective) should be pursued, society should be guided by the principles of self-reliance and cooperation, a healthy environment should be passed on to future generations, world peace should override commercial interests, and the world's resources should be redistributed to deal with world poverty. Its revised 1997 Constitution added to these: more decision making at the local level, open government, a basic income for all citizens, recycling and renewable energy, full implementation of the Good Friday Agreement, Workers' Co-ops and small family businesses, public transportation, and **nonviolent** direct action.

ITALY. The Italian Greens are among those green parties that have joined left-of-center coalitions, which have dominated Italian politics from 1996 to 2001 and have again been in power since 2006. In 1996, the Greens joined Romano Prodi's left-leaning "Olive Coalition." When the coalition won the election, the Greens gained their first ministerial portfolio: Environment (Edo Ronchi). Ronchi was environment minister at the time of the 1997 Kyoto Conference where the **Kyoto Protocol** was signed. He stayed in office until 2000. Another Green representative, Alfonso Pecararo Scanio, was appointed as agriculture minister from 2000–2001. He has served as environment minister since 2006.

A pivotal issue in the emergence of the green movement in Italy was the plan to develop dozens of nuclear power plants, announced by the government in 1975. This attracted strong opposition both from elite groups (scientists and intellectuals) and the public. Amici della Terra (**Friends of the Earth**) played an important role in organizing the campaign against the development of nuclear power. Prominent members of the Communist Party, which had become one of the dominant parties in Italy in the 1970s, joined in the campaign and even formed the Lega per l'Ambiente (Environmental League). Following the nuclear accident in 1986 at **Chernobyl**, the Lega per l'Ambiente organized a protest rally against the development of nuclear power with up to 150,000 people attending.

In 1987 environmental groups initiated a national campaign for a referendum on the development of nuclear power, and the overwhelming majority of citizens voted against the nuclear plans of the national government, voting instead for a decision that would be made at the local level. A majority also opposed the development of the Super-Phéonix nuclear reactor project. Apart from the focus on environmental protection and opposition to the development of nuclear power, green groups have campaigned on social justice issues and improving participation through the extension of democracy and self-government.

The history of Italy's Green Party goes back to various green groups that began to contest municipal elections in 1980 in the towns of Este, Lugo di Romagna, Mantove, and Usmaate. In 1983 they contested elections in 16 locations. At the 1985 local elections green groups put up 150 lists. They also competed in the regional elections, receiving 636,000 votes (2.1 percent). They gained 115 seats at the local level, 16 at the provincial level, and 10 at the regional level. In 1988 the Greens polled an average of 3.7 percent in local, regional, and provincial elections.

In November 1986, green groups in Italy formed the Federazione delle Liste Verdi (Federation of Green Lists), the forerunner of today's Italian Green Party, Federazione dei Verdi. This national federation widely came to be known as "the Greens." Other political organizations also campaigned successfully on a green platform; they include the Radical Party and Worker Democracy, which had been formed long before the green party. The Radical Party also collaborated with green groups in electoral campaigns.

The Italian electoral system has undergone various changes, but has always included a degree of proportional representation; this provided genuine opportunities for minority parties to gain seats. In the 1987 elections to the national parliament, green groups received around one million votes (2.5 percent) and gained 13 seats in the lower house and two in the Senate. In 1992 they procured a similar vote (2.8 percent) and thereby won 16 seats in the lower house and four in the Senate. They attracted a similar share of the vote in elections to the Chamber of Deputies in 1994 (2.7 percent and nine seats) and 1996 (2.5 percent and 14 seats in cooperation with parties such as the Democratic Left Party). Their share of seats in the Senate was seven out of 325 in 1994 and 14 out of 325 in 1996.

In the 2001 elections, when the right-of-center coalition led by Silvio Berlusconi was swept into power, the Greens, like all of the left, performed poorly. They had formed a short-lived common list with the Italian Democratic Socialists called Il Girasole (Sunflower) within the Olive Tree coalition. The combined list polled only 2.2

percent. Still, they were able to send eight delegates to the lower chamber and nine to the Senate.

In the 2006 legislative elections, with just 2.05 percent of the vote, the Federazione dei Verdi still won 15 seats in the Chamber of Deputies as part of the Union Coalition. Another green list, Ambianta Lista Ecologisti Democratici (Environmental List Ecological Democrats) ran as part of the conservative Cassa delle Libertà (House of Freedoms) coalition, but brought in only 17,574 votes (0.05 percent). In the Senate elections, the Greens joined forces with the Italian Communist Party and the United Consumers, forming a common list, "Together with the Union." Combined they won 11 seats (five of which went to Green delegates). Ambianta Lista Ecologisti Democratici ran as part of the conservative coalition and received .11 percent of the vote, insufficient to obtain any seats.

Electoral results have influenced decisions regarding the Greens' structure and orientation. After the 1989 European elections, the Greens received 3.8 percent of the vote, and a coalition of green associations, Verdi Arcobaleno (Rainbow Greens), gained a further 2.4 percent. The latter represented and reflected the connection between environmental issues and left-wing groups. After the election, in 1990 the Greens and the Verdi Arcobaleno joined forces and became the Federazione dei Verdi. Federazione dei Verdi remained a coalition of regional green groups until it officially became a party in 1996.

In the 1994 elections to the **European Parliament**, the Federazione dei Verdi attracted over a million votes (3.2 percent of the ballot) and secured three out of 87 seats. In the June 1999 election, however, they won only two seats. This contributed to a decision to restructure the party. The leadership of the party was turned over to Grazia Francescato (1999–2001), who had been a charismatic leader of **World Wide Fund for Nature (WWF)**-Italy, and a decision was made to shift the party to the far left. This prompted several former party noteworthies to leave the party, including Ronchi, Gianni Mattioli, Luigi Manconni, Massimo Scalia, and Franco Corleone. There was little change, however, in the party's electoral performance. In the 2004 European Parliamentary elections, the Greens won 2.5 percent of the vote (two seats). After the 2006 election, at the urging of Scanio, the party again shifted direction, trying to create a more open image.

The profile of supporters and voters for green groups is similar to that in many other European countries. In other words, the young and better educated are more likely than other sections of the community to support green groups. Green organizations are also more likely to do well in the more prosperous northern part of Italy than in the south. *See also* DIRECT DEMOCRACY.

– J –

JAPAN. In the Meiji era (1868–1912), there were numerous protest movements in Japan against pollution caused by mining activities, the most famous being the Ashio Copper Mine case. In the Taisho period (1912–1926), there were local protests against air pollution in cities and near industrial sites. Prewar militarism and a clamp down on leftist movements beginning in the mid-1920s largely silenced these protest activities. Japan's postwar development boom produced an economic miracle but a pollution nightmare. Japan was plagued by various pollution diseases. Four communities—Minamata, a small fishing village in Kumamoto Prefecture on the island of Kyushu; Niigata, a much larger city; rice farming villages along the Jinzu River in Toyama Prefecture; and the city of Yokkaichi—played a particularly large role in strengthening national awareness of the threats of industrial pollution to human health and in pressuring the government to take pollution more seriously. In all of these communities the industrial dumping of toxic pollutants into water bodies or release of emissions into the air (in the case of Yokkaichi) over long periods of time resulted in severe community health problems. Victims complained to the industries, requested compensation, and demanded the end of polluting activities. While victims received small payments from the industries, nothing was done to stop the pollution. After years of frustration and with the aid of lawyers and journalists, these communities took their cases to court, an unusual step in a relatively nonlitigious society. The national attention that these cases received, along with hundreds of other environmental movements that formed, resulted in major grassroots pressures for political change and the eventual adoption of new pollution-control legislation.

The antipollution movements that emerged in the 1960s and 1970s were locally oriented. They forced local and national governments to address noise pollution, vibration, and pollution in urban canals; protect the right to "sunshine" of houses in cities that were rapidly being modernized; ensure food safety; and require the installation of pollution control devices. The citizens' movements did not win all of their battles. Efforts to prevent the building, and later expansion, of Narita airport, delayed construction plans by years, but in the end the airport was built and expanded, if less fully than was originally planned. Citizens' movements also failed to prevent the building of many dams, nuclear power plants, roads, apartment complexes, and the like. The most difficult cases for the movements were those that went against the plans of the powerful economic and construction ministries.

A few national environmental nongovernmental organizations (NGOs) formed relatively early in Japan too. The largest and oldest NGO is the Wild Bird Society, established in 1934 with a membership of somewhat over 50,000. Other groups that established themselves relatively early include the Nature Conservation Society of Japan (1951); **World Wide Fund for Nature (WWF)**, Japan (1971); and **Friends of the Earth**, Japan (1980). Compared to the situation in North America or Europe, however, Japan's environmental NGOs were few in number and small in size, both in terms of membership and budget.

Since the late 1980s, Japan's NGO community has been growing and becoming more concerned with global environmental issues. Friends of the Earth, Japan, started to take on the Japanese government regarding official development assistance (ODA) projects that were environmentally destructive. In 1989 they initiated a campaign against the planned construction of a huge dam in Narmada, **India**, that was to receive financing from Japanese aid. Japanese ODA programs also triggered the formation of the Japan Tropical Forest Action Network (JATAN). At the urging of international environmental groups that were working to stop logging in Sarawak, Malaysia, 12 Japanese grassroots groups and individuals formed a coalition in 1987 and established JATAN. One of JATAN's first campaigns was an effort to stop the Japan International Cooperation Agency's funding of a subsidiary company of Itochu that was building a logging road in Sarawak that was threatening the survival of the Penan. In subsequent years they launched campaigns against larger Japanese importers of tropical hardwoods.

The Citizens' Alliance for Saving the Atmosphere and the Earth formed in 1988 and became one of the leading NGOs in Japan working on campaigns to phase out ozone-depleting chemicals and reduce greenhouse gas emissions. **Greenpeace** established an office in Tokyo in 1989 in time to begin lobbying the Japanese government to introduce a greenhouse gas stabilization target prior to the **United Nations Conference on Environment and Development (UNCED)**.

There were still relatively few Japanese NGOs at the time of the UNCED. By the time of the December 1997 third conference of the parties to the **United Nations Framework Convention on Climate Change (UNFCCC)** held in Kyoto, Japan, where the **Kyoto Protocol** was drafted, there were 170 Japanese civil society organizations participating.

The Tokaimura nuclear accident was the worst in Japan's history and the third worst in the world, although of a far less severe scale than what happened at **Chernobyl**. The incident followed several other nuclear mishaps, including a sodium leak and fire at the Monju prototype fast breeder reactor in Fukui Prefecture that was initially kept secret from the public. The ensuing public distrust and safety concerns led to the shutdown of the reactor in 1995 until a Supreme Court decision ruled in favor of the plant's reopening in December 2005.

The series of accidents has heightened public distrust of what had long been considered one of the safest nuclear power industries in the world. It also emboldened **antinuclear** activists, although it failed to bring them together as a strong national movement. The government and nuclear industry have found it more difficult to build nuclear power plants as local opposition has become quite strong. After the Tokaimura accident, the first-ever antinuclear activist was elected to the Tokaimura assembly, the pronuclear Atomic Energy Commission agreed to let a representative of the antinuclear Citizens' Nuclear Information Center serve as a commission member, and the Diet passed a Special Law of Emergency Preparedness for Nuclear Disasters.

Important to the empowerment of Japanese civil society has been the passage of the Access to Freedom of Information Act and the Nonprofit Organizational Law. These pieces of legislation have made it easier for NGOs to organize, obtain legal status as nonprofits, and gather information for their campaigns. The government has also started to change its attitude toward NGOs. In the past, government officials tended to view NGO activists as left-wing radicals. Now the government is beginning to consult NGOs and to bring them into decision making related to environmental and ODA policies and programs.

JOINT IMPLEMENTATION. This flexibility mechanism of the **Kyoto Protocol** allows Annex I countries—the 36 industrialized countries and economies in transition listed in Annex I of the **United Nations Framework Convention on Climate Change (UNFCCC)**— to obtain credit toward their domestic emission reduction requirements by taking steps to reduce emissions in other Annex I countries, which in practice means the economies in transition. The principle behind this flexibility mechanism is to make emissions reductions more cost effective. *See also* CLEAN DEVELOPMENT MECHANISM; EMISSIONS TRADING.

– K –

KELLY, PETRA (1947–1992). Born in West **Germany**, Petra Kelly grew up in the **United States** and engaged in protests there against the Vietnam War. After returning to Germany, she took part in the Social Democratic Party before becoming a founding member of Die Grünen in 1980. Kelly became the most famous member of Die Grünen and was invited to many countries to promote green political organizations and their causes. For a time she was also regarded as the leading figure in the green movement worldwide. From 1983 to 1990 she served as a parliamentary delegate for Die Grünen, though she always maintained that she was skeptical of the use of Parliament as a means for confronting environmental problems.

In a 1982 *Der Spiegel* magazine interview, she explained that Parliament was not where decisions were made about the arms race and it was important to continue to work at the grassroots level to develop alternative social and economic structures based on principles of self-help and environmental awareness. She felt that parliamentary democracy had to be broadened to include a party that was fundamentally opposed to war and committed to **nonviolence** and ecological principles. Later, in her book, *Fighting for Hope*, she referred to Die Grünen as an "anti-party" party. The idea was for Die Grünen to use Parliament as a forum for publicizing issues and simultaneously maintain the strong connections between the party and grassroots social movements. Kelly also insisted that Die Grünen not enter coalitions for sharing power with the major parties. In this respect, she appeared to be closer to the fundamentalists than to realists in the party. Kelly promoted the use of Parliament as a means to initiate inquiries and hearings into issues that concerned the public, and Die Grünen used this mechanism effectively.

Despite her insistence on **direct democracy** and her apparent proximity to the fundamentalists, she fought with her colleagues over the issue of the rotation of delegates out of office after they had served either in executive positions in the party organization or in Parliament. The argument presented by Kelly and the realists was that they should be allowed to retain their positions because of their accumulated knowledge, experience, and skills. She had numerous well-publicized disagreements with other members over what she perceived to be a lack of professionalism and factional brawling in the party. By 1990 she and her partner, Gerd Bastian, a former army general who also served as a delegate for Die Grünen, had become detached from the party. They also withdrew from public life. In October 1992 both Kelly and Bastian were found dead in their home. Bastian had apparently shot Kelly in her sleep before taking his own life. *See also* ECOLOGY.

KENYA. In recent years, Kenya has had some success at institutionalizing a green movement. In addition to the internationally renowned **Green Belt Movement**, OSIENALA, or Friends of Lake Victoria, teaches local people how their day-to-day activities affect the lake habitat and encourages local research on the lake. Nature Kenya, previously known as the East Africa Natural History Society, created the first natural history museum in Kenya. Nature Kenya lobbies the national government and has been successful on issues such as the Environment Management and Coordination Act, the Forests Bill, and the National Environment Action Plan. Funding comes from international groups in **Great Britain**. Wakuluzu specifically addresses **biodiversity**, especially primates. They educate the public about the causes of endangered species, including habitat loss, poaching, and road accidents.

While intense conflict existed between former Kenyan president Daniel arap Moi and environmental groups, the current president Mwai Kibaki came to power as part of the large National Rainbow Coalition, of which the renowned **Wangari Maathai** was a member. Kibaki appointed Maathai as Deputy Minister of Environment, Natural Resources, and Wildlife. In 2003, she founded the Mazingira Green Party of Kenya.

Kenya has instituted Community Based Natural Resource Management Programs, which encourage local empowerment to protect the environment. Although this results in fewer baseline environmental standards, it also means wiser use of land based on local needs, and it makes rural people more inclined to support the environmental movement. Kenya also has thousands of self-help groups, such as the Harambee movement, that work to improve standards of living. The groups teach sustainable living and emphasize the relationship between environmental degradation and poverty.

KOREA, REPUBLIC OF. The Republic of Korea was an authoritarian state until the democratization movement led by students, labor union activists, and elements of the Korean Church succeeded in transforming the political system with the elections of 1987 and 1992. Grassroots demands for environmental protection began to grow in the 1980s as Korea's rapid industrialization caused increasingly bad pollution problems. Protests erupted near major industrial complexes in Ulsan, Pusan, and Yeocheon. The antipollution protesters saw their struggles against industrial pollution as an integral component of the struggle against military dictatorship.

A few environmental nongovernmental organizations (NGOs) and research institutes formed in the 1980s. The Korea Pollution Research Institute was founded as the first professional environmental NGO in the country. The Korea Antipollution Movement Council, which formed in 1984, and the Korea Antipollution Civilian Movement Council, which formed in 1986, merged the next year to create the Korea Antipollution Movement Association.

There has been a rapid growth in the environmental movement since the late 1980s. Antipollution movements protested the Doosan Electrical Company's emissions of phenol that contaminated drinking water, plans for the development of an industrial complex on the NakDong River, and the designation of Dukjuk Island as a nuclear waste storage site.

Umbrella organizations began to form in the 1990s as well. In 1993 the Korea Federation for Environmental Movements formed and became the largest environmental group in the country. In 2001 it had 25 local branches and 25,000 members. It has been active in **antinuclear**, anti–golf course, and citizen education efforts among many other campaigns. It also has supported green candidates for election. The League of Environmental Movements, Green Korea United, and the Korea Wetlands Association are other groups that formed at this time. Compared with many other countries that have experienced democratic transition in the post–Cold War period, South Korea's environmental community is quite robust.

In 2004, the Korea Greens was formed by individuals, local council members, and civil movement activists intent on greening and democratizing Korean politics. They have also established a Young Greens Korea. Both Green Korea United and Korea Greens participated in the **Asia Pacific Greens Network** meeting held in Kyoto, Japan, in 2005.

KYOTO PROTOCOL. The Kyoto Protocol to the **United Nations Framework Convention on Climate Change (UNFCCC)** was formulated with the goal of reducing greenhouse gas emissions of the industrialized states by 5 percent of 1990 levels by 2012. By ratifying this protocol, countries have pledged to reduce carbon dioxide emissions as well as five other greenhouse gases. They can do this either by making cuts to domestic emissions, by participating in emissions trading, or by two other flexible implementation mechanisms known as the **clean development mechanism** and **joint implementation**. These permits industrialized states to obtain credit for reducing greenhouse gas emissions in developing countries or transition economies.

The treaty was negotiated in Kyoto, **Japan**, in 1997. It was opened for signature on 16 March 1998 and went into force on 16 February 2005. As of February 2006, a total of 161 countries had ratified the agreement. Only Annex I countries—that is, the industrialized states and some transition economies—were required to make emissions cuts under the agreement. Developing countries, including some major greenhouse gas emitters, such as **India** and the **People's Republic of China**, are not required to make emission cuts under the protocol. The states of the European Union (EU) agreed to reduce their total emissions by 8 percent relative to 1990 levels by 2012, and Japan agreed to a 6 percent reduction in the same period.

The **United States** signed but has not ratified the agreement. The George W. Bush administration attracted global criticism for pulling the United States out of the Kyoto Protocol. The Bush administration argued that the treaty would place an unnecessary strain on the American economy.

– L –

LALONDE, BRICE. *See* FRANCE.

LATIN AMERICA AND THE CARIBBEAN REGION. The Latin America and Caribbean (LAC) region, which includes the countries of Central and South America, as well as the island nations of the Caribbean, is rich in natural resources and home to some of the greatest ecological **biodiversity** in the world. Five of the 10 most biologically diverse nations in the world—**Brazil**, Colombia, Ecuador, **Mexico**, and Peru—and 40 percent of the Earth's species are in Latin America.

In 1992, the Commission on Development and Environment for LAC identified nine key environmental concerns facing the region: land use, forest resources, ecosystems and biological patrimony, water resources, sea and shoreline resources, the environment in human settlements, energy, nonenergy mineral resources, and industry.

The creation of state agencies responsible for the environment, such as the Ministry of Sustainable Development and Environment in Bolivia, the Secretariat of Environment, Natural Resources, and Fisheries in Mexico, the Natural Resources Conservation Department of Jamaica, the National Environmental Commissions in Chile and Guatemala, has been an important step toward environmental conservation and protection in the region.

Growing public participation has proved crucial in increasing environmental awareness and spurring environment policy initiatives. The role of nongovernmental organizations (NGOs) in policy formation as well as the creation and direct oversight and management of protected areas has grown substantially. The involvement of NGOs has been especially critical to the creation of protected areas such as the Atlantic Forest Biosphere Reserve of Brazil and biosphere reserves in Mexico. Furthermore, the governments of Guatemala, Honduras, and **Costa Rica**, as well as other countries, have begun to directly involve NGOs in the management of **national parks** and other protected areas. In an effort to ensure public participation, Mexico, Colombia, and Chile have passed legislation that requires the establishment of local environmental planning communities with broad social representation.

Green parties have emerged in a number of the countries of the region but on the whole have struggled to obtain a political foothold. They have done best in Brazil and in Mexico.

LATVIA. The Latvian Green Party (Latvijas Zaļā Partijas) was formed in 1990 prior to Latvia's official independence. Latvia has the distinction of having the first Green prime minister, Indulis Emsis, in the world. He became prime minister in February 2004 after the breakdown of the four-party government that was then in charge. His minority government, however, was forced to resign in the fall of the same year. The Latvian Green Party was a coalition partner of the national government from 1993 to 1998, during which time Emsis was environment minister, and from 2002 to 2004, the party was put in charge of four ministries. In 2006, Emsis became Speaker of Parliament.

LEAGUE OF CONSERVATION VOTERS. A bipartisan group that seeks to defeat antienvironmental candidates to the U.S. Congress and White House and to support proenvironmental ones. It produces a National Environmental Scorecard and Presidential Report Card to show the electorate how their representatives voted on environmental legislation.

LEOPOLD, ALDO (1886–1948). Born in 1886 in Iowa, Aldo Leopold is celebrated for a work entitled *A Sand County Almanac*, which has been highly influential in the development of the green movement and a source of inspiration for the perspective on the environment known as **deep ecology**. Leopold graduated from the Forestry School at Yale University and was then employed by the Forest Service in Arizona. His book *Game Management* (1933) focused on the effective management and conservation of forests and wildlife within them. His work on this topic was widely used by professionals.

In writing *A Sand County Almanac*, published in 1949, a year after he died, Leopold became recognized as a key figure in the development of an ethic for the relationship between human beings and their environment. He sought to develop a system of values that went beyond the predominant focus on economic relationships. The notion of a land ethic was meant to extend "the boundaries of community" to cover soil, water, plants, and animals. Leopold argued that the time was ripe for developing a land ethic and, like **Rachel Carson** in her 1962 bestseller *Silent Spring*, painted a bleak picture of the damage being inflicted on the environment. Leopold pointed to the destruction of many species of plants and animals, soil erosion, and the utilitarian approach that regarded water as a resource just "to turn turbines, float barges, and carry off sewage."

Above all, his land ethic sought to change perceptions of the role of human beings from that of "conqueror of the land-community to plain member and citizen of it." This would be based on love, respect, and admiration for the environment. There are strong parallels between the idea of a heightened awareness of the value of the "land" (which includes animals, plants, water, and the soil) and **biocentrism** and **spirituality**.

LIMITS TO GROWTH, THE. The title of a book published in 1972 based on a study commissioned by the **Club of Rome** and written by Dennis L. Meadows, Donella H. Meadows, Jorgen Randers, and William W.

Behrens III, a team of researchers at the Massachusetts Institute of Technology (MIT). The study tried to realize the goal of the Club of Rome to develop a better understanding of economic growth, industrialization, environmental degradation, population change, and natural resources. Above all, it investigated the complex interaction between these factors rather than examining them in isolation.

In its methodology, the study was deeply influenced by Jay Forrester who, in the 1940s and 1950s, developed a dynamic model of social and economic change. *The Limits to Growth* used computers and complex models to predict the pattern of economic change over the next century. Originally, Forrester had assumed that computer models were superior to mental ones, because they were better able to analyze patterns and predict outcomes of the interaction of complex systems. Critics of these computer models pointed precisely to their inability to take into account the complexity of mental processes and the ways in which human perceptions could change rapidly.

In their computer models, Dennis Meadows and his team examined four principal determinants of economic growth: **population growth**, pollution, industrialization, and natural resources. The study predicted that if the prevailing patterns of exponential economic growth were to continue, humankind would be faced with a catastrophe by the end of the 20th century. The principal causes of the imagined calamity were a rapid depletion of resources, the threat to human existence by pollution of the environment, massive shortages in the food supply, and the rapid growth in world population.

The findings were somewhat alarmist but noted several possibilities for avoiding catastrophe. The principal conclusion was that if the prevailing trends in the expansion and growth of population, industrialization, pollution, food production, and resource consumption were not altered, the basis for industrial societies would be eroded within a hundred years. The study went on to argue that these trends could be altered, particularly if there was a focus on sustainable systems of economic development and environmental protection.

Among the main recommendations of the study were huge reductions in industrial and agricultural investment as well as a significant decrease in the birthrate and the transfer of wealth from more developed to less developed countries.

In both its assumptions and recommendations, *The Limits to Growth* was not dissimilar to concerns expressed during the previous century, notably by **Thomas Malthus** in *An Essay on the Principle of Population*. *The Limits to Growth* also appealed to people who, in the 1960s, had led or been influenced by the new wave of concern about environmental protection as well as the antiauthoritarian and anti–Vietnam War protest movements.

The **Club of Rome** acknowledged that the report's findings were tentative; however, it welcomed the opportunity to engage the community in a heated debate about the implications of the study. They were entirely successful; media coverage of the book and arguments stimulated by it helped boost sales of the work. Within a few years, about four million copies of the book had been sold in 30 languages. Worldwide sales eventually amounted to 20 million. The report made an immense contribution to raising awareness of environmental issues. It also generated a great deal of opposition.

One line of attack against the study was that it failed to consider how changes in technology, alterations in consumer behavior, and the discovery of new resources and forms of energy might avert the predicted outcomes. Other critics have argued that *The Limits to Growth* thesis outlines the interests of "managerialism" and reformist capitalism. In other words, the underlying concern is the sustainability of capitalism and industrialism with no attempt to imagine a qualitatively different society and culture. Although *The Limits to Growth* argued for a fairer redistribution of wealth and resources toward less developed countries, critics of the study were unhappy about what they regarded as an attempt by more developed countries to prevent less developed countries from attaining wealth and prosperity through economic growth. In the more developed countries, businesses were angered by recommendations for reduction in industrial growth.

Despite its serious shortcomings, *The Limits to Growth* stimulated awareness of the fragility of the environment, motivated many people to join social and political movements concerned about environmental issues, and eventually prompted changes in the behavior of consumers and in government policies. It also accelerated efforts to develop more efficient technology, look for new reserves of natural resources, and become more creative in dealing with environmental problems. *See also* SUSTAINABLE DEVELOPMENT.

LOVE CANAL. One of the most profound environmental disasters in U.S. history, the Love Canal tragedy helped spur new state and federal regulations during the 1980s regarding the proper disposal of toxic chemicals and other forms of hazardous waste.

Love Canal is a 70-acre fenced site that contains the original 16-acre hazardous waste landfill in the southeast corner of the City of Niagara Falls, New York. In the 1920s, a halfway dug canal in the area was turned into a poorly designed and regulated dumpsite for municipal and industrial chemical waste.

In the late 1950s, a working-class community of about 100 homes and a school was built on the former dumpsite. Twenty-five years later, the reckless administration of the dumpsite began to have severe consequences for the Love Canal community as 82 different chemical compounds, including 11 carcinogens, began to seep out of their rotting drum containers. After one particularly heavy rainfall in 1978, corroding waste-disposal drums penetrated up through the soil, spilling poisonous chemicals in backyards, basements, and school grounds. Run-off drained into the Niagara River 2.8 miles upstream of the Niagara Falls' water treatment plant, which served 77,000 people.

The Love Canal issue turned into a national media event, followed by further revelations about abandoned chemical wastes throughout the **United States**. Environmental lobbying and growing public pressure for congressional response followed. A resident of Love Canal, Lois Gibbs, led the Love Canal Homeowners Association in a struggle against the local, state, and federal governments to close down the community and relocate its families.

In 1978 and 1980, President Jimmy Carter announced two environmental emergencies for the Love Canal area, resulting in the evacuation of 950 families from a 10-block area surrounding the landfill. In 1980, the site was declared an Emergency Declaration Area. Congress reacted to the Love Canal crisis by passing the Superfund legislation in 1980. This legislation included an appropriation of US$1.6 billion to clean up the nation's worst abandoned toxic and hazardous waste sites.

From 1977–1980, US$45 million was spent at the site, including resident relocation and health testing expenses, environmental studies, and clean-up grants. A slurry wall and cap to contain groundwater in the site was proposed in 1982 as the long-term solution. In July 1982, the EPA gave US$6.9 billion to New York State in order to study and rehabilitate the site.

As a result of the extensive clean-up efforts, the site no longer presents a threat to human health and the environment. New homeowners have now repopulated the habitable areas of the Love Canal.

LOVELOCK, JAMES. *See* GAIA HYPOTHESIS.

LUXEMBOURG. In 1979 green groups formed an umbrella organization, the Alternative Leescht: Wiert Ich, to compete at elections. As in several other European countries, the formation of a green party in Luxembourg (Dei Greng Alternativ) was an effort to articulate at the electoral level the protests of social movements, notably those concerned about the development of nuclear power. The party was founded in 1983, and a year later gained 6.1 percent of the vote in elections to the **European Parliament**. In concurrent elections to the national parliament, two deputies won seats: Jean Huss with 5.7 percent and Jup Weber with 6 percent of the vote. The average across the nation was 2.9 percent. The main issues that concerned supporters of Dei Greng Alternativ were nuclear power, damage to the environment caused by industrialization, and the corporatist structures for determining policies, which involved business, labor, and the state but appeared to exclude other groups.

Decisions within the party are made at the district, local or regional, and national levels. Members at the district level elect representatives for the National Coordinating Group, a key body that oversees the democratic processes within the party and its financial and administrative affairs. At the national level, there are three conventions, the National Convention (which has a broad agenda), the Full Convention (which takes place four times a year and focuses on specific policy issues), and the Extraordinary Convention.

Dei Greng Alternativ, like Die Grünen in **Germany**, has practiced the rotation of parliamentary delegates and party officers, stipulating that they may only serve a limited term in office. The aim is to ensure that power does not become entrenched. Parliamentary delegates are also subjected to the imperative mandate, a principle that is designed to make them accountable to members and decisions passed at the party conventions and to subject them to recall at any time. Delegates also have to give their parliamentary salaries to the party, which remunerates them according to its own formula. All these issues caused great difficulty within the party; delegate Jup Weber even eventually ended up as an independent in the Parliament.

Dei Greng Alternativ espouses five core principles, **ecology**, **direct democracy**, social reforms, solidarity, and peace. The main emphasis in the party program has been on the consequences of industrialization, particularly pollution caused by the steel industry. However, Dei Greng Alternativ has argued not so much for deindustrialization as for the exploitation of new opportunities and combining of development and environmental protection, for example, through the production of goods in ways that do not cause damage to the environment. Dei Greng Alternativ has been critical of other aspects of **industrial society**, notably the pollution caused by vehicles, destruction of communities resulting from poor planning of housing development, and the inefficient use of energy, particularly the failure to develop renewable sources of energy. Apart from environmental issues, Dei Greng Alternativ has focused on the rights of women and minorities and on democracy, particularly on how local communities can have a greater say in decisions about development. As with many other green parties, Dei Greng Alternativ has not participated in government but has played a crucial role in accelerating the process whereby major parties address environmental issues. *See also* ALTERNATIVE ENERGY.

– M –

MAATHAI, WANGARI (1940–). Born in Kenya, Wangari Maathai founded the **Green Belt Movement**, which since the 1970s has mobilized poor women to plant millions of trees in order to prevent soil degradation and slow desertification. The movement grew to become both an environmental and a women's rights movement. Maathai was awarded a doctorate in 1971 from the University of Kansas. In 1976 she became head of veterinary anatomy and in 1977 associate professor of anatomy at the University of Nairobi. In 1980 she was appointed chair of the Kenyan National Council of Women. In 1989, when she opposed plans to develop a huge multistory building in a park in the capital city of Nairobi, she angered the political authorities and in the following year was prevented from returning to her country after a trip overseas. She is the first African woman to be awarded the Nobel Peace Prize, which she received in 2004 for her efforts to promote **sustainable development**.

MALAYSIA. Environmental awareness is on the rise in this Asian tiger, but the economic development prerogatives of the government remain strong, and deforestation rates continue at alarming levels.

During the colonial period, large areas of tropical forest were replaced with rubber plantations. Sabah and Sarwark, which were more isolated, did experience some logging during this period, but loss of forested areas was contained. This began to change in the 1970s and 1980s as Japanese and other countries' demand for wood increased and logging concessions were handed out to politicians and their families. Logging concessions overlapped with the lands of Borneo's indigenous tribes, which are collectively known as the Dayak. Clashes between the indigenous groups and the logging firms turned violent. After three tribes—the Penan, Kayan, and Kelabit—joined forces and blockaded logging roads, the government reacted by making the blockading of roads a criminal offense punishable by two years in prison and a fine of 6,500 Malaysian dollars. International nongovernmental organizations (NGOs) were also largely kept out at this time due to restrictive visa rules and fears of imprisonment. By the mid-1990s international pressure on Malaysia was becoming increasingly strong and NGOs shifted their efforts to include applying pressures on importing states to only buy lumber for sustainable forests. One victory was the decision by the Malaysian and Indonesian governments in 1994 to establish one of the world's largest wildlife sanctuaries on Borneo, the Betung Kerihun National Park. *See also* SAHABAT ALAM MALAYSIA (SAM).

MALTA. The tiny islands of Malta, which have a population of less than half a million, joined the European Union (EU) in 2004. Malta has a green party, the Democratic Alternative, which was founded in 1989. The party has not performed well in national parliamentary elections (1.69 percent in 1992, 1.7 percent in 1996, 1.5 percent in 1998, 0.7 percent in 2003), but they do have representation in the local councils of Sliema, Sannat, and Swieqi. The party did remarkably well in the 2004 **European Parliament** elections, when they polled 9.33 percent. Their candidate, Arnold Cassola, however, failed to be elected as a member of the European Parliament. Interestingly, he was subsequently picked up by the Italian Federazione dei Verdi to run as an Italian expatriate in the European Constituency to the Italian Chamber of Deputies.

MALTHUS, THOMAS ROBERT (1766–1834). Arguments about *The Limits to Growth*, the "**Tragedy of the Commons**," and the problems of **population growth** have frequently recurred in debates articulated by the green movement. These controversies correspond to concerns expressed since the 18th century, notably by Thomas Malthus in *An Essay on the Principle of Population* (1798). Malthus was born in Guildford, England, in 1766 and died in 1834. After being educated at Cambridge University, he served briefly as a curate before becoming a professor of political economy at Haileybury College in 1805.

In his famous essay, Malthus argued that a sharp increase in population (as experienced by **Great Britain** in the transition from an agrarian and feudal to an industrial economy) was likely to outpace the capacity of the community to provide food for it. Should the provision of food be plentiful for the existing population, a further increase in the size of the population was unavoidable. However, if a community were unable to provide for a growing population, the consequences would include famine, disease, and armed conflicts. Malthus's essay was used as the basis for an attack on the system of poor relief. It was argued that the poor laws increased the population, lowered the general standard of living and raised the number of paupers. This in turn had a harmful social effect, undermining the spirit of independence of individuals and destroying their will to work hard.

Although these arguments are not widely accepted among environmentalists today, the basic concern about population growth and the possibilities of armed conflict has generated considerable discussion, as in the popular work by **Paul Ehrlich** entitled *The Population Bomb* (1968). Ehrlich has often been described as a neo-Malthusian for his views. Among the measures proposed by some environmentalists to deal with the question of population are financial incentives to discourage procreation, and educational campaigns to change beliefs and perceptions about this issue. There is, however, no general agreement in the green movement and in other political and social organizations about the desirability or necessity of introducing measures to curb population growth.

McTAGGART, DAVID (1933–). Born in Vancouver, Canada, David McTaggart was a leading badminton player in the 1950s. In the 1960s he became a highly successful entrepreneur in the U.S. building industry. After losing most of his fortune, he sailed around the South Pacific before responding to an appeal by **Greenpeace** for supporters to participate in actions against nuclear testing by the French government at Mururoa. McTaggart led a group of activists into the nuclear test zone, drawing the ire of the French government, leading to serious assaults on the protestors, and succeeding in attracting immense publicity for Greenpeace. McTaggart went on to become director of Greenpeace International and was largely responsible for ensuring that the organization developed a very high level of professionalism and competence in carrying out research and conducting campaigns over numerous environmental issues.

MENDES, CHICO (1944–1988). The son of a rubber tapper in **Brazil**, Chico Mendes followed his father's trade and then became the leader of a protest movement against the activities of developers, particularly cattle ranchers and settlers in the **Amazon** region in the 1970s. Although the activities by Mendes and his fellow workers were conducted on a sustainable basis—that is, they allowed for the renewal of the trees—the actions of the cattle ranchers had a devastating impact on the environment. Mendes conducted an electoral campaign in 1986 as a candidate of the Worker's Party and secured a significant proportion of the vote. In 1987 he focused his efforts on lobbying the U.S. Inter-American Development Bank, which was instrumental in providing funds to the developers for constructing highways through the Amazon region. He succeeded in persuading the U.S. Senate Appropriations Committee to reduce significantly the amount of funds allocated to the bank on environmental grounds. He also persuaded the Brazilian government to create reserves for protection of the traditional extractive trades in the region. His successes prompted a violent response from the ranchers, who murdered him in December 1988. Mendes left a strong legacy as others organized the defense of the rainforests.

MEXICO. Mexico's environmental movement began in the 1980s with the formation of the country's first environmental nongovernmental organizations (NGOs). These early green groups rallied and mobilized around specific environmental issues, such as Mexico City's air pollution problem and the construction of Mexico's first nuclear power plant. While they achieved little success early on, these nascent groups facilitated the emergence of a much larger and more powerful environmental community over the next two decades.

The environmental movement gained crucial momentum during the 1990s with the North American Free Trade Agreement (NAFTA), which created a free trade area in the world among the **United States**, Mexico, and **Canada**. Pressure from environmental groups in all three countries, coupled with U.S. and Canadian concerns regarding the potential negative trade implications of Mexico's lower environmental standards, forced the incorporation of an environmental agreement into NAFTA. In the following years, this environmental aspect of NAFTA substantially strengthened Mexico's green groups by facilitating cross-border cooperation and the forging of alliances between Mexican NGOs and their stronger, more established, and better-funded American counterparts.

Today, Mexico's environmental movement is stronger and more organized than it has ever been. Recent victories, such as President Ernesto Zedillo's permanent veto of a proposed salt production plant that would have endangered the welfare of the gray whale in 2000, demonstrate the growing influence of green groups in policy formulation. However, although the environmental movement has made considerable gains, it continues to be confronted with a number of challenges. Co-optation, oppression, and the provision of varying levels of access to different groups by the Mexican government contribute to the fragmentation of the environmental community, which in turn hinders cooperation and organization. In addition, lack of access to information and inadequate funding severely impedes the progress of Mexico's environmental movement.

The Ecologist Green Party of Mexico (Partido Revolucionario Institucional [PVEM]) was officially registered in 1991. It received 1.4 percent of the proportional representation vote for federal deputies in 1994 and 3.8 percent in 1997. It did sufficiently well in 1997 to elect one senator (the first in the Western Hemisphere) and eight deputies. It also did well in local and mayoral elections. In 2000, the National Action Party, a conservative, business-friendly party, formed an alliance with the PVEM (the Alliance for Change), and successfully backed Vicente Fox for president. The party also won five seats to the Senate. Fox did not make many environmental promises during his campaign, although he did call for making water and forests matters of national security. The alliance broke down one year into Fox's presidency. In the 2003 Chamber of Deputies election, the PVEM allied this time with the Institutional Revolutionary Party (PRI). The PVEM was able to send 17 representatives to the Chamber of Deputies. In the 2006 presidential election, PVEM entered an alliance with the PRI and both backed Roberto Madrazo as their candidate.

The party's record has not been without issue, however. The federal electoral tribunal found it in violation of the electoral code and the Constitution because of its restricted list of candidates and officials (most of whom came from one family). It was also fined for campaign offenses in the 2000 presidential election.

MILJØPARTIET DE GRØNNE. *See* NORWAY.

MILLENNIUM DEVELOPMENT GOALS. *See* WORLD SUMMIT ON SUSTAINABLE DEVELOPMENT.

MONTREAL PROTOCOL ON SUBSTANCES THAT DEPLETE THE OZONE LAYER. The Montreal Protocol to the **Vienna Convention for the Protection of the Ozone Layer** established target dates and reduction levels for various chemical substances that contribute to the depletion of the **ozone layer**. The ozone layer protects the Earth from the sun's harmful ultraviolet rays. The protocol was signed in 1987 by 47 nations; over 120 nations have since ratified it. It entered into force in 1989. It has since been amended five times—in 1990, 1992, 1995, 1997, and 1999—to accelerate the phase out of some chemicals and to add other chemicals to the list of chemicals requiring phase out. The initial convention agreed to reduce annual production of chlorofluorocarbons (CFCs) by 50 percent of 1986 levels by June 1999, return halon production to 1986 levels by early 1992, allow developing countries up to 10 additional years to comply with deadlines, restrict chemical trade with nonsignatory countries, and create a fund to assist developing countries' implementation of the treaty.

The Montreal Protocol is widely considered one of the most successful global environmental agreements. Levels of CFCs and other chlorinated hydrocarbons in the stratosphere have either leveled off or decreased, while halon concentrations have increased at a slower pace and are expected to decline by about 2020. There have been relatively few incidences of attempts to smuggle CFCs from undeveloped to developed nations, and the number of countries and compliance levels have been very high.

MOVEMENT FOR THE SURVIVAL OF THE OGONI PEOPLE (MOSOP). *See* SARO-WIWA, KENULE.

MUIR, JOHN (1838–1914). Born in Dunbar, Scotland, John Muir moved with his family to Wisconsin in 1849. In 1863, after three years at the University of Wisconsin, where he did well but did not complete his studies, he began to travel around the **United States**, taking on casual jobs and exploring the countryside. Beginning in 1867, following a serious eye injury from which he recovered, he embarked on lengthy journeys across America before settling in California, first in San Francisco and then in Yosemite. In 1874 he became well known as a writer of "studies in the Sierra." His interest in travel extended to numerous journeys to Alaska as well as trips to South America, **Australia**, Europe, and **Africa**.

Muir became a prolific writer, focusing on his travels, the dangers to the natural environment, the need for protection and **preservation** of nature, and the **spiritual** qualities of the wilderness. He played a central role in the campaign that led to the creation of the Yosemite National Park in 1890. In 1892 Muir and other preservationists formed the **Sierra Club** to protect areas like Yosemite National Park as well as the Petrified Forest and Grand Canyon National Parks in Arizona. Muir was elected the first president of the club and guided it through several important campaigns until his death in 1914. In 1903 President Theodore Roosevelt went to visit Muir in Yosemite and undertook several plans for **conservation**. *See also* NATIONAL PARKS.

– N –

NAESS, ARNE. *See* DEEP ECOLOGY.

NARMADA DAM. The government of **India** established plans to capture the power of the Narmada River and its tributaries for electricity generation and irrigation of drought-prone areas such as Gujarat, Kutch, Saurashtra, and North Gujarat with a series of 30 large, 135 medium-sized dams, and several thousand small dams. The tallest and most controversial of the dam projects is known as Sardar Sarovar; the approved height of the dam has been steadily creeping upward. As of 2006, height extensions had been approved to 121 meters. Construction of the dam has required the displacement of tens of thousands of individuals. Local and international protests against the construction of the dams have been extensive. The World Bank, which had initially funded a portion of the dam project, withdrew its support in the early 1990s.

A powerful new movement arose in India in reaction to the dam. The Narmada Bachao Andolan (Save the Narmada Movement) led by Medha Patkar has become the largest **nonviolent** peoples' movement in India and claims to speak for the hundreds of thousands of indigenous peoples and peasants who will be displaced by the series of dams. Narmada Bachao Andolan was criticized by the Indian Supreme Court in 1999 when the court ruled in favor of the government's plan to build the dam. The court also ruled, however, that construction of the dam must stop until those who were being displaced receive rehabilitation. Narmada Bachao Andolan continues to protest the construction of dams along the Narmada River and to fight for the rights of those who are being affected by the construction of the dams. The group also works to promote alternative energies and the empowerment of women. The Friends of River Narmada, an international group of individuals and organizations largely of Indian descent, and the International Rivers Network have supported the work of Narmada Bachao Andolan.

NATIONAL BLACK ENVIRONMENTAL JUSTICE NETWORK. This national preventive health, environmental, and economic justice network is focused on the black community in the **United States**. It has spotlighted environmental injustices associated with the response to Hurricane Katrina. *See also* ENVIRONMENTAL JUSTICE.

NATIONAL ENVIRONMENTAL COALITION OF NATIVE AMERICANS. An organization that aims to educate Native Americans and non–Native Americans on issues pertaining to the dumping of nuclear waste on Native American lands. It also works with local and national groups to generate awareness of nuclear waste issues.

NATIONAL ENVIRONMENTAL TRUST. Set up in 1994, this nonprofit works to inform U.S. citizens about environmental issues ranging from clean air to forests, oceans, and environmental health.

NATIONAL PARKS. The first efforts to set aside natural areas for conservation occurred in cities. In 1853 New York City authorized the creation of Central Park. Frederick Law Olmstead, Jr., who designed Central Park, first proposed that Yosemite should be a protected area in 1865.

John Muir was the first nature writer to form his ideas into a political ideology, and he was successful in advocating efforts to establish parks such as Yellowstone and Yosemite, as well as a National Park System and for preservation of wilderness. **Preservationism** grew with the popularity of outdoor recreation clubs but, while influential, like **conservationism**, it was essentially the concern of the upper class.

The conservation and preservation movements both contributed in different ways to the establishment of a national parks system. **Yellowstone National Park** was created as the world's first national park in 1872. Newly emerged environmental groups played an important role in forwarding efforts to protect nature. The **Sierra Club**, a California hiking society founded 1892 by John Muir and Robert Underwood Johnson, lobbied for protection of wild areas. Other groups such as the National Federation of Women's Clubs mobilized women around conservation and preservation, in 1904 petitioning Congress to save California's Calaveras Grove of Big Trees, and in 1913 winning a long campaign conducted in conjunction with the **Audubon Society** to ban exotic bird feathers in hats. In 1919 the National Parks Conservation Association was formed to enhance the national parks system. Two other major environmental groups that formed and played a role in promoting nature conservation were the **Wilderness Society** (founded by preservationist Robert Marshall and conservationist **Aldo Leopold**) and the **National Wildlife Federation**, both established in 1935.

The American environmental movement benefited greatly from President Theodore Roosevelt's enthusiasm for hunting and the out-of-doors. He was a great supporter of Gifford Pinchot's conservationism. Roosevelt believed that conservation was necessary to protect the long-range prosperity of the country. In 1903 Roosevelt joined Muir in a hike in the Yosemite Valley and became more open to preservationist lobbying, later introducing a bill to prevent exploitation and damage in the park. In 1908 he convened the first Governors' Conference on Conservation and established the National Conservation Commission.

The environmental movement in the **United States** was by no means always united in its efforts to set aside land. Tensions between preservationists and conservationists escalated in 1908 when the mayor of San Francisco planned a dam and reservoir in the Hetch Hetchy valley in central California in order to supply water to the Bay Area metropolis. In this case, Gifford Pinchot supported utilization of the resource, while Muir condemned it as undermining the significant aesthetic value of the valley. The dam was signed into law by President Woodrow Wilson in 1913, but the controversy was important to the establishment of the National Park Service under Stephen Mather in 1916.

These competing views—of use versus preservation—have colored many local debates regarding the use and preservation of land.

The establishment of Everglades National Park in 1934 was a victory for preservationists as the area was marked for protection, not so much because it was monumental or splendid but rather because it was considered ecologically important and an important wildlife habitat. There are now 56 national parks in the United States.

The national park movement quickly spread to other countries. **Australia** established the world's second national park in 1879; the Royal National Park. **Canada** established the third, Banff National Park in 1885; and **New Zealand** the fourth, Tongariro National Park in 1887. **Sweden** was the first European country to pass legislation for the protection of nature when it established nine separate parks in 1909. The Swiss created their first national park in 1914. Interestingly, while many European countries established historic preservation sites already in the first half of the 20th century, most did not create their first national park until after World War II. France established its first national park, Vanoise, in 1963.

Greenland National Park is the world's largest park. Australia has the world's largest marine protected area, the Great Barrier Reef Marine Park established in 1975. The second largest is the Northwestern Hawaiian Islands Coral Reef Ecosystem Reserve. **Brazil** established the world's largest tropical forest park in 2002, the Tumucumaque National Park.

The **International Union for the Conservation of Nature and Natural Resources/World Conservation Union (IUCN)** organizes a World Congress on National Parks and Protected Areas every decade. At the fourth World Congress held in Caracas, Venezuela, in 1992, a goal to expand the world's protected areas to cover at least 10 percent of each major biome by 2000 was proposed. This is one of the few global green goals that has actually been met and exceeded. At the fifth World Congress held in Durban, **South Africa**, it was announced that protected areas stood at 11.5 percent of the Earth's land surface. The problem is that many of these parks are concentrated in uninhabited areas with low ecosystem value.

Establishing national parks, moreover, does not ensure that poachers will not continue to shoot valuable game. This has been a serious problem in many parts of the developing world.

NATIONAL PARKS CONSERVATION ASSOCIATION. Established in 1919, this nonpartisan association with over 300,000 members and supporters works to address major threats to the National Park System in the **United States**.

NATIONAL WILDLIFE FEDERATION. With four million members and supporters, the National Wildlife Federation (NWF) is one of the largest environmental groups in the world. Founded in 1936, NWF works on a variety of conservation issues in the **United States** and internationally.

NATURAL RESOURCES DEFENSE COUNCIL (NRDC). Established in 1970 by John Adams, the NRDC has grown to a base of 1.2 million members and online activists. NRDC has campaigns addressing clean energy, **global warming**, clean water, wildlife, parks, forests, wildlands, health, nuclear weapons and waste, green living, and U.S. and international laws and policies. With a staff of environmental lawyers and scientists, NRDC is one of the most influential environmental groups in the **United States**.

NATURE CONSERVANCY. The primary objective of the Nature Conservancy in the **United States** is to buy land in order to protect it. Formed in 1951, the organization has, over a 40-year period, been able to protect over 5 million acres, which include over 1,000 sanctuaries and many endangered species. Its nonconfrontational approach to environmental protection has made the organization attractive to the more conservative members of American society, many of whom would consider the tactics of some environmental groups as too radical and conflictual. In 1995 the Nature Conservancy had over 600,000 members. A decade later, its membership had grown to over one million.

NETHERLANDS. Although, as in other advanced industrialized nations, there is a strong awareness of environmental problems and significant support for social movements concerned about issues like the development of nuclear energy, there have been many obstacles to the successful implementation of environmental protection measures in the Netherlands. Economic development in the 1950s and 1960s led to considerable pollution of the air and water. The location of petrochemical industries has further contributed to these difficulties. In addition, the Netherlands has both contributed to and been the recipient of pollution flowing through the Rhine River.

Another major problem has been how to deal with the consequences of the enormous success of the agricultural sector in producing more livestock (notably cattle, pigs, and poultry), relative to the territory available, than any other country in the world. The principal difficulty is the damage caused by the nutrients from the manure generated by the livestock. Nitrogen and phosphate have damaged surface waters and groundwater, and have contributed to air pollution in the form of ammonia acids.

The Netherlands has a strong environmental movement represented by well-known groups such as Greenpeace (the international office is located in Amsterdam), Milieu Defensie (**Environmental Defense**), and Stichting Milieu en Natuur (Society for Nature and the Environment); groups with a connection to the church, such as Werkgroep Kerk en Milieu (Working Group Church and Environment) and Time to Turn; and more radical groups, such as Vrienden van Groenfront! (Friends of the Greenfront!). The growth of the environmental movement helped to transform the Netherlands into an increasingly green-oriented country.

In the early 1970s concern about air and water pollution caused by heavy industry led to the formation of a Ministry for the Environment and introduction of the **polluter pays principle**. In addition, subsidies and levies were introduced to fund new technologies to deal with contamination and assist with the regulation and inspection of levels of pollution. Public opinion was generally supportive of these measures, as was the Christian Democratic Party, which dominated the coalition governments that had to be formed in the context of a multiparty system. Although environmental groups attracted many supporters and sympathizers, green political organizations were unable to exert a great deal of influence in the 1970s and 1980s due to their fragmentation and the particular circumstances surrounding their development.

Pressure on the major parties to address concerns about the environment resulted in the government's 1989 National Environmental Policy Plan. The plan put the Netherlands at the forefront of green planning by integrating all environmental issues into a single ecosystem-based policy, and linking this to public health and the economy. The plan recommended targets for reducing pollution, particularly **acid rain** and the depletion of the **ozone layer**. Other proposals were how to reduce drastically the use of pesticides and handle the transportation of hazardous wastes. The government used the findings of the **World Commission on Environment and Development (WCED)** on **sustainable development** to justify drastic action. The plan has since been modified several times. The focus has shifted increasingly toward the use of consultative decision making, through target group consultation and the establishment of covenants (voluntary agreements among stakeholders). Market-based mechanisms are also increasingly coming into use, such as with the use of emissions trading. More than 250,000 firms are involved in the plan through performance-based covenants that they reach with the government, addressing matters such as **climate change**, energy efficiency, air and water pollutants, resource recycling, and the like. The fourth National Environmental Policy Plan (2001) focuses on dealing with climate change (through energy efficiency improvements), agriculture and biodiversity, and natural resources.

The Netherlands was one of the stronger proponents within the European Union (EU) calling for action to address climate change. It was a strong proponent of the **Kyoto Protocol**. The country's ability to meet its Kyoto Protocol greenhouse gas targets, however, remains in question. In an effort to meet the goals, the Netherlands is combining an emphasis on local initiatives, covenants with industry, emissions trading, and **joint implementation**.

There is also a green political movement in the Netherlands. Two green parties formed in the 1980s. The first, De Groenen (The Greens), was founded in December 1983 and has generally failed to make much of an impression in elections. The second, Groen Links (Green Left), was an electoral alliance of left-wing parties in 1989, before turning itself into a new political party in November 1990. The history of the two organizations and the parties that existed prior to the formation of Groen Links are closely linked.

Although Groen Links was formed much later than De Groenen, it was composed of political organizations that arose much earlier. De Groenen was formed in 1983, partly as a reaction to the possibility that these (left-wing) organizations would exercise considerable influence over the direction of green politics. However, De Groenen failed to prevent this; the political organizations that came to form Groen Links comprised the left-wing political parties feared by De

Groenen. They included the Communist Party of the Netherlands; the Pacifist-Socialist Party, which had gained seats in parliamentary elections since the 1950s; and the Political Radical Party, which had been formed in 1968 and represented in Parliament since the early 1970s. Another minor party that joined this group was the Evangelical People's Party, founded in 1981.

The Pacifists opposed the military and began to engage in protests against environmental destruction in the 1960s. The Radicals had also concentrated on environmental issues. Both Pacifists and Radicals objected to the development of **nuclear energy** in the 1970s. Nonetheless, each of the minor parties in Groen Links retained its adherence to particular ideologies. The Communists remained loyal to many of the tenets of Marxism and Leninism. The Radicals and Pacifists espoused libertarian ideas. The main impetus to the merger between these parties was the growing evidence of their decline and the hope that they would make a far better showing in electoral politics as a united group. The combined membership of these political organizations had declined from a peak of around 36,000 in 1981 and 1982 to about 18,000 in 1989.

The existence of fairly coherent, small, left-wing parties, let alone of a coalition between them based on a proenvironment platform, has always made it difficult for De Groenen to establish itself as an influential minor party. In elections to the **European Parliament** in 1984, De Groenen polled 1.3 percent of the vote, whereas the coalition of left-wing minor parties, which then called itself the Groen Progressief Akkoord (Green Progressive Accord), secured 5.6 percent of the vote and two seats in the European Parliament. In the 1986 national elections De Groenen polled only 0.2 percent of the vote, in 1989 0.4 percent, and in 1994 only 0.1 percent. Their biggest success was the election of Martin Bierman, one of the party's founders, to the Senate in 1995. In 1988, they won no seats, however. Given its weak showing in elections, there was a proposal in November 2000 to form a Groenen Brug (Green Bridge) with Groen Links, but the proposal was rejected by the membership. Instead, they opted to cooperate with local, independent green branches. This strategy also failed the party, however, and so it has again sought to create an identity as an independent party.

By contrast, Groen Links has done reasonably well in elections, although it has been on a bit of a roller-coaster ride in terms of its performance. It secured 4.1 percent of the vote and six seats in the 1989 elections. In municipal elections in 1990, Groen Links obtained an impressive 300 councilor seats. The party won 5.2 percent in provincial elections in 1991 and 5.2 percent in the Senate elections, giving the party four seats. Like in many other western European countries, the mid-1990s were a difficult time for Groen Links. In 1994, it polled only 3.5 percent in the parliamentary election, dropping down to five seats. In the European Parliament elections as well, the party lost a seat.

The party rebounded in 1998 under the direction of Paul Rosenmoeller. The party won 11 seats in the Parliament. In 2002, however, Dutch politics took a noticeable shift to the right. Anti-immigrant sentiments were strong, and this buoyed the political fortunes of far-right politician Pim Fortuyn. His shocking murder one week before the elections sent sympathy voters flocking to Fortuyn's party list. Groen Links, which had expected to do well in the election, instead lost one of its seats. The party's fortunes further deteriorated in a special election held in 2003, when the party received only 5.2 percent of the vote and eight seats. In the 2006 elections, they dropped further to 4.6 percent (seven seats). At the European Parliament level, Groen Links secured two representatives.

De Groenen has always stood on a platform that attends first and foremost to environmental issues and links this to notions of self-sufficiency, decentralization, and grassroots democracy. De Groenen has not, however, been able to overcome its own problems in establishing a coherent organizational structure or the perception that Groen Links represents a much more viable and credible platform for addressing environmental issues.

Groen Links attempts to combine diverse convictions (including beliefs about control by the state of many large enterprises, the withdrawal of the Netherlands from the North Atlantic Treaty Organization (NATO), and the introduction of a **guaranteed minimum income**) with many of the aspirations of green parties throughout the world. The dissolution of the minor parties that formed Groen Links and development of environmental policies in the 1990s indicate that concerns about the environment are likely to dominate the agenda of the new political formation. Supporters of Groen Links share many of the characteristics of supporters of many other green parties: most are younger and/or have high levels of formal education, and large proportions are employed in the public sector. *See also* DIRECT DE-MOCRACY.

NEW POLITICS. The term *new politics* has been used to identify the articulation of issues that had previously been accorded relatively low status on the political agenda. Since the 1960s concern about the environment has been linked by social scientists to the emergence of the new politics. The new politics also includes preoccupation with **direct democracy**, decentralization, and **postmaterialism**. Postmaterialism provides clues to the difference between the old and the new politics. The old politics is concerned with questions of material prosperity, security, and law and order. The new politics focuses on a different set of considerations, aesthetic and intellectual development, and questions of **spirituality** and the **quality of life.** Nonmaterial values have been central to the new politics and reflect an attempt to move away from the focus on economic growth and material prosperity, including the production and consumption of goods.

The new politics also marks the entry of new social groups onto the political stage. Since the 1960s participation in these new movements has been high among women, minority groups, the young, the relatively affluent, and the well educated. New styles of political action have been adopted by these movements, hence the focus on participation and direct democracy, attempts to avoid hierarchical structures, and critique of the political patronage that characterizes traditional political organizations. In the green movement, the new forms of political organization have included the formation of **citizens' initiatives** and green political parties that have attempted to introduce innovative practices into conventional political settings.

NEW ZEALAND. The Values Party, formed in May 1972 in Wellington, New Zealand, was the first party to be established at the national level and champion both environmental protection and participatory democracy. At the November 1972 elections it competed in 43 of the 87 electorates. It polled 3.9 percent of the vote in these electorates and 2.7 percent of the vote across the nation. In 1975 the party improved its performance, obtaining 5.2 percent of the total vote and attracting many former Labour Party supporters. The pinnacle for the Values Party, in electoral terms, was a 9 percent vote in the January 1976 Nelson by-election. Thereafter, the party went into decline, receiving 2.8 percent of the vote in 1978 and only 0.2 percent in 1981. By then many of its members had questioned the worth of contesting elections, especially in a simple plurality electoral system that discriminated heavily against minor parties.

However, the Values Party had played a crucial part in directing attention away from the preoccupation with material prosperity and economic growth. The person primarily responsible for the formation of the party was Tony Brunt, a former journalist who, like many other young people, felt that traditional political organizations were failing to articulate the important issues of the day. Support for the party came from young people with high levels of formal education and upper-middle classes. It also came from former adherents of all the major parties, as well as from activists in radical left-wing political groups. Later, the adherents of the latter, especially in the city of Christchurch, began to exert a great deal of influence over the party.

In the early stages of its development, the party was influenced by ideas such as those propounded by the **Club of Rome**, the study *The Limits to Growth*, and the British publication *A Blueprint for Survival*. The 1972 party manifesto, *Blueprint for New Zealand*, adapted these ideas and focused on a wide range of **quality-of-life** issues, notably the depletion of nonrenewable resources, **population growth**, and the dangers associated with industrialization and technological change.

On a more positive note, the party focused on the need for a change in values with less emphasis on affluence and more on the fulfillment of spiritual needs. The party denounced the old political system for its short-term approach to policymaking, resorting to expediency and excessive focus on electoral contests. As regards environmental issues, during the 1972 election campaign, the Values Party mobilized opposition to the proposed development of a hydroelectric system that threatened Lake Manapouri on the South Island.

While this campaign helped to unify supporters of the party, the attempt to develop organizational structures presented a number of difficulties. Concern about participatory democracy and decentralization led to the party's almost ceasing to exist as a national organization until a new constitution was formulated and implemented at the 1974 party conference. By 1978 there was concern among many members that the party, particularly the groups based in Christchurch, had moved too far toward bureaucratization and conventional organizational practices.

In parallel with these tensions over organizational structures were divisions over policy. The Values Party had begun with a strong focus on quality-of-life issues. This approach had been partly undermined by the economic considerations that came to dominate the national and international political agenda following the oil crisis of 1973. The group in Christchurch, which had always been interested in economic issues from a socialist point of view, attempted to focus on developing a party program covering a wide range of economic and social questions. The kinds of issues addressed by social movements, such as campaigns against the introduction of nuclear power and restrictive laws on abortion, continued to play an important role.

The party was not very successful either in forming alliances with social movements or in retaining the allegiance of key groups within its own ranks. In 1979 the group from Christchurch, led by Toni Kunowski, having failed to force the majority into adopting a more professional approach to the organization of the party and having been defeated in a contest for the leadership of the party, formed a separate political organization called Socialist Network. The party never recovered from these divisions, even after it adopted the name Values: The Green Party of Aotearoa. Finally, in March 1990 members of the party participated in the creation of a new political organization, the Greens. In 1996 the Greens contested the elections as part of a coalition of parties called the Alliance. This association secured 10 percent of the vote and a total of 13 out of 120 seats in the Parliament.

Apart from its own internal conflicts and difficulties, the Values Party was negatively affected by the ability of the Labour Party to adapt to issues such as the widespread opposition to nuclear power. However, the possibility remained for the revival of a green political organization. In the 1987 elections the **antinuclear** stand of the Labour Party ensured its success in attracting environmentalists.

However, in 1990 neither this issue nor the reform of environmental legislation could prevent the Greens from running in the elections. Although it had virtually no policies and refused to appoint leaders in the conventional sense, the new party polled 6.6 percent of the national vote, thus demonstrating the enduring strength of the green political movement. The Greens had also polled almost 20 percent of the vote in some electorates. The constant problem, however, was the electoral system, which made it very difficult for them to gain any formal representation.

In May 1990, the Values Party merged with several new green groups to form the Green Party of Aotearoa New Zealand. Six months later, they won 7 percent of the vote. The first-past-the-post electoral system, however, meant the party was unable to win representation in Parliament. As a result, the party decided on the necessity of aligning with other parties, and they helped found the five-party Alliance. They ensured that the Alliance had a strong focus on **sustainable development**. In the 1996 general election, they succeeded in sending their first three green delegates to Parliament (Jeanette Fitzimons, Ron Donald, and Phillida Bunkle). By this time, they also had 20 greens in local government, including the mayor of Dunedin.

Feeling the need to maintain an independent image, the Green Party decided to leave the Alliance. This caused a split within the Green Party, and Phillida Bunkle decided to remain with the Alliance. The Green Party focused its 1999 campaign on safe foods and opposition to genetic engineering, nature conservation, and strong communities. In the end, the party won 5.2 percent of the vote and took seven seats. *See also* DIRECT DEMOCRACY; SPIRITUALITY.

NIGERIA. In Nigeria, oil extraction began in 1907. By 1938, the British colonizers had given BP and Shell Oil licenses to explore for and remove oil across all of Nigeria. Oil production began in 1957 and the companies discovered the Bomu oil field on the land of the Ogoni people in 1958. Nigeria's economy quickly became dependent on oil exports so that after independence in 1960, the new government continued to allow foreign oil companies to dominate the oil market in Nigeria. Environmental damage during the next several decades included oil waste pits, damage to buildings through seismic surveys, burial of chemical waste that contaminated the groundwater and arable land, gas flaring, and oil spills. Pollution and exploitation gave birth to the **Movement for the Survival of the Ogoni People (MOSOP)**. Reacting to the politics of exploitation, the Green Party of Nigeria was born in 2003. It was founded by Olisa Agbakoba. *See also* SARO-WIWA, KENULE.

NONVIOLENCE. The principle of nonviolence is an axiom espoused by many green political organizations. Some people believe that green political activists should renounce all forms of violence in the manner suggested by Mahatma Gandhi and his followers in the campaigns against British rule in **India**. There have been numerous suggestions for how to put nonviolence into practice. Green activists have argued that, in certain situations, it is necessary to engage in campaigns of civil disobedience, which could include noncompliance with tax regulations (for example in protest against the use of taxes to purchase military equipment and fund wars) and passive resistance, such as blocking the entrances to nuclear power plants to prevent the transportation of nuclear waste. There are also controversies over whether or not to sabotage nuclear plants in order to try to achieve similar objectives, and a small minority has carried out such threats.

Some green activists have suggested that no efforts should be made to arm citizens, even for their own defense, since this would already sow the seeds for violence. Others, however, have developed detailed proposals for eliminating "offensive" weapons that might be used to invade another country; maintaining "defensive" weapons (for instance, antiaircraft units); and preparing citizens to engage in resistance to armed invasion. *See also* EARTH FIRST!

NORWAY. Norway has benefited immensely from its oil and natural gas reserves. Unlike many oil-rich countries, it has a strong social democratic orientation and has invested much of its oil and gas wealth in the provision of social services and environmental protection. As one of the richest countries in the world, Norway consistently ranks as one of the countries with the highest **quality of life** and strongest orientation toward sustainable development. It is perhaps little wonder that Norway's **Gro Harlem Brundtland** led the commission that produced the famous 1987 report, *Our Common Future*. This report can be seen as a turning point in global awareness of the need to shift from current economic structures to more sustainable systems or risk severe ecological destruction and climate change. Given the relatively high degree to which environmental matters have been incorporated into the agendas of the main political parties, it has been difficult for the Norwegian Greens to gain a toehold in the political system.

Miljøpartiet De Grønne was formed in 1988 out of several local green lists. In one of the countries that consistently ranks as one of the most sustainable in the world, however, the party has had little success in establishing a unique image among voters. The party received only 0.1 percent of the vote in 2005. As with many of other green parties, Miljøpartiet De Grønne's party platform is based on such ideas as promotion of **grassroots democracy**, locally based and sustainable economics, ecological farming, and public transportation.

NUCLEAR DISARMAMENT PARTY (NDP). The principal objectives of the NDP in **Australia** are the closure of all foreign military bases, a ban on the stationing in or the passage through Australia of any nuclear weapons, and, of particular relevance to environmentalists, a halt to the mining and export of uranium. The NDP emerged from the peace and environment movements and represents one of the earlier efforts by green political activists to form a national political organization.

The peace movement has a longer history (as a new social movement) than the environmental movement and can be traced back to campaigns for disarmament in the 1950s both in Australia and in countries such as **Great Britain**. In the 1960s the Vietnam War provided a further focus for the peace movement. The young, better-educated, middle-class individuals and those with left-wing orientations have joined all these movements and the NDP in great numbers.

The NDP has had strong support among these social groups and endeavored to combine some of the ideas from both the peace and environmental movements. Uranium mining was one of the core issues that occupied the NDP, and this reflected an interest in both preserving the environment and peace and nuclear disarmament. However, the circumstances surrounding the formation of the NDP were favorable in some respects but problematic in others. The party was created in response to a 1984 decision by the Australian Labour Party (ALP) to permit the operation of a uranium mine. This was a breach of a pledge to proceed more cautiously in this domain and provoked a very strong response from opponents of uranium mining, many of whom were members of the ALP.

In a very short period of time, just six months after the formation of the NDP, 8,000 people had signed up as members, and 643,061 people, representing 7.2 percent of voters, had cast a first-preference vote for the party in elections to the Senate. There were, however, numerous disadvantages associated with this momentary shift in fortune. Although the profile, in social and economic terms, of those who voted for the NDP was similar to that of supporters of green political organizations in other countries, the party also shared some of their weaknesses. Apart from a pledge to rid the world of nuclear weapons and nuclear power, there had been an ineffectual debate in the NDP about how to implement policies. Little effort had been made to explain more fully the connection between policies about nuclear disarmament or uranium mining and questions relating to foreign policy and economic development.

In addition, the catalyst for the formation of the NDP was first and foremost a momentary reaction to the policies of one of the traditional political organizations, the ALP. The rapidity of the response to the policies of the ALP meant that there had been little debate about political differences among supporters of the NDP. These were largely repressed because of the need to compete hastily in an election campaign. Although there was much unity around the notion of nuclear disarmament, there had been little time to develop positions on other issues. Like many green political organizations, the NDP also lacked a coherent organizational structure. Party branches had been created in all states, yet there were no mechanisms to facilitate organizational coherence, the exchange of political ideas, and a dialogue with various social movements.

The overarching appeal to nationalism in a policy on nuclear weapons that was not influenced by the interests of foreign countries lasted for only a short while. Similarly, complaints against the ALP remained just a protest. Members of the traditional parties that had defected to the NDP felt they had achieved what they wanted simply by registering a protest vote against ALP policies. There had also been insufficient time and reflection for supporters of the green movement to become or remain loyal to the NDP. Many activists from the peace and environmental movements regarded the NDP as a useful adjunct to their campaigns, which took the form of social movements, lobby groups, mass political protests, and political networks.

Among those committed to the new party, conflicts arose between some who were solely concerned with the single issue of nuclear disarmament and others who wished to emulate the broader approach of Die Grünen in **Germany**. The failure by party activists to agree on basic organizational and political principles further undermined the chances of retaining the support of voters who had protested the traditional parties and of activists from social movements. A final obstacle to the further development of the NDP was, as in countries like those in Great Britain, an electoral system for the lower house, the House of Representatives, that disadvantaged minor parties. There were also hurdles to entering the upper house. After the 1984 elections, the NDP was allocated one seat in the Senate, following a favorable distribution of preferences to Jo Vallentine, its sole parliamentary delegate, in Western Australia. Yet, in New South Wales, where it attracted 249,722 votes, it was unable to secure another seat because of an unfavorable distribution of preferences by the ALP. Although the NDP continued to contest elections in the 1980s, it never recaptured the position it held in 1984.

The first national conference of the NDP, held in April 1985, was set up only to make recommendations that would be voted on by the membership at a later stage. The conference was not representative either of the membership or state branches. It had no mandate to draw up a constitution, form cohesive organizational structures, or decide on appropriate tactics for Jo Vallentine. Two issues prompted the exit of its only senator, along with about 40 other delegates, during the first conference. First, there was disagreement over procedures for the ratification of recommendations made by the conference. Those who walked out of the conference had argued that the entire membership should be involved through a postal ballot. Their preference for this method of voting rather than for ratification by branch meetings of the party was tied in with the other major stumbling block, the question of dual membership. There was concern over the disproportionate influence of the Socialist Workers Party over the NDP. To combat this threat, the NDP in Western Australia had introduced a proscription clause that allowed members of other parties into the NDP but prevented them from holding key positions. Postal balloting was regarded by many as a complementary mechanism to the proscription clause. The delegates in favor of postal balloting were, however, unable to secure a majority and walked out of the conference. Among them was Jo Vallentine, who went on to become an independent senator.

At the 1987 elections the NDP attracted only 102,480 votes, and Vallentine, as West Australian senator for nuclear disarmament, attracted 40,048 votes (4.8 percent) compared with 52,365 votes in 1984 (6.8 percent). Overall support for the NDP and for Vallentine dropped from 7.2 percent to 1.5 percent, yet the design of the electoral system ensured that both she and an NDP candidate from New South Wales were elected to the Senate. *See also* CAMPAIGN FOR NUCLEAR DISARMAMENT (CND).

NUCLEAR ENERGY. *See* ANTINUCLEAR PROTESTS; CAMPAIGN FOR NUCLEAR DISARMAMENT (CND).

– O –

OWEN, DAVID. *See* ECOLOGY.

OZONE LAYER. A term used to describe the concentration of a gas called ozone that occurs in the Earth's atmosphere, especially at a height of about 12 to 30 miles above the surface of the Earth. Ozone in the atmosphere is vital to the survival of life on Earth as we know it because it creates a protective shield against nearly all of the ultraviolet radiation emanating from the sun. The principal danger arising from any depletion of the ozone layer is a startling rise in skin cancer. Other dangers associated with any increase in radiation entering through the Earth's atmosphere include damage to the immune system of humans and animals and threats to plant life both on land and in the oceans. An increase in ultraviolet radiation is likely to contribute to chemical smogs and health problems, notably respiratory illnesses.

The principal cause of depletion of the ozone layer was the production, mainly in industrialized countries, of chlorofluorocarbons (CFCs). They had been used since the 1930s as an inexpensive and effective way of propelling substances in aerosol cans, such as deodorants, perfume, and paints. They were also used in a wide range of plastic foams for packing, in furniture, in the production of Styrofoam containers for fast-food outlets, and, in a liquefied form, as a coolant in refrigerators and freezers. Production of the most commonly used CFCs, chlorofluorocarbon 11 and chlorofluorocarbon 12, rose from around 5,000 tons in the 1930s to 45,000 tons in 1951, 750,000 tons in 1971, and over one million tons per annum in the early 1990s.

As far back as 1974 two researchers at the University of California, F. Sherwood Rowland and Mario Molina, discovered that the release of large volumes of CFCs into the atmosphere would probably destroy a significant proportion of the ozone layer. Studies by the U.S. National Academy of Sciences in 1976 and 1979 supported these findings. The **United States'** government did respond to this information by prohibiting, in 1978, the use of CFCs in nearly all aerosols. **Sweden**, **Canada**, **Norway**, and **Finland** took similar steps. These five countries, thereafter referred to as the Toronto Group, presented a variety of proposals for eliminating, across the world, the use of CFCs in aerosol cans and for phasing out their use in other products.

Initially, action by the Toronto Group had limited impact. First, their own ban on CFCs in aerosol cans did not lead to a reduction in the production of CFCs since they could be put to many other uses. Second, the Toronto Group faced opposition, notably by countries in the European Union (EU), on the grounds that more evidence was needed to prove the connection between CFCs and depletion of the ozone layer. The EU also perceived a variety of threats to its economic interests.

Major scientific breakthroughs occurred in the late 1970s and early 1980s. Scientists engaged in the British Antarctic Survey announced in 1982 a significant reduction in the concentration of ozone over the Antarctic. There remained, however, uncertainty over the reliability of this finding and whether CFCs, rather than other factors, were the cause of ozone depletion. The British scientists carried out exhaustive tests for two more years and, by the end of 1984, were convinced that there had been a 30 percent reduction in or thinning of the ozone layer in this region.

The threat to the ozone layer provided a huge impetus to the development of the green movement in the 1980s, as governments and industrialists became involved in negotiations on how to handle the problem, and environmental groups such as **Friends of the Earth** launched highly successful campaigns all over the world to persuade consumers to boycott products that contained CFCs. Apart from bringing about considerable pressure on governments, public opinion and consumer boycotts led to swift changes in the practices of major corporations. In **Great Britain**, some of the leading corporations removed CFCs from aerosol cans. In a campaign led by Friends of the Earth in the United States and over 30 other countries, environmental groups targeted the use of CFCs in Styrofoam packaging. In 1987 McDonalds, along with other fast-food outlets, agreed to eliminate packaging that was made with CFCs. However, the most significant steps in phasing out CFCs were to occur as scientists made further discoveries about their deleterious impact on the atmosphere and pressure mounted on governments to introduce drastic measures. This led to the **Vienna Convention for the Protection of the Ozone Layer** of 1985 and the **Montreal Protocol on Substances That Deplete the Ozone Layer** of 1987. Under these agreements, around 50 developed countries agreed to reduce their consumption of CFCs by 50 percent by the year 2000. Less developed countries, which contributed only marginally to the production and consumption of CFCs, were permitted to increase their consumption up to the end of the century, after which time they were also expected to phase out their CFCs.

Within a fortnight of the signing of the Montreal Protocol, on 30 September 1987, flights by the National Aeronautics and Space Administration over the Antarctic indicated that the problem of ozone depletion would need to be addressed in an even more radical manner. The scientists found that the "hole" in the ozone layer was roughly equivalent in size to the surface area of the United States and in depth to the height of Mount Everest. At certain levels and points, there was almost no ozone left at all. Above all, the connection was made between huge volumes of chlorine monoxide, a by-product of CFCs, and the depletion of ozone. Scientists soon became convinced that there would have to be a 100 percent reduction in CFCs. They were also aware that even if this were implemented, it would not be until well into the following century that the level of chlorine in the stratosphere would return to the levels registered in 1985. In 1988 and 1989 scientists discovered large volumes of chlorine monoxide in the Northern Hemisphere, over the Arctic. Though they could not identify any significant depletion in the ozone layer, they predicted a similar outcome as had occurred in the Southern Hemisphere. In 1989 the United States and countries belonging to the EU committed themselves to abandoning all production of CFCs by the year 2000.

The Montreal Protocol has been amended a number of times to include other ozone depleting chemicals and to speed up the phase out of harmful chemicals. Emissions of some substances, such as carbon tetrachloride, which can cause severe damage to the ozone layer, are not covered by the Montreal Protocol. Although the United States has banned this chemical, it is still produced by other countries.

One of the persisting issues related to the Montreal Protocol was how alternatives for CFCs could be introduced worldwide. Developing countries led by **India** insisted that the more developed nations make accessible to the less developed ones any alternatives at a low cost. A financial and technical assistance mechanism was built into the Montreal Protocol.

– P –

PAKISTAN. Pakistan has little history with environmental policies, and the minimal "Green Revolution" that occurred in the 1970s specifically dealt with land reform and self-sustainability among the farming community. Similar to the situation faced by other developing nations, Pakistan was forced to recognize and deal with land overuse and misappropriation among the wealthy. Land reform took place in the 1970s, but similar to other environmental legislation, it was unsuccessful. Major environmental legislation includes environmentally related portions of the 1973 Constitution, the 1983

Pakistan Environmental Protection Ordinance (PEPO), and the 1996 Environmental Protection Act. The Constitution, however, provided no concrete laws concerning the environment, PEPO created the Pakistan Environmental Protection Agency (EPA) yet it has remained weak, and the 1996 Environmental Protection Act was only put into effect at the start of the 21st century.

Founded in 2002, the Green Party of Pakistan, known as the Pakistan Greens, is a member of the Asia-Pacific Green Network and the Global Greens Network. As a very new party, the Pakistan Greens are only now gaining a foothold on Pakistani politics, and as there are other more powerful parties in existence, it will take time to gain the influence necessary to be elected to major offices.

Similar to the green parties of other Asian nations, the Pakistan Greens are courting the younger generation. The idea is that through the youth, the party can cultivate a belief in environmental responsibility. In 2005, at a meeting of the **Asia Pacific Greens Network**, the Young Greens Workshop involved members of greens from various states, including Pakistan. A theme of "Organizing the young" and "Move for change: Next generation politics" was created by representatives of the Pakistan Greens.

PARTIDO VERDE. *See* BRAZIL.

PEOPLE'S REPUBLIC OF CHINA (PRC). *See* CHINA, PEOPLE'S REPUBLIC OF (PRC).

PESTICIDE ACTION NETWORK (PAN). With regional centers in Africa, Asia/Pacific, Europe, and Latin America, PAN is a network of over 600 nongovernmental organizations (NGOs) in 90 countries that campaign to eliminate hazardous pesticides.

POLAND. Heavy industry and mining dominated Poland's economy in Soviet times, polluting the air and water. Poland's environmental problems are severe. In order to become a member of the European Union (EU), Poland was required to meet the demands of the *acquis communautaire*'s environmental chapter, but because of the serious pollution levels, was given an extension on meeting the air pollution requirements. Poland is also one of the largest sources of greenhouse gases in Europe.

The environmental movement in Poland from the 1950s to the 1970s was limited to groups that were considered nonthreatening by the state. They tended to focus on conservation issues. In 1980, with the rise of the Solidarity movement, more space opened for environmental activism and in 1980 the Polish Ecological Club was founded. Most environmental movements at the time were just that—movements and not organizations. These movements were active in the 1989 protests against the communist government. After the fall of communism in Poland, new environmental groups emerged, ranging from more radical groups, such as the Anarchist Foundation and Freedom and Peace, to ecological groups, such as the Green Federation. Poland's environmental movement, however, remains weak and poorly funded.

While there were early efforts to establish a political wing to the green movement in the early 1990s, it was not until 2004, that Zieloni, Poland's green party, was established by the efforts of the Ecological Forum of the Union for Freedom and various environmental groups. The party fielded candidates in the 2005 parliamentary elections, and won 3.89 percent of the vote, but this was not sufficient to win any seats.

POLLUTER PAYS PRINCIPLE. The polluter pays principle has been evoked by environmentalists and economists to address the consequences of damage to the environment. In essence, it refers to the idea that the full costs of goods and services, including the cost of repairing any damage inflicted on the environment, should be taken into consideration. For many governments, this means trying to ensure that the price of products includes the entire social and environmental costs of their production. The Federal Republic of **Germany** already recognized this principle in 1971. More recently, following the Maastricht Treaty on European Union in 1991, this principle was meant to apply to all member-states. According to the Maastricht Treaty, the cost of damage to the environment should be met by the producer. Governments set the standards, and polluters pay the relevant costs. The idea is that consumers will pay a price for products that reflect the full environmental and social costs.

POLLUTION CHARGES. In response to growing concern by expert communities and the public at large, governments either have begun to consider the possibility of or have actually implemented taxes and charges on products in order to reflect the costs to the environment. Green economists have long been concerned that the costs of goods and services have failed to reflect the real costs in terms of damage to the environment and have therefore argued and presented various mechanisms for valuing the environment. *See also* CARBON TAXES; POLLUTER PAYS PRINCIPLE.

POPULATION GROWTH. The notion of population growth as a central problem in modern societies has been a controversial one within the green movement. It underlies arguments about the "**Tragedy of the Commons**" and *The Limits to Growth*. The theme of overpopulation was publicized through best-selling works by **Paul Ehrlich** and by activists in green parties such as Sandy Irvine and Alec Ponton, members of the British Green Party. In *A Green Manifesto,* Irvine and Ponton declared that the expansion in human population represented the greatest of all threats to the survival of the living world. There is also a strong parallel to the arguments of **Thomas Malthus** in the 19th century. Irvine and Ponton outlined detailed measures, including financial disincentives to procreation and educational campaigns that lead to changes in perceptions about this issue. More recently, with statistics showing negative population growth throughout Europe as well as in **Japan** and the **Republic of Korea**, the environmental community in the North has stopped talking much about population growth even though the global population, estimated to be about 6.5 billion in 2006 could reach 9.1 billion by 2050 according to a medium-range estimate of the United Nations Population Division.

The challenge of population growth has been confronted most forcefully and controversially by the **People's Republic of China**, where a one-child policy was introduced in 1986 after the population hit the one-billion mark (compared with 550,000 in 1950). While exceptions were made for minority populations and enforcement was somewhat laxer in some rural communities, the one-child policy has helped to prevent an even more extreme population problem for the

People's Republic of China. This was done through education campaigns, closely monitored birth control measures, and in some cases, the reporting in workplaces of women's menstrual cycles. Most controversial have been the forced abortions and female infanticide that the policy also resulted in. Although China's population of 1.3 billion in 2006 is more likely to hit 1.6 billion or more in 2050 without continuation of a strict one child policy, the government has been relaxing the policy as it becomes worried about the reverse pyramid effect, a population that is top heavy with older people.

Population control efforts have been less successful in **India** than in the People's Republic of China. A government-sponsored sterilization program in 1975 that relied on coercive tactics and took advantage of illiteracy in rural communities seriously backfired; people lost trust in the government, and this problematized future government birth control programs. Compared to a population of 368 million in 1950, in 2006, India's population stood at 1.1 billion. Middle-range estimates are that it will be close to 1.6 billion in 2050.

The 1994 Cairo Programme of Action of the United Nations Conference on Population and Development reflects the ambiguity of international attitudes toward population matters. The program's nine principles include, among other things, the right to development, the importance of eradicating poverty for **sustainable development**, the right to decide freely and fairly the spacing of their children, and the family as the basic unit of society.

PORRITT, JONATHON. *See* GREAT BRITAIN.

PORTUGAL. Portugal has not been a leader within Europe on environmental matters. Nevertheless, Portugal too has a green party. The Partido Ecologistica-Os Verdes was formed in 1982 out of a green citizens' movement that was eager to add green concerns to local and national politics in Portugal. The party has used a coalition strategy to gain recognition at the polls. In the 2005 election, they formed a coalition with the Communists and combined won 7.57 percent of the vote. They were awarded two seats in Parliament. At the European Parliamentary level, they received 9.1 percent of the vote in the 2004 election.

POSTMATERIALISM. The concept of postmaterialism has been used by many writers to explain the change in values that has precipitated the advance of the green movement. The contrast between material and postmaterial values is as old as the study of politics. Aristotle suggested that once people had satisfied their basic material needs they might aspire to fulfill "higher" spiritual needs.

In empirical studies conducted since the 1970s, the political scientist Ronald Inglehart interpreted public opinion data from several European nations to suggest that materialist and postmaterialist values were strongly associated with new conflicts in society. Although scholars interested in the rise of postmaterialist values were initially concerned about the protest movements of the 1960s (the student and civil rights movements) rather than the green movement, the connection has often been made between postmaterial values and the ascent of the greens. Studies have repeatedly shown a strong connection between postmaterial values, as measured by Inglehart, and support for the green movement.

The term *postmaterialism* has been used to draw attention to a shift in value priorities from materialism to postmaterialism, from a prevalent way of thinking (oriented to economic growth) to an alternative environmentalist approach. Initially, Inglehart measured materialist and postmaterialist values by presenting survey respondents with a list of four goals for their country over the next 10 years and asking them to rank these goals in order of priority. The four items were "the maintenance of order in the nation," "giving people more say in government decisions," "fighting rising prices" and "protecting freedom of speech."

The second and fourth items were designed to find out who identified with the 1960s protests for more civil rights and liberty. Respondents who chose these two items as their first and second priorities were classified as postmaterialists. Those who chose "the maintenance of order" and "fighting rising prices" were deemed to be materialist. A third "mixed" category was used for those (namely, the majority) who were neither outright materialists nor postmaterialists. (Inglehart has added eight more items to the list, though the original four items are most commonly used.)

The scale identified the tendency of some to stress participation and individual freedom rather than economic and personal security. It has also been used to assess the connection between values and political behavior as well as economic and social circumstances. Like groups in the green movement, the 1960s social movements emphasized participation and freedom of speech in Western democracies. Numerous studies have shown that many of the backers of social movements in the 1960s also played a leading role in the green movement that began to attract many supporters in the 1970s. Inglehart's analysis of the impact of these earlier movements has proved to be of lasting importance, despite some shortcomings in his approach.

Inglehart adopted from the psychologist Abraham Maslow the notion of a "hierarchy of needs." At the base of this hierarchy we find primary or basic needs for survival, such as food, shelter, and security. They are labeled material needs. Once they have been met, people are more likely to seek fulfillment of secondary needs, including intellectual, aesthetic, and social needs. In affluent societies, basic material needs for food and shelter are usually met, if not by individuals receiving income as wage earners, at least by the welfare state, which is supposed to provide a basic safety net. People in affluent societies are therefore more likely than those in societies experiencing relatively high levels of material deprivation to be able to pursue intellectual, aesthetic, and social-postmaterialist goals.

However, during an economic recession, there is likely to be a diminishing emphasis on postmaterial values. Inglehart has postulated that this decline is not inevitable. The effect of poverty on values can be held in check by the socialization of individuals into certain values during particular phases of the life cycle. In other words, Inglehart has presented a parallel hypothesis based on the notion of socialization.

Although this and other arguments by Inglehart have been subject to many challenges, the distinction between materialism and postmaterialism has been influential in discussions about the rise of the green movement. Materialism is associated with economic growth, nonmaterialism is connected to self-fulfillment and self-actualization. The natural environment is valued either as a resource to be exploited for material ends or for its intrinsic or essential qualities. Though the notion of intrinsic qualities may appear somewhat nebulous, many argue that people are able to appreciate nature for aesthetic, spiritual, or even religious reasons.

For many activists in the green movement, it is not so much a question of dominating but of living in harmony with nature. *See also* DEEP ECOLOGY; SPIRITUALITY.

PRECAUTIONARY PRINCIPLE. The precautionary principle refers to the possibility of applying very stringent standards before permitting human interventions that may affect the environment. Governments, such as those of **Germany**, apply strict standards to minimize the dangers of pollution. In some cases, the application of the precautionary principle may entail a decision not to proceed with a project for development—say, the construction of a nuclear power plant. Most green parties have espoused the precautionary principle in debates over large-scale development projects. Some writers have argued that a concentrated emphasis on the precautionary principle may actually deprive human beings of the possibilities of dealing with certain problems. Since it is impossible to anticipate all the risks that might arise from the use of chemicals, a stringent application of the precautionary principle could lead to the denial of medical and other forms of relief to many people. In sum, there may be a need to consider the social and economic costs of implementing the precautionary principle.

PRESERVATIONISM. In the nineteenth century, a movement emerged advocating the protection of natural areas for their intrinsic worth. Preservationists believed that areas of natural beauty should be set aside as places where humans could commune with nature and be inspired by nature's splendors. John Muir is a famous preservationist. Whereas **conservationism** urged the protection of nature for economic purposes or leisure use, preservationism urged their protection on something close to moral grounds. *See also* SPIRITUALITY.

PRICE MECHANISM. *See* CARBON TAXES; POLLUTER PAYS PRINCIPLE; POLLUTION CHARGES; VALUING THE ENVIRONMENT.

PROBE INTERNATIONAL. Based in Canada, the organization provides information about the environmental effects of such projects such as the Three Gorges Dam in China and the Mekong River, especially where such investment activity pertains to Canada's aid and trade abroad. It seeks to make accountable the relevant actors through disclosure of information and advocacy work.

PROPERTY RIGHTS MOVEMENT. Opposition to the establishment of new environmental regulations in the **United States** has grown and new groups intent on protecting property rights or eliminating environmental restrictions altogether (the Wise Use movement) have proliferated since the 1980s. Using many of the same tactics that environmental groups have used, the property rights movement has worked to stop what they perceive as infringements on their constitutional rights. There are now numerous groups across the country that have as their goal defending property rights from what they see as environmental regulations that prevent them from using their property. The property rights movement worked during the 1990s to weaken the U.S. Endangered Species Act and was successful in restricting congressional funding for the enforcement of the act. The National Endangered Species Act Reform Coalition, representing 150 groups, including farmers, electric utilities, home builders, and others, have been campaigning to have the Endangered Species Act revised so that compensation will be provided to property owners when restrictions are placed upon them because of endangered species found on their land. The property rights movement was one of the voices opposed to U.S. involvement in the **Convention on Biological Diversity**.

– Q –

QUALITY OF LIFE. Following the Great Depression and World War II, there seemed little prospect of challenging predominant views about the connection between the quality of life and achievement of economic growth and industrial development. However, the green movement's challenging of established beliefs about economic development has led to a much broader definition of the quality of life. Apart from a strong focus on environmental protection and **preservationism** for aesthetic, spiritual, recreational, and cultural reasons, the definition of quality of life includes, and goes beyond, the enduring concerns about security of employment, food, and shelter.

Interest in the quality of life impinges on the symbiotic relationship between formal employment and the informal sector (the home, family, and other social networks). Questions are brought up about the location and character of employment (a job that offers the possibility of self-realization, safe work conditions, a setting that is relatively free of fear and harassment, a reduction of time spent commuting to work, and telecommuting), a more flexible approach to the working day (or night), how work relates to involvement with family and other commitments, and new arrangements for monitoring actual work performance. Pressure for reform in the workplace is occurring in parallel with changes in how we perceive family life, relationships between spouses, and the raising of children.

The broader definition of quality of life advocated by the green movement has often been adopted by traditional political parties that have become preoccupied not only with the economic welfare of those in formal paid employment and their dependents but also with the social, economic, and political concerns of minorities, immigrants, single parents, homosexuals, and women. Although some of these issues are not directly related to environmental protection, they reflect concerns about the quality of life introduced by environmentalists. Above all, the preoccupation with the quality of life reflects doubts about some of the definitions, categories, and dichotomies that have been used to influence human behavior over the past century.

Concerns with economic survival (the so-called traditional economic issues of unemployment, prices, inflation, and taxation) continue to play a significant and fundamental role in politics, yet a growing number of people view economic and other issues in terms of improving the quality of life. Issues such as the health system, education, and care for the aged are deemed important not purely for the sake of survival, but in the context of improvements in the quality of life. Rather than accept the traditional social reformers' dichotomy between the market and the state or the economic and the social, the definition of quality of life is being extended beyond meeting basic needs for survival. Environmentalism, along with concerns about the quality of health care, employment, and education, reminds us of this shift in priorities as certain needs have been met for growing sections of the population.

The rise in environmentalism is linked to much more than the obvious signs of deterioration in the physical environment. It is associated with changes in the social structure, efforts to adapt to technological change, and rising levels of education. *See also* POSTMATERIALISM.

– R –

RAINBOW AND GREENS JAPAN (NIJI TO MIDORI NO 500 NIN LISTO). This group was launched in 1998 by city councilors, prefectural members of parliament, and mayors who supported diversity and green politics. After their success in the April 1999 local elections when 133 of the 226 candidates they supported won, they launched the Rainbow and Green Local Government Policy Information Center and a newsletter. In the 2004 election they cooperated with another now-dissolved green group, Midori no Kaigi (Environmental Green Political Assembly, formerly the Sakigake Party), and ran their first candidate at the national level for the Upper House of the Diet. They did not, however, win any seats. *See also* JAPAN.

RAINFOREST ACTION NETWORK (RAN). With offices in San Francisco, California, and Tokyo, **Japan**, RAN works with environmental and human rights groups in 60 countries. Formed in 1985, one of their first campaigns was against Burger King. After sales dropped sharply, Burger King agreed to stop importing rainforest beef. RAN has used savvy campaigns to pressure large corporations to end practices that have harmed the world's rainforests. It also encourages citizen action through direct action, letter writing campaigns, boycotts, and **nonviolent** demonstrations.

RAINFOREST INFORMATION CENTRE. An Australian-based nongovernmental organization (NGO) working to protect rainforests and the indigenous people who depend upon them. The group was born out of the successful efforts in the early 1980s to protect the rainforests of New South Wales, **Australia**.

REGAN, TOM. *See* ANIMAL RIGHTS.

RENEWABLE ENERGY. *See* ALTERNATIVE ENERGY.

REPUBLIC OF KOREA. *See* KOREA, REPUBLIC OF.

ROMANIA. Romania's transition to democracy and away from state socialism and its accession to the European Union (EU), which has required adoption of the *acquis communautaire*, have dominated the nation's attention. The environment has not been the primary concern of people during this transition. Yet, as the site of one of the more grave environmental disasters to hit central and eastern Europe, the environmental movement has been galvanized into action, supported by environmental movements in western Europe. The trigger was a major cyanide spill in Baia Mare from a gold-extraction operation. The spill polluted several central European rivers, including the River Somes, the River Tisza in Hungary, and the Danube; the Danube eventually flows into the Black Sea, Several Romanian nongovernmental organizations (NGOs) have mobilized against a Canadian-Romanian mining company that is planning a large gold mine project in the Carpathian Mountains, making use of cyanide.

A nascent green party exists in Romania. Reflecting the country's break with communism, in contrast with some of its western European counterparts, which oppose neoliberal economics, the Romanian Green Party supports the free market and the elimination of government intervention, except as it pertains to environmental protection. In 2004, it attracted 60,000 votes in the national election.

ROYAL NATIONAL PARK. Formally dedicated in April 1879, the National Park (later renamed the Royal National Park) was the first **national park** in **Australia** and the second in the world. It was formed by an initiative of a former premier, Sir John Robertson. The park comprised 18,000 acres on the southern shores of Port Hacking, about 13 miles from the city of Sydney. The construction of a railway link in 1886 facilitated access to the park and there was a rapid rise in the number of visitors.

RUSSIA. In the early part of the twentieth century, ecologists in Russia promoted the establishment of nature preserves (*zapovedniks*) for scientific study. A few such preserves were established during the early Bolshevik years, but **conservationism** eventually lost out to Stalinism and its emphasis on conquering nature and heavy industrialization. As was the case in the West, in the late 1960s movements began to form to oppose pollution and development projects that threatened environmentally sensitive areas, including on Lake Baikal and along the Volga River. After the 1986 **Chernobyl** nuclear accident, environmental activism spread throughout the Soviet Union. With the political opening provided by perestroika, environmental activism temporarily flourished and environmental groups played a significant role in the collapse of the Soviet Union, especially in **Estonia**, **Latvia**, and Lithuania. They became a channel through which opposition voices could express their discontent with aspects of the socialist economy and communist political system.

The breakup of the Soviet Union left Russia as the largest former east bloc state. Despite Russia's large population, its vast territory means that population density is relatively low. Nevertheless, the legacies of Stalinist era industrialization left Russia scarred by severe pollution. Although Russia has democratized, strong authoritarian tendencies remain. This has affected Russia's green movement. President Vladimir Putin clamped down on environmental groups during the 1990s, arresting Alexander Nikitin and Grigory Pasko, who provided information to the international community about the Russian nuclear fleet's dumping of radioactive waste and the dangerous state of its Pacific nuclear submarine fleet. In 2000 Putin shut down the State Committee on the Environment.

Despite this harsh environment, some environmental groups have survived in Russia. Most have been dependent on international financial assistance. *See also* SOCIO-ECOLOGICAL UNION.

– S –

SAHABAT ALAM MALAYSIA (SAM). Founded in 1978 by S. Mohamed Idris, Sahabat Alam Malaysia represents the **Friends of the Earth** organization in that country. SAM is best known for its campaigns to prevent the destruction of tropical rainforests. The main focus of these activities has been in Sarawak, where indigenous people such as the Kayan, Penan, and Pelabit have been engaged in an enduring struggle with logging companies. The rapid destruction of the forests led in the 1980s to blockades by the native people of routes used by the logging companies. SAM assisted in these campaigns to defend the lifestyles and livelihood of the indigenous people and ensured that their concerns received a huge amount of publicity across the world. SAM has also been involved in legal battles over the land rights of the native people. Apart from these campaigns, SAM has focused on issues such as the depletion of resources, pollution of the soil, and reporting on the state of the environment through its publications.

SARO-WIWA, KENULE (1941–1995). Born in **Nigeria**, Ken Saro-Wiwa was an author, television producer, and environmental activist. He founded **Movement for the Survival of the Ogoni People (MOSOP)**, an organization developed to defend the environmental and human rights of the Ogoni people who live in the Niger Delta, which fostered a grassroots community-based political movement. Since Royal Dutch Shell struck oil in the Ogoni lands in 1958, it has extracted billions of dollars worth of oil, and Nigeria has become the seventh largest producer in the Organization of Petroleum Exporting Countries (OPEC), but very little of the oil revenue flowed into the Ogoni lands while the environmental situation continued worsening.

In January 1993, Saro-Wiwa organized 300,000 Ogoni to march peacefully to demand a share in oil revenues and some form of political autonomy. MOSOP began requesting environmental remediation and compensation for past damage from the oil companies. By 1993 the oil companies began pulling out of the Ogoni lands but the Nigerian government increased enforcement of military rule. In May 1994 the Nigerian government of General Sani Abacha abducted and jailed Saro-Wiwa in connection with the murder of four Ogoni leaders. In October 1995 a military tribunal tried and convicted him in a questionable trial. On 10 November 1995 Saro-Wiwa and eight of his Ogoni compatriots were hanged. International outrage and condemnation against the trial led to the immediate suspension of Nigeria from the Commonwealth of Nations.

Since Saro-Wiwa's death, the situation in the Ogoni lands has grown worse. In 2004 at least 600 people died in militia conflicts over oil. MOSOP continues to organize peaceful protests and demand the Ogonis' rights.

SAVE MY FOREST FOUNDATION (SAMFU). The high-quality wood in West Africa's rainforest has attracted the interest of international logging companies. The rainforest has an extremely diverse ecological system and is the habitat for a quarter of Africa's mammals. **Biodiversity** has suffered as loggers create pockets of rainforest, splitting species and causing interbreeding in populations. Liberia hosts about 44 percent of the rainforest that stretches across West Africa. Commercial loggers such as the Evergreen Trading Corporation have been granted access by the Liberian government to remove trees, even within **national parks**. To combat the deforestation, groups such as SAMFU have sprung up as both environmental and human rights advocates. SAMFU does research to determine the amount of logging occurring, motivates local people to become involved through political action and civil disobedience, and educates rural communities about the rights to land. By addressing the human suffering that has accompanied deforestation along with environmental concerns, SAMFU reaches a broader base of the population.

SAVE OUR ENVIRONMENT. A collaborative Internet advocacy network of some of the largest and most influential U.S.-based environmental advocacy groups, including American Rivers, the **Audubon Society**, **Defenders of Wildlife**, **Earth Justice**, **Friends of the Earth**, **Greenpeace**, **League of Conservation Voters**, **National Environmental Trust**, **National Parks Conservation Association**, **Natural Resources Defense Council (NRDC)**, **National Wildlife Federation**, the Ocean Conservancy, Physicians for Social Responsibility, **Sierra Club**, state Public Interest Research Groups (PIRGs), Union of Concerned Scientists, the **Wilderness Society**, and the **World Wide Fund for Nature (WWF)**, working on diverse environmental issues. Save Our Environment provides information on state and federal bills and their effects on the environment and encourages citizen action through letter-writing campaigns, editorials, state ballot initiatives, and the like.

SCHUMACHER, E. F. (1911–1977). Born in **Germany**, where he was trained as an economist, E. F Schumacher immigrated to **Great Britain** in 1937. After being interned during World War II, he worked in a number of public service agencies, and was employed for 20 years at the British National Coal Board. Schumacher is renowned as the author of the highly influential *Small Is Beautiful*. He was also the founder, in 1966, of the Intermediate Technology Development Group, which had as its principal focus the development of technologies that were appropriate to the needs of less developed countries.

SHIVA, VANDANA (1952–). Indian researcher and activist, Vandana Shiva, was a supporter of the **Chipko Andalan** Movement in **India** in the 1970s. She was an outspoken activist against the Green Revolution of the 1970s and is a firm critic of genetically modified seeds, which she argues contribute to **biodiversity** loss and force farmers to use nonrenewable seeds, thereby increasing poverty. In 1982 she formed the Research Foundation for Science, Technology, and **Ecology** (RFSTE) and in 2000 created Naydanya ("nine seeds"). The purpose of RFSTE and Naydanya are to educate people about **conservationism** and agricultural issues. Both are directed toward helping farmers pursue more ecofriendly farming. Shiva has received numerous awards, including the Right Livelihood Award, also known as the Alternative Nobel Prize, in 1993.

SIERRA CLUB. Founded in May 1892 by John Muir and his associates, the Sierra Club aimed to protect and preserve the natural environment, notably the Sierra Nevada, and encourage people to appreciate the region. From its inception, the Sierra Club campaigned and lobbied the highest levels of government to protect nature.

Its first success was in checking proposals to reduce Yosemite National Park in size. In 1910 it contributed to the successful campaign to establish Glacier National Park. In collaboration with other organizations it applied pressure for the formation of a National Park Service (which was achieved in 1916) and protection of redwood forests (in 1919). The Sierra Club contributed to or led campaigns for the expansion of Sequoia National Park (1926), Grand Canyon National Park (1975), and Redwood National Park (1978) and the creation of numerous parks and reserves: Admiralty Island (1932); Kings Canyon (1940); Point Reyes National Seashore, California (1962); Padre Island National Seashore, Texas (1962); Big Thicket Preserve, Texas (1974); Big Cypress Reserve, Florida (1974); and Hells Canyon Recreation Area (1975).

Over time the Sierra Club broadened its focus from supporting legislation that protected forests and wilderness, such as the 1964 Wilderness Act, which created a National Wilderness Preservation System, to lobbying for the enactment of the National Environmental Protection Act and foundation of the Environmental Protection Agency (EPA) (1970) and the reinforcement of the Clean Air Act (in 1977, 1987, and 1990). Other major campaigns include the protection of about 0.8 million acres of land managed by the Forest Service (Colorado Wilderness Act, 1993), reversal of a decision by the World Bank to loan US$500 million to **Brazil** for the construction of 147 new dams in the Amazon region, enactment of legislation to designate 6.8 million acres of wilderness in 18 states (1984), the successful prosecution of a suit against plans to remove 1.5 million acres of land from the Bureau of Land Management inventory of wilderness areas, and the enactment of the Alaska National Interest Lands Conservation Act (1980), which assigned 375 million acres as **national parks** refuges and wilderness areas.

The Sierra Club's success in these campaigns corresponds to a steady increase in membership. In 1897 the club had 350 members. In the first half of the century there was a steady rise to 7,000 in 1952 and 10,000 in 1956. In 1950 the club formed a chapter outside California for the first time. Between 1952 and 1969, under the proactive leadership of **David Brower** and in the context of a growing awareness of environmental problems (triggered by popular works such as *Silent Spring* and reaction to the economic development that followed the post–World War Il reconstruction), membership of the club increased tenfold, to 70,000. This trend continued and corresponded to the upsurge of new environmental groups and political organizations. In 1970 the club had 100,000 members; in 1976, 165,000; in 1985, 348,000; and in 1986, 400,000. By 1993–1994 the club had 550,000 members and a decade later, its membership had grown to 750,000.

Although the Sierra Club has continued to concentrate its campaigns on the preservation of lands and ancient forests, it has broadened its agenda to include issues such as the protection of endangered species, **population growth**, free trade agreements and their impact on the environment, policies by international agencies such as the World Bank, energy policy (and its impact on **climate change** and the **greenhouse effect**), pollution of air and water, and waste management and recycling.

Though independent of any political organization, the Sierra Club endorses politicians in congressional races and at times, for the presidency, as it did with its endorsement for William J. Clinton in 1992. In the 2006 U.S. congressional elections, the Sierra Club endorsed a large number of candidates, primarily Democrats, but also a handful of Republicans and Independents. This is not necessarily inconsistent with its mission statement: "To explore, enjoy and protect the wild places of the earth; to practice and promote the responsible use of the earth's ecosystems and resources; to educate and enlist humanity to protect and restore the quality of the natural and human environment; and to use all lawful means to carry out these objectives."

SILENT SPRING. It takes much more than a scientific discovery to bring about a shift in perceptions about environmental protection and create mass political support for it. One of the most important breakthroughs was the articulation of the discovery that the quality of human life could be seriously threatened by certain types of economic growth and forms of industrial development. *Silent Spring*, by **Rachel Carson**, provides a striking illustration of how such a discovery can be effectively disseminated. The publication of the book in 1962 has widely been credited with setting in motion the mass environmental movements in the latter half of the 20th century.

Although the book was a landmark scientific study, its impact is not solely attributable to its scientific character. Carson had for many years been disturbed by the impact of chemical pesticides such as dichloro-diphenyl-trichloroethane (DDT) on wildlife, its habitat, and human life. In sharing her findings with others, she went much further than presenting scientific evidence. She challenged the entire approach of the chemical and other industries, their "arrogance" in assuming that "nature exists for the convenience of man," and their failure to appreciate that "the history of life on earth has been a history of interaction between living things and their surroundings."

The book elicited an immediate response from the chemical industry. It spent hundreds of thousands of dollars to prevent the widespread dissemination of the work and in trying to discredit it. However, sales of hardback copies alone amounted to 500,000, and in

1963 it was published in 15 countries. Throughout the **United States** people were concerned that the use of DDT would lead to the extinction of treasured symbols such as the bald eagle. Publicity surrounding the book led to the establishment of a special panel of the Science Advisory Committee by President John F. Kennedy, which supported the arguments presented by Carson about the hazards of pesticides. The impact of the book went far beyond the chemical industry and the government. *Silent Spring* provided a major impetus to the environmental movement, serving for many as a manifesto for questioning the prevailing approaches to progress and the quality of life. There had already been warnings about the dangers of DDT to the environment. One important difference between prior accounts and *Silent Spring* lay in Carson's ability to place scientific discoveries in the context of a fundamental questioning of how people thought about the environment. The timing of the work may also have been an important factor; there was a more receptive audience in the 1960s than in the past. *See also* QUALITY OF LIFE.

SLOVAKIA. The Slovak Green Party's manifesto, which was drawn up in 1998 and revised in 2002, is based on the goals of **Agenda 21**. The party was established right after the Velvet Revolution in **Czechoslovakia**. The party first participated in elections in 1990, winning a higher percentage of the vote (3.5 percent) to the Narodna Rada (Parliament) than it has at any time since (1991: 1.1 percent; 2002: 1.0 percent). In 1990 it had six parliamentary representatives; in 2006, it had none. This is a big contrast with the situation of the Green Party in the neighboring, **Czech Republic**. The party has done better at the local than the national level.

SMALL IS BEAUTIFUL. The widespread use of the expression "small is beautiful" originates from the best-selling book of that title by British economist **E. F Schumacher**. Schumacher argued not so much against all large-scale endeavors as about their suitability. For some undertakings, it may well be necessary to advocate a vast structure, for example, developing certain institutions and agencies in a city may require a substantial amount of money.

Apart from his focus on the suitability or appropriateness of the size of cities, technology, and institutions and agencies, Schumacher was concerned about the tendency to assume that immensity corresponds to efficient and effective structures. He provided many illustrations of how small-scale structures (nation-states, cities, governments and NGOs, and technologies) may often be much more effective in achieving objectives such as prosperity and environmental protection than large-scale ones. Schumacher, rather than advocating an "idolatry of smallness," argues that we have simply gone too far, both in our beliefs and practices, in the opposite direction. His book also targets the values that arise from a preoccupation with materialism, and he links his thesis to debates about the plundering of the environment, thereby evoking some of the issues suggested in discussions of *The Limits to Growth*. *See also* POSTMATERIALISM.

SOCIAL ECOLOGY. The term *ecology* has been adapted in a variety of ways to characterize different modes of organizing or thinking about the green movement. Social ecology represents, in certain respects, a contrast to **deep ecology**. Whereas deep ecology is concerned about the exploitation of the environment, social ecology, as understood by anarchist-writer Murray Bookchin, represents the view that the endeavor of human beings to dominate nature has its origins in their attempt to dominate each other. Bookchin differentiates social ecology from efforts to deal with environmental concerns by adopting new technologies (such as solar or wind power). He uses social ecology to promote new social structures that include dismantling the power of centralized bureaucracies and hierarchies and focusing instead on the practice of **direct democracy**. There are strong parallels between arguments for social ecology and those proposed by fundamentalists in the green movement.

SOCIALIST REPUBLIC OF VIETNAM. *See* VIETNAM, SOCIALIST REPUBLIC OF.

SOCIALIZATION. The term *socialization* has been used in arguments by the political scientist Ronald Inglehart about a shift from material to postmaterial values. Inglehart's central argument is that postmaterialists are more likely than materialists to take economic security for granted and to place more emphasis on aesthetic and intellectual development than on the pursuit of material goals. These postmaterialist values are said to underpin the rise of the green movement. Socialization is based on the understanding that the nature of people's upbringing, or socialization, prior to adulthood will have a lasting impact and be relatively independent of changes in economic fortunes and political upheavals. Inglehart has postulated two hypotheses: the scarcity hypothesis and the socialization hypothesis. The first is based on the assumption that people in affluent societies are more likely than those in societies experiencing relatively high levels of material deprivation to be able to pursue intellectual, aesthetic, and social goals—postmaterialist goals. The second is that the decline in these values is not inevitable during an economic recession. The effect of poverty on values can be held in check by the socialization of individuals into certain values during particular phases of the life cycle.

People who are socialized in different historical eras, which may be characterized either by affluence or deprivation, will later in life react differently to the economic, social, and political environment. Studies of political behavior have shown, for example, that many people have continued to identify with the same political party from their youngest years to old age. Several studies have shown significant differences in value priorities between people who grew up during the Great Depression and those who were raised during the affluent postwar years. Those who experienced the Great Depression were more likely to have materialist values, even following improvements in socioeconomic conditions and radical changes in the political system.

One difficulty with the argument about the rise of **postmaterialism** has been Inglehart's apparent failure to specify the precise relationship between socialization and scarcity of material goods (which is said to be pivotal in influencing whether or not someone develops postmaterialist values). There is an apparent contradiction between the two notions; at the very least, they cannot be applied at the same time since socialization implies that values are constant or stable, whereas scarcity is based on the idea of a change in values under certain social and economic circumstances. Inglehart may have been too selective in applying these notions, overemphasizing socialization in relation to adult values and applying the scarcity argument to the formative years of a person's life. He may have failed to apply scarcity to adulthood and thereby neglected the analysis of change within a particular generation as a consequence of social and economic transformations.

SOCIETY FOR THE PRESERVATION OF WILD FAUNA OF THE EMPIRE. Founded in 1903, the Society for the Preservation of Wild Fauna of the Empire (later renamed the Flora and Fauna Preservation Society) was the first international environmental association. The society initially focused on protecting fauna in colonized territories. It was backed both by naturalists and hunters who regretted the consequences of their past practices. The association was the first of many endeavors to achieve cooperation in protecting wildlife in Africa. *See also* AFRICAN SPECIAL PROJECT; AFRICAN WILDLIFE.

SOCIO-ECOLOGICAL UNION. This international environmental organization was born in the Soviet Union. Its roots are in the Druzhina (People's Patrol) Movement for Environmental Protection, the only large-membership ecological movement that existed in the Soviet Union. In 1987, it had more than 100 student associations participating. When the Socio-Ecological Union was founded in 1988, it brought together people from 89 cities and 11 republics of the Soviet Union. The Socio-Ecological Union has since grown into an umbrella organization of 250 independent nongovernmental organizations (NGOs) in Azerbaijan, Armenia, Belarus, **Estonia**, **Georgia**, Kazhakstan, Kyrgyzstan, Moldova, **Russia**, Tadjikistan, Turkmenistan, **Ukraine**, Uzbekistan, and the **United States**. The organization campaigns against environmentally destructive projects, promotes environmental impact assessment, conducts environmental education, and works on issues related to **alternative energy, biodiversity, conservationism**, sustainable forestry, **ozone** and **climate change**, air and water pollution, and chemical and nuclear safety.

SOUTH AFRICA. Environmentalism had already begun in South Africa's dark, apartheid years. Whites in South Africa did not organize any waste removal or water cleaning for black neighborhoods. Out of necessity, blacks created their own environmental cleanup group, the National Environmental Awareness Campaign in 1978. The founder, Japhta Lekgheto, was one of the first local leaders to link apartheid to poor environmental conditions. The Cape Town Ecology Group, founded in 1987, but no longer active, cohosted South Africa's first conference on the environment, where the links between environmental degradation and politics were a main theme. For most blacks, however, obtaining basic rights and freedoms was the primary concern.

Postapartheid South Africa's relative stability has created space for the emergence of an environmental movement. Many international conservation groups are active in South Africa. Local ones have emerged as well. The **Environmental Justice** Networking Forum, a national network of civil society groups, has as its primary focus the eradication of environmental justices and promotion of **sustainable development**. The Bateleurs, an organization of pilots based in Johannesburg, for example, completes air missions for environmental causes. They take aerial photographs of mines, forests, or other places where access is difficult. Individuals and organizations with concern for the environment may request a mission in order to increase information, expose illegal activities, provide inspiring photographs of a protected area, track wildlife, or help nature reserves. The founder of the Bateleurs, Nora Kreher, won the Audi Terra Nova Award for Conservation and Preservation of Environment for 2005. Another group, Food and Trees for Africa, was begun in 1990 by South African citizens. They have planted trees and sustainable gardens through their programs EduPlant, the Urban Greening Project, and Trees for Homes. In May 2005, the Sustainability Watch Campaign was launched by a group of 20 organizations to promote environmental monitoring and awareness raising.

South Africa has a nascent green party that is a member of **Global Greens**. Also known as the Government by the People Green Party, the Green Party of South Africa was founded in 1999. Two earlier efforts to form green-oriented parties (The Ecology Party in 1989 and the Green Party in 1992) failed and the parties disbanded. The future of the Green Party of South Africa remains uncertain. The Cape Town Greens are a branch of the party, and have mobilized against the pebble-bed modular nuclear reactor being considered by South Africa.

Reflecting the circumstances of South Africa, the party lists its major concerns as not only the numerous pollution and environmental degradation issues affecting the country but also important health concerns, including HIV/AIDS and cancer tied to toxic pollutants.

SOVIET UNION. *See* RUSSIA.

SPACESHIP EARTH. Our planet has often been compared with a spaceship in order to emphasize how reliant we are on our natural surroundings and that we should be aware of the consequences of disregarding our need for resources such as air and water in order to survive. The term *spaceship Earth* was used in July 1965 in a famous address by Adlai Stevenson, the U.S. ambassador to the United Nations.

The idea was given an added environmental twist in 1966 in an essay on "The Economics of the Coming Spaceship Earth" by Kenneth Boulding, an economist from the University of Michigan. Boulding drew a sharp contrast between a "cowboy" economy based on production, consumption, and the careless exploitation of natural resources and a "spaceman" economy, which attached value to maintaining the quality and complexity of the total capital stock.

SPAIN. Along with **Greece** and **Portugal**, **Spain** is often considered to be less environmentally progressive than its northern neighbors. This image may be becoming outdated, however, as Spain becomes one of the world's largest consumers of **alternative energies**, including solar and wind power. The greens are in coalition government in Catalonia and the Spanish greens (Los Verdes) joined the green group in the **European Parliament** for the first time in 2004.

Reflecting the cultural and political divide between Catalonia and the rest of Spain, Spain has two green parties: Los Verdes and Iniciativa per Catalunya Verds. Los Verdes is still struggling to gain a foothold in Spanish politics, which for many years have been dominated by conservative governments. It has also suffered from the competition stemming from other left parties, and particularly the Communists, who have themselves taken on green issues. After the 2004 elections, they were represented by one member of Parliament (MP) and one senator.

Representing Catalonia, the Iniciativa per Catalunya Verds formed in 1987 as a federation of three parties: the Unified Socialist Party of Catalonia, the Communist Party, and the left-wing Nationalists Agreement. It became a formal party in 1990. The party's origins have shaped its platform, which focuses on communism, **ecology**, and republicanism (red, green, violet). The party also describes itself as being opposed to hierarchy, favoritism, and corruption. It calls for a revitalization of left-leaning politics, greater free time for citizens, the return of a focus on community, gender equality, and close working relationships with nongovernmental organizations (NGOs), trade unions, and student groups. In the 2004 elections, Iniciativa per Catalunya Verds won 5.85 percent of the vote, obtaining two seats in the Spanish Parliament. At the Catalan regional level, it performed even stronger, pulling in 9.7 percent of the vote (12 seats). It joined a coalition government with the Socialist Party of Catalunya. At the European level, the party won 7.9 percent of the vote (one delegate).

SPIRITUALITY. The notion of spirituality has been promoted by some sections of the green movement to refer to the spiritual qualities of nature. In the 19th century, the spiritual qualities of nature were highlighted by pioneers of the movement for **preservation** of wilderness areas, such as **John Muir**. Interest in them can be linked to ideas about a shift in values from materialism to **postmaterialism** and the notion of **deep ecology**. There is a parallel between the regard for the spiritual features of and holistic approaches to nature, the latter arguing that the whole is more than the sum of the parts. In *Breaking Through*, Walter and Dorothy Schwarz drew a distinction between industrial society, in which life is fragmented and materialistic, and an approach to life that is far more complete because it includes spirituality.

Spirituality is said to include the aesthetic, caring, and loving aspects of existence. The fact that it cannot be measured and categorized the way one can classify and gauge levels of pollution, votes for a green party, or the implementation of a waste management policy has meant that it has not generally been overtly used in promoting the green movement. When it has been advanced, as in the work by **Rudolf Bahro** on *Building the Green Movement*, it has been derided, often by supporters of the green movement.

STEADY-STATE ECONOMY. The term *steady-state economy* was used by American economist Herman Daly to outline a possibility for dealing with some of the problems identified in 1970s debates about *The Limits to Growth*. The argument for a steady-state economy is a plea for either a sustainable economy or **sustainable development**. There are two main aspects to Daly's argument for a sustainable economy. The predominant suggestion is that our economy is ultimately governed by the laws of thermodynamics. The other aspect is a principle-centered approach to human existence, derived from certain "moral first principles." The first law of thermodynamics is that in a closed system no energy is produced or consumed, only modified. The second law declares that heat may not of itself pass from a cooler to a hotter substance. Daly refers to this as the law of entropy, which entails the gradual decrease in the amount of usable energy as a result of the process of modification of matter.

The only addition to the power supply comes from solar energy. However, in our society the rate of modification of existing matter surpasses the rate of replacement by solar energy. Daly concludes that we are the only species living beyond our "solar budget" and are moving toward the irreparable destruction of the biosphere. To deal with these problems, Daly advocates a steady-state economy, which would be based on a specified size of population and wealth. There would be flexibility for changing these sizes according to the availability of technologies and changes in values. However, a pivotal concept underlying any specification in size of population and wealth would be the "throughput of resources." Throughput, he emphasizes, "begins with depletion (followed by production and consumption) and ends with an equal amount of waste effluent or pollution."

The specification of throughput of resources implies that human beings, through moral principles and technology, would determine the rate of economic growth to a much greater extent than a system in which the growth of population and capital tends to shape technological and moral development. Daly stresses the importance of ethical first principles such as knowledge, self-discipline, and restraint on the accumulation of desires. He joins other critics of modem industrial society in questioning preoccupation with the power of scientific knowledge and necessity for economic growth. Instead, he proposes a greater emphasis on sharing scarce resources and controlling population growth. Other first principles promoted by Daly include the notion of holism. Whatever the objections raised to his ideas, Daly has brought about a notable shift in perceptions about the limits to and possibilities for reshaping the economy and linking it to concern about the environment. *See also* POPULATION GROWTH; SPIRITUALITY; STEWARDSHIP.

STEWARDSHIP. The notion of the stewardship of nature is derived from the Judeo-Christian tradition. Although this tradition has often been linked to the secular belief in progress, it includes not only the notion of human dominion over nature but also of responsibility for it. A similar custodial view toward nature can be found in Aboriginal culture. Philosophers such as Robin Attfield, author of *The Ethics of Environmental Concern*, have drawn attention to examples in the teachings of the Eastern Church of a compassionate view toward animals, justified in terms of the common origins of humans and animals as "creatures of God." The best-known Western examples of this compassionate view can be found in the work of St. Francis of Assisi. Recognition of moral obligations to nature and future generations is present in the Christian tradition.

Stewardship has been adopted both by new political movements and established organizations. Despite the diversity of green parties and their focus on local concerns, some agreement on basic principles such as stewardship and the needs of future generations has emerged. In his influential work on a **steady-state economy**, American economist Herman Daly evokes as his first principles the notions of holism and stewardship as counters to the preoccupation with the power of scientific knowledge and necessity for economic growth. At the national government level there has been an acknowledgment in the 1990s of the notion of stewardship—for instance, in documents like the white paper prepared by the British government entitled, *This Common Inheritance*. *See also* GREAT BRITAIN.

STRANA ZELENYCH. *See* CZECH REPUBLIC.

STUDENT ENVIRONMENTAL ACTION COALITION (SEAC). Started in 1988, SEAC claims hundreds of high schools, colleges, universities, and community groups as members. SEAC aims to educate and empower students and youth to fight for environmental and social justice in schools and communities. The organization provides activist training for youths, information on various campaigns, and a forum for organizing campaigns and advocacy actions.

SUNFLOWER. This golden flower has become the symbol of many green parties as well as of a world free of nuclear weapons.

SUSTAINABLE DEVELOPMENT. This term has been used by international agencies ever since the 1972 **United Nations Conference on the Human Environment (UNCHE)** that was held in Stockholm. It became an integral part of the vocabulary of public policy in Western democracies by the end of the 1980s. Prior to that, national governments had considered the development of national strategies for conservation, with the aim of integrating conservation and development. Arguments for sustainable development are major efforts by governments and other established organizations to provide an alternative to favoring development over environmental protection.

Sustainable development was defined by the **World Commission on Environment and Development (WCED)**, which was formed in 1983 by the United Nations, as meeting "the needs of the present without compromising the ability of future generations to meet their own needs." The commission provided a comprehensive statement on how to address both environmental and economic concerns and to recommend that all organizations strive to incorporate ecological wisdom into their economic and social decisions. The commission attempted to demonstrate that emphasis on materialism and economic growth will not necessarily damage the environment if it is guided by principles of **ecology** and preoccupied with the renewability of resources. Economic growth was, however, "absolutely essential in order to relieve the great poverty that is deepening in much of the developing world."

In their attempts to influence the agenda for change that was being shaped by an increasingly powerful green movement, governments have exploited sustainable development much more fully than in the past. They have begun to formulate long-term plans for the integration and interdependence of conservation and development, retention of options for the future use of resources, and a focus on the underlying causes as well as the symptoms of environmental damage. Interest in these principles was rekindled by the reformulation of sustainable development by WCED and by growing awareness about environmental problems such as **climate change** and the depletion of the **ozone layer.**

Concern about these kinds of issues (especially among advanced industrialized nations) and the enduring questions about social justice and economic development that are repeatedly raised in discussions about the future direction of less developed countries have prompted intense efforts to define a new agenda based on the concept of sustainable development. There has consequently been an increase in awareness of the possibilities for promoting development without harming the environment or maintaining a balance between development and the environment.

The idea of sustainable development has been used to forge close links between economic and environmental concerns by governments, business organizations, and environmental groups. For some critics, however, sustainable development is a new form of managerialism, an attempt to quantify, according to economic criteria, the costs and benefits of environmental damage. This is seen in some quarters as a retrograde step. Others regard the debate over sustainable development as creating the possibility for resolving the tension between environmental protection and economic development. They argue that we need to pursue development within a framework that recognizes the basis of prosperity, both now and for future generations, as the proper maintenance of community resources.

Though sustainable development has been tailored by different social actors to suit their particular circumstances, the debate over this issue has created an opportunity for governments to move from a defensive posture (toward the green movement) to one that enables them to influence arguments about the environment and economy. Governments have adopted the role of arbiter between competing interests, calling for a "balance" between economic and environmental perspectives.

Government agencies have, in some countries, extended the definition of standard of living from pure economic and material measures such as income levels and consumption of goods to include the idea of **quality of life** (which may cover the environment, social justice, and personal freedoms) and embrace a variety of values including ecological, aesthetic, and ethical considerations. Governments, like environmental and business groups, have discovered opportunities for developing new markets, products, and technologies in response to these public concerns.

The adoption of concepts such as sustainable development is also linked to the attempt by governments to control or influence debates about the environment. Ideas such as sustainable development are open to a wide variety of interpretations. If these frameworks are too precise (or insufficiently vague), the potential for conflict might be increased. Although governments have placed more emphasis than ever before on environmental protection, they have not downplayed economic objectives. Rather, they have attempted to incorporate the environment into decision making and production processes and services. For some environmentalists, support for sustainable development represents a fraudulent attempt to divert efforts from the fundamental problems that affect our planet. Others, however, are prepared to consider the possibilities for overcoming the tension between development and environmental protection.

The strategies pursued by government agencies for implementing sustainable development may include legislation that ensures that environmental concerns form part of planning at all levels of government activity; rewards for government and private organizations that reduce levels of pollution and penalties for those who do not; and the promotion of initiatives to develop industries in the field of environmental protection.

In the 1990s, green organizations and political movements have also put forward numerous proposals for combining with environmental protection issues such as employment. Trade unions, business organizations, and industrial groups have become more aware of the importance of the burgeoning environmental protection industry and market for treating and recycling waste, reducing air pollution, and cleaning water.

Although many of these initiatives are significant changes in political, social, and economic life, it is worth noting that human societies have been engaged in forms of sustainable development for centuries. The practice of Aboriginals of setting fire to the bush served at least two purposes: to force out animals that could then be hunted and to bring about the renewal of vegetation and plant life that would in turn attract animals. Another example is the opposition by foresters in **Australia** at the turn of the century to the exploitation of forests on the grounds of preserving timber for future generations. The foresters were criticized for obstructing the tide of progress, namely, land settlement. There is a parallel between this position and the support for sustainable development by WCED. *See also* GREEN CONSUMERISM; POSTMATERIALISM; WORLD SUMMIT ON SUSTAINABLE DEVELOPMENT.

SWEDEN. Sweden is widely considered to be one of the pioneer countries that helped to place environmental matters on national and international political agendas.

Regarded for many decades as the archetype of a social democratic and corporatist state, Sweden has nonetheless experienced difficulties in accommodating the demands of the green movement. Although the Swedish government was primarily interested in production and economic development, in the 1960s it developed structures to address some environmental concerns such as the pollution of the air and water and mercury poisoning of fish and birds. A major legislative initiative, the Environment Protection Act, 1969, targeted, among other things, the problem of water pollution. There were also parallel efforts to coordinate the activities of diffuse government bodies by forming a National Environment Protection Board. Among the successes of these initiatives is the improvement in the quality of water through the treatment of effluents from sewage. This has been the result of massive expenditure by the state on sewage treatment plants.

Concern about other environmental issues can be traced to the 1940s, when the government, concerned about damage to its lakes and rivers by **acid rain**, created a network of observers across Europe to record levels of acid pollution. The Swedes were at the forefront of international efforts in the 1970s to convene the **United Nations Conference on the Human Environment (UNCHE)** held in Stockholm in 1972.

The most divisive environmental issue of the 1970s, and the one that exposed the weakness of the dominant corporatist regime in Sweden, was **nuclear energy**. The Swedish government has widely been regarded as one of the most open and responsive to environmental concerns. Anxiety about the development of nuclear power posed a dual threat to the government. First, Sweden relied more than most advanced industrial countries on very high levels of energy consumption for its economic development. Second, the major partners in the Swedish success story—the government, big business and the trade unions—appeared unable to include the new social movements, notably those concerned about nuclear power, in the corporatist system.

The issue of nuclear energy was first taken up by a major political party, the Center Party (formerly, the Agrarian Party), during the 1976 elections. The opposition of the Center Party to nuclear power proved decisive insofar as it led to the Social Democratic Party's loss of power for the first time in 44 years and to formation of a coalition government between the Center Party, the Moderate Party, and the People's Party. The failure of all the major parties to come to address the issue of nuclear power and the defeat of a referendum advocated by the Center Party to end the expansion of nuclear power projects were crucial in the formation of Miljöpartiet de Gröna.

Green groups in Sweden have attracted support in local elections since the early 1970s. The Stockholm Party, which focused on environmental issues, gained three seats in the 1979 municipal elections.

As in many other western European countries, antinuclear protests paved the way for the formation of green political parties, including Miljöpartiet. Sweden relied heavily on the development of nuclear power for its energy needs, a policy championed by the Social Democratic Party that had governed Sweden for several decades. In 1976, however, a decisive shift in electoral politics occurred. The Center Party, led by Thorbjörn Fälldin, campaigned on an antinuclear platform. It gained 24 percent of the vote and displaced the Social Democrats in the government after forming a coalition with the Conservative and Liberal parties.

However, these two parties did not share the same goals as the Center Party, at least on the question of nuclear power. The unwillingness of the Center Party to confront its coalition partners over this question undermined its credibility among environmentalists, and disagreement over the development of nuclear power eventually led to the collapse of the coalition.

In 1979, following the **Three Mile Island** accident in the **United States** and changing climate of opinion on the issue of nuclear power, the Social Democrats agreed to hold a national referendum. The March 1980 referendum offered three options. The Center Party and the Communist Party advocated an end to the expansion of nuclear power and phasing out of the six reactors in operation within 10 years. By contrast, the Social Democrats and the Liberals agreed to phase out nuclear power, subject to the following conditions: the twelve reactors in operation, completed or under construction, could be used and would be held under state control. The Conservatives agreed with the phasing out of nuclear power but, like the Social Democrats and the Liberals, argued for the utilization of the 12 reactors in operation, completed, or under construction. The position of the Center and Communist Parties attracted 38.7 percent of vote, that of the Social Democrats and Liberals, 39.1 percent, and that of the Conservatives, 18.9 percent. Following the referendum, the decision to close down all nuclear reactors by the year 2010 was made. However, the referendum also allowed the government to proceed with the construction of six more nuclear power plants, thereby strengthening the dependence of the country on this form of energy.

Following this disappointing result, the antinuclear movement lost faith in the Center Party and began to concentrate its efforts on creating a new party that would focus principally on environmental issues. Miljöpartiet de Gröna, the Swedish Green Party, was founded in September 1981. In the 1982 and 1985 national elections it polled only 1.7 and 1.5 percent, respectively. By contrast, in municipal elections held at the same time, it received a significantly higher proportion of votes and gained 167 seats in 1982 and 240 seats in 1985. In 1988, however, Miljöpartiet de Gröna overcame the 4 percent threshold for parties to enter Parliament and was the first new party in 70 years to gain representation. It was allocated 20 seats after acquiring 5.6 percent of the national vote. This success can be attributed to the significance attached to the environment during the election campaign, dangers posed to the Swedish population by the **Chernobyl** disaster in 1986, and strong reaction against the style of professional politics that characterized the major parties.

The catastrophes at Three Mile Island in 1979 and, even more significantly, Chernobyl in 1986 played a crucial role in shifting public opinion on environmental issues. The Chernobyl accident had a greater direct impact on Sweden than on any other country outside the Soviet Union, and many restrictions had to be introduced on the consumption of fresh fruit and vegetables as well as on both livestock imported into Sweden and that produced by Swedes. At the 1988 elections, environmental issues were prominent on the political agenda and included debates on how to bring about the closure of all nuclear power plants, legislation and taxation to combat all forms of pollution, investment in **alternative energy** (including greater use of natural gases, solar energy, and wind power), restrictions on the use of chemicals in agriculture, new automobile speed limits, reductions in chlorine emissions from pulp mills, and much stricter regulation of the use of **chlorofluorocarbons (CFCs).**

In 1991, however, the Miljöpartiet polled only 3.4 percent and lost all its seats. The environment was not a major issue during this election campaign, and many voters were apparently deterred from supporting the party because it had become more explicit in leaning toward the left. However, in 1994, the party recovered in a convincing manner by obtaining 5 percent of the vote and 18 seats. Among the main factors that contributed to the revival of Miljöpartiet were its strong stance in opposing Sweden's membership in the European Union (EU), the general mistrust of professional politicians, and, paradoxically, its ability to present itself as a conventional party and avoid some of the difficulties associated with divisions between fundamentalists and realists that have troubled other green parties. In the 1998 parliamentary elections, support for the party dropped slightly to 4.5 percent, but because of the weak showing of the Social Democratic Party, the Social Democrats invited the Greens and the Left Party into a coalition government. In the 2006 elections they won 5.24 percent of the vote and 19 seats.

Ironically, given the party's opposition to Sweden's membership in the EU and to the adoption of the euro and their calls for Sweden to hold another referendum on leaving the EU, the Greens won 17.2 percent in the Swedish elections to the **European Parliament** in 1995. This gave them four seats. In 1999, however, their support dropped to 9.4 percent (two seats) and in 2004 to 5.9 percent (one seat).

In the late 1980s Miljöpartiet polled well enough at the local (municipal) and regional levels to gain seats in all local councils and enter coalitions in local governments. The most impressive results for the party have been at the local level and in the 26 county councils. Beginning in 1994, the party came to hold the balance of power in numerous districts. As a consequence, it began to play an important role in the administration and provision of services such as health care, education, and housing, as well as in supervising arrangements for environmental standards.

Local branches provided the foundation of the party. Above these were the regions, which elected representatives to the Annual Congress and national Representative Committee. As in other green parties, a key principle was to ensure as much participation as possible. This was epitomized by the focus on decentralization and **direct democracy**. The principle of rotation of delegates highlights the party's emphasis on addressing the problem of the concentration of power.

The Annual Congress elects members to a variety of committees, including a political bureau and an administrative bureau. The idea is to reduce the concentration of power. For example, the political bureau focuses on policymaking in general, whereas the administrative concentrates on economic policy. Again, symbolizing the effort by Miljöpartiet to present itself as a clear alternative to the major parties, there is a tendency against the emergence of strong party leaders. In 1995 Miljöpartiet did elect two spokespersons, though they remain representatives who deal with the media rather than serve as party leaders. There are also numerous rules to ensure equal representation of men and women, especially at the highest levels of the party.

A large proportion of Miljöpartiet's members had formerly been supporters of the Center Party and the Social Democrats. Most are young, middle class, and well educated. Women and people employed in the public sector are among its most numerous members. However, like other green parties, Miljöpartiet has been vulnerable to the propensity of voters to switch parties between elections.

Miljöpartiet established itself as an antinuclear party and has taken on many other issues, including self-government at a local level, decentralization of the state, peace and disarmament, and a reduction in economic growth. Most people regard the party as first and foremost a voice for environmental concerns, though it has developed a distinctive profile on other issues as well. Above all, Miljöpartiet did not share the view of most major parties that Sweden should join the EU. The party also challenged assumptions about the state's involvement in owning enterprises, creating wage-earner funds, and promoting the arms industry and spending on defense. Miljöpartiet has continued to espouse collectivist goals such as social justice and fairer and more equal distribution of income and wealth.

As in other countries, the major parties in Sweden have adopted many of the policies advocated by new social movements and green political organizations. Noting the significant changes in public opinion, they have responded to the continuing success of green parties, particularly at the local and regional levels. Tension still remains in Sweden between the growing awareness of dangers to the environment and the imperative to remain competitive in economic growth and development.

SWITZERLAND. A proposal in the early 1970s to build a highway through the city of Neuchâtel mobilized the local population. Opponents of the project, unable to persuade the authorities to reverse their decision, entered the communal elections in 1972 and won eight of the 41 seats in the local parliament. This paved the way for the foundation of the first green party in Switzerland, the Mouvement populaire pour l'environnement (MPE).

Inspired by the activities of the MPE in Neuchâtel, Jean-Jacques Hédiguer founded an MPE in the canton of Vaud. The organization attracted 5.6 percent of the vote in Lausanne and won five of the 100 seats in the town council and 15 other seats in various communes. Divisions within the MPE-Vaud led to the formation of the Groupement pour la Protection de l'Environnement, which, in 1977 attracted 8.2 percent of the vote and won eight seats on the town council and in 1979 gained a seat in the national parliament—the first national parliamentary seat won by any Green in the world. Another green party, in the German-speaking part of Switzerland, was founded in 1978. The Grüne Partei Zürich made steady progress, and in 1987 won 22 out of 180 seats in the cantonal parliament.

Before the 1987 national elections, a federation of green groups (Föderation der Grünen Parteien der Schweiz) formed a national Swiss Green Party (Grüne Partei der Schweiz [GPS]) in May 1986. In 1987 it secured 119 seats in cantonal parliaments, and by 1991 the number had risen to 154 seats. This is only a partial measure of the strength of the green movement. The total number of seats held by all green and alternative parties was somewhat greater. In 1991, despite some pessimistic predictions about the influence of environmental issues on voting behavior, the GPS polled 6.2 percent and secured 14 seats at the national level. This was an improvement on the 5.1 percent it received in 1987, which procured nine seats, and the 2.6 percent of 1983 (and four seats). In 1987 a coalition of leftist environmental groups, the Grüne Bündnis Schweiz, polled 4.3 percent nationally and secured five seats. However, this was a fairly loose coalition, and by 1991 the GPS had become the most influential and well-known green party.

As was the case in many other countries, the mid-1990s proved a difficult time for the greens in Switzerland. The GPS secured only eight seats in the Parliament, but subsequently two other members of Parliament who had been elected on alternative lists joined the party, bringing their number to 10. With unemployment a major concern, voters shifted their support to the Social Democrats, which saw a surge of support. In 1999, the GPS won 5 percent of the vote and secured nine seats, plus one from another list.

In the 2003 elections, the greens won 7.4 percent of the vote, their highest ever. The highest support rates came from the French-speaking areas of Switzerland (Neuchatel 13.8 percent, Geneva 11.2 percent, Vaud 11.1 percent). The German-speaking regions (Zurich, Bern, Lucerne) had support rates in the 8.5 to 9.8 percent range, with the exception of Basel County where it was 12.6 percent. This meant the GPS could take 15 seats in the Nationalrat, the Swiss Parliament.

At the cantonal level in the past decade, the Greens have tended to win representation in 15 or 16 of the 26 cantons. They have also started to obtain representation in cantonal executive councils. In 1999, Verena Diener became the first green president of a cantonal government. In 2001, Daniel Brélaz was elected mayor of Lausanne, the first green mayor of a major city in Switzerland.

Over time, different environmental issues have been prominent on the political agenda. In the 1970s a powerful social movement against the development of **nuclear energy** arose. The most famous protests emerged in 1975 against the proposal to construct a nuclear power plant at Kaiseraugst. Eventually, environmental groups and other political organizations succeeded in persuading the government to offer compensation to the developers responsible for not completing this project and introducing a moratorium, lasting 10 years, on nuclear power.

Since the 1970s, environmental groups have campaigned to reduce pollution by automobiles—for example, by attempting to prevent the construction of new highways. By the 1990s a strong reaction against the restrictions imposed on motorists by the government occurred, expressed in significant support for the AutoPartei (Car Party) and for the Lega Ticinese (Ticino League). Both these political parties were also opposed to the loosening of restrictions on immigration and the admission of asylum seekers to Switzerland.

Support for environmental groups and political organizations remained strong. In the 1980s the destruction of forests by **acid rain** and the nuclear disaster at **Chernobyl** focused attention on the environment. Moreover, there is an enduring concern about air pollution and the contamination of water supplies.

Over time dominant parties adopted significant components of the green agenda. In addition, the well-established conservation groups and new social movements that maintain a watchful eye on environmental issues operate at a distance from both the GPS and dominant parties. This allows groups such as the **World Wide Fund for Nature (WWF)** to gain better access to government and develop an independent stance on many issues. The program of the GPS covers many of the issues brought up by environmental groups while trying to articulate a broader agenda for political reform.

Apart from the environmental issues mentioned above, the GPS has sought to develop policies on how to check economic growth and focus on **sustainable development**, using taxation, especially energy taxes, instead of indirect taxes; transportation (particularly on promoting public transport); and a range of social justice measures (including a **guaranteed minimum income**, more equitable distribution of wealth and resources, and the protection of minorities and disadvantaged groups). The GPS has also attempted to gain support by focusing on two issues that have preoccupied many people: first, the system of political patronage and control exercised by established political elites and interest groups and, second, concern about the impact that membership in the European Union (EU) would have on the environment as well as on certain valuable elements of Swiss culture and political life.

The GPS has, like other green parties, embraced the principles of decentralization, a precautionary approach to development projects, and the idea of government and industry on a small scale. Coalitions with other parties in order to form a government commonly occur in municipal and cantonal settings. There was successful collaboration, for instance between 1986 and 1990, in the canton of Bern over issues such as the conservation of energy, nuclear power, education, and transport.

Above all, the GPS has developed a pragmatic approach to politics along the lines espoused by the realists in other green parties. It has taken full advantage of entitlements to membership in parliamentary committees and participated in the formulation of policies as well as in the negotiation of compromises with other parties. The GPS, like many other green parties, seeks to balance a fundamental commitment to environmental protection with achieving changes in policy within the prevailing political structures and to meet the challenge of retaining a distinct identity as other parties adopt substantial elements of the green political agenda.

The organization of the party reflects the emphasis of the Swiss political system on federal structures. Regional bodies have immense flexibility in determining their own policy platforms. The national governing body is the Assembly of Delegates, which is drawn from all cantons and meets twice a year. This meeting elects the party president and other officials. The GPS has applied the principle of rotation to its officers. The party has been successful in combining some of the principles of **direct democracy** with the need to achieve a degree of coherence in all its operations, including the formulation of policy and electoral contests. *See also BLUEPRINT FOR SURVIVAL, A*; CARBON TAXES; PRECAUTIONARY PRINCIPLE; SMALL IS BEAUTIFUL.

– T –

THAILAND. A "second-generation tiger," Thailand has undergone rapid economic development over the past three decades. In the late 1980s a series of environmental disasters sparked protests and the birth of Thailand's green movement. Environmental nongovernmental organizations (NGOs) emerged and, along with other groups such as community development groups, began environmental activities. Groups involved in the green movement in Thailand are involved with many different kinds of work, including advocacy, conservation, education, water and energy issues, and public health. NGO movements in Thailand began with community development activities, with a focus on economic development. Later, with the onset of environmental disasters resulting from economic development, environmental issues were included on their agenda. The protection of local forests has become an issue of increasing importance.

There are over 70 NGOs registered with the Thai government and a number of these are environmental or are involved with environmental issues. Registered NGOs are allowed juristic person and may apply for governmental financial support. However, the high financial costs involved with becoming a registered organization prevent many of the smaller, local NGOs from attaining registered status. Most Thai environmental NGOs receive most of their funding from foreign donors. The National Environmental Board and Thailand Environmental Institute provide further representation for NGOs and assist them in coordinating efforts with the Thai government.

Like in **Malaysia**, there is a growing Buddhist **ecology** movement in Thailand. Buddhist monks in Thailand are becoming increasingly involved in deforestation prevention projects and other conservation issues, applying their Buddhist beliefs to environmentalism and promoting environmental ethics and environmentally sound practices in their communities.

The Thailand Environment Foundation, a Bangkok-based foundation was established in 1993 to promote **sustainable development** through grassroots action as well as policy research and promoting public awareness. The foundation operates through the Thailand Environmental Institute.

THINK GLOBALLY, ACT LOCALLY. This concept has been attributed to environmentalist René Dubos and used as a slogan by the green movement in its endeavors to establish alternative ways of social action at the local level and demonstrate both in symbolic and practical terms the possibility for transforming the world. The focus on acting locally corresponds to the focus on decentralization in influential works like *A Blueprint for Survival* and in writings on bioregionalism, as well as in the orientation of many green political organizations and social movements. The slogan has been used to great effect in mobilizing people to take action in their local communities with respect to environmental protection; the creation of alternative lifestyles, including the provision of social and other services; and campaigns directed against specific industries, notably the weapons industry, and enterprises that have a deleterious impact on the environment.

THREE GORGES DAM. The idea of damming the Yangtze, one of the world's great rivers, was originally conceived by Sun Yatsen in 1919. Planning for the dam began in 1954 under the leadership of Mao Tsetung. Construction began in 1994 but then was temporarily suspended in 1989 due to strong citizen opposition. After the 1989 Tiananmen Square incident and the subsequent clamp-down on protest activities, Premier Li Peng pushed through plans for the dam. The construction plans were approved by the National People's Congress in 1992 although one-third of the delegates either voted against it or abstained from voting, suggesting that there was still considerable opposition to the project.

Upon its completion in 2009, the Three Gorges Dam will be the world's largest dam and will also go down as one of its most expensive construction projects ever (an estimated US$25 billion). The dam was championed for a variety of reasons: upon its completion it should produce 84.7 billion kilowatt hours of electricity, equivalent to about one-tenth of the People's Republic of China's electricity consumption; it will control flooding that in the past has killed tens of thousands; and, it will offset carbon dioxide emissions that would otherwise be produced by burning coal to produce electricity. Critics of the dam have condemned the environmental destruction, historical and cultural loss, and human resettlement the dam will require.

Protest against the dam within the **People's Republic of China** has been suppressed by the state. Author Dai Qing was arrested for writing a book in 1989 criticizing the dam. International environmental groups, including the International Rivers Network, have urged international banks and export credit agencies not to fund the project, but they are fighting a losing battle. Electricity generation has already begun in the lower stretches of the dam.

THREE MILE ISLAND. The site of a nuclear power plant in Harrisburg, Pennsylvania, and of a near catastrophe in March 1979. Radioactive gases were emitted from the plant and pregnant women and young children in the surrounding district were evacuated. The accident was caused by defects in machinery and negligence on the part of those responsible for the efficient supervision of the equipment, particularly in dealing with the emergency situation. The publicity surrounding this incident helped to mobilize further antinuclear protests in the **United States** and other countries. An additional stimulus to these protests was provided by a popular film based on similar events, entitled *The China Syndrome*.

TORREY CANYON. In the 1960s a number of catastrophes served to draw attention to the need for both a more powerful green movement and improved action by governments dealing with environmental problems. The collision of the oil tanker *Torrey Canyon* in March 1967 with rocks off the southwestern coast of England led to the spill of 875,000 barrels of oil. Much of it ended up on the shores of Cornwall and Brittany. Attempts to deal with the catastrophe were slow and very costly. Although governments have responded, to some degree, to the concerns brought up by the green movement, there is still considerable room for improvement, as demonstrated by the more recent and disastrous spill from the oil tanker *Exxon Valdez*.

"TRAGEDY OF THE COMMONS." In a paper first published in 1968, biologist Garrett Hardin coined this term to describe the transition from a period when it was possible, without any deleterious consequences, to allow people to use common land to feed their cattle to one in which such action leads to catastrophe. In the first stage, population levels are low. It is therefore plausible to imagine unhindered access to common land. In the second stage, with an increase in population and animals, the attempt to maximize use of common land, while yielding some benefit to each individual, ultimately has devastating consequences on the community as a whole. Hardin argued that the principle of freedom in the use of the commons needs to be set aside in favor of coercion for the good of the entire community. He proposed a variety of mechanisms, including restrictions on access to the commons, the introduction of taxes and charges to reduce pollution and control waste disposal, and a highly controversial proposal to impose constraints on the right to bear children. *See also* POPULATION GROWTH.

TRAINER, TED. *See* DEINDUSTRIALIZATION.

– U –

UKRAINE. Ukraine attracted the West's attention as the result of its Orange Revolution, when in late 2004, hundreds of thousands of protestors gathered in the streets to protest electoral fraud, rigging the election in favor of Viktor Yanukovych. The Supreme Court annulled the election results and there was a revote that brought pro-Western, opposition rival Viktor Yuschenko into the presidency. Support for Yushenko's government, however, was relatively short-lived and the country is again shifting to the right, when more pro-Russian Yanukovych was able to stage a comeback. The fortunes of the Ukrainian Greens appear to have been influenced by these larger political changes.

The Chernobyl nuclear disaster and the many pollution problems related to the Soviet-era economy's reliance on heavy industry and mining gave birth to a widespread **ecological** movement. Scientists and activists formed environmental groups in almost every region of the country. In 1987 they joined in a national association, Green World (Zeleny Svit). In the tumultuous period of 1989, Zeleny Svit, led by the writer Yury Shcherbak, became a major political force.

While the community suffers from lack of access to adequate funding and governmental support, and faces numerous institutional barriers to their activities, there are several hundred environmental nongovernmental organizations (NGOs) in the Ukraine. The Ukrainian Green Party (Partija Zelenykh Ukrainy) was established in 1991 and has branches throughout the country. It became a member of the **European Federation of Green Parties** in 1994. As with the newly emerging green parties in other states that were behind the Iron Curtain, the party is eager to find ways to move the country away from the ecological nightmares that were produced by the Soviet economic model. Also, like many other green parties, it calls for development of an ecologically sustainable economic and social system. It also hopes to awaken stronger ecological values within society. This may be difficult for the party, however, as the country struggles through major political upheavals. In the 1998 parliamentary elections, the party did quite well with 5.5 percent of the vote. This enabled it to select 19 delegates from its party list. The 2002 elections, however, saw a reversal of fortunes and the party lost all of its seats. In the 2006 elections, the party received less than 1 percent of the national vote. The party continues to have local and regional representation, however.

UNITED KINGDOM. *See* GREAT BRITAIN.

UNITED NATIONS CONFERENCE ON ENVIRONMENT AND DEVELOPMENT (UNCED). The UNCED was held in Rio de Janeiro in June 1992. Often referred to as the Earth Summit, it was the largest international gathering of this kind, with delegates from 178 countries. It was also seen as the sequel to the **United Nations Conference on the Human Environment (UNCHE)**, which had been held in Stockholm in 1972 and brought together governments, government agencies, and environmental groups to debate environmental questions.

The decision to hold another conference was made following a December 1989 resolution by the United Nations General Assembly. The choice of Rio de Janeiro as the venue for the conference was also important as it gave due recognition to the significance of less developed countries in efforts to address environmental issues. The meeting, with its focus on environment and development, was also a response to the efforts of agencies such as the **World Commission on Environment and Development (WCED)** to bring about a new understanding of the relationship between these issues. The report by the WCED had already become, for many governments and some nongovernmental agencies, the basis for developing a dialogue between environmentalists and developers. There was considerable skepticism among the media and environmentalists about the possibility of effective action emerging from the Rio conference. Reports on the conference reflected the central role of the media in spreading awareness of environmental problems and expressing the impatience with the delays in the implementation of new policies. A major difficulty for the conference was to reconcile the divergent perspectives of developed and developing countries. The economic implications of environmental protection are particularly acute for the latter. The agenda in this sphere has been dominated by arguments over who should pay for environmental protection and over the "hypocrisy" of developed nations that consume a disproportionate share of resources and expect developing countries to take drastic measures to save the environment. There has also been tension between environmentalism in the developed world and the needs for survival and improvement of material conditions in developing nations. The goals of environmentalists in the West may also clash with the policies of particular regimes. For example, environmentalists and trade unionists in Western countries have attempted to prevent trade with countries such as Malaysia in rainforest timbers.

Another dimension of international conflict lies in the different positions adopted by major powers or trading blocs on environmental issues, illustrated by the divergent positions of the **United States** and the European Union (EU) over the signing of international treaties on the emission of carbon dioxide, aid programs to developing countries, and regulating species protection or **biodiversity**. Conferences like the one held in Rio de Janeiro have contributed to the growing realization that national governments are having great difficulty in dealing with international economic problems as well as with environmental ones. Still, with the endorsement of several agreements at the conference, governments representing over 150 countries signaled at least a commitment to combat global problems.

Among the major agreements emerging from the conference was the plan to implement **sustainable development**, outlined in a document entitled **Agenda 21**. This document covered a vast range of topics including international cooperation, combating poverty, consumption patterns, population, the atmosphere, the oceans, indigenous peoples, women, NGOs, technology transfer, education, public awareness, and training, as well as integrated decision making and international institutional arrangements. In an effort to ensure that member-states devised national plans of action to implement Agenda 21, the United Nations established the **Commission on Sustainable Development (CSD)** in December 1992. Every year all member-states are to report to this commission on measures they have adopted to implement Agenda 21.

Another key initiative of the 1992 conference was the **United Nations Framework Convention on Climate Change (UNFCCC)**, which outlined principles that would underlie efforts to deal with problems such as global warming, particularly the **greenhouse effect**. The convention was endorsed by 154 countries and the EU. One of the most significant recommendations contained in this convention was that developed countries should, by the year 2000, reduce their greenhouse gas emissions to 1990 levels. However, governments were able to evade this requirement if they could prove that this would cause them economic difficulties.

Other important agreements to emerge from the conference were the **Convention on Biological Diversity**, Declaration on Environment and Development, and enactment of Forest Principles. As with the agreement on climate change, the Convention on Biological Diversity included many escape clauses for nations that were unwilling to implement aspects of it. The **United States** refused to sign it on the grounds that it would undermine its biotechnology industry, though 155 nations as well as the EU did sign the agreement. The UNCED played a critical role in getting the environment onto the political agenda of nation-states and the international community.

The UNCED also had an impact on the global green movement. The First Planetary Meeting of Greens was held just prior to the UNCED leading for a call by the world's Green parties for governments to heed the "global state of emergency." A Green International Steering Committee was formed at the conference, which met the following year in Mexico City and created the first Global Green Network, laying the foundation for the later formation of the **Global Greens**.

UNITED NATIONS CONFERENCE ON THE HUMAN ENVIRONMENT (UNCHE). Held from 5 to 16 June 1972 in Stockholm, **Sweden**, UNCHE signaled a significant breakthrough in getting governments, governmental agencies, and environmental groups together to discuss and recognize the importance of environmental problems. Official delegates from 113 countries took part in the conference. Among the principal themes was how to address problems of pollution. On some issues, such as testing nuclear weapons and monitoring the use of toxic chemicals, there was disagreement between major powers such as the **United States** and other countries. A more popular measure, suggested by the United States, was a moratorium, lasting 10 years, on trading in whales.

One significant outcome of the conference was the focus by less developed countries on the connection between environmental protection and economic development (and their concern about any attempt by industrialized developed countries to slow the pace of development in poorer countries). This concern contributed to discussion about the possibility of **sustainable development** and a shift in perceptions among many environmental groups in more developed countries toward a more global view of environmental issues and problems. Another long-term outcome was the emergence, following the conference, of many more grassroots nongovernmental environmental groups in less developed nations. This can partly be attributed to the enthusiasm generated by the conference for further action pertaining to the environment and economic development.

The conference also led to further cooperation between nation-states. As regards the establishment of institutional mechanisms and structures to facilitate this cooperation, the formation of the **United Nations Environment Programme** (**UNEP**) was one of the most visible outcomes of the 1972 conference.

UNITED NATIONS CONFERENCE ON THE LAW OF THE SEA (UNCLOS). The United Nations has supported three conferences on marine law. The first two were in 1958 and 1960. The third lasted from 1973 to 1982, and took up issues such as the depletion of fish stocks, marine pollution, and the creation of exclusive economic zones for sovereign nations. Although the Convention of the Law of the Sea was signed by 189 countries in 1982, this did not include major industrialized powers (such as the **United States**, **Japan**, **Germany**, **Great Britain**, and **France**). The latter objected to a clause that attempted to turn into common ownership the mineral wealth deposited on the ocean beds. UNCLOS only came into force in 1994 and entailed the creation of exclusive economic zones stretching out 200 nautical miles from a nation's coastline. However, the effort to declare the oceans a common heritage remains a source of tension between nations.

UNITED NATIONS ENVIRONMENT PROGRAMME (UNEP). This program was established in 1972 following the **United Nations Conference on the Human Environment (UNCHE).** In order to develop further the cooperation that had been achieved between government and nongovernmental organizations (NGOs) by the conference, the United Nations General Assembly supported the creation of a Governing Council of UNEP. The council would include representatives from 58 countries. They would be elected by the General Assembly for a period of three years at a time. The primary roles of UNEP were to coordinate and stimulate activities across all agencies of the United Nations.

In 1973 the Governing Council proposed three core objectives for the organization. The first was to increase knowledge, through the interdisciplinary study of ecological systems, "for an integrated and rational management of the resources of the biosphere, and for safeguarding human well-being as well as ecosystems." The second was to "support an integrated approach to the planning and management of development, including that of natural resources," with an awareness of the effects on the environment and social and economic considerations. The third was to provide assistance, particularly to developing countries, "to help mobilize additional financial resources for the purpose of providing the required technical assistance, education, training and free flow of information and exchange of experience, with a view to promoting the full participation of developing countries in the national and international efforts for the preservation and enhancement of the environment" (from *UNEP: Two Decades of Achievement and Challenge*). In response to the 1972 UNCHE recommendations, UNEP developed three approaches, which were labeled environmental assessment, environmental management, and supporting measures.

UNEP also established mechanisms for the collection and exchange of information. The system came to be known as Earthwatch. An important element in this arrangement is the International Referral System, known as International Referral System (INFOTERRA). INFOTERRA has become the most extensive mechanism for the exchange of information on environmental issues in the world. Approximately 150 countries and 6,500 institutions participate in the system. INFOTERRA has also created additional networks for research and information, including the Global Environment Monitoring System, International Register of Potentially Toxic Chemicals, and Global Resource Information Database.

Promoting environmental management, UNEP has contributed to the drafting of numerous international treaties, such as the 1973 **Convention on International Trade in Endangered Species**, the 1979 Bonn Convention on the Conservation of Migratory Species of Wild Animals, the 1985 **Vienna Convention for the Protection of the Ozone Layer**, the 1987 **Montreal Protocol on Substances That Deplete the Ozone Layer**, the 1992 **United Nations Framework Convention on Climate Change (UNFCCC)**, and the 1992 **Convention on Biological Diversity**. In order to assist with the management of water resources, it initiated a scheme for the Environmentally Sound Management of Inland Waters, which led to an agreement between eight African countries to monitor the use of the Zambezi River Basin. Another important initiative by UNEP was its Regional Seas Program, which, beginning in the mid-1970s, brought together countries to protect the coastline and oceans around the world.

The success or failure of UNEP's initiatives depends to a large degree on financial support from national governments and the latter's willingness to implement agreements. A large proportion of the objectives that UNEP has set for itself remain to be realized. However, it has raised awareness about environmental issues among political elites; coordinated action by numerous agencies at the local, national, and international levels; and successfully implemented some of its plans.

UNITED NATIONS FRAMEWORK CONVENTION ON CLIMATE CHANGE (UNFCCC). The UNFCCC was developed at the **United Nations Conference on Environment and Development (UNCED)**, which was held in Rio de Janeiro in 1992. The UNFCCC's purpose was to reduce greenhouse gas emissions in order to fight **global warming**, but at the convention countries were only able to agree on the need for action. No specific goals, targets, or timetables were agreed upon. The UNFCCC was opened for signing in May 1992 and was enforced beginning in March 1994. As of April 2006, the convention has been ratified by 189 countries. Its ultimate objective is to "achieve stabilization of greenhouse gas concentrations in the atmosphere at a low enough level to prevent dangerous anthropogenic interference with the climate system."

The UNFCCC established a Conference of the Parties to prepare a protocol that would create legally binding obligations for developed countries to reduce their greenhouse gas emissions. **Japan** agreed to host the third Conference of the Parties in its old capital, Kyoto, and hence the agreement that was formed there has come to be known as the **Kyoto Protocol**.

Under the principal of common but differentiated responsibilities that recognizes the different historical contributions of developed and developing states to global environmental problems, countries that signed the UNFCCC were split into three groups: Annex I, Annex II, and Developing countries. Annex I countries are the states that were members of the Organisation for Economic Cooperation and Development (OECD) in 1992 plus economies in transition. These are the states that are expected under the agreement to take the first steps to reduce their greenhouse gas emissions. Annex II states are the same as those in Annex I minus the countries in transition. They are expected to provide financial and technical assistance to developing countries to reduce their greenhouse gas emissions and adapt to the effects of climate change. Developing countries have no restrictions under the UNFCCC. *See also* GREENHOUSE EFFECT.

UNITED NATIONS INTERNATIONAL CONFERENCE ON POPULATION AND DEVELOPMENT. *See* POPULATION GROWTH.

UNITED STATES OF AMERICA. The United States has one of the world's largest environmental movements, but green parties have done less well than in many European states. While there may be a cultural element to this, the nature of the winner-take-all electoral systems at the federal and state levels has also played a major role.

Many of the best-known environmental groups in the United States emerged in the first half of the 20th century, including the **Audubon Society** and the **Sierra Club**. Many of the groups were concerned with **conservationism**. Several major new environmental groups formed in the years after World War II ended, including the **Nature Conservancy** (1951), Resources for the Future (1952), and the **World Wide Fund for Nature (WWF)** in (1961).

These environmental groups began to lobby Congress for preservation of more wilderness areas and the protection of wildlife. Howard Zahniser, a staffer at the U.S. Biological Survey, became director of the **Wilderness Society**. He believed environmental organizations could more effectively further their cause by forming coalitions lobbying for similar goals. After **David Brower** assumed the directorship of the Sierra Club, Zahniser and Brower lobbied together to have Congress designate 50 million acres in the west as wilderness. In 1956 these environmental movements also defeated government plans to dam the Grand Canyon and Echo Park in Dinosaur National Monument. They successfully lobbied for the passage of the Wilderness Act of 1964, setting aside pristine forests for preservation. Environmental groups also successfully lobbied for the passage of the Land and Water Conservation Fund Act of 1964 to fund federal purchases of land in order that they be protected, the Endangered Species Act of 1966, and the Wild and Scenic Rivers Act of 1968 to protect rivers of special character.

Concern also began to grow about the impact that rapid industrialization and modernization were having on the Earth and living species. A series of publications began to change public attitudes about environmental protection. In 1948 Fairfield Osborne published one of the first books to make a wake-up call related to agricultural practices, *Our Plundered Planet*. **Rachel Carson**'s groundbreaking 1962 book *Silent Spring* became a national best-seller.

A series of accidents also helped to shock the public. In 1969 an explosion on an oil platform off the coast of Santa Barbara created a huge oil slick that affected 35 miles of California coastline, killing marine life and birds. The same year, the Cuyahoga River in Ohio, which was contaminated with chemicals, caught fire.

New environmental groups began to form and existing environmental groups expanded their range of activities. The environmental movement became part of a larger counterculture movement that included supporters of the peace movement against the Vietnam War, the civil rights movement, and the women's rights movement. Gus Speth, creator of the **Natural Resources Defense Council (NRDC)** (1970), one of the most powerful groups regularly involved in environmental litigation in the country, stated that he was inspired to create an organization lobbying and conducting lawsuits on behalf of the environment by the example of the National Association for the Advancement of Colored People.

Other new groups to form at this time included **Environmental Defense** Fund (1967), **Friends of the Earth** (1969), and **Greenpeace** USA (1971). The focus of the environmental movement broadened to include not only nature conservation and wildlife preservation, but also air and water pollution, **nuclear energy**, chemical use, incinerators, toxic landfills, and many other issues. It is important to note that while these groups are national, they often are major actors in local environmental cases that may have national ramifications.

These environmental groups became powerful political actors, making use of the federal government system to lobby policymakers at multiple levels. Environmental activists were empowered in the 1970s by Congress and the courts. The Administrative Procedures Act of 1946 had already provided citizens with some avenues to learn about, and be involved in decision making related to development, environment, and other issues. The environmental groups' ability to influence regulatory direction expanded substantially, first with the passage of the National Environmental Policy Act (NEPA) in 1969 and then with the Supreme Court's ruling in the 1972 "Mineral King" case brought by the Sierra Club. The NEPA is one of the most important pieces of environmental legislation in the United States. It requires that environmental impact assessments be conducted for all major federal projects. It also included provisions for citizen suits and transparency in decision making on environmental matters, provisions that were included in many subsequent pieces of environmental legislation as well. The Sierra Club lost the Mineral King case, but in its ruling the Supreme Court expanded its interpretation of the concept of "standing to sue," indicating that if an organization is able to show that its members would be affected by an action, even if not directly injured by the action, they could have standing to sue.

Based on this enabling legislation, environmental organizations undertook suits to compel administrative and corporate improvements. Key U.S. environmental organizations, such as the NRDC and Environmental Defense Fund (EDF, now Environmental Defense) were created to undertake NEPA cases in order to preserve local areas. In the process, they became strong national-level players that were able to transfer their concerns to other locales facing destructive development. U.S. environmental groups used these provisions to sue violators of environmental laws and government agencies that were not performing duties required of them by the law. The federal courts, in turn, became very active in reviewing executive actions on environmental policy and not infrequently requiring federal agencies and states to adopt new regulations.

The membership of environmental nongovernmental organizations (NGOs) has gone up during administrations that have particularly actively pursued a neoconservative economic agenda at the expense of the environment. Thus, both during the Ronald Reagan presidency and the George W. Bush presidency, environmental groups have been able to attract new members.

As was the case in Europe, Australia, and New Zealand, some activists also turned to the political system to seek change. The **Citizens Party** was the first large-scale attempt by social movements in the United States to contest elections on a platform that combined a focus on environmental questions and socialist ideas for restructuring the economy; green political activists became even more convinced of the value of focusing on local politics.

In 1984, about 60 activists gathered in Macalister College in Minneapolis to form the Committees of Correspondence, named after the small grassroots groups of the U.S. Revolutionary War. They also adopted the Green Ten Key Values. Although the committees wanted to achieve a degree of coordination and coherence at the national level, they differed from the Citizens Party by focusing principally on local political campaigns and shedding the preoccupation with left-wing agendas. While this to some degree weakened any efforts to develop broad platforms for political campaigns, it did create new opportunities for local and regional green parties to emerge throughout the United States over the following years.

Greens in California, for example, met in the San Francisco Bay area in late 1984 and 1985, leading to the foundation of the East Bay Green Alliance. Other groups began to form around California, giving birth to the idea of holding a large Greening the West gathering. Over 1,000 people attended the meeting, which was held in the fall of 1988. The following year, the California Greens held their first ever statewide conference, with 25 attendees. In 1990 about 60 delegates from 30 local green groups decided to start a state-level party. They achieved ballot-status for the first time in 1992, meaning that they met the requirement of obtaining 78,992 registrants. Taking advantage of Earth Day gatherings and anti–Gulf War protests, the party was able to register a sufficient number of members to gain ballot status. The party elected its first green to the city council of Arcata.

In 1996, an Association of State Green Parties was formed. This led to the establishment in 2001 of the Green Party of the United States, a federation of the state green parties. Decisions are made through a National Committee made up of accredited state green parties. The primary goal of the party is to aid in the development of green parties in all 50 states and the District of Columbia.

In 1985 there were three candidates running nationwide, but no electoral successes. By the early 1990s green parties had secured numerous seats on local councils and boards of education. In 1992 elections the greens secured 20 seats at the municipal and county levels, representing a winning ratio of one in five contests. In 2002 they won 80 of the 260 municipal and county elections in which they ran a candidate. In the 2004 elections, a presidential election year, there were 436 candidates running in 42 states. They won 71 seats.

In California, which due in part to its size has the largest green contingent in the United States, the 2006 elections were good to the Green Party. The Green Party achieved their first-ever directly elected mayor when Gayle McLaughlin defeated the incumbent mayor of Richmond. The party had 19 wins in the 2006 elections, upping their number of representatives to 50, ranging from mayor to city councils and boards of education. The Greens attracted attention because of their strong position against the war in Iraq.

According to statistics compiled by the Green Party of the United States, as of April 2006, there were at least 232 elected Green office-holders in 28 states. The largest number of these were in California (63), followed by Pennsylvania (32), and Wisconsin (22). There have been a growing number of Green Party candidates running in statewide and federal elections. While electoral success has been extremely difficult at this level, in 1999 Audie Bock became the first Green Party candidate elected to the California State Assembly (she has since lost her seat and also switched party affiliation), and in the 2002 and 2004 elections, John Eder was elected to the State House of Representatives in Maine as a Green Independent. Currently, Eder is the only Green representative in a state assembly.

Despite the diversity of green parties and their focus on local concerns, some consensus on basic principles, which have been adopted from the platforms of European green parties like **Die Grünen**, has emerged. Apart from the core principles noted earlier, they include a focus on decentralization, feminism, respect for diversity, stewardship, the needs of future generations, and ecologically sustainable lifestyles. There is strong emphasis on organizing the economy and social services on a community basis and for much greater sharing of ownership and control than is presently the case.

Green parties in the United States have also adopted ideas about taking into account fully, through taxation and other means, the environmental and social costs of pollution and the use of energy and other resources. They also call for a reform of the electoral system, particularly the introduction of proportional representation, to enable more parties to compete effectively in elections. *See also* ALTERNATIVE ENERGY; *BLUEPRINT FOR SURVIVAL, A*; CONSERVATIONISM; ENVIRONMENTAL JUSTICE; LOVE CANAL; NATIONAL PARKS; POLLUTER PAYS PRINCIPLE; THREE MILE ISLAND.

UNITED STATES PUBLIC INTEREST RESEARCH GROUP (U.S. PIRG). This is the federation of state public research interest groups that has been in operation since 1970. U.S. PIRG and the 47 state PIRGs mobilize citizens and students to aid in their numerous environmental and energy campaigns. The federation is very active in its efforts to prevent the passage of legislation harmful to the environment at the state and federal levels. Its campaigns cover a range of issues, including clean air, **global warming**, **alternative energy**, healthy communities, food safety, voting and democracy, nature, and ecological conservation.

UNITED TASMANIA GROUP (UTG). The United Tasmania Group was formed in March 1972 as a direct response to the failure by traditional political parties to consider the full implications of the destruction of Tasmania's Lake Pedder in order to promote a hydroelectric system. The UTG was formed by the Lake Pedder Action Committee and was the first political organization in Australian history to adopt a new politics platform. In the 1972 state elections it came close to winning a seat in the Tasmanian Parliament after contesting four seats and polling about 7 percent of the vote for them. Both the UTG and the **Values Party** (formed in 1972 in New Zealand) are regarded by some commentators as the first green parties. The UTG (and the Values Party) combined opposition to industrial development with some of the preoccupations of social movements from the 1960s, such as the need for political reform and social change.

The manifesto of the UTG represented some of the central tenets of the alternative environmental paradigm described by Stephen Cotgrove in *Catastrophe or Cornucopia* and the postmaterialist values identified by Ronald Inglehart in *The Silent Revolution*. The UTG espoused a "new ethic" that condemned "the misuse of power for individual or group prominence based on aggression against man or nature." It advocated an aesthetic and harmonious relationship between human beings and nature and undertook to create new institutions that were based on participatory democracy, justice, and equal opportunity.

Although the UTG participated in nine electoral contests between 1972 and 1976, it failed to gain any seats and by 1977 began to decline as a political organization. In its place emerged a new organization, the Tasmanian **Wilderness Society**, which provided a structure for mobilizing protestors, especially against development projects such as the **Franklin Dam**. The UTG had served as a vehicle for training a new generation of political activists who were to wage highly successful campaigns and influence environmental policymaking and new political organizations in Tasmania and in **Australia**. *See also* DIRECT DEMOCRACY; POSTMATERIALISM.

– V –

VALUES PARTY. *See* NEW ZEALAND.

VALUING THE ENVIRONMENT. Discussions about **sustainable development** have, in recent times, led to numerous efforts to place a value on the environment, through the introduction of measures such as **pollution charges** and **carbon taxes**, and reconceptualize or challenge economic beliefs in the power of the **gross national product (GNP)**.

One of the most concerted efforts to bring about a change in perceptions and policies came, perhaps surprisingly, under Chris Patten, the British Minister for the Environment in the 1989 Conservative government led by Margaret Thatcher. Patten appointed as his advisers a team led by Professor David Pearce. Their *Blueprint for a Green Economy* outlined a range of specific measures for achieving sustainable development by placing values on the environment. Their work also drew together suggestions made by many other economists about how to deal with the problems of "goods" such as water and the atmosphere that have no price attached to them and have therefore been overexploited.

Pearce and his collaborators pointed to the inefficiency of a market system that did place a value on certain resources. Among their proposed reforms was the introduction of market-based incentives, such as pollution charges and carbon taxes, for changing behavior toward the environment. *See also* "TRAGEDY OF THE COMMONS."

VEREINTE GRÜNE ÖSTERREICHS. *See* AUSTRIA.

VIENNA CONVENTION FOR THE PROTECTION OF THE OZONE LAYER. A 1985 meeting organized at the behest of concerned scientists led to the Vienna Convention and governmental recognition of the need to act to protect the **ozone layer**. Ozone was first discovered in the Earth's stratosphere around 1880, and CFCs have been produced since 1892. It was not until 1974 that Mario Molina and Sherwood Rowland proposed that CFCs could destroy significant amounts of stratospheric ozone. In 1985, the year the convention was opened for signature, the British Antarctic Survey presented evidence of a "hole" in the ozone layer over Antarctica. *See also* MONTREAL PROTOCOL ON SUBSTANCES THAT DEPLETE THE OZONE LAYER.

VIETNAM, SOCIALIST REPUBLIC OF. Vietnam has undergone rapid economic growth since the implementation of the *doi moi* economic reforms of the 1980s, which liberalized economic policies and created something resembling a market economy within the communist state. The country's development has resulted in environmental damage and resource management issues that compound many of the severe ecological destruction that resulted from the Vietnam War, including the widespread use of napalm and Agent Orange.

The activities of international and local nongovernmental organizations (NGOs) are monitored by the Vietnamese government. The Communist Party of Vietnam, which controls the government, requires the registration of all local and international NGOs and institutions. The party monitors these organizations and only permits them to engage in certain activities, such as providing community assistance. Many international NGOs are in Vietnam despite the strict government monitoring. Included among these are the **World Conservation Union (IUCN)**, **World Wide Fund for Nature (WWF)**, and Care International.

– W –

WARD, BARBARA (1914–1982). Well known as the author of several works on environmental protection, Barbara Ward coauthored, with René Dubos, the highly influential book *Only One Earth*. This publication contained a powerful critique of advanced industrialized market economies and influenced the environmental policy agenda of the United Nations, which had commissioned the work. In 1968 Ward was appointed to the position of Schweitzer Professor of International Economic Development at Columbia University and, in 1973, to the presidency of the International Institute for Environment and Development.

WILDERNESS SOCIETY. The power of social movements such as those concerned about the environment lies partly in their ability to mobilize people. By organizing popular protests, environmental groups have influenced political processes and parliamentary politics. Campaigns such as the one by the Tasmanian Wilderness Society against the flooding of the Franklin and lower Gordon rivers contributed to a rapid rise in the membership of this organization. By 1983 the society had 7,332 members and, reflecting its national appeal, changed its name to the Wilderness Society. Branches had been formed in all states, and campaigns for the preservation of forests were being conducted across **Australia**.

The radicalism of the Wilderness Society signaled the entry of a new generation of environmentalists on the political scene. Apart from mobilizing large numbers of people, new environmental groups raised substantial financial support. In 1982 the estimated annual budget for the Wilderness Society was around A$1 million. Of that, A$130,000 was spent on a campaign for a referendum on the proposed **Franklin Dam**. The Wilderness Society was able to sustain and develop its financial and popular base during the 1980s, bolstered by the entrepreneurial activities of Wilderness Shops, which took in several million dollars. After declining to 5,171 in 1985, membership of the Wilderness Society rose from 5,930 to 7,002 between 1987 and 1988 and up to 10,819 in 1989 and 16,377 in 1991. Since then, environmental groups have become aware of the limits to their growth and competition among them for supporters—a rise in numbers of one group may be at the expense of another.

The Wilderness Society was one among several environmental groups invited by the government in Australia to participate in discussion groups on ecologically **sustainable development**. However, the association has always expressed concern about the predominance of economic interests in these gatherings. The Wilderness Society has been sharp in its criticism of any attempt by government to initiate development projects in forests. The rise in support during the 1980s for groups such as the Wilderness Society has contributed to a stronger focus by traditional political organizations on environmental issues. The Wilderness Society has also played an important part in endorsing candidates for parties such as the Australian Democrats and green parties in Australia. *See also* FRANKLIN DAM.

WILDERNESS SOCIETY (UNITED STATES). Set up in 1935, the Wilderness Society works for the conservation of land in the **United**

States and for the benefit of related values such as **biodiversity** and clean air and water. The Wilderness Society played a pivotal role in the passage of the Wilderness Act of 1964. It has a membership of close to a quarter of a million. The Wilderness Society, like many other green groups in the United States, has turned to the web for advocacy campaigning on issues such as preservation of open spaces, stopping oil and gas pipelines, and protecting national forests.

WOMEN'S ENVIRONMENTAL NETWORK. A London-based organization that represents women and campaigns on issues that link women, environment, and health. Women's Environmental Network seeks to educate, inform, and empower women and men who care about the environment, and to enable people to use their consumer power as a force for environmental change.

WOMEN'S GLOBAL GREEN ACTION NETWORK. Launched in 2005 at the United Nations Commission for Sustainable Development 13th Session in New York, the Women's Global Green Action Network aims to empower and unite grassroots women advocates, entrepreneurs, and community leaders around the world working on environmental, economic, and social justice issues.

WORLD COMMISSION ON ENVIRONMENT AND DEVELOP-MENT (WCED). The World Commission on Environment and Development was formed following a September 1983 resolution by the United Nations General Assembly to explore further the connection between environmental protection and economic development. Former Norwegian prime minister **Brundtland** chaired the WCED. The 23-member commission included 12 representatives from less developed nations, seven from Western developed countries, and four from communist countries. Work by the commission focused on the following topics: **population growth** and human resources, food security, **biodiversity**, energy and industry, urbanization, the international economy, peace and security, and, above all, forms of cooperation among national governments for addressing these issues. It then provided backing for a large number of studies on these topics and arranged meetings in 10 countries to elicit the views of a wide range of individuals and organizations.

The outcome of these extensive deliberations was the 1987 publication *Our Common Future*. The report pointed out that prevailing institutional mechanisms centered on local, regional, and national governments were inadequate to deal with the serious problems of **acid rain**, the **greenhouse effect**, and depletion of the **ozone layer**. The commission felt that environmental protection and economic development had to be viewed as interdependent rather than conflicting principles. To convey this point of view it used the term "**sustainable development**."

Our Common Future became a key source for deliberations by established organizations that were under pressure to adapt to new challenges from the rising green movement. The WCED defined sustainable development as meeting "the needs of the present without compromising the ability of future generations to meet their own needs."

In many countries this report was also taken as a useful basis for developing a dialogue between environmentalists and developers. The commission had provided a comprehensive statement on how to address both environmental and economic concerns and how all organizations should strive to incorporate ecological wisdom into their economic and social decisions. The report attempted to demonstrate that emphasis on materialism and economic growth will not necessarily damage the environment if it is guided by principles of **ecology** and preoccupied with the renewability of resources. Economic growth was seen as "absolutely essential in order to relieve the great poverty that is deepening in much of the developing world."

The final chapter of the report made a number of proposals for "institutional and legal change." They included the incorporation of sustainable development as a term of reference for the principal agencies of national governments; the creation, where they were lacking, of national environmental protection and natural resources management agencies; the strengthening, through increased funding, of the **United Nations Environmental Programme (UNEP)**; a greater focus on global environmental assessment and reporting; strengthening international cooperation on this matter, broadening and intensifying the contribution to sustainable development by the scientific community and nongovernmental organizations (NGOs); greater cooperation with industry groups; strengthening and extending existing international conventions and agreements; and drafting and implementing a universal declaration and a convention on environmental protection and sustainable development. *See also LIMITS TO GROWTH, THE.*

WORLD CONSERVATION STRATEGY. The World Conservation Strategy was initiated by the **World Conservation Union (IUCN).** The strategy focused on how to identify and deal with threats to species and ecosystems and the preservation of genetic diversity for the purposes of agricultural development. The project was formulated in conjunction with the **United Nations Environment Programme (UNEP)** and the **World Wildlife Fund (WWF).** Its announcement in March 1980 in about 40 countries received considerable attention. In their attempts to set the agenda for change, some governments more fully exploited notions such as **sustainable development,** which had been promoted by organizations such as the IUCN. Sustainable development has been used by international agencies ever since the **United Nations Conference on the Human Environment (UNCHE)** in Stockholm, 1972. The publication of *World Conservation Strategy: Living Resource for Sustainable Development* in 1980 provided a major impetus to arguments about sustainable development. The report recommended the development of national strategies for conservation with the aim of integrating conservation and development.

Some governments implemented the recommendations of the World Conservation Strategy and developed national conservation strategies. The Australian government noted that the successful implementation of its national strategy presupposed widespread acceptance of the following principles: the integration and interdependence of conservation and development, the retention of options for future use, a focus on the underlying causes and symptoms of environmental damage, the accumulation of knowledge for the future, and education of the community about the integration of sustainable development and conservation. Although this initiative was largely forgotten for several years, like the World Conservation Strategy, it later formed an important part of the process of reconciling environment and development.

WORLD CONSERVATION UNION (IUCN). Founded in 1948 and known until 1956 as the International Union for the Protection of Nature and referred to as the International Union for the Conservation of Nature and Natural Resources until 1990, the IUCN is one of the most influential associations in promoting dialogue between national governments and nongovernmental organizations (NGOs). The primary objective of the International Union for the Protection of Nature was to promote education and research with a view to protecting the environment and raising awareness of how much we rely on nature, including natural resources, for our well-being. Max Nicholson and Julian Huxley were among the leading players in the foundation of the organization.

The focus on conservation, and hence the change in name, came in 1956. The IUCN began to concentrate on conserving wetlands and the creation of **national parks**. Lacking funds for these initiatives, Huxley and Nicholson, among others, established an international fund-raising organization for nature conservation, the **World Wildlife Fund (WWF)**. Early work by the IUCN targeted conservation in Africa. The **African Special Project**, initiated by the IUCN, had two important results. It rendered effective assistance to African governments concerned about the preservation of wildlife and development of land, and it established the credibility of the IUCN as an agency capable of providing guidance and expertise to less developed nations in their efforts to conserve and protect the environment. The IUCN was also instrumental in framing of the **African Convention on the Conservation of Nature and Natural Resources** signed by 33 African states in 1968.

The IUCN also demonstrated a capacity to adapt to changing perceptions of how to protect the environment. Apart from special projects, it developed a vision of the interdependence of development and the environment. One of the most important initiatives by the IUCN in the 1970s was the formulation of a **World Conservation Strategy**. Another was its pivotal role in helping to convene the **United Nations Conference on the Human Environment (UNCHE)** in 1972.

The IUCN, while not part of the more militant green movement that emerged in the 1970s, has played a crucial role in maintaining and articulating green issues. Though not formally a part of the United Nations, it has influenced that body's environmental policies. Recently, the IUCN has had to deal with the tensions that arise between business and environmental interests. Members of the IUCN must reconcile business groups' interests in contributing with environmentalists' suspicion of the involvement of business in environmental protection organizations. *See also* SUSTAINABLE DEVELOPMENT.

WORLD HERITAGE. The United Nations Educational, Scientific and Cultural Organization (UNESCO) adopted the Convention Concerning the Protection of the World Cultural and Natural Heritage in 1972. The goal is to convince countries to preserve their cultural and natural heritage by designating places of special cultural or natural significance as World Heritage sites. As of April 2006, there are 812 World Heritage sites, including 160 natural and mixed properties.

WORLD RESOURCES INSTITUTE (WRI). Launched in 1985 with the support of the John D. and Katherine T. MacArthur Foundation, the WRI is an environmental think tank researching and providing policy solutions in the fields of people and ecosystems, **climate change**, and markets and enterprise. WRI also pursues public access to information and decisions regarding the environment and natural resources.

WORLD SUMMIT ON SUSTAINABLE DEVELOPMENT. The Johannesburg "Earth Summit" was held in South Africa from 26 August to 4 September 2002. It was a sequel to the **United Nations Conference on Environment and Development (UNCED)** that took place in Rio de Janeiro in June 1992. Considered ineffectual by some, the Summit on Sustainable Development was attended by representatives of over 190 countries. It is also commonly known as Rio+10.

One of the most important aspects of this conference was discussing the findings of the **Commission on Sustainable Development (CSD)**, which was formed in 1992 to monitor the plans initiated by the UNCED, particularly to monitor the financial and technical resources for sustainable development projects given to developing nations. The summit also provided an opportunity to review the progress made toward implementing **Agenda 21** and assess the workings of the World Bank and the World Trade Organization in terms of **sustainable development** goals.

It was almost universally agreed going into the conference that the implementation of sustainable development had suffered since 1992, with a widening poverty gap between the North and the South and further environmental degradation. This led to the Millennium Development Goals, which include among many other issues, halving the number of people living in extreme poverty, decreasing the proportion of people without basic sanitation or access to safe drinking water, and maintaining and restoring depleted fish stocks by 2015. The World Summit was used to advance the idea of public-private partnerships for sustainable development. For example, the **World Resources Institute** announced a partnership initiative that aimed at supporting credible decision making for the Millennium Development Goals. This initiative was backed by eight countries and the World Bank.

WORLDWATCH INSTITUTE. This independent research organization founded by Lester Brown in 1974 works for an environmentally sustainable and socially just society. It annually publishes *The State of the World.*

WORLD WIDE FUND FOR NATURE (WWF). Known as World Wide Fund for Nature in much of the world, WWF is called the **World Wildlife Fund (WWF)** in the United States and Canada. The stimulus to the formation of the WWF, which is now one of the largest conservation organizations in the world, was provided by eminent British ornithologist Julian Huxley after a visit he made to East Africa in 1960. Huxley wrote three articles in *The Observer* weekly magazine in which he disclosed his concerns about the destruction of wildlife caused by agricultural practices and poaching. In collaboration with Max Nicholson, the director general of the Nature Conservancy Council in **Great Britain**, Huxley brought together a group of well-known scientists (including ornithologist Peter Scott, who was vice president of the **World Conservation Union (IUCN)** to establish an international fund-raising organization for nature conservation. To emphasize the independence of the new organization, its headquarters were established in **Switzerland**, which enjoyed the reputation of a neutral country in international affairs.

Officially founded on 11 September 1961, the WWF aimed to establish offices in as many countries as possible to facilitate the process of fund raising and oversee various projects. The objective was to cooperate with nongovernmental organizations (NGOs) such as the IUCN, the International Council for Bird Preservation (later named Birdlife International), the International Waterfowl Research Bureau, and International Youth Federation for the Study and Conservation of Nature.

Assisted by dignitaries such as the Duke of Edinburgh, the WWF rapidly succeeded in raising large sums of money: within three years it had secured about US$1.9 million to support conservation projects all over the world, including **India**, **Kenya**, and the Galapagos Islands. The WWF also excelled in promoting itself, notably through the use of its black and white panda logo. Forty years later, in 2005, the WWF had close to five million supporters, 30 autonomous national organization offices, and five associate offices (NGOs that work closely with WWF). Since 1985 and as of 2005, WWF reports investing more than US$1.165 million in more than 11,000 projects in 130 countries.

The WWF has continuously lobbied governments on conservation issues, has often been granted access to the policymaking process, and has been successful in bringing about significant changes in policy and its successful implementation. From its inception, the WWF has influenced governments to establish and protect **national parks** and conservation areas. In the 1970s it was instrumental in assisting the Indian government to establish reserves for tigers. It launched campaigns to protect tropical rainforests and create sanctuaries for whales, dolphins, and seals. It also contributed to the effective operation of the Trade Records Analysis of Fauna and Flora in Commerce, an organization that drew attention to the trade in wildlife and wildlife products, notably ivory and rhino horn, which might lead to the extinction of certain species. The WWF has also cooperated in initiatives such as the **World Conservation Strategy**, launched by the IUCN and the **United Nations Environmental Programme (UNEP)**.

Throughout its existence, the WWF has been highly innovative in raising funds. In 1970 the president of WWF International, Prince

Bernhard of the Netherlands, initiated the 1001 fund, which in effect asked 1,001 individuals to contribute US$10,000 each and thereby raise US$10 million. In 1979 a "Save the Rhino" campaign raised US$1 million. In 1983 the WWF came up with the idea of persuading postal organizations in over 130 countries to depict threatened species on postage stamps, an initiative that by the early 1990s had raised another US$10 million. The WWF also organized agreements between less developed and wealthy nations so that instead of repaying part of their national debt to the developed nations, the emerging nations spent an agreed sum on conservation measures, so called **debt-for-nature swaps**.

In order to make known its commitment to addressing a wide range of environmental issues, the organization changed its name from World Wildlife Fund to the World Wide Fund for Nature in 1986, though in **Canada** and the **United States** it kept the original name.

In its mission statement for the 1990s the WWF set out three goals: preservation of biological diversity, particularly the preservation of tropical forests, wetlands, coasts, and coral reefs; sustainable use of natural resources, with a view both to improving the **quality of life** for human beings and preserving the foundations for the regeneration of resources; and reducing pollution and waste. In the 2000s, the focus of the work has shifted somewhat to include slowing **climate change**, reducing toxins in the environment, protecting oceans and fresh waters, stopping deforestation, and saving species. *See also* AFRICAN WILDLIFE; BIODIVERSITY.

WORLD WILDLIFE FUND (WWF). *See* WORLD WIDE FUND FOR NATURE (WWF).

– Y –

YELLOWSTONE NATIONAL PARK. Following an act of Congress, endorsed in 1872, Yellowstone National Park was created in Wyoming. The park covered an area of 800,000 hectares and was the first **national park** to be formally created by a government.

Bibliography

CONTENTS

I. INTRODUCTION

The influence of the green movement has not only been enhanced by but has also stimulated writings on the reshaping of the economy, relationships between human beings and nature, ways of reforming the political system, and the introduction of new policies to deal with a wide range of issues, including damage to the environment and the emergence of new social structures.

Although there are many books on the development of the green movement, a considerable portion of the available information appears in a more ephemeral form: articles and monographs. The regular publications that have emerged in the wake of the green movement contain many useful articles on the concepts and issues that occupy scholars, for example, journals such as *Environmental Politics*, *Global Environmental Politics*, and *Environmental Values*. There are numerous magazines and journals that have contributed to the articulation of green issues, not least *The Ecologist*.

Interest in environmental issues among policymakers has been stimulated by highly influential works that have attempted to reconcile development with the environment. The section of this bibliography that focuses on the economy includes the report by the World Commission on Environment and Development, *Our Common Future*, which has become a standard point of reference for policymakers. There are many other important works that offer ideas on how to reshape the economy. David Pearce and his collaborators have produced several influential books, including *Blueprint for a Green Economy*. Stephan Schmidheiny, in *Changing Course: A Global Business Perspective on Development and the Environment*, and Ernst Ulrich von Weiszäcker, in *Earth Politics*, present a wide range of ideas on how business and government can work toward addressing many of the key concerns of the green movement. Also included are pivotal works on economics such as those by Herman Daly on *Steady-State Economics*, Arthur Cecil Pigou on *The Economics of Welfare*, and E. J. Mishan on *The Costs of Economic Growth*. More recent thinking on ecological modernization, paths to sustainability, and environmental security are included as well.

The section on green concepts includes works that gave a powerful impetus to the green movement. Among these works are *Silent Spring* by Rachel Carson, *The Population Bomb* by Paul Ehrlich, *A Sand County Almanac* by Aldo Leopold, *The Limits to Growth* by Dennis Meadows and his collaborators, and *Small Is Beautiful* by E. F. Schumacher. Extracts from influential works are contained in several valuable collections of essays, for instance, in *The Green Reader*, edited by Andrew Dobson; in *The Politics of the Environment*, edited by Robert Goodin; and *Green Planet Blues*, edited by Ken Conca and Geoffrey Dabelko. A compilation of famous speeches by pioneering thinkers can be found in *Environmental Speeches That Moved the World*, edited by Alan Tol. This section on green concepts also includes critiques and alternatives to some of the ideas of proponents of the green movement, for example, *The Green Crusade: Rethinking the Roots of Environmentalism* by Charles T. Rubin, *Green Political Theory* by Robert Goodin, and *The Post-Industrial Utopians* by Boris Frankel. It also includes more recent developments in green thinking, such as Walter F. Baber and Robert V. Bartlett's *Deliberative Environmental Politics: Democracy and Ecological Rationality* and Robyn Eckersley's *The Green State: Rethinking Democracy and Sovereignty*. Andrew Jamison's *The Making of Green Knowledge: Environmental Politics and Cultural Transformation* is an excellent analysis of how green ideas have developed over time.

The section on the green movement is divided into three parts. The first "general" section includes mainly sociological accounts of how the green movement can be regarded a social movement that redefines the boundaries of political action. A special issue of the journal *Social Research*, edited by Jean Cohen and published in 1985, includes valuable essays by writers such as Klaus Eder, Claus Offe, and Jean Cohen that introduce the reader to key early analysts of the field. Other important early sociological approaches to the green movement can be found in works such as Alberto Melucci's *Nomads of the Present* and Alain Touraine's *Anti-Nuclear Protest*. Several overview and more comparative studies of the green movement have appeared in the past several years. These include Brian Doherty's *Ideas and Actions in the Green Movement*; Timothy Doyle's *Environmental Movements*; and John Dryzek, David Downs, Hans-Kristian Hernes, and David Schlosberg's *Green States and Social Movements: Environmentalism in the United States, United Kingdom, Germany, and Norway*.

The next section focuses on the related concept of green groups, including environmental nongovernmental organizations (NGOs). It includes some specific studies of groups, such as Derek Wall's *Earth First! and the Anti-Roads Movement* and more general studies, such as Michele Betsill and Elisabeth Corell's work on NGOs in international environmental negotiations.

The section entitled "New Politics" includes works that attempt to understand the green movement as a novel political phenomenon or the articulation of concerns that had for many years received limited attention on the political agenda. A useful collection of analytical studies in this field can be found in *New Politics*, edited by Ferdinand Müller-Rommel and Thomas Poguntke.

The section on green parties is divided into books and articles covering different countries and regions. Among the works that bring together accounts of early developments in green parties in various countries are *Green Parties: An International Guide*, by Sara Parkin; *New Politics in Western Europe: The Rise and Success of Green Parties and Alternative Lists*, edited by Ferdinand Müller-Rommel; and *The Green Challenge: The Development of Green Parties in Europe*, edited by Dick Richardson and Chris Rootes. An excellent contemporary look at the state of green parties in Europe can be found in the special issue of the *European Journal of Political Research* (45, S1 [2006]) on this theme. Articles, chapters, and some books on green parties in specific countries and regions can also be found in this section.

The next section, on green politics and policies, is divided into a general section, a comparative section, and works on different countries. There are significant early studies, such as Herbert Kitschelt's *The Logics of Party Formation*, which compares developments in Belgium and West Germany, as well as a series of monographs on *Green Politics* edited by Wolfgang Rüdig, which are an important source of information and investigation of green political organizations around the world. Classics include David Vogel's *National Styles of Regulation: Environmental Policy in Great Britain and the United States*, Martin Jänicke's *State Failure*, and Albert Weale's *The New Politics of Pollution*. A significant number of studies examine green politics in the United States and the European Union, such as Sonja Boehmer-Christiansen's *Designs on Nature: Science and Democracy in Europe and the United States*, or the book edited by Norman Vig and Michael Faure, *Green Giants? Environmental Policies of the United States and the European Union*. There are many excellent books comparing various European states on their green politics, policies, and movements. One of the more recent is edited by Andrew Jordan, Rudiger K. W. Würzel, and Anthony Zito and entitled *New Instruments of Environmental Governance: National Experiences and Prospects*. Others examine other parts of the world, such as Matthew Auer's *Restoring Cursed Earth: Appraising Environmental Policy Reform in Eastern Europe and Russia*.

The final section, on international relations, contains works that focus on specific issues or on the global aspects of environmental diplomacy as well as more general overviews of the field. These include studies by such big names in the field as Oran Young, Ronnie Lipschutz, Ken Conca, Karen Litfin, and Pamela Chasek, among many others.

II. PROFESSIONAL JOURNALS

The Ted Case Studies: An Online Journal, http://gurukul.ucc.american.edu/ted/class/all.htm.
Examines the relationship between trade and the environment.

Environment. Heldref Publications.
This journal offers both peer-reviewed articles and commentaries.
Environmental History. Forest History Society and the American Society for Environmental History.
The leading journal dealing with historical aspects of society's relationship to the environment.
Environmental Politics. Routledge.
Examines environmental movements and parties and environmental policy making and implementation. The focus is primarily on industrialized states.
Environmental Values. White Horse Press.
A refereed journal concerned with the basis and justification of environmental policy.
Environmentalist. Springer.
Presents the critical views of industrialists and ecologists, trying to bridge between them.
European Environment. John Wiley & Sons.
Includes both technical and more policy-oriented contributions.
Global Environmental Politics. MIT Press.
An interdisciplinary journal focused on global political forces and environmental change.
Journal of Environment and Development. Sage.
An interdisciplinary journal focused on sustainable development, the implementation of Agenda 21, national and international environmental policies, and a range of environmental issues.
Journal of Environmental Law. Oxford.
A scholarly and peer-reviewed journal with an emphasis on legal and policy developments and case law pertaining to the environment.
Organization and Environment: International Journal for Ecosocial Research.
A peer-reviewed journal that examines social organizing as it relates to the natural world.
Zeitschrift für Uwmeltpolitik und Umweltrecht. Verlagsgruppe Deutscher Fachverlag.
Introduces environmental policy and legal issues in Germany, Europe, and internationally.

III. BIOGRAPHY

Foreman, Dave. *Confessions of an Eco Warrior.* New York: Three Rivers Press, 1993.
Parkin, Sara. *The Life and Death of Petra Kelly.* London: Pandora Press, 1994.
Pearce, Fred. *Green Warriors.* London: Bodley Head, 1991.

IV. ECONOMY

Anderson, Terry L., and Donald R. Leal. *Free Market Environmentalism.* San Francisco: Pacific Research Institute for Public Policy, 1991.

Audley, John. *Green Politics and Global Trade: NAFTA and the Future of Environmental Politics.* Washington, D.C.: Georgetown University Press, 1997.

Bass, Stephen, Hannah Reid, David Satterthwaite, and Paul Steele, eds. *Reducing Poverty and Sustaining the Environment: The Politics of Local Engagement.* London: Earthscan, 2005.

Baumol, W. J., and W. E. Oates. *The Theory of Environmental Policy.* 2nd ed. Cambridge: Cambridge University Press, 1988.

Boulding, Kenneth E. "The Economics of the Coming Spaceship Earth." In *Environmental Quality in a Growing Economy,* edited by Henry Jarrett, 3–14. Baltimore: Johns Hopkins University Press, 1966.

Clapp, Jennifer, and Peter Dauvergne. *Paths to a Green World: The Political Economy of the Global Environment.* Cambridge, Mass.: MIT Press, 2005.

Cline, William R. *Global Warning: The Benefits of Emission Abatement.* Paris: OECD, 1992.

Daly, Herman. *Steady-State Economics.* San Francisco: Freeman, 1977.

———. "Steady-State Economics vs. Growthmania: A Critique of the Orthodox Conceptions of Growth, Wants, Scarcity and Efficiency." *Policy Sciences* 5 (1974): 149–67.

———. "The Steady-State Economy: What, Why and How?" In *The Sustainable Society,* edited by Dennis Pirages, 107–14. New York: Praeger, 1977.

Daly, Herman, and John B. Cobb. *For the Common Good: Redirecting the Economy toward Community, the Environment and a Sustainable Future.* Boston: Beacon Press, 1989.

Daly, Herman E., and Kenneth N. Townsend. *Valuing the Earth: Economics, Ecology, Ethics.* Cambridge, Mass.: MIT Press, 1993.

DeSimone, Livio D., and Frank Popoff. *Eco-Efficiency: The Business Link to Sustainable Development.* Cambridge, Mass.: MIT Press, 2000.

Driesen, David M. *The Economic Dynamics of Environmental Law.* Cambridge, Mass.: MIT Press, 2003.

Eckersley, Robyn. "Free Market Environmentalism: Friend or Foe?" *Environmental Politics* 2, no. 1 (1993): 1–19.

Fiorino, Daniel J. *The New Environmental Regulation.* Cambridge, Mass.: MIT Press, 2006.

Helm, Dieter. *Economic Policy towards the Environment.* Oxford: Blackwell, 1991.

Jones, Kent. *Who's Afraid of the WTO?* Oxford: Oxford University Press, 2004.

Jorgenson, Dale W. *Growth,* Vol. 2: *Energy, the Environment, and Economic Growth.* Cambridge, Mass.: MIT Press, 1998.

Lofdah, Corey L. *Environmental Impacts of Globalization and Trade: A Systems Study.* Cambridge, Mass.: MIT Press: 2002.

Lyon, Thomas P., and John W. Maxwell. *Corporate Environmentalism and Public Policy.* Cambridge: Cambridge University Press, 2004.

MacNeill, Jim, Pieter Winsemius, and Taizo Yakushiji. *Beyond Interdependence: The Meshing of the World's Economy and the Earth's Ecology.* Oxford: Oxford University Press, 1991.

Martinez-Alier, Juan. *Ecological Economics.* Oxford: Blackwell, 1990.

Mazmanian, Daniel A., and Michael E. Kraft, eds. *Toward Sustainable Communities: Transition and Transformations in Environmental Policy.* Cambridge, Mass.: MIT Press, 1999.

Mishan, E. J. *The Costs of Economic Growth.* Harmondsworth, U.K.: Penguin, 1967–1969.

Mol, Arthur P. J. *Globalization and Environmental Reform: The Ecological Modernization of the Global Economy.* Cambridge, Mass.: MIT Press, 2003.

Nordhaus, William D., and Joseph Boyer. *Managing the Global Commons: The Economics of Climate Change.* Cambridge, Mass.: MIT Press, 1994.

———. *Warming the World: Economic Models of Global Warming.* Cambridge, Mass.: MIT Press, 2003.

Oates, Wallace E. *The Economics of the Environment.* Aldershot: Edward Elgar, 1992.

Paehlke, Robert C. *Democracy's Dilemma: Environment, Social Equity, and the Global Economy.* Cambridge, Mass.: MIT Press, 2003.

Pearce, David. *Blueprint 2: Greening the World Economy.* London: Earthscan in association with the London Environmental Economics Centre, 1991.

———. *Economic Values and the Natural World.* London: Earthscan, 1993.

Pearce, David, April Markandya, and Edward B. Barbier. *Blueprint for a Green Economy.* London: Earthscan, 1989.

Pearce, David, and R. Kerry Turner. *Economics of Natural Resources and the Environment.* Hemel Hempstead: Harvester Wheatsheaf, 1990.

Pearce, David, and Jeremy Warford. *World without End: Economics, Environment and Sustainable Development.* Oxford: Oxford University Press and World Bank, 1993.

Pigou, Arthur Cecil. *The Economics of Welfare.* London: Macmillan, 1920.

Pirages, Dennis, and Ken Cousins, eds. *From Resource Scarcity to Ecological Security: Exploring New Limits to Growth.* Cambridge, Mass.: MIT Press, 2005.

Princen, Thomas, Michael F. Maniates, and Ken Conca, eds. *Confronting Consumption.* Cambridge, Mass.: MIT Press, 2002.

Redclift, Michael. *Sustainable Development.* London: Methuen, 1987.

Rich, Bruce. *Mortgaging the Earth: The World Bank, Environmental Impoverishment, and the Crisis of Development.* Boston: Beacon Press, 1994.

Sampson, Gary. *Trade, Environment, and the WTO: The Post-Seattle Agenda.* Baltimore: Johns Hopkins University Press, 2000.

Schelling, Thomas C., ed. *Incentives for Environmental Protection.* Cambridge, Mass.: MIT Press, 1983.

Schmidheiny, Stephan, with the Business Council for Sustainable Development. *Changing Course: A Global Business Perspective on Development and the Environment.* Cambridge, Mass.: MIT Press, 1992.

Schmidt-Bleek, Friedrich, and Heinrich Wohlmeyer, eds. *Trade and the Environment.* Laxenburg, Austria: IIASA, 1992.

Smart, Bruce, ed. *Beyond Compliance: A New Industry View of the Environment.* Washington, D.C.: World Resources Institute, 1992.

Starke, Linda. *Signs of Hope: Working towards Our Common Future.* Oxford: Oxford University Press, 1990.

Swanson, Timothy M., and Edward B. Barbier, eds. *Economics for the* Wilds. London: Earthscan, 1992.

Turner, R. Kerry. *Sustainable Environmental Economics and Management: Principles and Practice.* London: Belhaven Press, 1993.

UNCED. *Report of the UN Conference on Environment and Development.* A/CONF/151/26. 5 vols. New York: UN, 1992.

von Weizsäcker, Ernst U. *Earth Politics.* London: Zed Books, 1994.

von Weizsäcker, Ernst U., and Jochen Jessinghaus. *Ecological Tax Reform: A Policy Proposal for Sustainable Development*—A study prepared for Stephan Schmidheiny. London: Zed Books, 1992.

Wicke, Lutz. *Umweltökonomie.* 3rd ed. Munich: Vahlen, 1991.

World Commission on Environment and Development. *Our Common Future.* Melbourne: Oxford University Press, 1990.

V. GREEN CONCEPTS

Attfield, Robin. *The Ethics of Environmental Concern.* Oxford: Blackwell, 1983.

Baber, Walter F. and Robert V. Bartlett. *Deliberative Environmental Politics: Democracy and Ecological Rationality.* Cambridge, Mass.: MIT Press, 2005.

Bahro, Rudolf. *Building the Green Movement.* London: Heretic Books, 1986.

———. *Socialism and Survival.* London: Heretic Books, 1982.

Beck, Ulrich. *Risk Society.* Newbury Park, Calif.: Sage, 1992.

Benton, Ted. *Natural Relations: Animal Rights and Social Justice.* London: Verso, 1993.

Biehl, Janet. *Ecofascism: Lessons from the German Experience.* Dordecht: Kluwer Academic, 1998.

Boggs, Carl. "The Green Alternative and the Struggle for a Post-Marxist Discourse." *Theory and Society* 15 (1986): 869–99.

Bookchin, Murray. *Post-Scarcity Anarchism.* Berkeley, Calif.: Ramparts Press, 1971.

———. *Toward an Ecological Society.* Montreal: Black Rose Books, 1980.

Bramwell, Anna. *Ecology in the 20th Century: A History.* London: Yale University Press, 1989.

Cahill, Michael, and Tony Fitzpatrick, eds. *Environmental Issues and Social Welfare.* Oxford: Blackwell, 2002.

Čapek, Stella. "The Environmental Justice Frame: A Conceptual Discussion and an Application." *Social Problems 40* (1993): 5–24.

Capra, Fritjof. *The Turning Point.* London: Fontana, 1983.

Carson, Rachel. *Silent Spring.* Boston: Houghton Mifflin, 1962.

Commoner, Barry. *The Closing Circle: Nature, Man, and Technology.* New York: Knopf, 1971.

Conca, Ken, and Geoffrey Dabelko, eds. *Green Planet Blues: Environmental Politics from Stockholm to Johannesburg.* Boulder, Colo.: Westview Press, 2004.

Cotgrove, Stephen. *Catastrophe or Cornucopia.* Chichester: Wiley, 1982.

Council on Environmental Quality. *The Global 2000 Report to the President.* Harmondsworth, U.K.: Penguin, 1982.

Dean, Hartley. "Green Citizenship." In *Environmental Issues and Social Welfare,* edited by Michael Cahill and Tony Fitzpatrick, 22–37. Oxford: Oxford University Press, 2002.

Dobson, Andrew, ed. *The Green Reader.* London: André Deutsch, 1991.

———. *Justice and the Environment: Conceptions of Environmental Sustainability and Theories of Distributive Justice.* Oxford: Oxford University Press, 1998.

Dobson, Andrew, and Derek Bell, eds. *Environmental Citizenship.* Cambridge, Mass.: MIT Press, 2005.

Dobson, Andrew, and Paul Lucardie, eds. *The Politics of Nature: Explorations in Green Political Theory.* London: Routledge, 1993.

Dodds, Felix, and Tim Pippard, eds. *Human and Environmental Security: An Agenda for Change.* London: Earthscan, 2005.

Dolčak, Nives, and Elinor Ostrom, eds. *The Commons in the New Millennium: Challenges and Adaptation.* Cambridge, Mass.: MIT Press, 2003.

Dryzek, John. *The Politics of the Earth: Environmental Discourses.* Oxford: Oxford University Press.

———. *Rational Ecology: Environment and Political Economy.* Oxford: Blackwell, 1987.

Dubos, René. *Celebrations of Life.* New York: McGraw-Hill, 1981.

———. *The Wooing of Earth: New Perspectives on Man's Use of Nature.* New York: Scribner's, 1980.

Dunlap, Riley, and Karl van Liere. "The 'New Environmental Paradigm.'" *Journal of Environmental Education* 9 (1978): 10–19.

Durant, Robert F., Daniel J. Fiorino, and Rosemary O'Leary, eds. *Environmental Governance Reconsidered: Challenges, Choices, and Opportunities.* Cambridge, Mass.: MIT Press, 2004.

Eckersley, Robyn. *Environmentalism and Political Theory.* London: UCL Press, 1992.

———. *The Green State: Rethinking Democracy and Sovereignty.* Cambridge, Mass.: MIT Press, 2004.

Ehrlich, Paul R. *The Population Bomb.* New York: Ballantine, 1968.

Ehrlich, Paul R., and Anne Ehrlich. *The Population Explosion.* New York: Simon and Schuster, 1990.

Elliot, Robert. "Faking Nature." *Inquiry* 25, no. 1 (1982): 81–93.

Fairfax, Sally K., Lauren Gwin, Mary Ann King, Leigh Raymond, and Laura A. Watt. *Buying Nature: The Limits of Land Acquisition as a Conservation Strategy, 1780–2004.* Cambridge, Mass.: MIT Press, 2005.

Feinberg, Joel. "The Rights of Animals and Unborn Generations." In *Philosophy and Environmental Crisis,* edited by William T. Blackstone, 43–68. Athens: University of Georgia Press, 1974.

Fox, Warwick. *Toward a Transpersonal Ecology.* Boston: Shambhala, 1990.

Frankel, Boris. *The Post-Industrial Utopians.* Cambridge: Polity Press, 1987.

Goldsmith, Edward. *The Great U-Turn: De-Industrializing Society.* Bideford, U.K.: Green Books, 1988.

Goldsmith, Edward, Robert Allen, Michael Allaby, John Davoll, and Sam Lawrence. "A Blueprint for Survival." *Ecologist* 2, no. 1 (1972): 8–22.

Goodin, Robert E. *Green Political Theory.* Cambridge: Polity Press, 1992.

———. "The High Ground Is Green." *Environmental Politics 1,* no. 1 (1992): 1–8.

———, ed. *The Politics of the Environment.* Aldershot, U.K.: Edward Elgar, 1994.

Gorz, André. *Capitalism, Socialism, Ecology.* London: Verso, 1994.

Guha, Ramachandra, and Juan Martinez-Alier. *Varieties of Environmentalism: Essays North and South.* Oxford: Oxford University Press, 1998.

Hardin, Garrett. "The Tragedy of the Commons." *Science* 162, no. 3859 (13 December 1968): 1243–48.

Hardin, Garrett, and J. Baden. *Managing the Commons.* San Francisco: Freeman, 1980.

Huber, Josef. *Die verlorene Unschuld der Ökologie.* Frankfurt: Fischer, 1982.

Jamison, Andrew. *The Making of Green Knowledge: Environmental Politics and Cultural Transformation.* Cambridge: Cambridge University Press, 2001.

Jonas, Hans. *The Imperative of Responsibility: In Search of an Ethics for the Technological Age.* Chicago: University of Chicago Press, 1985.

Kelly, Petra. *Fighting for Hope*. London: Chatto and Windus, Hogarth Press, 1984.

Leopold, Aldo. *A Sand County Almanac*. 1949. Reprint, Oxford: Oxford University Press, 1977.

Liddick, Donald R. *Eco-Terrorism: Radical Environmental and Animal Liberation Movements*. New York: Praeger, 2006.

Light, Andrew, and Avner de-Shalit, eds. *Moral and Political Reasoning in Environmental Practice*. Cambridge, Mass.: MIT Press, 2003.

Lovelock, J. *Gaia: A New Look at Life on Earth*. Oxford: Oxford University Press, 1979.

———. *Healing of Gaia: Practical Medicine for the Planet*. New York: Harmony Books, 1991.

Lovins, Amory B. *Soft Energy Paths: Towards a Durable Peace*. London: Penguin, 1977.

Maddox, John. *The Doomsday Syndrome*. London: Macmillan, 1972.

Malthus, Thomas. *An Essay on the Principle of Population*. 1798. Reprint edited by Philip Appleman. New York: W. W. Norton, 1976.

Marsh, George Perkins. *Man and Nature*. 1864. Reprint, Cambridge, Mass.: Harvard University Press, 1965.

Meadows, Donella H., Dennis L. Meadows, Jorgen Randers, and William W. Behrens III. *The Limits to Growth*. New York: New American Library, 1972.

Mellor, Mary. "Green Politics: Ecofeminist, Ecofeminine or Ecomasculine?" *Environmental Politics 1*, no. 1 (1992): 229–51.

Merchant, Carolyn. *The Death of Nature*. New York: Harper and Row, 1980.

———. *Radical Ecology: The Search for a Livable World*. London: Routledge, 1992.

Meyer, John M. *Political Nature: Environmentalism and the Interpretation of Western Thought*. Cambridge, Mass.: MIT Press, 2001.

Morrison, Denton E., and Riley E. Dunlap. "Environmentalism and Elitism: A Conceptual and Empirical Analysis." *Environmental Management* 10 (1986): 581–89.

Müller-Rommel, Ferdinand. "Die Posmaterialismusdiskussion in der empirischen Sozialforschung: Politisch and wissenschaftlich überlebt oder noch immer zukunftsweisend?" *Politische Vierteljahresschrift* 24 (1983): 218–28.

Myers, Nancy J., and Carolyn Raffensperger, eds. *Precautionary Tools for Reshaping Environmental Policy*. Cambridge, Mass.: MIT Press, 2005.

Myers, Norman. *The Sinking Ark: A New Look at the Problem of Disappearing Species*. Oxford: Pergamon Press, 1979.

Naess, Arne. *Ecology, Community, and Lifestyle*. Cambridge: Cambridge University Press, 1989.

———. "The Shallow and the Deep, Long-Range Ecology Movement: A Summary." *Inquiry* 16, no. 1 (1973): 95–100.

Najam, Adil, and Nick Robins. "Seizing the Future: The South, Sustainable Development and International Trade." *International Affairs* 77, no. 1 (2001): 93–111.

Nicholson, Max. *The New Environmental Age.* Cambridge: Cambridge University Press, 1987.

Ophuls, William. "The Politics of the Sustainable Society." In *The Sustainable Society,* edited by Dennis Pirages. New York: Praeger, 1977.

O'Riordan, Tim. *Environmentalism.* London: Pion, 1981.

Owen, Denis. *What Is Ecology?* 2nd ed. Oxford: Oxford University Press, 1980.

Paehlke, Robert. *Environmentalism and the Future of Progressive Politics.* New Haven, Conn.: Yale University Press, 1989.

Passmore, John. "Attitudes to Nature." In *Nature and Conduct,* edited by R. S. Peters, 251–64. London: Macmillan, 1975.

———. *Man's Responsibility for Nature.* 2nd ed. London: Duckworth, 1980.

Pepper, David. *Eco-Socialism: From Deep Ecology to Social Justice.* London: Routledge, 1993.

———. *The Roots of Modern Environmentalism.* London: Routledge, 1986.

Ponting, Clive. *A Green History of the World.* Harmondsworth, U.K.: Penguin, 1991.

Porritt, Jonathan. *The Coming of the Greens.* London: Fontana, 1988.

———. *Seeing Green: The Politics of Ecology Explained.* London: Blackwell, 1984.

Potowski, Matthew, and Aseem Prakash. "Green Clubs and Voluntary Governance: ISO 14,001 and Firms' Regulatory Compliance." *American Political Science Review* 49, no. 2 (2005): 235–48.

Redclift, Michael, and Ted Benton, eds. *Social Theory and the Environment.* London: Routledge, 1994.

Richardson, Dick. "The Green Challenge: Philosophical, Programmatic and Electoral Considerations." In *The Green Challenge: The Development of Green Parties in Europe,* edited by Dick Richardson and Chris Rootes, 4–22. London: Routledge, 1995.

Rubin, Charles T. *The Green Crusade: Rethinking the Roots of Environmentalism.* New York: Free Press, 1994.

Sagoff, Mark. "On Preserving the Natural Environment." *Yale Law Journal* 84, no. 2 (1974): 205–67.

Sale, Kirkpatrick. *Dwellers in the Land: The Bioregional Vision.* Philadelphia: New Society, 1991.

———. *The Schumacher Lectures,* Vol. 2. London: Random Century, 1974.

Sandbach, Francis. *Environment: Ideology and Policy.* Oxford: Blackwell, 1980.

Schumacher, E. F. *Small Is Beautiful: Economics as if People Mattered.* New York: Harper and Row, 1973.

Shutkin, William A. *The Land That Could Be: Environmentalism and Democracy in the Twenty-First Century.* Cambridge, Mass.: MIT Press, 2001.

Simonis, Udo, E. "Ecological Modernization of Industrial Society: Three Strategic Elements." *International Social Science Journal* 121 (1989): 347–61.

Sylvan, Richard, and David Bennett. *The Greening of Ethics.* Cambridge: White Horse Press, 1994.

Trainer, Ted. *Abandon Affluence!* London: Zed Books, 1985.

Tol, Alan, ed. *Environmental Speeches That Moved the World.* New Brunswick, N.J.: Rutgers University Press, 2006.

Ward, Barbara, and René Dubos. *Only One Earth.* Harmondsworth, U.K.: Penguin, 1972.

Whiteside, Kerry H. *Precautionary Politics: Principle and Practice in Confronting Environmental Risk.* Cambridge, Mass.: MIT Press, 2006.

World Commission on Environment and Development. *Our Common Future.* Melbourne: Oxford University Press, 1990.

Yearley, Steven. *The Green Case: A Sociology of Environmental Issues, Arguments and Politics.* London: Harper Collins, 1991.

Young, Stephen C. "The Different Dimensions of Green Politics." *Environmental Politics 1,* no. 1 (1992): 9–44.

VI. GREEN ISSUES

Adger, W. Neil, Jouni Paavola, Saleemul Huq, and M. J. Mace, eds. *Fairness in Adaptation to Climate Change.* Cambridge, Mass.: MIT Press, 2006.

Agarwal, Bina. "Environmental Action, Gender Equity and Women's Participation." *Development and Change* 28, no. 1 (1997): 1–44.

Bandyopadhyay, Jayanta, and Vandana Shiva. "Chipko: Rekindling India's Forest Culture." *Ecologist* 17 (1987): 26–34.

Barry, John. *Rethinking Green Politics: Nature, Virtue, and Progress.* London: Sage, 1999.

Barry, John, and Robyn Eckersley, eds. *The State and the Global Ecological Crisis.* Cambridge, Mass.: MIT Press, 2005.

Benton, Ted. *Natural Relations: Ecology, Animal Rights and Social Justice.* London: Verso, 1993.

Bergeron, Kenneth D. *Tritium on Ice: The Dangerous New Alliance of Nuclear Weapons and Nuclear Power.* Cambridge, Mass.: MIT Press, 2004.

Bolton, Geoffrey. *Spoils and Spoilers: Australians Make Their Environment, 1780–1980.* Sydney: Allen and Unwin, 1981.

Buttel, Fred. "Environmentalization: Origins, Processes, and Implications for Rural Social Change." *Rural Sociology* 57 (1992): 1–27.

Cole, H. S. D., Christopher Freeman, Marie Hohoda, and K. L. R. Pavitt. *Thinking about the Future: A Critique of "The Limits to Growth."* London: Chatto & Windus, 1973.

Corburn, Jason. *Street Science: Community Knowledge and Environmental Health Justice.* Cambridge, Mass.: MIT Press, 2005.

Deere, Carolyn L., and Daniel C. Esty, eds. *Greening the Americas: NAFTA's Lessons for Hemispheric Trade.* Cambridge, Mass.: MIT Press, 2002.

Ehrlich, Paul R., and Anne H. Ehrlich. *Population, Resources, Environment.* San Francisco: Freeman, 1970.

Ekins, Paul. *A New World Order: Grassroots Movements for Global Change.* London: Routledge, 1992.

Garcia-Johnson, Ronnie. *Exporting Environmentalism: U.S. Multinational Chemical Corporations in Brazil and Mexico.* Cambridge, Mass.: MIT Press, 2000.

Gerrard, Michael B. *Whose Backyard, Whose Risk: Fear and Fairness in Toxic and Nuclear Waste Siting.* Cambridge, Mass.: MIT Press, 1996.

Hofrichter, Richard, ed. *Reclaiming the Environmental Debate: The Politics of Health in a Toxic Culture.* Cambridge, Mass.: MIT Press, 2000.

International Union for Conservation of Nature and Natural Resources. *World Conservation Strategy: Living Resource Conservation for Sustainable Development.* Gland, Switzerland: International Union for Conservation of Nature and Natural Resources, the United Nations Environment Programme, and the World Wildlife Fund, 1980.

Irvine, Sandy. *Beyond Green Consumerism.* London: Friends of the Earth, 1987.

Kemp, Ray. *The Politics of Radioactive Waste Disposal.* Manchester: Manchester University Press, 1992.

Krenzler, Horst G., and Anne MacGregor. "GM Food: The Next Major Transatlantic Trade War?" *European Foreign Affairs Review* 5 (2000): 287–316.

Lang, Tim, and Michael Heasman. *Food Wars: Public Health and the Battles for Mouths, Minds, and Markets.* London: Earthscan, 2004.

Leggett, Jeremy. "The Environmental Impact of War: A Scientific Analysis and Greenpeace's Reaction." In *Environmental Protection and the Law of War,* edited by Glen Plant, 75–81. London: Belhaven Press, 1992.

Lerner, Steve. *Beyond the Earth Summit: Conversations with Advocates of Sustainable Development.* Bolinas, Calif.: Common Knowledge Press Commonweal, 1991.

———. *Eco-Pioneers: Practical Visionaries Solving Today's Environmental Problems.* Cambridge, Mass.: MIT Press, 1998.

Lewidov, Les, and Susan Carr. "Unsound Science? Transatlantic Regulatory Disputes over GM Crops." *International Journal of Biotechnology* 2 (2000): 257–73.

Lewidow, Les, S. Carr, and D. Weld. "Genetically Modified Crops in the EU: Regulatory Conflicts and Precautionary Opportunities." *Risk Research* 3 (2000): 189–208.

Marshall, A. J. *The Great Extermination: A Guide to Anglo-Australian Cupidity, Wickedness and Waste.* London: Heinemann, 1966.

Meadows, Donella H., Dennis L. Meadows, and Jorgen Randers. *Beyond the Limits.* London: Earthscan, 1992.

Mesarovic, Mihailo D., and Eduard Pestel. *Mankind at the Turning Point: The Second Report to the Club of Rome.* London: Hutchinson, 1975.

Miller, Clark, and Paul N. Edwards, eds. *Changing the Atmosphere: Expert Knowledge and Environmental Governance.* Cambridge, Mass.: MIT Press, 2001.

Mintzer, Irving M., ed. *Confronting Climate Change: Risks, Implications and Responses.* Cambridge: Cambridge University Press, 1992.

Mounfield, Peter. *World Nuclear Power.* London: Routledge, 1991.

Nelkin, Dorothy, and Michael Pollack. *The Atom Besieged.* Cambridge, Mass.: MIT Press, 1981.

———. "Political Parties and the Nuclear Debate in France and Germany." *Comparative Politics* 2 (1980): 127–42.

Oberthür, Sebastian, and Thomas Gehring, eds. *Institutional Interaction in Global Environmental Governance: Synergy and Conflict among International and EU Policies.* Cambridge, Mass.: MIT Press, 2006.

Pearce, Fred. *Turning Up the Heat.* London: Bodley Head, 1989.

Peters, Rob, and Thomas Lovejoy, eds. *Global Warming and Biodiversity.* New Haven, Conn.: Yale University Press, 1992.

Pickering, Kevin T., and Lewis A. Owen. *An Introduction to Global Environmental Issues.* London: Routledge, 1994.

Plumwood, Val. "Nature, Self, and Gender: Feminism, Environmental Philosophy, and the Critique of Rationalism." *Hypatia* 6, no. 1 (1991): 3–27.

Prins, Gwyn, ed. *Defended to Death: A Study of the Nuclear Arms Race.* Harmondsworth, U.K.: Penguin, 1983.

Regan, Tom. *The Case for Animal Rights.* London: Routledge, 1988.

Ringius, Lasse. *Radioactive Waste Disposal at Sea: Public Ideas, Transnational Policy Entrepreneurs, and Environmental Regimes.* Cambridge, Mass.: MIT Press, 2000.

Roddewig, Richard. *Green Bans. The Birth of Australian Environmental Politics.* Sydney: Hale and Ironmonger, 1978.

Rosendal, G. Kristin. "Governing GMOs in the EU: A Deviant Case of Environmental Policymaking?" *Global Environmental Politics* 5, no. 1 (2005): 82–104.

Schellnhuber, Hans Joachim, Paul J. Crutzen, William C. Clark, Martin Claussen, and Hermann Held, eds. *Earth System Analysis for Sustainability.* Cambridge, Mass.: MIT Press, 2004.

Schneider, Stephen. *Global Warming: Are We Entering the Greenhouse Century?* San Francisco: Sierra Club Books, 1989.

Schreurs, Miranda. "The Climate Change Divide: The European Union, the United States, and the Future of the Kyoto Protocol." In *Green Giants? Environmental Policies of the United States and the European Union,* edited by Norman J. Vig and Michael G. Faure, 207–30. Cambridge, Mass.: MIT Press, 2004.

Shiva, Vandana. *Close to Home: Women Reconnect Ecology, Health, Development Worldwide.* Philadelphia, PA: New Society, 1994.

———. *Monocultures of the Mind: Perspectives on Biodiversity and Biotechnology.* London: Zed Books, 1993.

———. *Staying Alive: Women, Ecology and Development.* London: Zed Books, 1989.

———. *The Violence of Green Revolution: Third World Agriculture, Ecology, and Politics.* London: Zed Books, 2006.

Shrivastava, Paul. *Bhopal: Anatomy of a Crisis.* London: Paul Chapman, 1992.

Simon, Julian L. *Population Matters: People, Resources, Environment, and Immigration.* New Brunswick, N.J.: Transaction, 1989.

Taylor, Richard. *Against the Bomb.* Oxford: Clarendon Press, 1988.

United Nations Environment Programme. *Convention on Biological Diversity.* 5 June 1992. Na. 92–7807. Nairobi: UNEP, 1992.

———. *UNEP: Two Decades of Achievement and Challenge.* Nairobi: UNEP, 1992.

Weber, Edward P. *Bringing Society Back In Grassroots Ecosystem Management, Accountability, and Sustainable Communities.* Cambridge, Mass.: MIT Press, 2003.

Yamin, Farhana, and Joanna Depledge. *The International Climate Change Regime: A Guide to Rules, Institutions and Procedures.* Cambridge: Cambridge University Press, 2004.

Yaroshinskaya, Alla. *Chernobyl: The Forbidden Truth*. Oxford: John Carpenter, 1994.

VII. GREEN MOVEMENT

A. General

Alario, Margarita. *Environmental Destruction, Risk Exposure, and Social Asymmetry: Case Studies of the Environmental Movement's Action*. Lanham, Md.: University Press of America, 1995.

Auer, Matthew R. "Environmentalism and Estonia's Independence Movement." *Nationalities Papers* 26, no. 4 (1998): 659–76.

Boggs, Carl. *Social Movements and Political Power*. Philadelphia: Temple University Press, 1986.

Bramwell, Anna. *Blood and Soil: Walther Darré and Hitler's Green Party*. Bourne End, U.K.: Kensal Press, 1985.

Brand, Karl-Werner. "Cyclical Aspects of New Social Movements: Waves of Cultural Criticism and Mobilization Cycles of New Middle-Class Radicalism." In *Challenging the Political Order*, edited by Russell Dalton and Manfred Kuechler, 23–42. Cambridge: Polity Press, 1990.

———. *Neue Soziale Bewegungen: Entstehung, Funktion and Perspektive neuer Protestpotentiale*. Opladen, Germany: Westdeutscher Verlag, 1982.

Brand, Karl-Werner, Detlef Bilsser, and Dieter Rucht. *Aufbruch in eine neue Gesellschaft: Neue soziale Bewegungen in der Bundesrepublik Deutschland*. Frankfurt: Campus, 1986.

Caniglia, Beth S. "Informal Alliances vs. Institutional Ties: The Effects of Elite Alliances on Environmental TSMO Networks." *Mobilization: An International Journal* 6, no. 1 (2001): 37–54.

Capra, Fritjof, and Charlene Spretnak. *Green Politics: The Global Promise*. London: Hutchinson, 1984.

Christen, Catherine, Seline Herculano, Kathryn Hochsteler, Renae Prell, Marie Price, and J. Timmons Roberts. "Latin American Environmentalism: Comparative Views." *Studies in Comparative International Development* 33, no. 2 (1998): 58–87.

Cohen, Jean L. "Strategy or Identity: New Theoretical Paradigms and Contemporary Social Movements." *Social Research* 52, no. 4 (1985): 663–716.

Collinson, Helen, ed. *Green Guerillas: Environmental Conflicts and Initiatives in Latin America and the Caribbean*. Montreal, Que.: Black Rose Books, 1997.

Dalton, Russell. "Alliance Patterns of the European Environmental Movement." In *Green Politics Two*, edited by Wolfgang Rüdig, 5985. Edinburgh: Edinburgh University Press, 1992.

Dalton, Russell J., Paula Garb, Nicholas P. Lovrich, and John C. Pierce. *Critical Masses: Citizens, Nuclear Weapons Production, and Environmental Destruction in the United States and Russia.* Cambridge, Mass.: MIT Press, 1999.

Dawson, Jane. *Eco-Nationalism: Anti-Nuclear Activism and National Identity in Russia, Lithuania, and Ukraine.* Durham, N.C.: Duke University Press, 1996.

Diani, Mario, and Doug McAdam, eds. *Social Movements and Networks: Relational Approaches to Collective Action.* Oxford: Oxford University Press, 2003.

Doherty, Brian. *Ideas and Actions in the Green Movement.* London: Routledge, 2002.

Doyle, Timothy. *Environmental Movements.* London: Routledge, 2002.

Dryzek, John, David Downs, Hans-Kristian Hernes, and David Schlosberg, *Green States and Social Movements: Environmentalism in the United States, United Kingdom, Germany, and Norway.* Oxford: Oxford University Press, 2003.

Eder, Klaus. "The 'New Social Movements': Moral Crusades, Political Pressure Groups, or Social Movements." *Social Research* 52, no. 4 (1985): 869–90.

Escobar, Arturo, Dianne Rocheleau, and Smitu Kothari. "Environmental Social Movements and the Politics of Place." *Development* 45, no. 1 (2002): 28–35.

Faber, Daniel J. *The Struggle for Ecological Democracy: Environmental Justice Movements in the United States.* New York: Guilford Press, 1998.

Fitzpatrick, Tony, and Michael Cahill, eds. *Environment and Welfare: Towards a Green Social Policy.* Basingstoke: Palgrave MacMillan, 2002.

Fox, Stephen. *John Muir and His Legacy: The American Conservation Movement.* Boston: Little, Brown, 1981.

Guggenberger, Bemd. *Bürgerinitiativen in der Parteiendemokratie.* Stuttgart: Kohlhammer, 1980.

Guggenberger, Bemd, and Udo Kempf, eds. *Bürgerinitiativen and Repräsentatives System.* 2nd ed. Opladen, Germany: Westdeutscher Verlag, 1984.

Harrison, Kathryn, and Werner Antweiler. "Incentives for Pollution Abatement: Regulation, Regulatory Threats, and Non-Governmental Pressures." *Journal of Policy Analysis and Management* 22 (2003): 361–82.

Hochstetler, Kathryn. "After the Boomerang: Environmental Movements and Politics in the La Plata River Basin." *Global Environmental Politics* 2, no. 2 (2002): 35–57.

Jamison, Andrew, Ron Eyerman, and Jacqueline Cramer. *The Making of the New Environmental Consciousness: A Comparative Study of the Environmental Movements in Sweden, Denmark and the Netherlands.* Edinburgh: Edinburgh University Press, 1991.

Keck, Margaret E., and K. Sikkink. *Activists beyond Borders: Advocacy Networks in International Politics.* Ithaca, N.Y.: Cornell University Press, 1998.

———. "Transnational Advocacy Networks in International and Regional Politics." *International Social Science Journal* 51, no. 159 (1999): 89–101.

Khagram, Sanjeev, James V. Riker, and Kathryn Sikkink, eds. *Restructuring World Politics: Transnational Social Movements, Networks and Norms.* Minneapolis: University of Minnesota Press, 2002.

Melucci, Alberto. *Nomads of the Present: Social Movements and Individual Needs in Contemporary Society.* London: Century Hutchison, 1989.

Naguib Pellow, David, and Robert J. Brulle, eds. *Power, Justice, and the Environment: A Critical Appraisal of the Environmental Justice Movement.* Cambridge, Mass.: MIT Press, 2005.

Obach, Brian K. *Labor and the Environmental Movement: The Quest for Common Ground.* Cambridge, Mass.: MIT Press, 2004.

Offe, Claus. "New Social Movements: Challenging the Boundaries of Institutional Politics." *Social Research* 52, no. 4 (1985): 817–68.

Pakulski, Jan. *Social Movements: The Politics of Moral Protest.* Melbourne: Cheshire, 1991.

Peet, Richard. *Liberation Ecologies: Environment, Development, Social Movements.* London: Routledge, 2004.

Raustiala, Kal. "Non-State Actors and the Framework Convention on Climate Change." In *International Relations and the Climate Change Regime,* edited by Detlef Sprinz and Urs Luterbacher. Cambridge, Mass.: MIT Press, 2001.

Roberts, J. Timmons, and Melissa Tollofson-Weiss. *Chronicles from the Environmental Justice Frontline,* Cambridge: Cambridge Press, 2001.

Romero, Aldemaro, and Sarah West, eds. *Environmental Issues in Latin America and the Caribbean.* Dordrecht, The Netherlands: Springer, 2005.

Rose, Fred. *Coalitions across the Class Divide: Lessons from the Labor, Peace, and Environmental Movements.* Ithaca, NY: Cornell University Press, 2000.

Sandler, Ronald, and Phaedra C. Pezzullo, eds. *Environmental Justice and Environmentalism: The Social Justice Challenge to the Environmental Movement.* Cambridge, Mass.: MIT Press, 2006.

Scott, Alan. *Ideology and the New Social Movements.* London: Unwin Hyman, 1990.

Smith, Jackie G., Charles Chatfield, and Ron Pagnucco. *Transnational Social Movements and Global Politics: Solidarity beyond the State.* Syracuse, N.Y.: Syracuse University Press, 1997.

Taylor, Bron Raymond, ed. *Ecological Resistance Movements: The Global Emergence of Radical and Popular Environmentalism.* Albany: State University of New York Press, 1995.

Taylor, Dorceta. "American Environmentalism: The Role of Race, Class and Gender in Shaping Activism, 1820–1995." *Race, Gender & Class* 5, no. 1 (1997): 16–62.

Tilly, Charles. *Social Movements, 1768–2004.* Boulder, Colo.: Paradigm, 2004.

Touraine, Alain. *Anti-Nuclear Protest.* Cambridge: Cambridge University Press, 1983.

Wall, Derek. *Babylon and Beyond: The Economics of Anti-Capitalist, Anti-Globalist, and Radical Green Movements.* Ann Arbor, Mich.: Pluto Press, 2005.

Wapner, Paul. *Environmental Activism and World Civic Politics.* Albany: State University of New York Press, 1996.

———. "Horizontal Politics: Transnational Environmental Activism and Global Cultural Change." *Global Environmental Politics* 2, no. 2 (2002): 37–62.

Yearley, Steven. "Social Movements and Environmental Change." In *Social Theory and the Global Environment,* edited by Michael R. Redclift and Ted Benton. Abingdon, Oxford, U.K.: Taylor and Francis, 1994.

Yearley, Steven, and John Forrester. "Shell: A Sure Target for Global Environmental Campaigning?" In *Global Social Movements,* edited by R. Cohen and S. M. Rai, 134–45. London: Atlone Press, 2000.

B. Green Groups and Nongovernmental Organizations

Arts, Bas. "'Green Alliances' of Business and NGOs. New Styles of Self-Regulation or 'Dead End Roads'?" *Corporate Social Responsibility and Environmental Management* 9, no. 1 (2002): 26–36.

Banuri, Tariq, and Frédérique Apffel Marglin, eds. *Who Will Save the Forests? Knowledge, Power and Environmental Destruction.* London: Zed Books, 1993.

Betsill, Michele M., and Elisabeth Corell. "NGO Influence in International Environmental Negotiations: A Framework for Analysis." *Global Environmental Politics* 1, no. 4 (2001): 65–85.

Bombay, Peter. "The Role of Environmental NGOs in International Environmental Conferences and Agreements: Some Important Features." *European Environmental Law Review* 10, no. 7 (2001): 228–31.

Bramble, Barbara, and Gareth Porter. "Non-Governmental Organisations and the Making of U.S. International Environmental Policy." In *The International Politics of the Environment: Actors, Interests and Institutions,* edited by Andrew Hurrell and Benedict Kingsley, 313–53. Oxford: Clarendon Press, 1992.

Breitmeier, Helmut, and Volker Rittberger. "Environmental NGOs in an Emerging Global Civil Society." In *The Global Environment in the Twenty-First Century: Prospects for International Cooperation,* edited by Pamela S. Chasek, 130–63. Tokyo: United Nations University Press, 2000.

Byrne, Paul. *The Campaign for Nuclear Disarmament.* London: Croom Helm, 1988.

Clark, Ann M. "Non-Governmental Organizations and their Influence on International Society." *Journal of International Affairs* 48, no. 2 (1995): 507–25.

Clarke, Gerard. "Non-Governmental Organizations (NGOs) and Politics in the Developing World." *Political Studies* 46 (1995): 36–52.

Colchester, Marcus, and Larry Lohmann, eds. *The Struggle for the Land and the Fate of the Forests.* Penang: World Rainforest Movement; London: Zed Books, 1993.

Corell, Elisabeth. "Non-State Actor Influence in the Negotiations of the Convention to Combat Desertification." *International Negotiation* 4, no. 2 (1999): 197–223.

Corell, Elisabeth, and Michele. M. Betsill. "A Comparative Look at NGO Influence in International Environmental Negotiations: Desertification and Climate Change." *Global Environmental Politics* 1, no. 4 (2001): 86–107.

Cullen, Pauline P. "Coalitions Working for Social Justice: Transnational Non-Governmental Organizations and International Governance." *Contemporary Justice Review* 2, no. 2 (1999): 159–77.

Dalton, Russell J. *The Green Rainbow: Environmental Groups in Western Europe.* New Haven, Conn.: Yale University Press, 1994.

Diani, Mario. *Green Networks: A Structural Analysis of the Italian Environmental Movement.* Edinburgh: Edinburgh University Press, 1995.

Doh, Jonathan P., and Hildy Teegen. *Globalization and NGOs: Transforming Business, Government and Society.* Westport, Conn.: Greenwood/Praeger, 2003.

———. "Nongovernmental Organizations as Institutional Actors in International Business: Theory and Implications." *International Business Review* 11, no. 6 (2002): 665–84.

Dunlap, Riley E., and Angelo G. Mertig, eds. *American Environmentalism: The U.S. Environmental Movement 1970–1990.* New York: Taylor and Francis, 1992.

Edwards, Michael, and David Hulme. *Making a Difference: NGOs and Development in a Changing World.* London: Earthscan, 1992.

Ekins, Paul. *A New World Order: Grassroots Movements for Global Change.* London: Routledge, 1992.

Fisher, Julie. *The Road from Rio: Sustainable Development and the Non-governmental Movement in the Third World.* Westport, Conn.: Praeger, 1993.

Foreman, David, and Bill Haywood, eds. *Ecodefense: A Field Guide to Monkeywrenching.* Tucson, Ariz.: Ned Ludd Books, 1985.

Fox, Jonathan A. and L. David Brown, eds. *The Struggle for Accountability: The World Bank, NGOs, and Grassroots Movements.* Cambridge, Mass.: MIT Press, 1998.

Fox, Stephen. *John Muir and His Legacy: The American Conservation Movement.* Boston: Little, Brown, 1981.

Gemmill, Barbara, and Bamidele-Izu, Abimbola. "The Role of NGOs and Civil Society in Global Environmental Governance." In *Global Environmental Governance: Options and Opportunities,* edited by Daniel C. Esty and Maria H. Ivanova. New Haven, Conn.: Yale School of Forestry and Environmental Studies, 2002.

Ghai, Dharam, and Jessica M. Vivian, eds. *Grassroots Environmental Action: People's Participation in Sustainable Development.* London: Routledge, 1992.

Gottlieb, Robert. *Forcing the Spring: The Transformation of the American Environmental Movement.* Washington, D.C.: Island Press, 1993.

Jancar, Barbara. "Chaos as an Explanation of the Role of Environmental Groups in East European Politics." In *Green Politics Two,* edited by Wolfgang Rüdig, 156–84. Edinburgh: Edinburgh University Press, 1992.

Kitschelt, Herbert. "Political Opportunity Structures and Political Protest: Antinuclear Movements in Four Democracies." *British Journal of Political Science* 16 (1986): 57–85.

Kong, Nancy, Oliver Salzmann, Aileen Ionescu-Somers, and Oliver Salzmann. "Moving Business/Industry towards Sustainable Consumption: The Role of NGOs." *European Management Journal* 20, no. 2 (2002): 109–27.

Lowe, Philip, and Jane Goyder. *Environmental Groups in Politics.* London: Allen and Unwin, 1983.

Mazey, Sonia, and Jeremy Richardson. "Environmental Groups and the EC: Challenges and Opportunities." In *Environmental Policy in the European Union.* 2nd ed., edited by Andrew Jordan, 106–21. London: Earthscan, 2005.

McCormick, John. *The Global Environmental Movement.* 2nd ed. London: Wiley, 1995.

———. "International Nongovernmental Organizations: Prospects for a Global Environmental Movement." In *Environmental Politics and the International Arena: Movements, Parties, Organizations and Policy,* edited by Sheldon Kamieniecki, 131–43. Albany: State University of New York Press, 1993.

Mercer, Claire. "NGOs, Civil Society and Democratization: A Critical Review of the Literature." *Progress in Development Studies* 2, no. 1 (2002): 5–22.

Milbrath, Lester. *Environmentalists: Vanguard for a New Society.* Albany: State University of New York Press, 1984.

Minnion, John, and Philip Bolsover, eds. *The CND Story.* London: Allison and Busby, 1983.

Newell, Peter. "Environmental NGOs and Globalization." In *The Governance of TNCs. Global Social Movements,* edited by Robin Cohen and Shirin M. Rai, 117–33. London: Atlone Press, 2000.

Parmentier, Rèmi. "Greenpeace and the Dumping of Waste at Sea: A Case of Non-State Actors' Intervention in International Affairs." *International Negotiation* 4, no. 3 (1999): 433–55.

Predelli, Line Nyhagen. "Ideological Conflict in the Radical Environmental Group Earth First!" *Environmental Politics* 4, no. 1 (1995): 123–29.

Princen, Thomas, and Matthias Finger, with contributions by Jack P. Manno and Margaret L. Clark. *Environmental NGOs in World Politics: Linking the Local and the Global.* London: Routledge, 1994.

Raustiala, Kal. "States, NGOs and International Environmental Institutions." *International Studies Quarterly* 41, no. 4 (1997): 719–740.

Rochon, Thomas. *Mobilizing for Peace: Antinuclear Movements in Western Europe.* Princeton, N.J.: Princeton University Press, 1988.

Rucht, Dieter. "Ecological Protest as Calculated Law-breaking: Greenpeace and Earth First! in Comparative Perspective." In *Green Politics Three,* edited by Wolfgang Rüdig, 66–89. Edinburgh: Edinburgh University Press, 1995.

———. "Environmental Movement Organizations in West Germany and France." In *Organizing for Change: International Social Movement Research Series,* vol. 2, edited by Bert Klandermans, 61–94. Greenwich, Conn.: JAI Press, 1989.

Rüdig, Wolfgang. *Anti-Nuclear Movements.* London: Longman, 1990.

Sale, Kirkpatrick. *The Green Revolution: The American Environmental Movement 1962–1992.* New York: Hill and Wang, 1993.

Seel, Benjamin, Matthew Paterson, and Brian Doherty, eds. *Direct Action in British Environmentalism.* Routledge: London, 2000.

Shabecoff, Philip. *A Fierce Green Fire: The American Environmental Movement.* New York: Hill and Wang, 1993.

Taylor, Richard, and Colin Pritchard. *The Protest Makers: The British Nuclear Disarmament Movement of 1958–1965 Twenty Years On.* Oxford: Pergamon, 1980.

Wall, Derek. *Earth First! and the Anti-Roads Movement.* London: Routledge, 1999.

Wapner, Paul. "The Transnational Politics of Environmental NGOs: Governmental, Economic and Social Activism." In *The Global Environment in the Twenty-First Century: Prospects for International Cooperation,* edited by P. S. Chasek, 87–108. Tokyo, United Nations University Press, 2000.

Warhurst, John. "The Australian Conservation Foundation: The Development of a Modem Environmental Interest Group." *Environmental Politics* 3, no. 1 (1994): 68–90.

Wells, Edward R., and Alan M. Schwartz. *Historical Dictionary of North American Environmentalism.* Lanham, Md.: Scarecrow Press, 1997.

Winston, Morton. "NGO Strategies for Promoting Corporate Social Responsibility." *Ethics and International Affairs* 16, no. 1 (2002): 71–87.

Wright, Brian G. "Environmental NGOs and the Dolphin-Tuna Case." *Environmental Politics* 9, no. 4 (2000): 82–103.

Yamin, Farhana. "NGOs and International Environmental Law: A Critical Evaluation of their Roles and Responsibilities." *Review of European Community International Law* 10, no. 2 (2001): 149–62.

C. New Politics

Barnes, Samuel H., Max Kaase, and Klause R. Allerbeck. *Political Action.* Beverly Hills, Calif.: Sage, 1979.

Dalton, Russell. *Citizen Politics: Public Opinion and Political Parties in Advanced Industrial Democracies.* 2nd ed. Chatham, N.J.: Chatham House, 1996.

———. "Cognitive Mobilization and Partisan Dealignment in Advanced Industrial Democracies." *Journal of Politics* 46 (1984): 264–84.

Dalton, Russell, and Manfred Kuechler, eds. *Challenging the Political Order: New Social Movements in Western Democracies.* Cambridge: Polity Press, 1990.

Inglehart, Ronald. *Culture Shift in Advanced Industrial Society.* Princeton, N.J.: Princeton University Press, 1990.

———. *The Silent Revolution.* Princeton, N.J.: Princeton University Press, 1977.

———. "The Silent Revolution in Europe: Intergenerational Change in Post-Industrial Societies." *American Political Science Review* 65, no. 4 (1971): 991–1017.

———. "Value Change in Industrial Societies." *American Political Science Review* 81, no. 4 (1987): 1289–1303.

Jacobs, Michael, ed. *Greening the Millennium? The New Politics of the Environment.* Oxford: Blackwell, 1997.

Jahn, Detlef. "The Rise and Decline of New Politics and the Greens in Sweden and Germany." *European Journal of Political Research* 24, no. 2 (1993): 177–94.

Lafferty, William. "Basic Needs and Political Values: Some Perspectives from Norway on Europe's Silent Revolution." *Acta Sociologica* 19 (1976): 117–36.

Marsh, Alan. *Protest and Political Consciousness.* Beverly Hills, Calif.: Sage, 1977.

———. "The Silent Revolution, Value Priorities, and the Quality of Life in Britain." *American Political Science Review* 32, no. 1 (1975): 1–30.
Müller-Rommel, Ferdinand, and Thomas Poguntke, eds. *New Politics.* Aldershot, U.K.: Dartmouth, 1995.
Poguntke, Thomas. "New Politics and Party Systems." *West European Politics* 10, no. 1 (1987): 76–88.

VIII. GREEN PARTIES

A. General

Earth Friendly Guides. *Voting Green.* Napa, Calif.: Lulu Press, 2005.
Icke, David. *It Doesn't Have to Be Like This: Green Politics Explained.* London: Green Print, 1990.
Rootes, Chris. "Environmental Consciousness, Institutional Structures and Political Competition in the Formation and Development of Green Parties." In *The Green Challenge: The Development of Green Parties in Europe,* edited by Dick Richardson and Chris Rootes, 232–52. London: Routledge, 1995.
Talshir, Gayil. *The Political Ideology of Green Parties: From the Politics of Nature to Redefining the Nature of Politics.* New York: Palgrave, 2002.

B. Comparative

Alber, Jens. "Modernization, Cleavage Structures, and the Rise of Green Parties and Lists in Europe." In *New Politics in Western Europe: The Rise and Success of Green Parties and Alternative Lists,* edited by Ferdinand Müller-Rommel, 195–210. Boulder, Colo.: Westview Press, 1989.
Dalton, Russell J. *The Graying of the Greens? The Changing Base of the Green Party Support.* Berkeley, Calif.: Center for German and European Studies, University of California, 1993.
Doherty, Brian. "The Fundi-Realo Controversy: An Analysis of Four European Green Parties." *Environmental Politics* 1, no. 1 (1992): 95–120.
Kitschelt, Herbert. "Left-Libertarian Parties: Explaining Innovation in Competitive Systems." *World Politics* 15 (1988): 194–234.
———. *The Logics of Party Formation: Ecological Politics in Belgium and West Germany.* Ithaca, N.Y.: Cornell University Press, 1989.
———. "Organizational Strategy of Belgian and German Ecology Parties." *Comparative Politics* 20, no. 2 (1988): 127–54.
Kitschelt, Herbert, and Staf Hellemans. *Beyond the European Left.* Durham, N.C.: Duke University Press, 1990.

Kreuzer, Markus. "New Politics: Just Post Materialist? The Case of the Austrian and Swiss Greens." *West European Politics* 13, no. 1 (1990): 12–30.

Müller-Rommel, Ferdinand. "Green Parties and Alternative Lists under Cross-National Perspective." In *New Politics in Western Europe: The Rise and Success of Green Parties and Alternative Lists,* edited by Ferdinand Müller-Rommel, 5–22. Boulder, Colo.: Westview Press, 1989.

———, ed. *Green Parties in National Government.* London: Frank Cass, 2002.

———. *Grüne Parteien in Westeuropa: Entwicklungsphasen and Erfolgsbedingungen.* Opladen, Germany: Westdeutscher Verlag, 1993.

———. "New Political Movements and 'New Politics' Parties in Western Europe." In *Challenging the Political Order,* edited by Russell Dalton and Manfred Kuechler, 209–31. Cambridge: Polity Press, 1990.

———, ed. *New Politics in Western Europe: The Rise and Success of Green Parties and Alternative Lists.* Boulder, Colo.: Westview Press, 1989.

———. "Social Movements and the Greens." *European Journal of Political Research* 13, no. 1 (1985): 53–67.

Müller-Rommel, Ferdinand, and Thomas Poguntke, eds. *Green Parties in National Governments,* special issue of *Environmental Politics* 11, no. 1 (2002): 112–32.

O'Neill, Michael. *Green Parties and Political Change in Contemporary Europe: New Politics, Old Predicaments.* Aldershot, Hampshire, U.K.: Ashgate, 1997.

Parkin, Sara. *Green Parties: An International Guide.* London: Heretic Books, 1989.

Poguntke, Thomas. *Green Parties in National Governments: from Protest to Acquiescence?* Keele: SPIRE, Keele University, 2001.

———. "The 'New Politics Dimension' in European Green Parties." In *New Politics in Western Europe: The Rise and Success of Green Parties and Alternative Lists,* edited by Ferdinand Müller-Rommel, 175–94. Boulder, Colo.: Westview Press, 1989.

Rootes, Chris. "Environmental Consciousness, Institutional Structures and Political Competition in the Formation and Development of Green Parties." In *The Green Challenge: The Development of Green Parties in Europe,* edited by Dick Richardson and Chris Rootes, 232–52. London: Routledge, 1995.

Rudig, Wolfgang. "Between Ecotopia and Disillusionment: Green Parties in European Government." *Environment* 44, no. 3 (2002): 20–33.

———. Is Government Good for Greens? Comparing the Electoral Effects of Government Participation in Western and East Central Europe." *European Journal of Politial Research* 45, S1 (2006): 127–54.

Rüdig, Wolfgang, and Mark Franklin. "Green Prospects: The Future of Green Parties in Britain, France and Germany." In *Green Politics Two,* edited by Wolfgang Rüdig, 37–58. Edinburgh: Edinburgh University Press, 1992.

Sellers, Jeffrey. "Place, Post-Industrial Change and the New Left." *European Journal of Political Research* 22, no. 2 (1998): 187–217.

Webb, Paul. *Political Parties in Advanced Industrial Democracies.* Oxford: Oxford University Press, 2002.

C. Australia

Bean, Clive, and Elim Papadakis. "Minor Parties and Independents: Electoral Bases and Future Prospects." Special issue on "Party Systems, Representation and Policy Making: Australian Trends in Comparative Perspective," edited by Ian Marsh and John Uhr. *Australian Journal of Political Science* 30 (1995): 111–26.

Commonwealth of Australia. *Our Country: Our Future.* Canberra: Australian Government Publishing Service, 1989.

Hay, P. R. "Vandals at the Gate: The Tasmanian Greens and the Perils of Sharing Power." In *Green Politics Two,* edited by Wolfgang Rüdig, 86–110. Edinburgh: Edinburgh University Press, 1992.

Hutton, Drew, ed. *Green Politics in Australia.* Sydney: Angus and Robertson, 1987.

Papadakis, Elim. *Environmental Politics and Institutional Change.* Cambridge: Cambridge University Press, 1996.

———. *Politics and the Environment: The Australian Experience.* Sydney: Allen and Unwin, 1993.

Papadakis, Elim, and Clive Bean. "Minor Parties and Independents: The Electoral System." Special issue on "Party Systems, Representation and Policy Making: Australian Trends in Comparative Perspective," edited by Ian Marsh and John Uhr. *Australian Journal of Political Science* 30 (1995): 97–110.

Turnborn, Nick, and Ariadne Vromen. "The Australian Greens: Party Organisation and Political Processes." *Australian Journal of Politics and History* 52, no. 3 (2006): 455–70.

D. Austria

Frankland, E. Gene. "The Austrian Greens: From Electoral Alliance to Political Party." In *Green Politics Three,* edited by Wolfgang Rüdig, 192–216. Edinburgh: Edinburgh University Press, 1995.

Haerpfer, Christian. "Austria: The 'United Greens' and the 'Alternative List/Green Alternative.'" In *New Politics in Western Europe: The Rise and Success of Green Parties and Alternative Lists,* edited by Ferdinand Müller-Rommel, 23–38. Boulder, Colo.: Westview Press, 1989.

Lauber, Volkmar. "The Austrian Greens." *Environmental Politics* 3, no. 1 (1995): 313–19.

Waller, Michael. "The Dams on the Danube." *Environmental Politics* 1, no. 1 (1992): 121–27.

E. Belgium

Buelens, Jo, and Kris Deschouwer. "Belgium." In *Green Parties in National Governments,* edited by Ferdinand Müller-Rommel and Thomas Poguntke, special issue of *Environmental Politics* 11, no. 1 (2002): 112–32.

Deschouwer, Kris. "Belgium: The 'Ecologists' and 'AGALEV.'" In *New Politics in Western Europe: The Rise and Success of Green Parties and Alternative Lists,* edited by Ferdinand Müller-Rommel, 39–54. Boulder, Colo.: Westview Press, 1989.

Hooghe, Marc. "The Green Parties in the Belgian General Elections of 24 November 1991: Mixed Blessings." *Environmental Politics* 1, no. 1 (1992): 287–91.

———. "The Greens in the Belgian Elections of 21 May 1995: Growing Doubts." *Environmental Politics* 4, no. 4 (1995): 253–57.

Kitschelt, Herbert. "The Medium Is the Message: Democracy and Oligarchy in Belgian Ecology Parties." In *Green Politics One,* edited by Wolfgang Rüdig, 82–114. Edinburgh: Edinburgh University Press, 1990.

Rihoux, Benoit. "Belgium: Greens in a Divided Society." In *The Green Challenge: The Development of Green Parties in Europe,* edited by Dick Richardson and Chris Rootes, 91–108. London: Routledge, 1995.

F. Czechoslovakia

Jelicka, Petr, and Tomas Kostelecky. "Czechoslovakia: Greens in a Post-Communist Society." In *The Green Challenge: The Development of Green Parties in Europe,* edited by Dick Richardson and Chris Rootes, 208–31. London: Routledge, 1995.

———. "The Development of the Czechoslovak Green Party since the 1990 Election." *Environmental Politics* 1, no. 1 (1992): 72–94.

G. Denmark

Schüttemeyer, Suzanne S. "Czechoslovakia: Greens in a Post-Communist Society." In *The Green Challenge: The Development of Green Parties in*

Europe, edited by Dick Richardson and Chris Rootes, 208–31. London: Routledge, 1995.

———. "Denmark: 'De Grønne.'" In *New Politics in Western Europe: The Rise and Success of Green Parties and Alternative Lists,* edited by Ferdinand Müller-Rommel, 55–60. Boulder, Colo.: Westview Press, 1989.

H. Europe/European Union

Barry, John, and Brian Doherty. "The Greens and Social Policy: Movements, Politics, and Practice?" In *Environmental Issues and Social Welfare,* edited by Michael Cahill and Tony Fitzpatrick, 119–39. Oxford: Oxford University Press, 2002.

Benoît, Rihoux, and Wolfgang Rüdig. *Analysing Greens in Power: Setting the Agenda. European Journal of Politial Research* 45, S1 (2006): 1–33.

Benoît, Rihoux. "Governmental Participation and the Organisational Adaptation of Green Parties." *European Journal of Politial Research* 45, S1 (2006): 69–98.

Bomberg, Elizabeth. "The Europeanisation of Green Parties: Exploring the EU's Impact." *West European Politics* 25, no. 3 (2002): 29–50.

———. *Green Parties and Policies in the European Union.* London: Routledge, 1998.

Bomberg, Elizabeth, and Neil Carter. "Greens in Brussels: Shapers or Shaped?" *European Journal of Politial Research* 45, S1 (2006): 99–125.

Bowler, Shaun, and David M. Farrell. "The Greens at the European Level." *Environmental Politics* 1, no. 1 (1992): 132–36.

Buck, Karl H. "Europe: The 'Greens' and the 'Rainbow Group' in the European Parliament." In *New Politics in Western Europe: The Rise and Success of Green Parties and Alternative Lists,* edited by Ferdinand Müller-Rommel, 176–94. Boulder, Colo.: Westview Press, 1989.

Burchell, Jon. *The Evolution of Green Politics: Development and Change within European Green Parties.* London: Earthscan, 2002.

———. "Evolving or Conforming? Assessing Organisational Reform within European Green Parties." *West European Politics* 24, no. 3 (2001): 113–34.

Carter, Neil. "The Greens in the 1994 European Parliamentary Elections." *Environmental Politics* 3, no. 1 (1994): 495–502.

Curtice, John. "The 1989 European Election: Protest or Green Tide?" *Electoral Studies* 8 (1989): 217–30.

Dumont, Patrick, and Hanna Bäck. "Why So Few, and Why So Late? Green Parties and the Question of Governmental Participation." *European Journal of Politial Research* 45, S1 (2006): 35–67.

Gaffney, John. *Political Parties and the European Union.* London: Routledge, 1996.

Liefferink, Duncan, and Mikael Skou Anderson. "Strategies of 'Green' Member States in EU Environmental Policy-making." In *Environmental Policy in the European Union.* 2nd ed., edited by Andrew Jordan, 49–66. London: Earthscan, 2005.

Rüdig, Wolfgang. "The Greens in Europe: Ecological Parties and the European Elections of 1984." *Parliamentary Affairs* 38 (1985): 56–72.

Van der Eijk, Cees, and Mark N. Franklin. "European Community Politics and Electoral Representation: Evidence from the 1989 European Elections Study." *European Journal of Political Research* 19, no. 1 (1991): 105–27.

I. Finland

Paastela, Jukka. "Finland." In *Green Parties in National Governments,* edited by Ferdinand Müller-Rommel and Thomas Poguntke, special issue of *Environmental Politics* 11, no. 1 (2002): 17–38.

———. "Finland: The 'Vihreät.'" In *New Politics in Western Europe: The Rise and Success of Green Parties and Alternative Lists,* edited by Ferdinand Müller-Rommel, 81–86. Boulder, Colo.: Westview Press, 1989.

J. France

Boy, Daniel, "France." In *Green Parties in National Government,* edited by Ferdinand Müller-Rommel, 63–77. London: Frank Cass, 2002.

Cole, Alistair, and Brian Doherty, "France: *Pas commes les* autres-the French Greens at the crossroads." In *The Green Challenge: The Development of Green Parties in Europe,* edited by Dick Richardson and Chris Rootes, 45–65. London: Routledge, 1995.

Hainsworth, Paul. "Breaking the Mould: The Greens in the French Party System." In *French Political Parties in Transition,* edited by Alistair Cole, 91–105 Aldershot, U.K.: Dartmouth, 1990.

Holliday, Ian. "Dealing in Green Votes: France, 1993." *Government and Opposition* 29, no. 1 (1994): 64–79.

Kitschelt, Herbert. "La Gauche libertaire et les écologistes." *Revue Franpaise de Science Politique* 40, no. 3 (1990): 339–65.

Prendiville, Brendan. "France: 'Les Verts.'" In *New Politics in Western Europe: The Rise and Success of Green Parties and Alternative Lists,* edited by Ferdinand Müller-Rommel, 87–100. Boulder, Colo.: Westview Press, 1989.

———. "French Ecologists at the Crossroads: The Regional and Cantonal Elections of March 1992 in France." *Environmental* Politics 1, no. 3 (1992): 448–57.

————. "The French Greens, Inside Out." *Environmental Politics* 1, no. 1 (1992): 283–87.

Szarka, Joseph. *The Shaping of Environmental Policy in France.* New York: Berghahn Books, 2001.

K. Germany

Alber, Jens. "Modernisierung, neue Spannungslinien and die politischen Chancen der Grünen." *Politische Vierteljahresschrift* 26, no. 3 (1985): 211–26.

Allen, Christopher S. *Transformation of the German Political Party System: Institutional Crisis of Democratic Revival.* New York: Berghahn Books, 1999.

Blüdorn, Ingolfor. "'New Green Pragmatism' in Germany-Green Politics beyond the Social Democratic Embrace?" *Government and Opposition* 39, no. 4 (2004): 564–86.

Bürklin, Wilhelm. "Governing Left Parties Frustrating the Radical Non-Established Left: The Rise and Inevitable Decline of the Greens." *European Sociological Review* 3, no. 2 (1987): 109–26.

Chandler, William, and Alan Siaroff. "Postindustrial Politics in Germany and the Origins of the Greens." *Comparative Politics* 18 (1986): 303–25.

Dicke, Klaus, and Tobias Stoll. "Freies Mandat, Mandatsverzicht des Abgeordneten and das Rotationsprinzip der GRÜNEN." *Zeitschrift für Parlamentsfragen* 16, no. 4 (1985): 451–65.

Fogt, Helmut. "Basisdemokratie oder Herrschaft der Aktivisten? Zum Politikverständnis der Grünen." *Politische Vierteljahresschrift* 25, no. 1 (1984): 97–114.

Frankland, E. Gene. "Federal Republic of Germany: 'Die Grünen.'" In *New Politics in Western Europe: The Rise and Success of Green Parties and Alternative Lists,* edited by Ferdinand Müller-Rommel, 61–80. Boulder, Colo.: Westview Press, 1989.

————. "Germany: The Rise, Fall and Recovery of Die Grünen." In *The Green Challenge: The Development of Green Parties in Europe,* edited by Dick Richardson and Chris Rootes, 23–44. London: Routledge, 1995.

Frankland, E. Gene, and Donald Schoonmaker, eds. *Between Protest and Power: The Green Party in Germany.* Boulder, Colo.: Westview Press, 1992.

Green, Simon. *Governance in Contemporary Germany.* Cambridge: Cambridge University Press, 2005.

Hülsberg, Werner. "After the West German Elections." *New Left Review* 152 (1987): 85–99.

————. *The German Greens.* London: Verso Press, 1988.

Ismayr, Wolfgang. "Die Grünen im Bundestag: Parlamentarisierung and Basisanbindung." *Zeitschrift für Parlamentsfragen* 16, no. 3 (1985): 299–321.

Jahn, Detlef. "Green Politics and Parties in Germany." *Political Quarterly* 68(b) (1997): 174–82.

Jesinghausen, Martin. "General Election to the German Bundestag on 16 October 1994: Green Pragmatists in Conservative Embrace or a New Era for German Parliamentary Democracy?" *Environmental Politics* 3, no. 1 (1995): 108–13.

Kolinsky, Eva. "The Greens in Germany: Prospects of a Small Party." *Parliamentary Affairs* 37, no. 4 (1984): 434–47.

———. *The Greens in West Germany: Organisation and Policy-Making.* Ithaca, N.Y.: Cornell University Press, 1989.

———. "The West-German Greens—A Women's Party?" *Parliamentary Affairs* 41, no. 1 (1988): 129–49.

Lees, Charles. *The Red-Green Coalition in Germany: Politics, Personalities, and Power.* Manchester: Manchester University Press, 2001.

Mayer, Margit, John Ely, and Michael Schattzschneider. *The German Greens: Paradox between Movement and Party.* Philadelphia: Temple University Press, 1998.

Mewes, Horst. "The West German Green Party." *New German Critique* 28 (1983): 51–85.

Müller-Rommel, Ferdinand. "The German Greens in the 1980s: Short-term Cyclical Protest or Indicator of Transformation?" *Political Studies* 37, no. 1 (1989): 114–22.

Papadakis, Elim. *The Green Movement in West Germany.* London: Croom Helm, 1984.

———. "Social Movements, Self-limiting Radicalism and the Green Party in West Germany." *Sociology* 22, no. 3 (1988): 433–54.

Patterson, William E., Gordon Smith, and Stephen Padgett. *Developments in German Politics 3.* Basingstoke: Palgrave Macmillan, 2003.

Poguntke, Thomas. *Alternative Politics. The German Green Party.* Edinburgh: Edinburgh University Press, 1993.

———. "Goodbye to Movement Politics? Organisational Adaptation of the German Green Party." *Environmental Politics* 2, no. 1 (1993): 379–404.

———. "The Organization of a Participatory Party—the German Greens." *European Journal of Political Research* 15 (1987): 609–33.

———. "Party Activists versus Voters: Are the German Greens Losing Touch with the Electorate?" In *Green Politics One,* edited by Wolfgang Rüdig, 29–46. Edinburgh: Edinburgh University Press, 1990.

Raschke, Joachim. *Die Grünen: Wie sie wurden, was sie Bind.* Cologne: Bund Verlag, 1993.

Rebe, Bernd. "Die erlaubte verfassungwidrige Rotation." *Zeitschrift fur Parlamentsfragen* 16, no. 4 (1985): 468–74.

Reutter, Werner. *Germany on the Road to "Normalcy": Policies and Politics of the Red-Green Federal Government (1998–2002).* New York: Palgrave Macmillan, 2004.

Roberts, Geoffrey K. "The Green Party in Germany: 1990–1991." *Environmental Politics* 1, no. 1 (1992): 128–31.

Rüdig, Wolfgang. "Germany." In *Green Parties in National Governments,* edited by Ferdinand Müller-Rommel and Thomas Poguntke, special issue of *Environmental Politics* 11, no. 1 (2002): 78–111.

Scharf, Thomas. *The German Greens: Challenging the Consensus.* Oxford: Berg, 1994.

Wiesenthal, Helmut. *Realism in Green Politics: Social Movements and Ecological Reform in Germany.* New York: St. Martin's Press, 1993.

L. Great Britain

Agyeman, Julian, and Robert Evans. "'Just Sustainability': The Emerging Discourse of Environmental Justice in Britain?" *Geographical Journal* 170 (2004): 155–64.

Bennie, Lynne, Mark Franklin, and Wolfgang Rüdig. "Green Dimensions: The Ideology of the British Greens." In *Green Politics Three,* edited by Wolfgang Rüdig, 217–39. Edinburgh: Edinburgh University Press, 1995.

Byrne, Paul. "Great Britain: The 'Green Party.'" In *New Politics in Western Europe: The Rise and Success of Green Parties and Alternative Lists,* edited by Ferdinand Müller-Rommel, 101–12. Boulder, Colo.: Westview Press, 1989.

Frankland, E. Gene. "Does Green Politics Have a Future in Britain? An American Perspective." In *Green Politics One,* edited by Wolfgang Rüdig, 7–28. Edinburgh: Edinburgh University Press, 1990.

McCulloch, Alistair. "The Ecology Party in England and Wales: Branch Organisation and Activity." *Environmental Politics* 2, no. 1 (1993): 20–39.

———. "The Green Party in England and Wales: Structure and Development, the Early Years." *Environmental Politics* 1, no. 1 (1992): 418–36.

Rawcliffe, Peter. "The Role of the Green Movement in Ecological Modernization: A British Perspective." In *The Emergence of Ecological Modernization,* edited by Stephen C. Young, 65–86. London: Routledge, 2001.

Robinson, Mike. *The Greening of British Party Politics.* New York: St. Martin's Press, 1992.

Rootes, Chris. "Britain: Greens in a Cold Climate." In *The Green Challenge: The Development of Green Parties in Europe,* edited by Dick Richardson and Chris Rootes, 66–90. London: Routledge, 1995.

———. "The New Politics and the New Social Movements: Accounting for British Exceptionalism." *European Journal of Political Research* 22 (1992): 171–91.

Rüdig, Wolfgang, and Philip Lowe. "The Withered 'Greening' of British Politics: A Study of the Ecology Party." *Political Studies* 34 (1986): 262–84.

M. Greece

Demertzis, Nicolas. "Greece: Greens at the Periphery." In *The Green Challenge: The Development of Green Parties in Europe,* edited by Dick Richardson and Chris Rootes, 193–207. London: Routledge, 1995.

N. Ireland

Farrell, David M. "Ireland: The 'Green Alliance.'" In *New Politics in Western Europe: The Rise and Success of Green Parties and Alternative Lists,* edited by Ferdinand Müller-Rommel, 123–30. Boulder, Colo.: Westview Press, 1989.

O. Italy

Biorcio, Roberto. "Italy." In *Green Parties in National Governments,* edited by Ferdinand Müller-Rommel and Thomas Poguntke, special issue of *Environmental Politics* 11, no. 1 (2002): 39–62.

Diani, Mario. "Italy: The 'Liste Verdi.'" In *New Politics in Western Europe: The Rise and Success of Green Parties and Alternative Lists,* edited by Ferdinand Müller-Rommel, 113–22. Boulder, Colo.: Westview Press, 1989.

Pridham, Geoffrey. "Italian Small Parties in Comparative Perspective." In *Small Parties in Western Europe: Comparative and National Perspectives,* edited by Ferdinand Müller-Rommel and Geoffrey Pridham, 71–94. London: Sage, 1991.

Rhodes, Martin. "The Italian Greens: Struggling for Survival." *Environmental Politics* 3, no. 1 (1995): 305–12.

———. "Italy: Greens in an Overcrowded Political System." In *The Green Challenge: The Development of Green Parties in Europe,* edited by Dick Richardson and Chris Rootes, 168–92. London: Routledge, 1995.

———. "Piazza or Palazzo? The Italian Greens and the 1992 Elections." *Environmental Politics* 1 (1992): 437–42.

P. Luxembourg

Hirsch, Mario. "The 1984 Luxembourg Election." *West European Politics* 8, no. 1 (1985): 116–18.

Koelble, Thomas. "Luxembourg: The 'Greng Alternative.'" In *New Politics in Western Europe: The Rise and Success of Green Parties and Alternative*

Lists, edited by Ferdinand Müller-Rommel, 131–38. Boulder, Colo.: Westview Press, 1989.

Q. Netherlands

Lucardie, Paul. "General Elections in the Netherlands, May 1994: The Triumph of Grey Liberalism." *Environmental Politics* 3, no. 1 (1995): 119–22.

Lucardie, Paul, Jelle van der Knoop, Wijbrandt van Schuur, and Gerrit Voerman. "Greening the Reds or Reddening the Greens? The Case of the Green Left in the Netherlands." In *Green Politics Three,* edited by Wolfgang Rüdig, 90–111. Edinburgh: Edinburgh University Press, 1995.

Lucardie, Paul, Gerrit Voerman, and Wijbrandt van Schuur. "Different Shades of Green: A Comparison between Members of Groen Links and De Groenen." *Environmental Politics* 2, no. 1 (1993): 40–62.

Voerman, Gerrit. "The Netherlands: Losing Colours, Turning Green." In *The Green Challenge: The Development of Green Parties in Europe,* edited by Dick Richardson and Chris Rootes, 109–27. London: Routledge, 1995.

R. New Zealand

Bayle, Tim. "The Greens. " In *New Zealand Government and Politics.* 3rd ed., edited by Raymond Miller, 283–92. Oxford: Oxford University Press.

Rainbow, Stephen L. "The New Zealand Values Party: Challenging the Poverty of Progress 1972–1989." In *Green Politics Two,* edited by Wolfgang Rüdig, 111–33. Edinburgh: Edinburgh University Press, 1992.

———. "Why Did New Zealand and Tasmania Spawn the World's First Green Parties?" *Environmental Politics* 1, no. 1 (1992): 321–46.

S. Scotland

Bennie, Lynne G. *Understanding Political Participation: Green Party Membership in Scotland.* Aldershot: Ashgate, 2004.

T. Spain

Aguilar-Fernández, Susana. "The Greens in the 1993 Spanish General Election: A Chronicle of a Defeat Foretold." *Environmental Politics* 3, no. 1 (1994): 153–58.

U. Sweden

Affigne, Anthony. "Environmental Crisis, Green Party Power: Chernobyl and the Swedish Greens." In *Green Politics One,* edited by Wolfgang Rüdig, 115–52. Edinburgh: Edinburgh University Press, 1990.

Bennulf, Martin. "Sweden: The Rise and Fall of *Miljöpartiet de gröna.*" In *The Green Challenge: The Development of Green Parties in Europe,* edited by Dick Richardson and Chris Rootes, 128–45. London: Routledge, 1995.

———. "The 1994 Election in Sweden: Green or Grey?" *Environmental Politics* 3, no. 1 (1995): 114–18.

Bennulf, Martin, and Sören Holmberg. "The Green Breakthrough in Sweden." *Scandinavian Political Studies* 13 (1990): 165–84.

Burchett, Jon. "'Small Steps' or 'Giant Leaps': How the Swedish Greens Are Learning the Lesson of Government Participation." *Scandinavian Political Studies* 24, no. 3 (2001) 239–54.

Vedung, Evert. "The Environmentalist Party and the Swedish Five Party Syndrome." In *When Parties Fail,* edited by Kay Lawson and Peter Merkl, 76–109. Princeton, N.J.: Princeton University Press, 1988.

———. "Sweden: The Miljöpartiet de Gröna." In *New Politics in Western Europe: The Rise and Success of Green Parties and Alternative Lists,* edited by Ferdinand Müller-Rommel, 139–54. Boulder, Colo.: Westview Press, 1989.

V. Switzerland

Church, Clive. H. "The Development of the Swiss Green Party." *Environmental Politics* 1, no. 1 (1992): 252–82.

———. "Switzerland: Greens in a Confederal Polity." In *The Green Challenge: The Development of Green Parties in Europe,* edited by Dick Richardson and Chris Rootes, 146–67. London: Routledge, 1995.

Finger, Matthias, and Simon Hug. "Green Politics in Switzerland." *European Journal of Political Research* 21, no. 3 (1992): 289–306.

Hug, Simon. "The Emergence of the Swiss Ecological Party: A Dynamic Model." *European Journal of Political Research* 18, no. 6 (1990): 645–70.

Ladner, Andreas. "Switzerland: The 'Green' and 'Alternative Parties.'" In *New Politics in Western Europe: The Rise and Success of Green Parties and Alternative Lists,* edited by Ferdinand Müller-Rommel, 155–75. Boulder, Colo.: Westview Press, 1989.

W. United States

Hawkins, Howie. *Independent Politics: The Green Party Strategy Debate.* Chicago: Haymarket Books, 2006.

Lowe, Philip. "Red-Green U.S. Style: The Rise and Demise of the Citizens Party, 1979–1984." In *Green Politics Three,* edited by Wolfgang Rüdig, 112–53. Edinburgh: Edinburgh University Press, 1995.

Rensenbrink, John. *The Greens and the Politics of Transformation.* San Pedro, Calif.: R. & E. Miles, 1992.

Sifry, Micah L. *Spoiling for a Fight: Third Party Politics in America.* New York: Routledge, 2003.

IX. GREEN POLICIES AND POLITICS

A. General

Axelrod, Regina S., David Leonnard Downie, and Norman Vig. *The Global Environment: Institutions, Law and Policy.* Washington, D.C.: Congressional Quarterly Press, 2004.

Carter, Neil. *The Politics of the Environment: Ideas, Activism, Policy.* Cambridge: Cambridge University Press, 2001.

Darst, Robert G. *Smokestack Diplomacy: Cooperation and Conflict in East-West Environmental Politics.* Cambridge, Mass.: MIT Press, 2001.

Downs, Anthony. "Up and Down with Ecology: The Issue-Attention Cycle." *Public Interest* 28 (1972): 38–50.

Doyle, Timothy. *Environment and Politics.* 2nd ed. London: Routledge, 2001.

Garner, Robert. *Environmental Politics.* New York: Prentice-Hall, 1995.

Gorz, André. *Ecology as Politics.* London: Pluto, 1980.

Grove, Richard H. *Green Imperialism: Colonial Expansion, Tropical Island Edens and the Origins of Environmentalism, 1600–1868.* Cambridge: Cambridge University Press, 1995.

Irvine, Sandy, and Alec Ponton. *A Green Manifesto.* London: Macdonald, 1988.

Jasanoff, Sheila, and Marybeth Long Martello, eds. *Earthly Politics: Local and Global in Environmental Governance.* Cambridge, Mass.: MIT Press, 2004.

Klandermans, Bert, Hanspeter Kriesi, and Sidney Tarrow, eds. *From Structure to Action: Comparing Movement Research across Cultures.* Greenwich, Conn.: JAI Press, 1988.

Lafferty, William. *Sustainable Communities in Europe.* London: Earthscan, 2001.

Lowe, Philip, and Wolfgang Rüdig. "Political Ecology and the Social Sciences." *British Journal of Political Science* 16, no. 4 (1986): 513–50.

Raustiala, Kal. "The 'Participatory Revolution' in International Environmental Law." *Harvard Environmental Law Review* 21 (1997): 537–71; 584–86.

Rohrschneider, Robert. "Citizens' Attitudes towards Environmental Issues: Selfish or Selfless?" *Comparative Political Studies* 21, no. 3 (1988): 347–67.

———. "Public Opinion toward Environmental Groups in Western Europe: One Movement or Two?" *Social Science Quarterly* 72, no. 2 (1991): 251–66.

———. "The Roots of Public Opinion toward New Social Movements: An Empirical Test of Competing Explanations." *American Journal of Political Science* 34, no. 1 (1990): 1–30.

Rüdig, Wolfgang, ed. *Green Politics One.* Edinburgh: Edinburgh University Press, 1990.

———. *Green Politics Two.* Edinburgh: Edinburgh University Press, 1992.

———. *Green Politics Three.* Edinburgh: Edinburgh University Press, 1995.

Ryle, Martin. *Ecology and Socialism.* London: Random Century, 1988.

Young, Stephen C. *The Politics of the Environment.* Manchester: Baseline Books, 1993.

B. Comparative

Boehmer-Christiansen, Sonja A. "Anglo-German Contrasts in Environmental Policymaking." *International Environmental Affairs* 4, no. 4 (1992): 140–59.

———. *Designs on Nature: Science and Democracy in Europe and the United States.* Princeton, N.J.: Princeton University Press, 2005.

Boehmer-Christiansen, Sonja A., and Jim Skea. *Acid Politics: Environmental and Energy Policies in Britain and Germany.* London: Belhaven Press, 1991.

Caldwell, Lynton D. *International Environmental Policy: Emergence and Dimensions.* 2nd ed. Duke Press Policy Studies. Durham, N.C.: Duke University Press, 1990.

Chertow, Marian R., and Daniel C. Esty. *Thinking Ecologically: The Next Generation of Environmental Policy.* New Haven, Conn.: Yale University Press, 1997.

Clark, Ann Marie, and Elisabeth Jay Friedman. "Sovereign Limits and Regional Opportunities for Global Civil Society in Latin America." *Latin American Research Review* 36, 3 (2001): 7–35.

Clark, William C., Jill Jaeger, Josee van Eijndhoven, and Nancy M. Dickson, eds. *Social Learning Group, Learning in the Management of Global Environmental Risk: A Comparative History of Social Responses to Climate Change, Ozone Depletion, and Acid Rain*, Vol. 1. Cambridge, Mass.: MIT Press, 2001.

———, eds. *Social Learning Group, Learning in the Management of Global Environmental Risk: A Comparative History of Social Responses to Climate Change, Ozone Depletion and Acid Rain,* Vol. 2. Cambridge, Mass.: MIT Press, 2001.

Conca, Ken. *Governing Water: Contentious Transnational Politics and Global Institution Building.* Cambridge, Mass.: MIT Press, 2005.

Dasgupta, Partha, and Karl-Goran Maler, eds. *The Environment and Emerging Development Issues.* New York: Clarendon Press, 1997.

de Bruijn, Theo, and Vicki Norberg-Bohm, eds. *Industrial Transformation: Environmental Policy Innovation in the United States and Europe.* Cambridge, Mass.: MIT Press, 2005.

Desai, Uday. *Environmental Politics and Policy in Advanced Industrialized Countries.* Cambridge, Mass.: MIT Press, 2002.

Dietz, Frank J., Udo E. Simonis, and Jan van der Straaten, eds. *Sustainability and Environmental Policy-Restraints and Advances.* Berlin: Edition Sigma, 1992.

Dunlap, Thomas. *Nature and the English Diaspora: Environment and History in the United States, Canada, Australia, and New Zealand.* Cambridge: Cambridge University Press, 1999.

Eckersley, Robyn, ed. *Markets, the State and the Environment: Towards Integration.* Melbourne: Macmillan, 1995.

Fiorino, Daniel J. "Environmental Policy and the Participation Gap." In *Democracy and the Environment,* edited by William M. Lafferty and James Meadowcroft, 194–212. Cheltenham, U.K.: Edward Elgar, 1996.

———. *Making Environmental Policy.* Los Angeles: University of California Press, 1995.

Fischer, Frank, and Michael Black, eds. *Green Environmental Policy: The Politics of a Sustainable Future.* New York: St. Martin's Press, 1995.

Gonzalez, George, G., Sheldon Kamieniecki, and Robert O. Vos. *Flashpoints in Environmental Policy Making.* Albany: State University of New York Press, 1997.

Holland, Kenneth M., F. Morton, and Brian Galligan, *Federalism and the Environment: Environmental Policymaking in Australia, Canada, and the United States.* Westport, Conn.: Greenwood Press, 1996.

Jänicke, Martin. "Conditions for Environmental Policy Success: An International Comparison." *Environmentalist* 12, no. 1 (1992): 47–58.

———. *State Failure. The Impotence of Politics in Industrial Society.* Cambridge: Polity Press, 1990.

Jänicke, Martin, Harrold Mönch, Thomas Ranneberg, and Udo E. Simonis. "Structural Change and Environmental Impact: Empirical Evidence on 31 Countries in East and West." *Intereconomics* 24 (1989): 24–34.

Jänicke, Martin, and Helmut Weidner, eds. *National Environmental Politics. A Comparative Study of Capacity-Building.* Berlin: Springer, 1997.

———. *Successful Environmental Policy: A Critical Evaluation of 24 Cases.* Berlin: Edition Sigma, 1995.

Joppke, Christian. "Social Movements during Cycles of Issue Attention: The Decline of the Antinuclear Energy Movements in West Germany and the USA." *British Journal of Sociology* 42, no. 1 (1991): 43–60.

Jordan, Andrew, Rudiger K. W. Würzel, Anthony R. Zito, eds. *New Instruments of Environmental Governance? National Experiences and Prospects.* London: Frank Cass, 2003.

Lipschutz, Ronnie D., and Ken Conca, eds. *The State and Social Power in Global Environmental Politics*. New York: Columbia University Press, 1993.

McBeath, Jerry, and Jonathan Rosenberg, *Comparative Environmental Politics*. Dordrecht, The Netherlands: Springer, 2006.

Münch, Richard, with Christian Lahusen, Markus Kurth, Cornelia Borgards, Carsten Stark, and Claudia Jauss. *Democracy at Work: A Comparative Sociology of Environmental Regulation in the United Kingdom, France, Germany, and the United States*. Westport, Conn.: Praeger, 2001.

Reich, Michael R. "Mobilizing for Environmental Policy in Italy and Japan." *Comparative Politics* 16 (1984): 379–402.

Scheberle, Denise. *Federalism and Environmental Policy: Trust and the Politics of Implementation*. Washington, D.C.: Georgetown University Press.

Schreurs, Miranda A. *Environmental Politics in Japan, Germany, and the United States*. Cambridge: Cambridge University Press, 2002.

Schreurs, Miranda A., and Elizabeth Economy, eds. *The Internationalization of Environmental Protection*. Cambridge: Cambridge University Press, 1997.

Smith, Zachary A. *The Environmental Policy Paradox*. Englewood Cliffs, N.J.: Prentice-Hall, 1992.

So, Yok-shiu F., and Alvin Y. So. *Asia's Environmental Movements: Comparative Perspectives*. Armonk, N.Y.: M. E. Sharpe, 1999.

Toke, Dave. *The Politics of GM Food: A Comparative Study of the UK, USA, and EU*. London: Routledge, 2004.

Vig, Norman, and Michaele Faure, eds. *Green Giants? Environmental Policy of the United States and the European Union*. Cambridge, Mass.: MIT Press, 2004.

Vogel, David. *National Styles of Regulation: Environmental Policy in Great Britain and the United States*. Ithaca, N.Y.: Cornell University Press, 1986.

von Weizsäcker, Ernst Ulrich. *Earth Politics*. London: Zed Books, 1994.

Weale, Albert. "The Greening of the European Polity." *West European Politics* 14, no. 4 (1991): 193–98.

———. *The New Politics of Pollution*. Manchester: Manchester University Press, 1992.

Weale, Albert, Timothy O'Riordan, and L. Kramme. *Controlling Pollution in the Round: Change and Choice in Environmental Regulation in Britain and Germany*. London: Anglo-German Foundation for the Study of Industrial Society, 1991.

Weidner, Helmut, and Martin Jänicke, eds. *Capacity Building in National Environmental Policy: A Comparative Study of 17 Countries*. Berlin: Springer, 2002.

Weiss, Edith Brown, and Harold K. Jacobson, eds. *Engaging Countries: Strengthening Compliance with International Environmental Accords*. Cambridge, Mass.: MIT Press, 2000.

C. Social Bases

Cotgrove, Stephen, and Andrew Duff. "Environmentalism, Middle-Class Radicalism and Politics." *Sociological Review* 28, no. 2 (1980): 333–51.

———. "Environmentalism, Values and Social Change." *British Journal of Sociology* 32, no. 1 (1981): 92–110.

Eckersley, Robyn. "Green Politics and the New Class: Selfishness or Virtue?" *Political Studies* 37, no. 2 (1989): 205–23.

Galtung, Johan. "The Green Movement: A Socio-Historical Explanation." *International Sociology* 1, no. 1 (1986): 75–90.

Jones, Robert, and Riley Dunlap. "The Social Bases of Environmental Concern." *Rural Sociology* 57, no. 1 (1992): 28–47.

Kriesi, Hanspeter. "New Social Movements and the New Class in the Netherlands." *American Journal of Sociology* 94, no. 5 (1989): 1078–1116.

Parkin, Frank. *Middle Class Radicalism: The Social Bases of the Campaign for Nuclear Disarmament.* Manchester: Manchester University Press, 1968.

Van Liere, Kent, and Riley E. Dunlap. "The Social Bases of Environmental Concern: A Review of Hypotheses, Explanations and Empirical Evidence." *Public Opinion Quarterly* 44, no. 2 (1980): 181–98.

D. Africa

Darkoh, Michael, and Apollo Rwomire, eds. *Human Impact on Environment and Sustainable Development in Africa.* Aldershot, Hampshire, U.K.: Ashgate, 2003.

Fabricius, Christo, Eddie Koch, Stephen Turner, and Hector Magome, eds. *Rights, Resources, and Rural Development: Community-Based Natural Resource Management in Southern Africa.* London: Earthscan, 2005.

Fairhead, James, and Melissa Leach. *Misreading the African Landscape: Society and Ecology in a Forest-Savanna Mosaic.* Cambridge: Cambridge University Press, 1996.

———. *Science, Society, and Power: Environmental Knowledge and Policy in West Africa and the Caribbean.* Cambridge: Cambridge University Press, 2003.

Keeley, James, and Ian Scoones. *Understanding Environmental Policy Processes: Case Studies from Africa.* London: Earthscan, 2003.

Levine, Arielle, and Geoffrey Wandesforde-Smith, eds. "Wildlife, Markets, States and Communities in Africa." *Journal of International Wildlife Law and Policy* (2004): 135–216.

Oates, John. *Myth and Reality in the Rainforest: How Conservation Strategies Are Failing in West Africa.* Berkeley: University of California Press, 1999.

Ribot, Jesse C. "Decentralisation, Participation and Accountability in Sahelian Forestry: Legal Instruments of Political-Administrative Control." *Africa* 69, no. 1 (1999): 23.

Salih, M. A. Mohamed. *Environmental Politics and Liberation in Contemporary Africa.* Dordrecht, The Netherlands: Kluwer Academic, 1999.

E. Australia

Bean, Clive, Ian McAllister, and John Warhurst, eds. *The Greening of Australian Politics: The 1990 Federal Election.* Melbourne: Longman Cheshire, 1990.

Burnam Burnam. "Aboriginal Australia and the Green Movement." In *Green Politics in Australia,* edited by Drew Hutton, 91–104. Sydney: Angus and Robertson, 1987.

Doyle, Timothy. *Green Power: The Environmental Movement in Australia.* Sydney: New South Wales University Press, 2000.

Economou, Nicholas M. "Accordism and the Environment: The Resource Assessment Commission and National Environmental Policymaking." *Australian Journal of Political Science* 28, no. 3 (1993): 399–412.

Galligan, Brian, and Georgina Lynch. *Integrating Conservation and Development: Australia's Resource Assessment Commission and the Testing Case of Coronation Hill.* Canberra: Federalism Research Centre Discussion Paper No. 14, 1992.

Hay, Peter R., Robyn Eckersley, and Geoff Holloway, eds. *Environmental Politics in Australia and New Zealand.* Hobart: Centre for Environmental Studies, 1989.

Hay, Peter R., and M. G. Haward. "Comparative Green Politics: Beyond the European Context." *Political Studies* 36, no. 4 (1988): 433–48.

McAllister, Ian. "Dimensions of Environmentalism: Public Opinion, Political Activism and Party Support in Australia." *Environmental Politics* 3, no. 1 (1994): 22–42.

McAllister, Ian, and Donley Studlar. "Trends in Public Opinion on the Environment in Australia." *International Journal of Public Opinion Research* 5, no. 4 (1993): 353–61.

Papadakis, Elim. "Development and the Environment." Special issue on "The 1993 Federal Election," edited by Clive Bean. *Australian Journal of Political Science* 29 (1994): 66–80.

———. "Does the New Politics Have a Future?" In *Australia Compared,* edited by Francis G. Castles, 239–57. Sydney: Allen and Unwin, 1991.

———. "Environmental Policy." In *Consensus and Restructuring: Hawke and Australian Public Policy,* edited by Christine Jennett and Randal Stewart, 339–55. Melbourne: Macmillan, 1990.

———. "Minor Parties, the Environment and the New Politics." In *The Greening of Australian Politics,* edited by Clive Bean, Ian McAllister, and John Warhurst, 33–53. Melbourne: Longman Cheshire, 1990.

———. "New Aspirations, Changing Patterns of Representation and Electoral Behaviour." In *Governing in the 90s,* edited by Ian Marsh, 3–29. Melbourne: Longman Cheshire, 1992.

Pybus, Cassandra, and Richard Flanagan, eds. *The Rest of the World Is Watching.* Sydney: Pan Macmillan, 1990.

Toyne, Philip. *The Reluctant Nation.* Sydney: ABC Books, 1994.

Walker, Ken. *Australian Environmental Policy.* Sydney: University of New South Wales Press, 1992.

F. Canada

Boardman, Robert, ed. *Canadian Environmental Policy: Ecosystems, Politics, and Process.* Toronto: Oxford University Press, 1992.

Doern, G. Bruce, ed. *Getting It Green: Case Studies in Canadian Environmental Regulation.* Toronto: C. D. Howe Institute, 1990.

Hoberg, George. "Sleeping with an Elephant: The American Influence on Canadian Environmental Regulation." *Journal of Public Policy* 11, no. 1 (1991): 107–32.

Lee, Eugene E., and Anthony Perl. *The Integrity Gap: Environmental Policy and Institutions.* Vancouver: University of British Columbia, 2004.

McKenzie, Judith I. *Environmental Politics in Canada: Managing the Commons into the Twenty-first Century.* Oxford: Oxford University Press, 2001.

Skogstad, Grace, and Paul Kopas. "Environmental Policy in a Federal System: Ottawa and the Provinces." In *Canadian Environmental Policy,* edited by Robert Boardman, 43–59. Toronto: Oxford University Press, 1992.

Toner, Glen, and Bruce Doern. "Five Political and Policy Imperatives in Green Plan Formation: The Canadian Case." *Environmental Politics* 3, no. 1 (1994): 395–420.

G. Central and Eastern Europe/Russia/Soviet Union

Andonova, Liliana B. *Transnational Politics of the Environment: The European Union and Environmental Policy in Central and Eastern Europe.* Cambridge, Mass.: MIT Press, 2003.

Auer, Matthew. *Restoring Cursed Earth: Appraising Environmental Policy Reform in Eastern Europe and Russia.* New York: Rowman and Littlefield, 2005.

Baumgartl, Bernd. "Green Mobilization against Red Politics: Environmentalists' Contribution to Bulgaria's Transition." In *Green Politics Three,* edited by Wolfgang Rüdig, 154–91. Edinburgh: Edinburgh University Press, 1995.

Carmin, Joann, and Stacy D. VanDeveer, eds. *EU Enlargement and the Environment: Institutional Change and Environmental Policy in Central and Eastern Europe.* London: Routledge, 2005.

Carter, Frank W., and David Turnock. *Environmental Problems in Eastern Europe.* London: Routledge, 1993.

———. *Environmental Problems in Eastern Europe.* 2nd ed. London: Routledge, 2002.

Dalton, Russell J., Paula Garb, Nicholas P. Lovrich, and John C. Pierce. *Critical Masses: Citizens, Nuclear Weapons Production, and Environmental Destruction in the United States and Russia.* Cambridge, Mass.: MIT Press, 1999.

Eckerberg, Katarina. "Environmental Problems and Policy Options in the Baltic States: Learning from the West?" *Environmental Politics* 3, no. 1 (1994): 445–78.

Fagin, Adam. "Environment and Transition in the Czech Republic." *Environmental Politics* 3, no. 1 (1994): 479–94.

Feshbach, Murray, and Alfred Friendly, Jr. *Ecocide in the USSR: Health and Nature under Siege.* London: Aurum Press, 1992.

Fisher, Duncan. *Paradise Deferred: Environmental Policymaking in Central and Eastern Europe.* London: Royal Institute of International Affairs/Ecological Studies Institute, 1992.

Gutner, Tamar. *Banking on the Environment: Multilateral Development Banks and Their Performance in Central and Eastern Europe.* Cambridge, Mass.: MIT Press, 2002.

———. *Environmental Management in the Soviet Union and Yugoslavia.* Durham, N.C.: Duke Press Policy Studies, 1987.

Jancar-Webster, Barbara. "Eastern Europe and the Former Soviet Union." In *Environmental Politics in the International Arena: Movements, Parties, Organisations, and Policy,* edited by Sheldon Kamieniecki, 199–222. New York: State University of New York Press, 1993.

———. ed. *Environmental Action in Eastern Europe: Responses to Crises.* New York: M. E. Sharpe, 1993.

Kára, Jan. "Geopolitics and the Environment: The Case of Central Europe." *Environmental Politics* 1, no. 1 (1992): 186–95.

Kostelecký, Tomáš. *Political Parties after Communism: Developments in East-Central Europe.* Washington, D.C.: Woodrow Wilson Center Press, 2002.

Làng-Pickvance, Katy. *Democracy and Environmental Movements in Eastern Europe: A Comparative Study of Hungary and Russia.* Boulder, Colo.: Westview Press, 1998.

Mnatsakanian, Ruben A.. *Environmental Legacy of the Former Soviet Republics.* Edinburgh: Centre for Human Ecology, University of Edinburgh, 1992.

Oldfield, Jonathan. *Russian Nature: Exploring the Environmental Consequences of Social Change.* Aldershot, Hamsphire, U.K.: Ashgate, 2005.

Pryde, Philip R. *Environmental Management in the Soviet Union.* Cambridge: Cambridge University Press, 1991.

Russell, Jeremy. *Energy and Environmental Conflicts in East/Central Europe: The Case of Power Generation.* London: Royal Institute of International Affairs/World Conservation Union, 1991.

Sandberg, Mikael. *Green Post-Communism? Environmental Aid, Polish Innovation, and Evolutionary Political Economics.* London: Routledge, 1999.

Stewart, John Massey, ed. *The Soviet Environment: Problems, Policies and Politics.* Cambridge: Cambridge University Press, 1992.

Waller, Michael, and Frances Millard. "Environmental Politics in Eastern Europe." *Environmental Politics* 1, no. 1 (1992): 159–85.

Ziegler, Charles E. *Environmental Policy in the USSR.* London: Frances Pinter, 1987.

H. Central Asia

Weinthal, Erika. *State Making and Environmental Cooperation: Linking Domestic and International Politics in Central Asia.* Cambridge, Mass.: MIT Press, 2002.

I. China

Economy, Elizabeth. *The River Runs Black: The Environmental Challenge to China's Future.* Ithaca, N.Y.: Cornell University Press, 2004.

Gallagher, Kelly Sims. *China Shifts Gears: Automakers, Oil, Pollution, and Development.* Cambridge, Mass.: MIT Press, 2006.

Yang, Guobin. "Environmental NGOs and Institutional Dynamics in China." *China Quarterly,* no. 181 (March 2005): 46–66.

J. European Union

Baker, Susan. "Environmental Policy in the European Union: Institutional Dilemmas and Democratic Practice." In *Democracy and the Environment,* edited by William M. Lafferty and James Meadowcroft, 213–33. Cheltenham, U.K.: Edward Elgar, 1996.

———. "Punctured Sovereignty, Border Regions and the Environment within the European Union." In *Nations and States: Borders, Frontiers of Sovereignty in the New Europe*, edited by Liam O'Dowd and Tom Wilson, 19–50. Aldershot, U.K.: Avebury, 1996.

Baldock, David, and Tony Long. *The Mediterranean Environment under Pressure: The Influence of the CAP on Spain and Portugal and the "IMPs" in France, Greece and Italy.* London: Institute for European Environmental Policy, 1987.

Collins, Ken, and David Eamshaw. "The Implementation and Enforcement of European Community Environmental Legislation." *Environmental Politics* 1, no. 4 (1992): 213–49.

Commission of the European Communities. *Administrative Structures for Environmental Management in the European Community.* Luxembourg: Office for Official Publications of the European Communities, 1993.

———. *The State of the Environment in the European Community.* Brussels: EC Commission, 1992.

———. *Towards Sustainability: A European Community Programme of Policy and Action in Relation to the Environment and Sustainable Development.* Brussels: EC Commission, 1992.

Faure, John, John Vervaele, and Albert Weale, eds. *Environmental Standards in the European Union in an Interdisciplinary Framework.* Antwerp: Maklu, 1994.

Gupta, Joyeeta, and Michael Grubb, eds. *Climate Change and European Leadership: A Sustainable Role for Europe?* Dordrecht: The Netherlands, 2000.

Haigh, Nigel. *The EC and Integrated Environmental Policy.* London: Institute for European Environmental Policy, 1992.

———. *EEC Environmental Policy and Britain.* London: Longman, 1989.

———. *Manual of EC Environmental Policy.* London: Institute for European Environmental Policy, 1992.

Jehlicka, Petr, and Andrew Tickle. "Environmental Implications of Eastern Enlargement: The End of Progressive EU Environmental Policy?" *Environmental Politics* 13, no. 1 (2004): 77–95.

Johnson, Stanley P, and Guy Corcell. *The Environmental Policy of the European Communities.* International Environmental Law and Policy Series. London: Graham and Trotman, 1989.

Jordan, Andrew, ed. *Environmental Policy in the European Union.* 2nd ed. London: Earthscan, 2005.

Jordan, Andrew, and Duncan Liefferink, eds. *Environmental Policy in Europe: The Europeanization of National Environmental Policy.* London: Routledge, 2004.

Judge, David, ed. *A Green Dimension for the European Community.* London: Frank Cass, 1993.

Knill, Christopher, and Andrea Lenschow. "Adjusting to EU Environmental Policy: Change and Persistence of Domestic Administrations." In *Transforming Europe: Europeanization and Domestic Change,* edited by Maria Green Cowles, James Caporaso, and Thomas Risse, 116–36. Ithaca, N.Y.: Cornell University Press, 2001.

Lodge, Juliet. "Environment: Towards a Clean Blue-Green EC." In *The European Community and the Challenge of the Future,* edited by Juliet Lodge, 319–26. London: Pinter, 1989.

Sands, Philippe. "European Community Environmental Law: Legislation, the ECJ and Common Interest Groups." *Modern Law Review* 53, no. 5 (1990): 685–98.

Sbragia, Alberta M. "Institution-building from Below and Above: The European Community in Global Environmental Politics." In *Environmental Policy in the European Union.* 2nd ed., edited by Andrew Jordan, 201–24. London: Earthscan, 2005.

Schreurs, Miranda. "Environmental Protection in an Expanding European Community: Lessons from Past Accessions." *Environmental Politics* 13, no. 1 (2004): 27–51.

Skogstad, Grace. "Legitimacy and/or Policy Effectiveness? Network Governance and GMO Regulation in the European Union." *Journal of European Public Policy* 10, no. 3 (2003): 321–38.

Skou Andersen, Mikael, and Duncan Liefferink, eds. *European Environmental Policy: The Pioneers.* Manchester: Manchester University Press, 1997.

Van Der Straaten, Jan. "A Sound European Environmental Policy: Challenges, Possibilities and Barriers." In *A Green Dimension for the European Community,* edited by David Judge, 65–83. London: Frank Cass, 1993.

Vandermeersch, Dirk. "The Single European Act and the Environmental Policy of the European Economic Community." *European Law Review* 12, no. 6 (1987): 407–29.

Verhoeve, Barbara, et al. *Maastricht and the Environment: The Implications for the EC's Environmental Policy of the Treaty on European Union Signed at Maastricht on 7 February 1992.* London: Institute for European Environmental Policy, 1992.

Weale, Albert, Geoffrey Pridham, Martin Porter, Michelle Cini, and Dimitrios Konstadakapolus. *Environmental Governance in Europe: An Ever Closer Ecological Union?* Oxford: Oxford University Press, 2003.

Wilkinson, D. *Maastricht and the Environment.* London: Institute for European Environmental Policy, 1992.

Wurzel, Rüdiger. "Environmental Policy." In *The European Community and the Challenge of the Future.* 2nd ed., edited by Juliet Lodge, 178–99. London: Pinter, 1993.

K. France

Bridgford, Jeff. "The Ecologist Movement and the French General Election 1978." *Parliamentary Affairs* 31, no. 3 (1978): 314–23.

Cerney, Philip G., ed. *Social Movements and Protest in France.* London: St. Martin's Press, 1982.

Hayes, Graeme. *Environmental Protest and the State of France.* Houndmills, Basingstoke, Hampshire, U.K.: Palgrave Macmillan, 2002.

Müller-Rommel, Ferdinand, and Helmut Wilke. "Sozialstruktur and 'Postmaterialistische' Werteorientierungen von Ökologisten: Eine empirische Analyse am Beispiel Frankreichs." *Politische Vierteljahresschrift* 22, no. 3 (1981): 383–97.

Prendiville, Brendan, and Tony Chafer. "Activists and Ideas in the Green Movement in France." In *Green Politics One,* edited by Wolfgang Rüdig, 177–209. Edinburgh: Edinburgh University Press, 1990.

Whiteside, Kerry H. *Divided Natures: French Contributions to Political Ecology.* Cambridge, Mass.: MIT Press, 2002.

L. Germany

Aguilar, Susana. "Corporatist and Statist Designs in Environmental Policy: The Contrasting Roles of Germany and Spain in the European Community Scenario." *Environmental Politics* 2, no. 1 (1993): 223–47.

Boehmer-Christiansen, Sonja. A. "Taken to the Cleaners: The Fate of the East German Energy Sector since 1990." *Environmental Politics* 1, no. 1 (1992): 196–228.

Bruggemeier, Franz-Josef, Mark Cioc, and Thomas Zeller, eds. *How Green Were the Nazis? Nature, Environment, and Nation in the Third Reich.* Athens: Ohio University Press, 2005.

Bürklin, Wilhelm P "The Split between the Established and the Non-Established Left in Germany." *European Journal of Political Research* 13 (1985): 283–93.

Federal Ministry for the Environment, ed. *Environmental Protection in Germany.* Bonn: Economica Verlag, 1992.

Markovits, Andrei, and Philip S. Gorski. *The German Left: Red, Green, and Beyond.* Cambridge: Polity Press, 1993.

Papadakis, Elim. "Green Issues and Other Parties: *Themenklau* or New Flexibility?" In *Policy Making in the West German Green Party,* edited by Eva Kolinsky, 61–85. Oxford: Berg, 1989.

Rehbinder, Eckhard. "Rethinking Environmental Policy." In *Developments in German Politics,* edited by Gordon Smith, William Paterson and Stephen Padgett, 227–46. London: Macmillan, 1992.

Weidner, Helmut. *25 Years of Modern Environmental Policy in Germany. Treading a Well-worn Path to the Top of the International Field.* WZB-Discussion papers FS 1195–301. Berlin: Wissenschaftszentrum Berlin, 1995.

M. Great Britain

Doherty, Brian. "Manufactured Vulnerability: Eco-Activist Tactics in Britain." *Mobilization* 4, no. 1 (1999) 75–89.

———. "Paving the Way: The Rise of Direct Action and the Changing Character of British Environmentalism." *Political Studies* 47, no. 2 (1999): 275–91.

Flynn, Andrew, and Philip Lowe. "The Greening of the Tories: The Conservative Party and the Environment." In *Green Politics Two,* edited by Wolfgang Rüdig, 9–36. Edinburgh: Edinburgh University Press, 1992.

Jordan, Andrew. "Integrated Pollution Control and the Evolving Style and Structure of Environmental Regulation in the UK." *Environmental Politics* 2, no. 1 (1993): 405–27.

McCormick, John. *British Politics and the Environment.* London: Earthscan, 1991.

Robinson, Mike. *The Greening of British Party Politics.* Manchester, U.K.: Manchester University Press, 1992.

Rootes, Christopher A. "The Greening of British Politics." *International Journal of Urban and Regional Research* 15, no. 2 (1991): 287–97.

Rose, Chris. *The Dirty Man of Europe: The Great British Pollution Scandal.* London: Simon and Schuster, 1990.

N. India

Agarwal, Bina. "Environmental Management, Equity and Ecofeminism: Debating India's Experience." *Journal of Peasant Studies* 25, no. 4 (1998).

———. "The Gender and Environment Debate: Lessons from India." *Feminist Studies* 18, no. 1 (1992): 119–58.

O. Ireland

Baker, Susan. "The Evolution of the Irish Ecology Movement." In *Green Politics One,* edited by Wolfgang Rüdig, 47–81. Edinburgh: Edinburgh University Press, 1990.

P. Japan

Barrett, Brendan, ed. *Ecological Modernisation in Japan.* London, UK: Routledge, 2005.

Dauvergne, Peter. *Shadows in the Forest: Japan and the Politics of Timber in Southeast Asia.* Cambridge, Mass.: MIT Press, 1997.

Hasegawa, Kōichi. *Constructing Civil Society in Japan: Voices of Environmental Movements.* Melbourne: Trans Pacific Press, 2004.

Imura, Hidefumi, and Miranda A. Schreurs, eds. *Environmental Policy in Japan.* Cheltenham, U.K.: Edward Elgar, 2005.

Peng-er, Lam. *Green Politics in Japan.* London: Routledge, 1999.

Schreurs, Miranda A. "Assessing Japan's Role as a Global Environmental Leader." Special issue on "Policy Leadership in Japan," edited by S. Javed Maswood and Hayden Lesbirel. *Policy and Society* 23, no. 1 (2004): 88–110.

Steiner, Kurt. *Political Opposition and Local Politics in Japan.* Princeton, N.J.: Princeton University Press, 1980.

Weidner, Helmut. *Basiselemente einer erfolgreichen Umweltpolitik. Eine Analyse and Evaluation der Instrumente der japanischen Umweltpolitik.* Berlin: Edition Sigma, 1996.

Wilkening, Ken. *Acid Rain Science and Politics in Japan: A History of Knowledge and Action toward Sustainability.* Cambridge, Mass.: MIT Press, 2004.

Q. Latin America

De Onis, Juan. *The Green Cathedral: Sustainable Development of Amazonia.* New York: Oxford University Press, 1992.

Goldrich, Daniel, and David V. Carruthers. "Sustainable Development in Mexico? The International Politics of Crisis or Opportunity." *Latin American Perspectives* 72, no. 19 (1992): 97–122.

Goodman, David, and Michael Redclift, eds. *Environment and Development in Latin America: The Politics of Sustainability.* Manchester, U.K.: Manchester University Press, 1991.

Griffith, Kathleen A. "NAFTA, Sustainable Development, and the Environment: Mexico's Approach." *Journal of Environment and Development* 2, no. 1 (1993): 193–203.

Haenn, Nora. *Fields of Power, Forests of Discontent: Culture, Conservation, and the State in Mexico.* Tucson: University of Arizona Press, 2005.

Hogenboom, Barbara. "Cooperation and Polarisation beyond Borders: The Transnationalisation of Mexican Environmental Issues during the NAFTA Negotiations." *Third World Quarterly* 17, no. 5 (1996): 989–1005.

———. *Mexico and the NAFTA Environment Debate: The Transnational Politics of Economic Integration.* Amsterdam: Universiteit van Amsterdam, 1998.

Mumme, Steven P. "Environmental Policy and Politics in Mexico." *Ecological Policy and Politics in Developing Countries. Economic Growth, Democracy, and Environment,* edited by Uday Desai, 183–203. Albany: State University of New York, 1998.

Mumme, Steven P., C. Richard Bath, and Valerie J. Assetto. "Political Development and Environmental Policy in Mexico." *Latin American Research Review* 23, no. 1 (1988): 7–34.

Mumme, Stephen P., and Donna Lybecker. "Environmental Capacity in Mexico: An Assessment." In *Capacity Building in National Environmental Policy: A Comparative Study of 17 Countries,* edited by Helmut Weidner and Martin Jänicke, 311–28. Berlin: Springer, 2002.

Pacheco-Vega, Raul. *Democracy by Proxy: Environmental NGOs and Policy Change in Mexico. Environmental Issues in Latin America and the Caribbean.* Dordrecht, The Netherlands: Springer, 2005.

Pádua, Jose. "The Birth of Green Politics in Brazil: Exogenous and Endogenous Factors." In *Green Politics Two,* edited by Wolfgang Rüdig, 134–55. Edinburgh: Edinburgh University Press, 1992.

Steinberg, Paul F. *Environmental Leadership in Developing Countries: Transnational Relations and Biodiversity Policy in Costa Rica and Bolivia.* Cambridge, Mass.: MIT Press, 2001.

Stern, M. A. 1993. "Mexican Environmental Policy Revisited." *Journal of Environment and Development* 2, no. 2 (2002): 185–96.

R. Netherlands

Driessen, Peter P. J., and Pieter Glasbergen, eds. *Greening Society: The Paradigm Shift in Dutch Environmental Politics.* Dordrecht, The Netherlands: Kluwer Academic, 2002.

Pridham, Geoffrey, Susannah Verney, and Dimitrios Konstadakopulos. "Environmental Policy in Greece: Evolution, Structures and Process." *Environmental Politics* 4, no. 2 (1995): 244–70.

Van der Straaten, Jan. "The Dutch National Environmental Policy Plan: To Choose or to Lose." *Environmental Politics* 1, no. 1 (1992): 45–71.

S. New Zealand

Dann, Christine. "The Environmental Movement." In *New Zealand Government and Politics.* 3rd ed., edited by Raymond Miller, 368–77. Oxford: Oxford University Press.

Rainbow, Stephen L. *Green Politics.* Auckland: Oxford University Press, 1994.

T. Norway

Skjaerseth, Jon Birger. *International Regimes and Norway's Environmental Policy.* Aldershot, Hampshire, U.K.: Ashgate, 2004.

U. Southern Europe

Aguilar, Susana. "Corporatist and Statist Designs in Environmental Policy: The Contrasting Roles of Germany and Spain in the European Community Scenario." *Environmental Politics* 2, no. 1 (1993): 223–47.

Diani, Mario. "The Italian Ecology Movement: From Radicalism to Moderation." In *Green Politics One,* edited by Wolfgang Rüdig, 153–76. Edinburgh: Edinburgh University Press, 1990.

Eder, Klaus, and Maria Kousis. *Environmental Politics in Southern Europe: Actors, Institutions, and Discourses in a Europeanizing Society.* Dordrecht, The Netherlands: Kluwer Academic, 2001.

Koufakis, Loanna. "Country Reports: Greece." *European Environmental Law Review* (October 1994): 244–45.

Pridham, Geoffrey, Susannah Verney, and Dimitrios Konstadakopulos. "Environmental Policy in Greece: Evolution, Structures and Process." *Environmental Politics* 4, no. 2 (1995): 244–70.

V. United States

Allen, Barbara L. *Uneasy Alchemy Citizens and Experts in Louisiana's Chemical Corridor Disputes.* Cambridge, Mass.: MIT Press, 2003.

Barton, Greg. *American Environmentalism.* San Diego, Calif.: Greenhaven Press, 2002.

Blatt, Harvey. *America's Environmental Report Card: Are We Making the Grade?* Cambridge, Mass.: MIT Press, 2004.

Brulle, Robert J. *Agency, Democracy, and Nature: The U.S. Environmental Movement from a Critical Theory Perspective.* Cambridge, Mass.: MIT Press, 2000.

Cole, Luke, and Sheila Foster. *From the Ground Up: Environmental Racism and the Rise of the Environmental Justice Movement.* New York: NYU Press, 2000.

DeSombre, Elizabeth R. *Domestic Sources of International Environmental Policy: Industry, Environmentalists, and U.S. Power.* Cambridge, Mass.: MIT Press, 2000.

Dowie, Mark. *Losing Ground: American Environmentalism at the Close of the Twentieth Century.* Cambridge, Mass.: MIT Press, 1996.

Dunlap, Riley E. "Public Opinion and Environmental Policy." In *Environmental Politics and Policy,* edited by J. P Lester, 87–134. Durham, N.C.: Duke University Press, 1989.

Dunlap, Riley E., and Angela G. Mertig. "The Evolution of the U.S. Environmental Movement from 1970 to 1990: An Overview." Special issue on "Two

Decades of American Environmentalism." *Society and Natural Resources* 4 (1991): 209–18.

Eckstein, Barbara, and James A. Throgmorton, eds. *Story and Sustainability: Planning, Practice, and Possibility for American Cities.* Cambridge, Mass.: MIT Press, 2003.

Gore, Albert. *Earth in the Balance: Ecology and the Human Spirit.* Boston: Houghton Mifflin, 1992.

Guber, Deborah Lynn. *The Grassroots of a Green Revolution: Polling America on the Environment.* Cambridge, Mass.: MIT Press, 2003.

Kassman, Kenn. *Envisioning Ecotopia: The U.S. Green Movement and the Politics of Radical Social Change.* Westport, Conn.: Praeger, 1997.

Minteer, Ben A. *The Landscape of Reform: Civic Pragmatism and Environmental Thought in America.* Cambridge, Mass.: MIT Press, 2006.

Nash, Roderick. *American Environmentalism: Readings in Conservation History.* 3rd ed. New York: McGraw Hill, 1989.

———. "The American Invention of National Parks." *American Quarterly* 22, no. 3 (1970): 726–35.

———. *Wilderness and the American Mind.* New Haven, Conn.: Yale University Press, 1973.

Pellow, David N. *Garbage Wars: The Struggle for Environmental Justice in Chicago.* Cambridge, Mass.: MIT Press, 2002.

Portney, Kent E. *Controversial Issues in Environmental Policy.* Newbury Park, Calif.: Sage, 1992.

———. *Taking Sustainable Cities Seriously: Economic Development, the Environment, and Quality of Life in American Cities.* Cambridge, Mass.: MIT Press, 2003.

Rabe, Barry. *Statehouse and Greenhosue: The Emerging Politics of American Climate Change Policy.* Washington, D.C.: Brookings Institution.

Ringquist, Evan J. *Environmental Protection at the State Level: Policies and Progress in Controlling Pollution.* New York: M. E. Sharpe, 1993.

Taylor, Dorceta. "American Environmentalism: The Role of Race, Class and Gender in Shaping Activism, 1820–1995." *Race, Gender & Class* 5, no. 1 (1997): 16–62.

Vittes, Elliot. "After the 1992 US Elections: Clinton and Environmental Policy." *Environmental Politics* 3, no. 1 (1994): 146–52.

W. Vietnam

O'Rourke, Dara. *Community-Driven Regulation: Balancing Development and the Environment in Vietnam.* Cambridge, Mass.: MIT Press, 2003.

X. INTERNATIONAL RELATIONS

Axelrod, Regina S., David L. Downie, and Norman J. Vig, eds. *The Global Environment: Institutions, Law, and Policy.* Washington, D.C.: Congressional Quarterly Press, 2004.

Benedick, Richard Eliot. *Ozone Diplomacy: New Directions in Safeguarding the Planet.* Cambridge, Mass.: Harvard University Press, 1991.

Brenton, Tony. *The Greening of Machiavelli: The Evolution of International Environmental Politics.* London: Earthscan/Royal Institute of International Affairs, 1994.

Chasek, Pamela S., Janet Welsh Brown, and David L. Downie. *Global Environmental Politics.* 4th ed. Boulder, Colo.: Westview Press, 2006.

DeSombre, Elizabeth. *Global Environmental Institutions.* London: Routledge, 2006.

Elliott, Lorraine. *The Global Politics of the Environment.* London: Macmillan, 1998.

Johnson, Stanley. *The Earth Summit: The United Nations Conference on Environment and Development.* London: Graham and Trotman/Martinus Nijhoff, 1993.

Käkönen, Jyrki, ed. *Perspectives on Environmental Conflict and International Politics.* London: Pinter, 1992.

Lipschutz, Ronnie D., and Ken Conca, eds. *The State and Social Power in Global Environmental Politics.* New York: Columbia University Press, 1993.

Litfin, Karen T., ed. *The Greening of Sovereignty in World Politics.* Cambridge, Mass.: MIT Press, 1998.

Miles, Edward L., Arild Underdal, Steinar Andresen, Jorgen Wettestad, Jon Birger Skjaerseth, and Elaine M. Carlin. *Environmental Regime Effectiveness: Confronting Theory with Evidence.* Cambridge, Mass.: MIT Press, 2001.

Mitchell, Ronald B., William C. Clark, David W. Cash, and Nancy M. Dickson, eds. *Global Environmental Assessments: Information and Influence.* Cambridge, Mass.: MIT Press, 2006.

O'Neill, Kate. *Waste Trading among Rich Nations: Building a New Theory of Environmental Regulation.* Cambridge, Mass.: MIT Press, 2000.

Porter, Gareth, and Janet Welsh Brown. *Global Environmental Politics.* 2nd ed. Boulder, Colo.: Westview Press, 1996.

Rowlands, Ian H., and Malory Greene, eds. *Global Environmental Change and International Relations.* Basingstoke: Macmillan, with *Millennium: Journal of International Studies,* 1992.

Sand, Peter. *The Effectiveness of International Environmental Agreements: Survey of Existing Legal Instruments.* Cambridge: Grotius, 1992.

———. *Lessons Learned in Global Environmental Governance.* New York: World Resources Institute, 1990.

Sands, Philippe. *Principles of International Environmental Law.* 2nd ed. Cambridge: Cambridge University Press, 2003.

Susskind, Lawrence. *Environmental Diplomacy: Negotiating More Effective Global Agreements.* New York: Oxford University Press, 1994.

Victor, David G., Kal Raustiala, and Eugene B. Skolnikoff, eds. *The Implementation and Effectiveness of International Environmental Commitments: Theory and Practice.* Cambridge, Mass.: MIT Press, 1998.

Vogler, John. *The Global Commons: A Regime Analysis.* Chichester, U.K.: Wiley, 1995.

Vogler, John, and Mark Imber, eds. *The Environment and International Relations.* London: Routledge, 1996.

Young, Oran, ed. *The Effectiveness of International Environmental Regimes: Causal Connections and Behavioral Mechanisms.* Cambridge, Mass.: MIT Press, 1999.

———, ed. *Global Governance: Drawing Insights from the Environmental Experience.* Cambridge, Mass.: MIT Press, 1997.

———. *The Institutional Dimensions of Environmental Change: Fit, Interplay, and Scale.* Cambridge, Mass.: MIT Press, 2002.

———. *International Cooperation: Building Regimes for Natural Resources and the Environment.* Ithaca, N.Y.: Cornell University Press, 1989.

———. *International Governance: Protecting the Environment in a Stateless Society.* Ithaca, N.Y.: Cornell University Press, 1994.

XI. ENVIRONMENTAL WEBSITES

A. Environmental Databases

The American Society of International Law
www.asil.org/resource/env1.htm
Guide to electronic resources for international law.

Analysis, Integration and Modeling of the Earth System (AIMES)
www.aimes.ucar.edu/
AIMES is the International Geosphere-Biosphere Programme's (IGBP) project to develop quantitative understandings of the role of human perturbations to the Earth's biogeochemical cycles and their interactions with the physical

climate system. AIMES's data bases include the Global Emissions Inventory Analysis (www.geiacenter.org/).

Carnegie Mellon University Libraries—Environmental History
www.library.cmu.edu/Research/Humanities/History/environment.html
A useful website related to environmental history and related documents.

Center for International Earth Science Information Network (CIESIN Columbia University)
www.ciesin.org/
CIESIN provides interactive data access and mapping tools via the Internet, and the website provides links to various databases and a search engine for locating data. The website also provides links to related research groups and organizations. The organization supports interdisciplinary approaches to the study of the environment, develops global and regional information systems, and provides training and technical support services.

Central Intelligence Agency (CIA)
https://www.cia.gov/cia/publications/factbook/appendix/appendix-c.html
A list of international environmental agreements and parties to those agreements.

Earth Summit Info
www.earthsummit.info/
A compendium of information and links related to sustainable development and biodiversity.

EarthTrends
http://earthtrends.wri.org/
A comprehensive online database of the World Resources Institute that focuses on the environmental, social, and economic trends that shapes our world.

Envirolink
www.envirolink.org
Provides a wide array of information in the fields of agriculture, air quality, climate change, ecosystems, environmental legislation, sustainable living, wildlife, and many other categories. Includes links to environmental groups by topic area.

Environmental Groups
www.nrdc.org/reference/environGroups.asp
An extensive set of links to various environmental groups compiled by the Natural Resources Defense Council.

Environmental Information Systems in Sub-Saharan Africa (EIS-SSA)
www.grida.no/prog/global/eis-ssa/index.htm
The EIS-SSA program aims at developing African capacity for the management of environmental information to support the process of sustainable

development in sub-Saharan Africa. The program supports African countries by assessing their priority needs and finding adequate sustainable and long-term solutions to deal with these issues.

Environmental Performance Index

www.yale.edu/epi/

This index identifies specific targets for environmental performance and measures how close each country comes to these established goals. The index was developed by the Center for Environmental Law and Policy at Yale University and the Center for International Earth Science Information Network (CIESIN) at Columbia University in collaboration with the World Economic Forum and the Joint Research Centre of the European Commission.

Environmental Sustainability Index

www.yale.edu/esi/

This project created by Yale University's Daniel C. Esty in collaboration with the Center for Earth Science Information Network (CIESIN) at Columbia University, and the World Economic Forum produces a periodic Environmental Sustainability Index (ESI). The ESI is a composite index that tracks socioeconomic, environmental, and institutional indicators. Countries are rank ordered.

Environmental Treaties and Resource Indicators (ENTRI)

http://sedac.ciesin.columbia.edu/entri/

Produced by the Center for Earth Science Information Network (CIESIN) at Columbia University and the Socio Economic Data and Applications Center (SEDAC), this search engine locates treaties according to search criteria in various issue and topical areas and provides full-text access to treaties.

European Green Parties

www.heldref.org/html/greenparties.html

Provides information about European green parties' histories, party platforms, and electoral results.

European Union (EUROPA)

http://europa.eu.int/comm/environment/index_en.htm

The European Union's environmental portal which provides up-to-date information on the state of the environment, policy initiatives, and legislative issues.

Hieros Gamos—World Environmental Law

www.hg.org/environ.html

A resourceful database of international environmental treaties, as well as environmental laws in different regions in the world.

IUCN Red List of Threatened Species

www.iucnredlist.org/

Compiled on a regular basis, this data base indicates species that are threatened with extinction.

New Ideas in Pollution Regulation
www.worldbank.org/nipr/index.htm
The World Bank's Economics of Pollution Control research team's website on methods of pollution regulation.
Pew Center on Global Climate Change
www.pewclimate.org
The Pew Center on Global Climate Change is a leading organization addressing climate change and provides much research on its website for the public and policymakers.
Pollution Scorecard
www.scorecard.org/
Allows the visitor to the site to input a U.S. ZIP code and assess pollution levels in their communities.
Social Movements and Culture website
www.wsu.edu/~amerstu/smc/enviro.html
Provides links to social movements and environmental justice websites.
Sustainable Africa
http://allafrica.com/sustainable/
An Internet channel of the AllAfrica Foundation to promote the advancement and diffusion of knowledge and understanding.

B. Environmental News

Capitol Reports
www.caprep.com/
Summaries of daily environmental news, focuses on U.S. government activity.
Earthwatch Radio
http://ewradio.org/
Produced at the University of Wisconsin-Madison by staff and students, they cover a wide range of subjects that concern science and the environment and give special attention to global climate change, and the Great Lakes and oceans.
Earthwire Africa
www.earthwire.org/africa/
Environmental news portal on Africa.
E Magazine
www.emagazine.com/
The online home of *E/The Environmental Magazine*.
ENDS Environmental Daily
www.environmentdaily.com/articles/
Europe's environmental news service.

EnviroLink Network

www.envirolink.org/

The EnviroLink Network is a nonprofit organization that provides access to thousands of online environmental resources since 1991.

Environment Daily (Europe)

www.environmentdaily.com/articles/index.cfm

Europe's environmental news service.

Environmental Law Reporter

www.elr.info/index.cfm

A high-quality journal on environmental law.

Environmental Media Services

www.ems.org/

A nonprofit organization dedicated to providing journalists with the most current information on environmental issues.

Environmental News Network (ENN)

www.enn.com/

ENN provides balanced and nonpartisan news, information, and interactive resources for individuals, organizations, and corporations interested in the environment.

Environmental News Service (ENS)

www.ens-newswire.com/index.asp

An international daily newswire for the latest environmental news, current issues, climate, water, food, forests, species, energy, and education.

The Frugal Environmentalist

www.frugalgreen.com/

A quarterly magazine dedicated to empowering people to make affordable, ecofriendly lifestyle choices.

Grist Magazine

www.grist.org/

Environmental news and commentary with a bit of humor and political twist.

Guardian Unlimited

http://politics.guardian.co.uk/green/

Current news from the United Kingdom on Green Parties.

Milieu Kontakt Oost-Europa

www.militeukontakt.nl/index.php?show=news&country_id=0

Provides overviews of the environmental and green movements for each of 23 Eastern European countries plus their relationship to the European Union (in English).

Nature's Voice

www.nrdc.org/naturesvoice/

A bulletin of environmental campaigns and victories.

Planet Ark
    www.planetark.com/index.cfm
    The website provides news and information about world environmental is-
    sues, campaigning activities in Australia and the United Kingdom, and sci-
    entific findings.
PlanetSave
    www.planetsave.com/
    Daily environmental news from the United States and the world.
Society for Environmental Journalists
    www.sej.org/news/index.htm
    A resourceful site for journalists reporting on the environment. Complete
    with daily environmental news.

C. Federations of Green Parties

Federacion de Partidos Verdes de las Americas/Federation of the Green Parties
of the Americas
    www.fpva.org.mx/
Global Greens
    www.globalgreens.info/federations.php
Green Islands Network (Britain, Ireland, and associated Islands)
    www.greenislands.net/gpni_hx.htm
The Greens/European Free Alliance (European Parliament)
    www.greens-efa.org/index.htm

D. Green Parties (Outside the United States)

Australia: Australian Greens
    www.greens.org.au/
Austria: Die Grüne
    www.gruene.at/
    www.europeangreens.org/cms/default/dok/148/148544.austria@en.htm
Belgium: Ecolo
    www.ecolo.be/
    www.europeangreens.org/cms/default/dok/148/148548.belgium@en.htm
Belgium: Groen!
    www.groen.be
    www.europeangreens.org/cms/default/dok/148/148541.belgium@en.htm
Benin: Les Verts du Bénin/Benin Greens
    www.greensbenin.org

Brazil: Partido Verde de Brazil
www.partidoverde.org.br/
Bulgaria: Zelena Partiya v Bulgariya
www.greenparty.bg/
Canada: Green Party of Canada
www.greenparty.ca/
Cyprus: Kinima Oikologon Periballontiston
www.cyprusgreens.org/
www.europeangreens.org/cms/default/dok/148/148622.cyprus@en.htm
Czech Republic: Strana Zelenych
www.zeleni.cz/
www.europeangreens.org/cms/default/dok/148/148625.czech_republic@en.htm
Denmark: De Grønne
www.groenne.dk/
www.europeangreens.org/cms/default/dok/148/148628.denmark@en.htm
Dominican Republic: Partido Verde Dominican
www.verdedominicano.com/
Estonia: Erakond Eestimaa Roelised
www.roheline.erakond.ee
www.europeangreens.org/cms/default/dok/148/148631.estonia@en.htm
Egypt: The Greens Party
www.egyptiangreens.com/docs/firstpage/index.php
Finland: Vihrea De Gröna
www.vihreat.fi/en
www.europeangreens.org/cms/default/dok/148/148636.finland@en.htm
France: Les Verts
http://lesverts.fr/
www.europeangreens.org/cms/default/dok/148/148640.france@en.htm
Georgia: Sakartvelo's mtsvaneta partia
www.greensparty.ge/en/home.asp?pg=hm
www.europeangreens.org/cms/default/dok/149/149870.georgia@en.htm
Germany: Bündnis 90/Die Grünen
www.gruene.de/cms/default/rubrik/0/3.htm
www.europeangreens.org/cms/default/dok/149/149871.germany@en.htm
Greece: Oikologoi Prasinoi
www.ecogreens.gr/gr/
www.europeangreens.org/cms/default/dok/148/148839.greece@en.htm
Hungary: Zöld Demokraták Szövetsége
www.zd.hu/
www.europeangreens.org/cms/default/dok/148/148852.hungary@en.htm
India: Indian National Green Party
www.tgouwp.edu/greens/

Iran: Green Party of Iran
    www.iran-e-sabz.org/eindex.html
Ireland: Irish Green Party/Comhaontas Glas
    www.greenparty.ie/
    www.europeangreens.org/cms/default/dok/148/148863.ireland@en.htm
Ireland: Young Greens/Oige Ghlas
    www.younggreens.ie/main/index.php
Israel: Ha-Yerukim
    www.green-party.org.il/
Italy: Federazione dei Verdi
    www.verdi.it/apps/news.php
    www.europeangreens.org/cms/default/dok/148/148866.italy@en.htm
Japan: Niji to Midori
    www.nijitomidori.org/
Kosovo: Partia e të Gjelbërve të Kosovës
    www.pgjk.org/index_en.htm
Latvia: Lativijas Zala Partija
    www.zp.lv/info.asp?en
    www.europeangreens.org/cms/default/rubrik/9/9034.htm
Luxembourg: Dei Greng
    www.greng.lu/
    www.europeangreens.org/cms/default/dok/148/148885.1uxembourg@en
    .htm
Malta: Alternattiva Demokratika (Democratic Alternative)
    www.alternattiva.org.mt/page.asp?p=5189&1=1
Mexico: Partido Verde Ecologista de Mexico
    www.pvem.org.mx/
Morocco: Les Verts du Maroc
    www.lesvertsmaroc.tk/
Nepal: Green Nepal Party
    www.greens.org/nepal/
Netherlands: De Groenen
    www.degroenen.nl/
    www.europeangreens.org/cms/default/dok/148/148897.netherlands@en
    .htm
Netherlands: GroenLinks
    www.groenlinks.nl/
    www.europeangreens.org/cms/default/dok/148/148897.netherlands@en.htm
New Zealand: Green Party of Aotearoa New Zealand
    www.greens.org.nz/
Nicaragua: Verdes en Alianza/Greens in Alliance
    www.verdesenalianza.org/

Northern Ireland: Green Party of Northern Ireland
www.greens-in.org/articles/?type=article
Norway: Miljøpartiet De Grønne
www.gronne.no/wordpress/
www.europeangreens.org/cms/default/dok/148/148902.norway@en.htm
Peru: Partido Ecologista Alternativa Verde
www.verdes.org.pe/index3.htm
Philippines: Green Philippines
www.geocities.com/chrisjsimon/greenphil/
Poland: Zieloni 2004
www.zieloni2004.pl/portal/index.php
www.europeangreens.org/cms/default/dok/148/148903.poland@en.htm
Portugal: Os Verdes
www.osverdes.pt/
www.europeangreens.org/cms/default/dok/148/148905.portugal@en.htm
Romania: Partidul Verdi
www.verzii.ro/
www.europeangreens.org/cms/default/dok/148/148906.romania@en.htm
Russia: Zelenaya Alternativa (Interregional Green Party of Russia)
www.resist.ru
www.europeangreens.org/cms/default/dok/148/148991.russia@en.htm
Scotland: Scottish Green Party
www.scottishgreens.org.uk/
www.europeangreens.org/cms/default/dok/149/149867.united_kingdom@en
.htm
Slovakia: Strana Zelenych na Slovensku
www.stranazelenych.sk/
www.europeangreens.org/cms/default/dok/148/148996.slovakia@en.htm
Slovenia: Stranka Mladih Slovenije
www.sms.si
www.europeangreens.org/cms/default/dok/149/149873.slovenia@en.htm
Somalia: Somalia Green Party
www.africagreenparty.20m.com/
South Africa: Green Party of South Africa
www.greenparty.org.za/
Spain: Iniciatava per Catalunya Verds
www.iniciativa.cat/
www.europeangreens.org/cms/default/dok/149/149011.spain@en.htm
Spain: Los Verdes
www.verdes.es/
www.europeangreens.org/cms/default/dok/149/149007.spain@en
.htm

Sweden: Miljöpartiet de Gröna
  www.mp.se/
  www.europeangreens.org/cms/default/dok/149/149017.sweden@en.htm
Switzerland: Grüne Partei der Schweiz/Les Verts
  www.gruene.ch/d/index.asp
  www.europeangreens.org/cms/default/dok/149/149030.switzerland@en
  .htm
Taiwan: Green Party Taiwan
  http://gptaiwan.yam.org.tw/english_version/index_e.html
Turkey: Yesiller
  www.yesiller.org/about.htm
Ukraine: Partiya Zelenykh Ukrainy
  www.greenparty.org.ua/
United Kingdom: Green Party of England and Wales
  www.greenparty.org.uk/news
  www.europeangreens.org/cms/default/dok/149/149722.united_kingdom@en
  .htm
United Kingdom: Green Party London
  http://london.greenparty.org.uk/news
United Kingdom: Wales Green Party/Plaid Werdd Cymru
  www.walesgreenparty.org.uk/

E. Green Parties in the United States

The Greens/Green Party USA
  www.greenparty.org/index.php
Alabama Green Party
  www.alabamagreenparty.org/
Arizona Green Party
  www.azgp.org/
Georgia Green Party
  www.accgreens.org/gpga/
Green Party of Alaska
  www.alaska.greens.org/
Green Party of Arkansas
  www.arkgreens.org/
Green Party of California
  www.cagreens.org/
Green Party of Colorado
  www.greens.org/colorado/
Green Party of Connecticut
  www.ctgreens.org/index.shtml

Green Party of Delaware
http://gpde.us/index.php
Green Party of the District of Columbia
www.dcstatehoodgreen.org/
Green Party of Florida
www.floridagreens.org/
Green Party of Louisiana
www.lagreens.org/
Green Party of Michigan
www.migreens.org/
Green Party of Minnesota
www.mngreens.org/
Green Party of Nevada
www.nevadagreenparty.org/
Green Party of New Jersey
www.gpnj.org/
Green Party of New Mexico
www.greenpartynm.org/
Green Party of New York State
www.gpnys.org/
Green Party of Ohio
www.ohiogreens.org/
Green Party of Oklahoma
www.okgreens.org/
Green Party of Pennsylvania
www.greenpartypa.org/
Green Party of Rhode Island
www.greens.org/ri/
Green Party of Tennessee
www.tn.greens.org/
Green Party of Texas
www.txgreens.org/
Green Party of Virginia
www.vagreenparty.org/
Green Party of Washington
www.wagreens.us/home/
Green-Rainbow Party of Massachusetts
www.green-rainbow.org/
Idaho Green Party
www.idahogreenparty.org/ (Under Construction but still workable)
Illinois Green Party
www.ilgp.org/

Indiana Green Party
www.indianagreenparty.org/
Iowa Green Party
www.greens.org/iowa/
Maine Green Independent Party
www.mainegreens.org/
Maryland Green Party
www.mdgreens.org/
Montana Green Party
www.mtgreens.org/
Nebraska Green Party
www.nebraskagreens.org/
North Carolina Green Party
www.ncgreenparty.org/
Pacific Green Party of Oregon
www.pacificgreens.org/
Progressive Party of Missouri
www.ppmo.org/index.php
South Carolina Green Party
www.scgreenparty.org/
Vermont Green Party
www.vermontgreens.org/
Wisconsin Green Party
www.wisconsingreenparty.org/

F. Environmental Nongovernmental Organizations and Green Movements

Abolition 2000
www.abolition2000.0rg/site/c.cdJIKKNpFqG/b.1315003/k.BCFA/Home.htm
Audubon Society
www.audubon.org/
Action! Network
http://actionnetwork.org/
African American Environmentalist Association (AAEA)
www.aaenvironment.com/
African Wildlife Foundation
www.awf.org
The Center for International Environmental Law (CIEL)
www.ciel.org/
Citizens Network for Sustainable Development (CITNET)
www.citnet.org/

Clean Water Action
www.cleanwateraction.org/
Clean Water Network
www.cwn.org/cwn/
Conservation International
www.conservation.org/xp/CIWEB/home
Defenders of Wildlife
www.defenders.org/about
Earth First!
www.earthfirst.org/about.htm
Earth Island Institute
www.earthisland.org/
Earth Justice
www.earthjustice.org/
EarthRights International
www.earthrights.org/
Environmental Defense
www.edf.org
Environmental Law Institute
www2.eli.org/index.cfm
Provides information services, advice, publications, training courses, seminars, research programs, and policy recommendations to engage and empower environmental leaders.
Environmental Media Association
www.ema-online.org/index.html
This organization has as its goal inspiring the global entertainment industry to educate people about the environment.
Free the Planet!
www.freetheplanet.org/
Friends of the Earth, U.S.
www.foe.org
Friends of the Earth, International
www.foei.org/
Global Environment Facility (GEF)
www.gefweb.org/index.html
GLOBE International (Global Legislators' Organisation for a Balanced Environment)
www.globeinternational.org
Green Cross International
www.gci.ch/index.htm
Green Korea United
www.greenkorea.org/

Green Belt Movement (GBM) (Kenya)
www.greenbeltmovement.org/
Green Institute
www.greeninstitute.net/
Green Movement of Sri Lanka
www.greensl.net/index.htm
Green Power
www.greenpower.org.hk/index_e.html
Founded in 1988 in Hong Kong to promote environmental education.
Greenpeace International
www.greenpeace.org/international/
Intergovernmental Panel on Climate Change
www.ipcc.ch/
International Institute for Environment and Development
www.iied.org/
International Institute for Sustainable Development
www.iisd.org/about/
Korea Greens
www.greens.or.kr/english/sub/sub1.htm
League of Conservation Voters
www.lcv.org/
Movement for the Survival of the Ogoni People
www.dawodu.net/mosop.htm
National Black Environmental Justice Network
www.nbejn.org/index.html#
National Environmental Coalition of Native Americans
http://oraibi.alphacdc.com/necona/
National Environmental Trust
www.net.org/
National Parks and Conservation Association (NPCA)
www.npca.org/
National Wildlife Federation (NWF)
www.nwf.org/
Natural Resources Defense Council (NRDC)
www.nrdc.org/
The Nature Conservancy
www.nature.org/
Pesticide Action Network
www.pan-international.org/
Probe International
www.probeinternational.org/pi/index.cfm?DSP=content&ContentID=2700

Rainforest Action Network
www.ran.org
Rainforest Information Centre
www.rainforestinfo.org.au/aboutthe.htm
Save Our Environment
www.saveourenvironment.org/
Sea Shepherd Conservation Society
www.seashepherd.org
Sierra Club
www.sierraclub.org/
Socio-Ecological Union
www.seu.ru/index.en.htm
Student Environmental Action Coalition
www.seac.org/
Union of Concerned Scientists
www.ucsusa.org/
United States Public Interest Research Group (U.S. PIRG)
www.uspirg.org/
Wilderness Society (Australia)
www.wilderness.org.au/
Wilderness Society (United States)
www.wilderness.org/
Women's Environmental Network (WEN)
www.wen.org.uk/
Women's Global Green Action Network
www.wggan.org/
World Resources Institute (WRI)
www.wri.org.
World Wide Fund for Nature/World Wildlife Fund (WWF)
www.wwf.org/
Worldwatch Institute
www.worldwatch.org/

G. Regional Economic and Trade-Related Associations' Environmental Websites

Association of Southeast Asian Nations (ASEAN)
www.aseansec.org/8919.htm
European Union (EU)
http://europa.eu.int/comm/environment/international_issues/agreements_en
.htm

North American Agreement on Environmental Cooperation (North American Free Trade Agreement [NAFTA])
  www.sice.oas.org/trade/nafta/env-9141.asp
World Trade Organization (WTO)
  www.wto.org/english/thewto_e/whatis_e/tif_e/bey2_e.htm

H. Global Conferences, Declarations, and International Agreements

African Convention on the Conservation of Nature and Natural Resources
  www.iucn.org/themes/wcpa/wpc2003/pdfs/outputs/africa/africa_pasconvention.pdf
Agenda 21
  www.un.org/esa/sustdev/documents/agenda21/
Convention on Biological Diversity
  www.biodiv.org/default.shtml
Convention on Long-Range Transboundary Air Pollution
  www.unece.org/env/lrtap/
Montreal Protocol on Substances That Deplete the Ozone Layer
  http://unfccc.int/cop3/fccc/climate/fact17.htm
United Nations Conference on Environment and Development (UNCED)
  www.un.org/geninfo/bp/enviro.html
United Nations Conference on the Human Environment (Stockholm, Sweden 1972)
  www.unep.org/Documents.Multilingual/default.asp?documentid=97&1=en (UNEP report)
  www.unep.org/Documents.multilingual/Default.asp?DocumentID=97&ArticleID=1503 (Declaration of the United Nations Conference on the Human Environment)
United Nations Framework Convention on Climate Change
  http://unfccc.int/2860.php (FCCC website)
  www.ciesin.org/TG/PI/TREATY/framwork.html

About the Authors

Miranda Schreurs (BA, MA University of Washington; PhD University of Michigan) is director of the Environmental Policy Research Center and professor of comparative politics at the Freie Universität Berlin (University of Berlin), Germany. Prior to this she was associate professor in the Department of Government and Politics at the University of Maryland, College Park. Schreurs is author of *Environmental Politics in Japan, Germany, and the United States* (2002), which received the 2005 Harold and Margaret Sprout Award, Honorable Mention for the best book on environmental politics from the International Studies Association. She is coeditor of *The Environmental Dimension of Asian Security: Conflict and Cooperation over Energy, Resources, and Pollution* (2007); *Environmental Policy in Japan* (2005); *Ecological Security in Northeast Asia* (1998); and *The Internationalization of Environmental Protection* (1997). She has held fellowships from the SSRC-MacArthur Foundation Program in International Peace and Security Affairs, the Fulbright Foundation, and the National Science Foundation/Japan Society for the Promotion of Science. Her main research areas are in the comparative studies of environmental and energy decision making, environmental and energy security, and international environmental cooperation.

Elim Papadakis (BA Hons. University of Kent at Canterbury; PhD London University) is executive director at the Australian Research Council and holds a professorship in European studies at the Australian National University. His principal areas of expertise are environmental politics and policy, public opinion, and the development of the welfare state. Apart from serving as vice president of the Australian Sociological Association, he has held positions on the editorial boards of the *Australian Journal of Political Science* and the *Australian and New Zealand*

Journal of Sociology. His publications include *Environmental Politics and Institutional Change* (1996), *Politics and the Environment: The Australian Experience* (1993), and *The Green Movement in West Germany* (1984). In 1999 he was a corecipient of the Robert M. Worcester Prize, awarded annually for the year's outstanding contribution to the *International Journal of Public Opinion Research*, the official journal of the World Association for Public Opinion Research); and in 2002 he was a corecipient of the Henry Mayer Prize for the best article published in the *Australian Journal of Political Science.*